IDEAS IN CONTE?

THE POLITICAL THOUGHT OF
THE DUTCH REVOLT 1555–1590

This book is a comprehensive study of the history of the political thought of the Dutch Revolt (1555–90). It explores the development of the political ideas which motivated and legitimized the Dutch resistance against the government of Philip II in the Low Countries, and which became the ideological foundations of the Dutch Republic as it emerged as one of the main powers of Europe. It shows how notions of liberty, constitutionalism, representation and popular sovereignty were of central importance to the political thought and revolutionary events of the Dutch Revolt, giving rise to a distinct political theory of resistance, to fundamental debates on the 'best state' of the new Dutch commonwealth and to passionate disputes on the relationship between church and state which prompted some of the most eloquent early modern pleas for religious toleration.

In conclusion the author situates the political thought of the Revolt within the history of the European tradition, arguing that sixteenth-century Dutch political theory, inspired by the indigenous legacy of its constitutionalism and civic culture, and the intellectual legacy of the late Middle Ages, Renaissance and Reformation, should be considered as one of the principal foundations of modern political thought.

IDEAS IN CONTEXT

Edited by Quentin Skinner (general editor), Lorraine Daston,
Wolf Lepenies, Richard Rorty and J. B. Schneewind

The books in this series will discuss the emergence of intellectual traditions and of related new disciplines. The procedures, aims and vocabularies that were generated will be set in the institutions. Through detailed studies of the evolution of such traditions, and their modification by different audiences, it is hoped that a new picture will form of the development of ideas in their concrete contexts. By this means, artificial distinctions between the history of philosophy, of the various sciences, of society and politics and of literature may be seen to dissolve.

The series is published with the support of the Exxon Foundation.

A list of books in the series will be found at the end of the volume.

THE POLITICAL THOUGHT OF THE DUTCH REVOLT

1555–1590

MARTIN van GELDEREN

*Assistant Professor at the Department of History,
the Technical University, Berlin*

CAMBRIDGE
UNIVERSITY PRESS

CAMBRIDGE UNIVERSITY PRESS
The Edinburgh Building, Cambridge CB2 2RU, UK
40 West 20th Street, New York NY 10011-4211, USA
477 Williamstown Road, Port Melbourne, VIC 3207, Australia
Ruiz de Alarcón 13, 28014 Madrid, Spain
Dock House, The Waterfront, Cape Town 8001, South Africa

http://www.cambridge.org

First published 1992
First paperback edition 2002

A catalogue record for this book is available from the British Library

Library of Congress Cataloguing in Publication data
Gelderen, Martin van.
The political thought of the Dutch revolt. 1555-1590 / Martin van
Gelderen.
p.   cm. - (Ideas in context)
Includes bibliographical references and index.
ISBN 0 521 39204 7 hardback
1. Netherlands - Politics and government - 1556-1648.   I. Title.
II. Series.
DH186.5.G37   1992
949.2′03-dc20   91-45932   CIP

ISBN 0 521 39204 7 hardback
ISBN 0 521 89163 9 paperback

Transferred to digital printing 2002

For Anne

Contents

vii

Preface

The origins of this monograph can be traced to a stormy November afternoon in 1981. Browsing through the bookshop of the Erasmus-university in Rotterdam I came across Quentin Skinner's study on *The foundations of modern political thought*. Although the two volumes dealt with the political thought of the Renaissance and the Reformation, and therefore had little to do with the theories of John Rawls and Robert Nozick, high up on the charts of the Rotterdam curriculum of normative political theory, I was permitted to put them on the examination list.

As always during an oral examination I was asked to criticize the books I had studied. Trying to think of something original, I hazarded that the section on the Dutch Revolt in the superb study of Quentin Skinner was rather poor. Somehow that remark must have stirred a tender chord, as it was suggested that I do a study of the political thought of the Dutch Revolt for my graduate thesis. Reading about four treatises published during the Revolt to justify the resistance against Philip II should suffice. Such was the beginning of what became, in 1984, the topic of my Ph.D. research.

Throughout the past years several people have helped me to find my way through Dutch sixteenth-century history, the history of European political thought and the main collections of sixteenth-century literature in the Netherlands and Belgium. I should like to thank my supervisor, Gisela Bock, for her confidence and support, Bertjan Verbeek for sharing many years of study and three years in Italy, Guido Marnef for commenting on Chapter 3, Professor Woltjer for many detailed comments on the Ph.D. version of this monograph and Eco Haitsma Mulier for continuous debate and many thoughtful comments on the previous versions of this monograph.

In addition, I should like to thank the European University Institute for three years of financial support, a stimulating atmosphere, a great deal of academic freedom and beautiful summers, and the Department of History at the Technical University, Berlin, and Volker Hunecke in particular, for giving me the opportunity to revise my thesis and turn it into a monograph while living and working in one of the most arresting capitals of Europe. Credit should also be given to the staff of the libraries I visited, and especially to the staff of the department of 'Oude Drukken' at the Royal Library in The Hague for their assistance throughout the past years.

In particular, I should like to thank Quentin Skinner, for major intellectual inspiration and for his support and patience as editor, and Wim Blockmans, who throughout the past years has stimulated and supported me in a way which combined the best virtues of the Burgundian Netherlands. Last, but as always not least, I want to thank Anne for continuous support, stimulation and, above all, patient love.

M. v. G.

Abbreviations

AGN	*Algemene Geschiedenis der Nederlanden*, 15 vols. (Haarlem, 1977–83)
BLL	British Library, London
BMGN	*Bijdragen en Mededelingen betreffende de Geschiedenis der Nederlanden*
BRN	*Bibliotheca Reformatoria Neerlandica*
CAA	City Archives of Antwerp
HPT	*History of Political Thought*
JHI	*Journal of the History of Ideas*
KN	W. P. C. Knuttel, *Catalogus van de Pamfletten-verzameling berustende in de koninklijke bibliotheek*, i (The Hague, 1889)
LCHY	*The Low Countries History Yearbook*
MPM	Museum Plantin-Moretus, Antwerp
RLB	Royal Library, Brussels
RLTH	Royal Library, The Hague
TvG	*Tijdschrift voor Geschiedenis*
ULA	University Library of Amsterdam (Gemeente Universiteit)
ULG	University Library of Ghent
ULL	University Library of Leiden
ULL, THYS	University Library of Leiden, Thysius collection
ULU	University Library of Utrecht

CHAPTER I

Introduction

I.I. PRELIMINARY

On 26 July 1581 the States General of the United Provinces in the Netherlands[1] passed a resolution which declared Philip II, King of Spain, Duke of Brabant, Duke of Guelders, Count of Flanders, Count of Holland and Zeeland, Lord of Friesland etc. forfeited of his sovereignty over the provinces. The resolution, better known as the Act of Abjuration, ascertained that, 'despairing of all means of reconciliation and left without any other remedies and help', the States had been forced

in conformity with the law of nature and for the protection of our own rights and those of our fellow countrymen, of the privileges, traditional customs and liberties of the fatherland, the life and honour of our wives, children and descendants so that they should not fall into Spanish slavery – to abandon the King of Spain and to pursue such means as we think likely to secure our rights, privileges and liberties.[2]

Like many resolutions of the States General, the Act of Abjuration was the outcome of a lengthy decision-making process, marked by discussion and bargaining, slowness and carefulness. A so-called 'committee of conciliation' had prepared the Act, and all provinces had been asked to give their opinion on the question of relinquishing Philip II. Many had cautioned against provocation. Although they

---

[1] In this study the words 'Dutch', 'Netherlands' and 'Low Countries' refer to the so-called 'Seventeen Provinces' in the north-west of continental Europe which were united in 1548 by the Transaction of Augsburg in a separate Burgundian Circle of the Holy Roman Empire and, following the 1549 Pragmatic Sanction, were the patrimony of Philip II. The 'Seventeen Provinces' included the present Benelux and French Flanders, in the north-west of present-day France.

[2] Act of Abjuration, in E. H. Kossmann and A. F. Mellink (eds.), *Texts concerning the Revolt of the Netherlands* (Cambridge, 1974), 225.

accepted the Act of Abjuration as such, the States were of the opinion
that its proclamation must not arouse too much passion and certainly
should not damage the trade with the Spanish enemy which was
considered of vital economic interest for the provinces. And so it
happened. Without any pomp and circumstance, a number of
mainly well-to-do Dutch citizens, deputies of provinces and towns,
declared the King of Spain forfeited of his sovereignty over their
provinces.

The Act of Abjuration stands out as a milestone in Dutch history.
It was one of the key events in what nowadays is called the Dutch
Revolt, the period of protest and resistance against Philip II, leading
to the abjuration and ultimately to the emergence of the Dutch
Republic of the United Provinces.

As one of the Netherlands' finest hours, the Revolt belongs to the
most extensively studied subjects of the history of the Low Countries.
Over the past centuries it has continued to fascinate historians,
theologians, jurists, playwrights and others. This attention has not
been limited to the Netherlands and Belgium. As far as historical
research is concerned the monumental and exultant work of the
American historian Motley in the nineteenth century, or more recent
studies of the British historians Geoffrey Parker and Helmut
Koenigsberger (and many others),[3] stand out as principal examples
of the attention the Dutch Revolt has attracted throughout the
world.

However, despite the general recognition of the rise of the Dutch
Republic as being of major political and economic importance for the
course of European history, the intellectual dimensions of the
emergence of the Republic have been rather neglected. This is
especially manifest in the history of political thought. In twentieth-
century texts on early modern European political thought, the Dutch
Revolt has been virtually discarded. In Allen's *History of political
thought in the sixteenth century* the Dutch Revolt is not mentioned at all.
Mesnard's *L'essor de la philosophie politique au XVIe siècle* has six pages
on 'Calvinist theories and the revolt of the Netherlands', which
basically stress the international co-ordination of Calvinist political
doctrines and the influence of French Huguenot treatises on the rest
of Europe.[4] In Quentin Skinner's magisterial study *The foundations of*

---

[3] See J. L. Motley, *The rise of the Dutch Republic*, 3 vols. (Leipzig, 1858). For the studies of
Parker and Koenigsberger see Bibliography.

[4] Pierre Mesnard, *L'essor de la philosophie politique au XVIe siècle*, 3rd edn. (Paris, 1969), 370.

modern political thought, which covers both the Renaissance and the Reformation, only two pages are devoted to a discussion of the justification of the Dutch Revolt, leading to the rapid conclusion that Dutch treatises 'were basically derived from French sources'.[5] The view seems to be dominant that as far as the justification of the Dutch Revolt was concerned, Dutch political thought was essentially an application of French monarchomachic ideas.[6]

Amongst Dutch and Belgian historians the intellectual history of the political thought of the Dutch Revolt has not attracted widespread attention.[7] Nor has it been esteemed very highly. In more recent Dutch contributions to the topic it has been concluded that, whatever its value and importance may have been, late sixteenth- (and early seventeenth-) century Dutch political thought hardly qualifies as political theory.[8] In spite of 'all their application and ingenuity', Dutch pamphleteers succeeded in working out neither a 'royalist nor a parliamentary constitutional theory'.[9] Thus Dutch political thought does not match classical works such as the *Vindiciae contra tyrannos* (1579), Hotman's *Francogallia* (1573), Althusius' *Politica* (1603), let alone Bodin's *Six livres de la République* (1576). It has been said that the Dutch did not develop 'political ideas of a certain coherence and a certain level of abstraction, which might have guided political practice', but that, as one of the most outstanding Dutch intellectual historians has argued recently, they were always

---

[5] Quentin Skinner, *The foundations of modern political thought*, ii: *The age of Reformation* (Cambridge, 1978), 338. Skinner (wisely) added that 'the possibility of mutual influence [between Dutch and French treatises] ought not to be ruled out. A great deal more research in the Dutch sources will be needed, however, before it will be possible to pronounce with confidence on this point.'

[6] See e.g. Carlos M. N. Eire, *War against the idols: the reformation of worship from Erasmus to Calvin* (Cambridge, 1986), 304, who reasserts that 'the significance of the Dutch Revolt... lies in its application of the Calvinist theory of resistance rather than in its formulation'.

[7] The only two previous monographs on the topic are A. C. J. de Vrankrijker, *De motiveering van onzen opstand* (Nijmegen, 1933; repr. 1979); P. A. M. Geurts, *De Nederlandse Opstand in de pamfletten 1566–1584* (Utrecht, 1983; first pub. 1956).

[8] See E. H. Kossmann, 'Bodin, Althusius en Parker, of: over de moderniteit van de Nederlandse Opstand', in E. H. Kossmann, *Politieke theorie en geschiedenis: verspreide opstellen en voordrachten* (Amsterdam, 1987; first pub. 1958), 93–111; E. H. Kossmann, 'Popular sovereignty at the beginning of the Dutch *ancien régime*', *LCHY* 14 (1981), 1–28. For a different and much more qualified view see M. E. H. N. Mout, 'Van arm vaderland tot eendrachtige republiek: de rol van politieke theorieën in de Nederlandse Opstand', *BMGN* 101 (1986), 345–65, and also Nicolette Mout, 'Ideales Muster oder erfundene Eigenart: republikanische Theorien während des niederländischen Aufstands', in H. G. Koenigsberger (ed.), *Republiken und Republikanismus im Europa der frühen Neuzeit* (Munich, 1988), 169–94.

[9] Kossmann, 'Popular sovereignty', 2.

behind 'the course of history'.[10] Moreover, Dutch sixteenth-century political thought has been argued to be 'unmodern', not to say conservative. Unlike Bodin's theory, which turned the new state into a creative force, Dutch authors, and 'Calvinist constitutionalists' in general, merely sought 'to stabilize the dynamic of the state as it developed in power and scope, and to make the process of political decision-making objective'.[11]

These interpretations have contributed greatly to the intellectual history of the Dutch Revolt. One of their problems is that they leave their underlying notion of 'political theory' rather unclarified. At times it seems that 'political theory' is held to be a coherent, relatively abstract set of political ideas with both explanatory and normative, if not predictive, power.[12] Undoubtedly such a view is legitimate, although it seems to narrow the study of political thought and probably leads to the conclusion that very few sixteenth- and seventeenth-century political thinkers qualify as political theorists.[13]

I.2. SCOPE AND OBJECTIVES OF THE RESEARCH

In this book I attempt to contribute to the intellectual history of the Dutch Revolt by offering a different perspective on the political thought of the Revolt on the basis of an analysis of about 800 political treatises published between 1555 and 1590.[14] My aim is threefold.

First, I focus on how Dutch authors justified first the protest and later the armed resistance against the government of Philip II and how they underpinned the latter's abjuration. The essential question

---

[10] Mout, *Van arm vaderland*, 365.

[11] Kossmann, 'Popular sovereignty', 28; also Kossmann, 'Bodin', 109.

[12] Thus the leading question of Kossmann's classic study on 'political theory in the seventeenth-century Netherlands' is whether the Dutch 'have succeeded in explaining and defending the exceptional construction [i.e. the Republic], which dominated their community life, in a theory which indicated its place in the larger context of the world's forms of states? Have they been able to define precisely what their state was and how it should develop itself?' See E. H. Kossmann, *Politieke theorie in het zeventiende-eeuwse Nederland* (Amsterdam, 1960), 7. It is striking that this notion of political theory does not seem to differentiate between empirical and normative political theory.

[13] In fact not many 20th-century political thinkers will do. For example, it is doubtful whether John Rawls, generally considered to be a leading political philosopher, can qualify as 'political theorist' since his 'theory for justice' seems at many points to be out of touch with political reality (see William A. Galston, 'Moral personality and liberal theory', *Political Theory*, 10 (1982), 492–519). It can of course be questioned whether Rawls' 'theory of justice' in fact demands normative political theory to be empirically explanatory (and if so, how far). See John Rawls, *A theory of justice* (Oxford, 1973), in particular pp. 46–54.

[14] For information on the primary sources used in this study, see Appendix: a note on primary sources.

in this respect is whether, and if so how, Dutch authors articulated a right of resistance and of abjuration. Thus ideas on political obedience and resistance are central to the book.

Secondly, I reconstruct the ideas of the Revolt's advocates on the authority and character of what may be called the 'good government' for the Netherlands. In this respect I pay special attention to discussions concerning the form of government, the issue of sovereignty and the debate on the relationship between political and ecclesiastical authorities. In other words, the second focus of this book is on ideas about the character of the Dutch political order.

Finally, by way of conclusion, I locate the political thought of the Dutch Revolt, as interpreted here, in the intellectual context of some of the main streams of sixteenth-century European political thought. By relating it to monarchomach ideology and to the Italian republicanism of the Machiavellian moment, the aim is to arrive at some conclusions about the character and origins of the political thought of the Dutch Revolt, and to indicate its significance for the development of modern European political thought.

In its approach this study attempts to benefit from the profound methodological changes that have affected the history of political thought in recent times due to the debate whose origins can be traced to the 1960s when J. G. A. Pocock and Quentin Skinner in particular launched their attacks against the prevailing orthodoxies in the history of political thought.[15]

The first orthodoxy to be attacked was textualism, which basically claimed that the text itself forms 'the sole necessary key to its own meaning'.[16] In order to understand a text one only needs to focus on the text itself. With its focus on the eternal wisdoms old texts are claimed to enshrine, this orthodoxy, so Skinner emphasized, has failed to acknowledge the historicity of texts. It has failed to recognize

---

[15] Skinner's main methodological articles, some critical responses and Skinner's own reply have been assembled in James H. Tully (ed.), *Meaning and context: Quentin Skinner and his critics* (Oxford, 1988). In addition see John G. Gunnell, *Political theory: tradition and interpretation* (Cambridge, 1979); Andrew Lockyer, 'Traditions as context in the history of political theory', *Political Studies*, 27 (1979), 201–17; Peter L. Janssen, 'Political thought as traditionary action: the critical response to Skinner and Pocock', *History and Theory*, 24 (1985), 115–46; Richard Ashcraft, 'Introduction', in Richard Ashcraft, *Revolutionary politics and Locke's 'Two Treatises of Government'* (Princeton, NJ, 1986), 3–16. Pocock's main methodological articles are listed in the Bibliography. A lucid interpretation of the changes in the field of intellectual history is Donald R. Kelley, 'Horizons of intellectual history: retrospect, circumspect, prospect', *JHI* 48 (1987), 143–69.

[16] Quentin Skinner, 'Meaning and the understanding of speech acts', in Tully (ed.), *Meaning and context*, 29.

that a text is the embodiment of a particular use of words and sentences by a particular author at a particular time. To understand this particular, historical use of words and sentences, the student of political thought has to move beyond the text itself.

This should not, however, lead to embracing the second orthodoxy, contextualism, which held that, in order to understand a text, appropriate knowledge of its social and political context suffices. According to Skinner, contextualism failed to see that to explain why an author has written a text is not the same thing as understanding the text itself.[17] Thus, whereas textualism ignored the historicity of human action, contextualism misconceived of the relationship between text and context. If the aim is to recover the historical identity of texts, the hermeneutic enterprise of intellectual history should be guided by what Skinner has labelled a 'historical and intertextual approach'.[18]

In attempting to construct such an approach, which acknowledges the importance of both the historicity of texts and the relationship between text and context, Pocock and Skinner have underlined the importance of linguistic and intellectual contexts. A principal starting-point for their approaches is the recognition that each political author has to be seen, as Pocock has put it, 'as inhabiting a universe of *langues* that give meaning to the *paroles* he performs in them'.[19] Although this sounds rather linguistic, the essential point is in fact to recognize the highly normative, political character of *langues*, of 'languages' used in political discourse. According to Pocock, *langues* 'will exert the kind of force that has been called para-digmatic... That is to say, each will present information selectively as relevant to the conduct and character of politics, and it will encourage the definition of political problems and values in certain ways and not in others.'[20] Basically, this argument means that each author of political texts lives in a society where one or more modes of political discourse, or (the term preferred in this study) ideologies, are either available or in development. These 'modes of discourse', which together can be said to make up what Skinner has called the

[17] See Quentin Skinner, 'Motives, intentions and the interpretation of texts', and 'Social meaning and the explanation of social action', both in Tully (ed.), *Meaning and context*, where it is argued that there is a 'sharp line' to be drawn between the motives of an actor to do action *x* and the intentions the author has in doing act *x*. Contextual factors can show the reasons, the motives, for performing act *x*. They do not, however, unveil the 'point' of act *x*.

[18] Quentin Skinner, 'A reply to my critics', in Tully (ed.), *Meaning and context*, 232.

[19] J. G. A. Pocock, 'Introduction: the state of the art', in J. G. A. Pocock, *Virtue, commerce and history* (Cambridge, 1985), 5.   [20] Pocock, *Virtue, commerce and history*, 8.

'normative vocabulary' of a society, will contain certain fundamental assumptions about human nature, about politics and about society. They will stress certain problems, they will use certain concepts with a more or less fixed meaning to discuss these problems, they will have certain modes of argument and certain ways of proceeding to do this and they will come up with certain solutions.[21]

Recapturing the normative vocabulary of the society and culture to which an interpreted text belonged is one of the basic steps in the process of interpretation.[22] Having recovered this normative vocabulary of ideologies, it may become possible to see what an author was historically 'doing' in a certain text, that is, it may become possible to ascertain what sort of intellectual moves he was making in his text, compared to the available ideologies. Thus, the study of political ideas very much becomes focused on the moves authors make within ideologies, on how authors endorse, refute, elaborate or ignore 'the prevailing assumptions and conventions of political debate'[23] or, in other words, on how authors accept, modify and innovate ideologies. The history of political thought thereby changes its nature. In being focused on the formation and transformation of modes of political discourse, the history of political thought is turned into a history of continua of political discourse, as Pocock has called it,[24] or, to quote Skinner, into the history of the growth and development of ideologies.[25]

In this new history of ideologies, ideology is conceived of as 'a language of politics', which means that an ideology will contain a number of basic assumptions about human nature, politics and society, that it will focus on certain political problems, that it will employ certain concepts to discuss these problems, that it will have certain modes of argument to do so and that it will come up with certain solutions. As such, ideology entails a belief system and can still be described as 'a more or less coherent conglomerate of assumptions, attitudes, sentiments, values, ideals and goals accepted and perhaps

---

[21] Quentin Skinner, 'Hermeneutics and the role of history', *New Literary History*, 7 (1975–6), 221.

[22] According to Pocock, *Virtue, commerce and history*, 9, 'it is a large part of our historian's practice to learn to read and recognize the diverse idioms of political discourse as they were available in the culture and at the time he is studying: to identify them as they appear in the linguistic texture of any one text and to know what they would ordinarily have enabled that text's author to propound or "say"'.

[23] Quentin Skinner, *The foundations of modern political thought*, vol. i, p. xiii. In making this point Skinner is greatly indebted to recent developments in the theory of speech-acts and to the work of Austin in particular.   [24] Pocock, *Virtue, commerce and history*, 28.

[25] Skinner, *The foundations of modern political thought*, vol. i, p. xiii.

acted upon by a more or less organized group of persons'.[26] At the same time, however, the intrinsic connections between ideology and language are emphasized in Skinner's conception of ideology, which is built on the recognition that meaning is primarily constructed within language, and as such has the crucial advantage of bringing the social character of ideology to the fore. By focusing on the links between normative vocabulary, social context and individual ideological moves, the collective aspects of ideology are underlined. In many ways the relationship between ideology and individual ideological moves is seen in terms of a duality. On the one hand, the normative vocabulary enables individuals to structure and interpret the world they live in, both in an empirical and in a normative sense; it allows them to make sense of and to evaluate the changing world around them.[27] Thus individual ideological moves are generated, which, on the other hand, reproduce or transform particular ideologies. Thus, a study of what an author was 'doing' in a text is to an important extent a study of how an author reproduces or transforms ideologies.[28]

As a language of politics, an ideology has some specific characteristics. It has, to begin with, a specific subject. Although the assumptions on human nature, society, politics etc. on which ideology is grounded will be embedded in everyday practices, ideology connects them with a specific domain, the reflection on 'the binding and authoritative allocation of values in society', to invoke a classic definition of politics.[29] It means that an ideology is praxis-oriented. On the one hand, political praxis 'sets the main problems for the political theorist';[30] on the other hand, ideology tries to come to terms with these problems. Moreover, ideological writings explicitly advocate certain solutions and it is their aim to persuade an audience to adopt these solutions. Therefore, ideological writings will anticipate the audience they intend to persuade. In these respects

[26] Donald R. Kelley, *The beginning of ideology: consciousness and society in the French Reformation* (Cambridge, 1981), 4.   [27] See Ashcraft, *Revolutionary politics*, 5.

[28] According to Pocock it should be noted that acts of 'rule or paradigm innovation may be performed explicitly or implicitly, overtly or covertly, intentionally or unintentionally, and much depends upon reception and reader response; the reader and interpreter may have the resources of rhetoric at his disposal too. Many an author has found himself a more radical innovator than, or even than, he intended to be or ever admitted he was.' J. G. A. Pocock, 'The concept of language and the *métier d'historien*: some considerations on practice', in Anthony Pagden (ed.), *The languages of political theory in early modern Europe* (Cambridge, 1987), 34.

[29] David Easton, *A framework for political analysis* (Chicago, Ill., 1979), 50, 57.

[30] Skinner, *The foundations of modern political thought*, vol. i, p. xi.

ideological treatises can be said to form a distinctive genre of publications, with a proper subject, a specific strategy and a strong alignment to the practical necessities of society.

Skinner has emphasized that this alignment between ideology and political praxis should be seen in terms of a dynamic mutual dependence. Political thought is not simply a mirror, reflecting the whims of political action. Take the 'hardest case' where professed political principles will only serve as a mere legitimization of political action. No matter how revolutionary this action may have been, if its agent wants to legitimize it, he has 'to show that a number of the existing range of favourable evaluative–descriptive terms can somehow be applied as apt descriptions of his own apparent untoward actions'.[31] His legitimization,. that is, has to take the normative vocabulary as its starting-point, which the agent can then try to manipulate. This means that any course of action which cannot be legitimized out of the existing normative vocabulary will be strongly inhibited. Consequently, the scope of the possible courses of action is limited by the normative vocabulary. Even if the agent in question is as shrewd in manipulating this normative vocabulary as can be, he still

cannot hope to stretch the application of existing principles indefinitely; correspondingly, he can only hope to legitimate a restricted range of actions. It follows that to study the principles which the agent finally chooses to profess must be to study one of the key determinants of his decision to follow out any one particular line of action.[32]

The restructuring of the history of political thought as propounded by Pocock and Skinner (and many others) has been a source of major intellectual and methodical inspiration for this study. Thus this study not only presents and analyses the important political treatises of the Dutch Revolt, it will also specifically focus on how they are interconnected. It is a principal objective to explore if, and how far, the political treatises of the Dutch Revolt shared basic assumptions on human nature, politics and society, formulated similar problems, employed similar modes of argument, reasserted and innovated arguments and developed similar (or contrasting) solutions for key political problems. In other words, this is essentially a study of the growth and development of ideologies of the Dutch Revolt.

---

[31] Quentin Skinner, 'Some problems in the analysis of political thought and action', in Tully (ed.), *Meaning and context*, 112.   [32] Ibid., 117.

This has important consequences for the selection of material presented here. As it is physically impossible to include all the treatises which have, in one way or another, contributed to the political thought of the Dutch Revolt, I concentrate on those treatises which have contributed significantly to the formation and trans-formation of political ideologies of the Dutch Revolt, either by developing, substantially reasserting, refuting or innovating argu-ments on the issues which are central to this study, such as obedience, resistance, forms of government, sovereignty and the relationship between church and political authorities.[33]

1.3. OUTLINE

If, as Pocock has put it, 'political speech is of course practical and informed by present necessities'[34] it will be useful to start by offering a synthesis of the political context of the political thought of the Dutch Revolt, not only because it will provide the reader with information about the actual circumstances in which treatises were written but also because it will show which practical political necessities and problems treatises were responding to, and, finally, because it will provide necessary background information about institutional and political arrangements and developments to which treatises might allude. Thus this study opens with an introductory chapter on the Dutch Revolt, sketching the basic features of the political culture and the institutional framework of the Burgundian Netherlands and outlining the main political developments of the Revolt.

Chapter 3 is an attempt to reconstruct the answers that Reformed Protestants articulated with regard to the questions of obedience and resistance with which they were increasingly confronted during the 1550s and 1560s due to the policy of severe persecution of protestants. The purpose of this chapter is to establish whether there was a more or less distinct Reformed approach to the questions of obedience and resistance, and, if so, what the Reformed ideas on political authority, obedience and resistance amounted to.

Chapter 4 explores the political justification of the Dutch Revolt. It reconstructs the political arguments that were developed to justify and motivate the protest and resistance against Philip II and his

---

[33] The result of this process of selection has been that, of all 800 treatises studied, about 250 titles are presented in this study.   [34] Pocock, *Virtue, commerce and history*, 13.

government, which finally led to the 1581 abjuration. Thus, Chapter 4 reconstructs the political ideologies of resistance of the Revolt.

Chapter 5 is devoted to an analysis of the quest for 'the best state of the commonwealth' as undertaken by Dutch political treatises from about 1578, when, more and more, the break with Philip II was recognized to be inevitable. This chapter probes and analyses the answers of Dutch political treatises with regard to the problems and future of the political order of the Netherlands.

Chapter 6 again focuses on politics and religion. It examines the debates in the Dutch Provinces of the 1570s and 1580s on the key issues of religious peace, the relationship between church and political government and the paramount issue of toleration.

Chapter 7, finally, attempts, by way of conclusion to relate the political thought of the Dutch Revolt to some of the main streams of sixteenth-century European political thought. By confronting the political thought of the Revolt with the Huguenot monarchomachic ideology and the Italian republicanism of the Machiavellian moment in particular, this chapter sums up the main findings of the book and gives an interpretation of the significance of the political thought of the Dutch Revolt for the development of modern European political thought.

It should be emphasized that this interpretation of the political thought of the Dutch Revolt obviously neglects a number of important dimensions of the intellectual history of the late sixteenth-century Low Countries. For example, since this book deals with the political thought of the *proponents* of the Dutch Revolt, the political ideas of those who, at one point or another, wanted to remain faithful to Philip II are (if only for reasons of economy) much neglected. Thus I will not examine in detail whether there was any substantial intellectual debate between proponents and opponents of the Revolt. Evidently some treatises of proponents of the Revolt were explicitly directed against adversaries but most of these were distinguished by accusation and insinuation rather than by intellectual debate. Occasional references to 'Spanish-minded' authors occur, but do not indicate an extensive intellectual debate. None the less, it should be recognized that the material, as presented here, makes it unwarranted to draw definite conclusions with regard to the magnitude of intellectual debate between proponents and opponents of the Revolt.

Moreover, in studying the political thought of the proponents of the Dutch Revolt this book certainly does not cover all of its dimensions. Although questions on obedience and resistance and the character of the Dutch political order were undoubtedly of overwhelming concern, some other topics such as the social thought of the advocates of the Dutch Revolt would, considering the tradition of Christian humanism on this point,[35] certainly be worth studying. In fact, some treatises dealt exclusively with social issues; others, especially the treatises of Reformed Protestant ministers, included sections on such issues as charity.

Finally, even though the study of the political treatises published between 1555 and 1590 is essential for the interpretation of the Revolt's intellectual history, the importance of other sources for the history of political thought, conceived as a history of ideologies, should not be underestimated. Coins, letters, paintings, plays, printings, sermons and songs were all important as means of political expression and as vehicles of developing and transmitting political ideas.[36] I have made complementary use of some other forms of primary sources, though not systematically. A principal example is the analysis of Reformed Protestant thought on the issues of obedience and resistance (Chapter 3), which makes extensive use of church protocols. None the less, it is probably fair to say that to focus on the Revolt's political treatises is but to study 'the tip of an ideological iceberg'.[37]

---

[35] See e.g. Margo Todd, *Christian humanism and the Puritan social order* (Cambridge, 1987), ch. 2, which offers a reconstruction of 'Christian humanism as a social ideology', with singular attention for Erasmus and Vives.

[36] For a similar argument, see Ashcraft, *Revolutionary politics*, 6–7.

[37] Kelley, *The beginning of ideology*, 41.

CHAPTER 2

The Dutch Revolt: historical contexts[1]

2.1. THE NETHERLANDS AROUND 1555

'The people of this country are in general of beautiful stature, well made and proportioned, and amongst their other beautiful features they have the most beautiful men and women. In general their personage is upright but many exceed the normal and are tall, principally in Holland and Friesland where they are extremely tall.'[2]

In these terms the Florentine merchant Lodovico Guicciardini praised the physical features of the inhabitants of the Low Countries. Lodovico, who was a member of the famous Guicciardini dynasty and a nephew of Francesco Guicciardini, spent most of his life in the Netherlands, especially in Antwerp where he lived for forty-eight years. In 1567 he published his *Descrittione di tutti i Paesi Bassi*, which contained a meticulous description of the Low Countries, their towns and rivers, their economy, their political system and their inhabitants. According to Guicciardini the Dutch were rather 'cold' and sober-minded people, who wisely took the world and Fortune as it came. They were neither ambitious nor haughty, but polite and open, enjoying good company which sometimes led to licentiousness, especially since their main vice was drinking. Passion, even when love came into play, seemed alien to them: 'As persons of cold

---

[1] In addition to J. L. Motley's classic *The rise of the Dutch Republic* (various edns.) two more recent syntheses of the history of the Dutch Revolt in the English language are Pieter Geyl, *The Revolt of the Netherlands, 1555–1609* (London, 1932; repr. 1988) and Geoffrey Parker, *The Dutch Revolt*, rev. edn. (Harmondsworth, 1985). Recent Dutch syntheses are found in *AGN* vi and S. Groenveld, H. L. P. Leeuwenberg, N. Mout and W. M. Zappey, *De kogel door de kerk? De opstand in de Nederlanden 1559–1609*, 2nd rev. edn. (Zutphen, 1983). See also A. T. van Deursen and H. de Schepper, *Willem van Oranje: een strijd voor vrijheid en verdraagzaamheid* (Weesp, 1984), which combines an introduction to the Revolt with a short biography of William of Orange.

[2] Lodovico Guicciardini, *Descrittione di tutti i Paesi Bassi* (Antwerp, 1581), 39.

nature they are very temperate in the matters of Venus, and they strongly abhor adultery.'[3]

Guicciardini had a keen eye for Dutch women. He described them as beautiful, gracious and of good manners. According to Guicciardini women had an important position in Dutch society, as they not only took care of family matters, but also had their 'hand and mouth in all other masculine affairs' like commerce and business. They did so with such dexterity and diligence 'that in many parts, like in Holland and in Zeeland, the men leave almost everything for them to take care of'.[4]

It is estimated that in Guicciardini's times the Low Countries had about 3 million inhabitants. Two-thirds of them lived in the core provinces: Flanders, Brabant and Holland. By sixteenth-century standards these three provinces had an extremely high level of urbanization. Almost half of the population lived in towns. In 1566 Antwerp was by far the biggest town with 90,000 inhabitants. Brussels, with about 50,000 inhabitants came next, followed by Ghent (30,000) and Bruges and Amsterdam (both about 25,000).[5] Economically the towns were of principal importance. Although, as in all pre-industrial societies, agriculture was still the main foundation of economy and society and although agriculture played an important role in the economic upsurge of the Low Countries,[6] the urban element was undoubtedly the dominant factor in the economy and culture of the Low Countries. Once again the three core provinces (and Zeeland, which was enclosed by them) took the lead. Antwerp had become the trading and financial centre of Europe, and Amsterdam was starting to become the centre for the Baltic grain trade. Already in the fourteenth and fifteenth century economic life in the core provinces had begun to transcend the confines of feudalism. Commercial capitalism and domestic industrialization prospered in Brabant, Flanders and Holland.[7] During the 'beautiful sixteenth century', the period between 1490 and 1565, the economy flourished.

---

[3] Ibid. 43.
[4] Ibid. 44. For a recent study see Sherrin Marshall, 'Protestant, Catholic and Jewish women in the early modern Netherlands', in Sherrin Marshall (ed.), *Women in Reformation and Counter-Reformation Europe* (Bloomington, Ind., 1989), 120–39.
[5] Ghent and Bruges were on the way back. In the 14th century, Ghent, then the second largest city of Europe, had 64,000 and Bruges 46,000 inhabitants.
[6] See Jan de Vries, *The Dutch rural economy in the Golden Age, 1500–1700* (New Haven, Conn., 1974), esp. pp. 236–43.
[7] See Walter Prevenier and Wim Blockmans, *The Burgundian Netherlands* (Cambridge, 1985), 124, and Hugo de Schepper, *Belgium nostrum 1500–1650: over integratie en desintegratie van het Nederland* (Antwerp, 1987), 8.

The revival of the internal market and the gradual shift of the centre of the world economy from the Mediterranean to the Atlantic coasts of north-western Europe were important stimuli for the trading sector. Transit trade in particular experienced a remarkable growth. Later, structural improvements within the agricultural and manufacturing sectors of the Dutch economy itself became of great importance.

The benefits of the economic upsurge were not evenly distributed. In fact it has been argued that the economic growth of the 'beautiful sixteenth century' contributed to a growing polarization within Dutch society.[8] The main group to profit was the urban elite. For the merchants of Antwerp and other cities the period between 1490 and 1565 indeed was beautiful. Economic prosperity gave them the possibility of becoming the patrons of lavish arts and sciences. Small peasants and craftsmen were the main victims. For them the economic developments and the ascent of commercial capitalism meant growing poverty and increasing proletarianization. The rise of the textile industry in booming villages such as Hondschoote led to the formation of an industrial proletariat in the south-western part of Flanders. Here traditional mechanisms of social control broke up and the feudal order more than ever became a mirage.

In the 1560s economic growth came to an end. The agrarian sector was unable to sustain its pattern of growing production and the internal market for manufactured products collapsed. A severe commercial conflict with the English government had grave consequences for the textile industry, while the Danish–Polish–Swedish war had a dramatic impact for the Baltic grain trade. When in 1565 the harvest failed and the winter turned out to be extremely grim, a severe economic crisis followed, marked by sharply rising prices and massive unemployment. Of course the battles, sieges, plunderings and mutinies of the Dutch Revolt did not help to improve the situation. The years between 1565 and 1575 were the most problematic. However, as far as purchasing power was concerned, even during the Dutch Revolt the situation in Holland and also in

---

[8] See Hugo Soly, 'Le Grand essor du capitalisme commercial: villes et campagnes', in E. Witte (ed.), *Histoire de Flandre* (Brussels, 1983), 105–20 and J. A. van Houtte, 'Die Städte der Niederlande im übergang vom Mittelalter zur Neuzeit', in J. A. van Houtte, *Essays on medieval and early modern economy and society* (Louvain, 1977), 219–20. For a qualified view see E. Scholliers and C. Vandenbroecke, 'Structuren en conjuncturen in de Zuidelijke Nederlanden, 1480–1800', in *AGN* v. 252–310.

Antwerp was not as bad as in the rest of Europe.[9] Only the immediate years after 1586 were times of economic crisis, marked by decreasing purchasing power, rising prices and massive migration from the south to the new Republic, which not only wrecked the economy of the southern provinces but at first also contributed to the unemployment in the north.[10]

2.2. THE FORMATION OF THE BURGUNDIAN STATE

The growing economic unification of the core provinces was an important factor in the process of state formation in the Low Countries. Economic contacts and interests stimulated the growth of a sense of interdependence, and contributed to the rise of supraprovincial institutions, especially in the realm of jurisdiction and representation. More and more civil cases were put forward to supraprovincial courts for arbitration. More and more local authorities and private citizens, especially those of the core provinces, sent requests to the princely authority to settle certain issues. Thus, in a way reminiscent of what Elias has labelled the 'Königsmechanismus',[11] the need for co-operation and arbitration created the possibility of establishing and gradually strengthening a central state apparatus. The Burgundian–Habsburg dynasty was both eager and able to exploit this possibility.

The territorial unification of the Low Countries was started in the late fourteenth century. In 1384 Philip the Bold, Duke of Burgundy, acquired Flanders and Artois. Before the turn of the century Philip also acquired control over Brabant and Limburg. Under his grandson Philip the Good a personal union between these provinces was forged in 1430. Three years later Philip became Count of Holland, Zeeland and Hainaut, thus unifying the core provinces of the Low Countries.

---

[9] See L. Noordegraaf, *Hollands welvaren? Levensstandaard in Holland 1450–1650* (Bergen, NH, 1985), 172–3. This conclusion was confirmed in the subsequent debate about Noordegraaf's book. See 'Welvarend Holland: discussie over L. Noordegraaf, "Hollands welvaren? Levensstandaard in Holland 1450–1650"', *BMGN* 102 (1987), 229–58.

[10] See L. Noordegraaf, 'Dearth, famine and social policy in the Dutch republic at the end of the sixteenth century', in Peter Clark (ed.), *The European crisis of the 1590s* (London, 1985), 67–83.

[11] Norbert Elias, *Uber den Prozess der Zivilisation*, 2 vols., 8th edn. (Frankfurt am Main, 1982), ii. 222–79, esp. p. 236. See also W. P. Blockmans, 'Breuk of continuiteit? De Vlaamse privilegien van 1477 in het licht van het staatsvormingsproces', in W. P. Blockmans (ed.), *1477: le privilège général et les privilèges régionaux de Marie de Bourgogne pour les Pays-Bas*, Ancien pays et assemblées d'états, lxxx (Kortrijk-Heule, 1985), 114.

From the outset the Burgundian dynasty had combined territorial expansion with a policy of centralization and state-building. Philip the Good and his son Charles the Bold systematically sought to create and strengthen institutions at the central level. To an important extent this policy proved to be successful. By 1473 an impressive network of central financial and judicial institutions had been created. The subsequent defeat and death of Charles the Bold in the 1477 battle of Nancy, however, not only led to the loss of the Duchy of Burgundy to the French king, it also led to a profound political crisis within the Low Countries themselves. In this crisis a sort of 'legal revolution'[12] took place. By means of the Grand Privilege, which applied to the Burgundian Netherlands as a whole, four provincial privileges and dozens of urban privileges, the towns and States assemblies imposed upon Mary of Burgundy, Charles' heiress, a number of institutional reforms which strongly curtailed central power. The Burgundian state as such, however, was not destroyed. On the contrary, the States General immediately recognized Mary as the legitimate successor of her father, and took measures to protect the Netherlands against the French king.

The 1477 restriction of central power, however, was temporary. Between 1490 and 1506 Philip the Fair was able to regain much of the ground that had been lost in the 1477 crisis. The marriage of his mother, Mary, with Maximilian of Austria had meant a fusion between the Burgundian and the Habsburg dynasties. The consequences proved to be enormous. Unexpectedly the marriage of Philip himself with Juana of Castile, intended to seal the alliance between the Habsburgs and the Spanish monarchs against the King of France, led to a personal union with Spain when through a twist of fate Juana became Queen of Castile. Thus the Low Countries were united with Spain. Moreover, Charles, the son of Philip the Fair and Juana of Castile, not only became King of Spain, he was also elected Holy Roman Emperor. During his reign Charles V completed the territorial unification of the Low Countries. He acquired Tournai, Friesland, Utrecht, Overijssel, Groningen, Drenthe and finally, in 1543, Guelders.

The emperor also established the administrative independence of the Netherlands. In 1529 with the treaty of Cambrai Francis I

---

[12] See Maurice-A. Arnould, 'Le lendemains de Nancy dans les "pays de par deçà", Janvier–Avril 1477', in Blockmans (ed.), *1477*, 1–2. Arnould's article contains a detailed analysis of the crisis of 1477.

formally renounced his feudal rights over certain parts of the Low
Countries, namely Artois, Tournai and most of Flanders. In 1548
with the Transaction of Augsburg the Habsburg dominions in the
Low Countries were brought together in a separate Burgundian
Circle, whose ties with the Holy Roman Empire were virtually non-
existent. Most of all the Augsburg Transaction freed the Netherlands
from imperial legislation and jurisdiction. A year later, in 1549, it was
decided that the Dutch Provinces would have the same hereditary
succession. Finally, the Netherlands had become 'one and inseparable'.

The proliferation of the Burgundian state apparatus implied the
growth of a corps of professional civil servants. Already, during the
fourteenth and fifteenth century, jurists with a university training in
Roman and canon law strongly contributed to the growth of central
state power, especially in the judicial and financial domains.
Gradually the political importance of this group waxed. This led to
frictions with the nobility, another pillar of the Burgundian state.

During the Burgundian era the nobility was unable to retain the
paramount position it had had before 1300. An enormous decrease in
its purchasing power, due primarily to the dramatic fall in the value
of large rents, turned the nobility into a vulnerable group. Its support
for the Burgundian cause could easily be bought with money, offices
and honorific titles such as Knight of the Order of the Golden Fleece,
founded in 1430 by Philip the Good. The support of the nobility was
enlisted and Burgundian power thereby consolidated. The nobles
were used as power-brokers, not only to create a form of national
conscience but also, by means of offices such as provincial governors,
to function as the first 'levers' for the integration of the diverse
regional networks of power and patronage.

Patronage surely was the 'cement of the Burgundian state'.[13]
Despite the proliferation of the state apparatus and the rise of
powerful bureaucrats, the Burgundian state was too weak to
implement its policy in all regions by itself. It had to rely on more
informal mechanisms of integration such as patronage, venality of
offices and corruption to achieve its goals, and to overcome the forces
of regionalism and particularism.

[13] Prevenier and Blockmans, *The Burgundian Netherlands*, 264. See also H. F. K. van Nierop,
   'Willem van Oranje als hoog edelman: patronage in de Habsburgse Nederlanden?' *BMGN*
   99 (1984), 651–76, and Wim Blockmans, 'Corruptie, patronage, makelaardij en venaliteit
   als symptomen van een ontluikende staatsvorming in de Bourgondische Nederlanden',
   Tijdschrift voor Sociale Geschiedenis, 11 (1985), 231–47.

2.3. THE POLITICAL STRUCTURE AND CULTURE OF THE NETHERLANDS AROUND 1555

When Philip II succeeded his father, Charles V, in 1555, he did not formally become lord of the Netherlands. He acquired a large number of titles, such as Duke of Brabant, Duke of Guelders, Count of Flanders, Count of Holland and Lord of Friesland, which together made him the sovereign over the Low Countries. Despite the long and powerful tradition of centralization of the Burgundian–Habsburg dynasty the governmental structure Philip inherited was still a classic example of the late medieval system of *dominium politicum et regale*,[14] exemplified by a rather complicated set of political institutions.

In theory the sovereign had a broad authority, which covered what was called 'policy, justice and grace'.[15] The sovereign was the chief legislator, the supreme judge and the only one competent to grant pardon and reprieve; he had the right of appointment with regard to important ecclesiastical posts and he claimed to have the unique authority to convene the States General.

As both Charles V and Philip II were frequently absent from the Netherlands – Philip left the Netherlands for good in 1559 – they appointed a Governor-General, usually a close relative, to govern the Low Countries in their name and place. In theory the sovereign delegated his authority to the Governor-General. In practice neither Charles V nor Philip II wished to loosen their control over the government of the Netherlands. By secret instruction several important issues, such as convening the States General and making important political and ecclesiastical appointments, remained the unique prerogative of the sovereign and, through letters or secret dispatches, Charles and Philip continually passed orders to their Governor-Generals to steer daily politics.

[14] *Dominium politicum et regale* as developed by Sir John Fortescue in his 15th-century treatise on *The governance of England* refers to a type of government whose essence was that, especially with regard to taxation, 'the king should rule by such laws as he makes himself (*dominium regale*), but such laws should receive the assent of his people (*dominium politicum*)'. See H. G. Koenigsberger, *Dominium regale or Dominium politicum et regale: monarchies and parliaments in early modern Europe* (London, 1975), which also discusses the Netherlands (pp. 16–21). Koenigsberger has argued that the reign of Charles V over the Netherlands was a 'typical example' of *dominium politicum et regale*. See H. G. Koenigsberger, 'Why did the States General of the Netherlands become revolutionary in the sixteenth century?' *Parliaments, Estates and Representation*, 2 (1982), 103.

[15] See Hugo de Schepper, 'De burgerlijke overheden en hun permanente kaders, 1480–1579', in *AGN* v. 157.

The Governor-Generals were to be guided by the advice of three governmental councils, the Collateral Councils, which Charles V had created in 1531. The Collateral Councils fitted well into the pattern of Burgundian government.[16] Their creation was an attempt not only to check the Governor-General but also to channel the power of the high nobility for the benefit of Burgundian policy. In appointing ten nobles to the Council of State, the most important of the three councils, Charles V sought to prevent the high nobility becoming a source of opposition to the Governor-General and thus to himself. As members of the Collateral Councils the high nobles themselves had been turned into officers of central policy.

The Collateral Councils were also intended to split the nobles and the professional civil servants into different councils, in order to stop a growing animosity between these groups. However, the Council of State, the council of the nobles, could not withdraw itself from the process of bureaucratization. In later years a number of jurists, the so-called *togati*, entered the ranks of the Council of State.[17] Functions such as president and secretary of the Council, the formulation of proposals and the implementation of decisions required legal expertise, and while the nobles were frequently unable to participate in the deliberations of the Council if only because they served the sovereign on the battlefield, the jurists soon became its permanent members. Although the nobility continued to play an important role in the Council of State throughout the sixteenth century, the influence of the jurists increased. Top civil servants gradually became top politicians.

The competence of the Council of State was defined rather vaguely; its task was to advise the sovereign and the Governor-General on 'the great and principal affairs of state'. The Council was of primary importance in dealing with foreign affairs and with matters of defence and public order. Quite often it also gave the final advice in matters which belonged with the other Collateral Councils. In fact, whenever the Governor-General, who convened the Council, deemed it necessary, the Council was asked for advice.

[16] See M. Baelde, *De collaterale raden onder Karel V en Filips II, 1531–1578: bijdrage tot de geschiedenis van de centrale instellingen in de zestiende eeuw* (Brussels, 1965), who shows (pp. 4–12), that the Collateral Councils were not created out of the blue but were the outcome of a tendency to a conciliary form of central government, starting well into the 15th century.

[17] In 1555 seven nobles and five jurists were members of the Council of State (Baelde, *De collaterale raden onder Karel V en Filips II*, 76). The Bishop of Arras, Antoine de Perrenot, Prince William of Orange, Count Lamoraal of Egmont, Count Hendrik of Brederode, Count Charles of Berlaymont and the Frisian jurist Viglius, who would all in one way or another play an important role in the Dutch Revolt, were amongst them.

The Privy Council, whose members were all trained professional jurists, was an important and loyal institution in constructing and implementing the Burgundian–Habsburg policy of centralization. It played a pivotal role in preparing and implementing legislation and it had a number of tasks in public administration. The Privy Council was also important as a court, especially as a court of appeal. Finally, the Council dealt with matters touching sovereignty, such as granting privileges, patents and acts of grace.

The Council of Finances administered the domains and finances of the sovereign. It took care of the financial administration of the Crown's properties, it took part in the negotiations with the States assemblies over tax propositions and it controlled the process of taxation as a whole. The Council also supervised lower financial institutions and advised in major financial transactions.

The rise of the professional civil servant was also noticeable in the governmental institutions at the provincial level. Each province had its own Council of Justice dealing with the administration of justice and with public administration in general. In the homologation of law and justice, both crucial to the process of integration, these councils were of great importance. They had an advisory and implementing role in legislative affairs and they functioned both as a court of first instance and as a court of appeal for local sentences. Nobles had been members of the Councils of Justice, but in the course of the sixteenth century the policy was adopted in general to appoint only professional jurists as members. The growing importance of the Councils of Justice had its repercussions for the provincial Governor or Stadtholder. Traditionally the Stadtholder, a post normally occupied by a high noble, had been the principal representative of central government at the provincial level. As in theory the Stadtholder was the direct substitute of the sovereign in the province, his authority, derived from sovereign authority, gave him wide powers. Thus he had the right to appoint, in co-operation with the court at Brussels, the public officials in the province and probably also the military governors. During the reigns of Charles V and Philip II, however, systematic attempts were made to curtail the competence of the Stadtholder, to the benefit of the central government and of its more loyal representatives in the provinces, the Councils of Justice. This policy was quite successful. In 1559, for example, the formal powers of William of Orange, who was appointed Stadtholder of Holland and Zeeland, were strongly curtailed.

It was much more difficult for the central government to deal with the provincial States assemblies. The provincial States came into being during the late Middle Ages. Their origins were diverse. In the north, for example, the States assemblies had arisen, in the course of the fifteenth century, out of the advisory council of the provincial lord, in which his vassals and *ad hoc* representatives of towns participated, and out of the diverse assemblies of freeholders, well known in provinces like Holland, Zeeland, Drenthe and Friesland.[18] In all regions, however, with the exception of Brabant and Hainaut, the diverse regional assemblies were only turned into provincial States after the assimilation of the regions in the Burgundian state.

In late medieval theory the States were considered to be the representative assembly of the people, of the complex of the three feudal estates. Therefore, in theory, all three estates, clergy, nobility and citizenry, were represented in the States. In practice there were enormous differences between the provinces at this point. Even in Brabant, Flanders, Hainaut, Utrecht, Zeeland, Luxemburg, Namur and Artois, where all three estates were represented in the provincial States, there occurred great differences in actual power relations. In Brabant and Hainaut every estate had one vote, and unanimity in the decision-making process was required, yet the Brabant towns were much more involved in political life. Having dominated the duchy between 1261 and 1430, the four capitals Louvain, Brussels, Antwerp and Bois-le-Duc were, since then, constantly engaged in a precarious political struggle with the provincial nobility and the duke.[19] In Flanders the cities of Bruges, Ghent and Ypres controlled the States together with the Franc de Bruges. In Holland the clergy was missing in the States assembly, while in Friesland, even less affected by feudalism, both nobility and clergy were missing. In the north their places were occupied by freeholding farmers.

Thus in the core provinces of Flanders and Holland, and to a lesser extent in Brabant, the cities played a dominant role in the States. In the more rural provinces of the east and south (the north, with Friesland and Overijssel, was an apparent exception) the nobility preserved much of its strength and in the south also the clergy retained its position. The States assemblies of the core provinces also

---

[18] See P. H. D. Leupen, 'De representatieve instellingen in het noorden, 1384–1482', in *AGN* iv. 164–72.

[19] See R. van Uytven, 'Vorst, adel en steden: een driehoeksverhouding in Brabant van de twaalfde tot de zestiende eeuw', *Bijdragen tot de Geschiedenis*, 59 (1976), 93–122.

had a higher level of activity than the States assemblies in more rural areas such as Hainaut and Artois, which met less frequently.[20]

The provincial States considered themselves to be the *contrepoids* of the sovereign. With great eagerness they guarded their provincial rights and freedoms. They were of the opinion that important political decisions concerning, for example, successions, monetary questions and matters of war should never be taken without their co-operation and consent.

An important source of power of the States was the fact that for levying taxes the sovereign needed the explicit consent of the States assemblies. Although it was not so easy for them to reject a proposal, taxes could only be levied after the States had adjudged an aid or a subsidy. As the frequency of requests for even bigger subsidies increased during the sixteenth century, the States were able to strengthen their positions. The States of Flanders, Brabant, Holland and Zeeland, for example, acquired a certain control over the administration of the revenues and expenditures of the taxes.

In an attempt to escape from provincialism and to foster the idea of unity amongst the provinces, Philip the Good started to gather the provincial States in joint assemblies. From 1464 the States General of the Low Countries met on a regular basis. Formally the States General did not have any specific sphere of competence. In 1477 the Grand Privilege contained three articles dealing with its authority. They said that the prince of the Low Countries could not declare war without explicit consent of the States General and gave both provincial States and States General the freedom to assemble at their own initiative to 'discuss the matters, well-being and profit of our common countries'. Finally, article 20 ordained that new tolls demanded the consent of the countries.[21] In practice the prince informed the States General about the pivotal matters of state, such as questions regarding war and peace, foreign relations and important dynastic affairs. Such explanations often served to motivate requests for taxes which up to 1523 were generally addressed to the

---

[20] W. P. Blockmans, 'Le régime représentatif en Flandre dans le cadre européen au bas Moyen Age avec un projet d'application des ordinateurs', in *Album Elemér Mályusz: studies presented to the International Commission for the History of Representative and Parliamentary Institutions*, lvi (Brussels, 1976), 217–21.

[21] See the modern edition of the Grand Privilege in Blockmans (ed.), *1477*, 92–3. These articles were reconfirmed and extended in 1488. Soon, however, the validity of the Grand Privilege became controversial. Once the Burgundian–Habsburg dynasty had recovered from the blow of 1477, it started to denounce it, although the privilege explicitly proclaimed itself as being valid for eternity.

States General.[22] The States General, however, had no authority of its own to decide on these requests.

Its constitutive elements, the provincial States, saw the States General primarily as a useful instrument for increasing their influence in central policy. In the negotiations with the prince their deputies never had full powers to act. The basic rule of the decision-making process was that provincial deputies could only grant what their principals far away in the provinces had allowed them to. This not only made it almost impossible for the sovereign to exert the charismatic powers of his office, it also turned the negotiations into a time-consuming affair with great possibilities for creative obstructionism, especially as the decision-making process within the provincial States themselves was characterized by the same mechanism. Deputies of towns in the States assemblies normally had limited powers and took decisions only by order and after due consultation with the town governments, in which they themselves often played important roles.

The relation between the towns and the central government was a precarious balance of power. Custom, privileges and their economic and financial power had enabled the great towns to retain a large part of their independence. Guicciardini even compared the city government of Antwerp to that of a free republic: 'Antwerp has as her lord and prince the Duke of Brabant, margrave of the Holy Empire, but with so many and great privileges, obtained from antiquity on, that she governs and rules herself almost in the way of a free city and republic.'[23]

It was, for example, difficult for the prince to influence the composition of the town magistrate, as appointments were based in general on lists of candidates, proposed by the town government itself. On the other hand the towns needed the central government for co-ordination and arbitration and from time to time they also needed its coercive power to preserve public order. It is probably safe to conclude, as Guy Wells has done in his study on Antwerp, that central and local authority were 'inextricably bound up together to the extent that neither side could really function without the other's collaboration'.[24]

There was no uniform pattern of town government in the

[22] After 1523 requests for aids were often directly presented to the provincial States.
[23] Guicciardini, *Descrittione di tutti i Paesi Bassi*, 132.
[24] Guy Wells, *Antwerp and the government of Philip II, 1555–1567* (Ann Arbor, Mich., 1982), 136.

Netherlands.[25] The town magistrate consisted of aldermen, whose number varied from six to seventeen in the case of Antwerp, and normally one or more burgomasters. The town magistrate handled daily affairs of public administration and the court of aldermen administered justice. For important decisions the approval was needed of a larger town council, whose origins and composition varied throughout the Netherlands. In the north and especially in Holland and Zeeland the so-called *vroedschap*, which literally meant 'practical wisdom', developed. In the beginning this was a group of prominent and wealthy citizens, often former members of the town government, which was called for advice in important and contentious matters. Gradually this body developed into a distinct town council and in the sixteenth century it became the ultimate decision-making body in municipal affairs. It also made up the list of nominees out of which the sovereign yearly had to elect the new magistrate. In principle, members of the *vroedschap* were appointed for life and in case of vacancies the body itself appointed new members. The *vroedschap* was the essential part of the social and political elite of the town. None the less, as in the case of Gouda, the *vroedschappen* pretended to be representative institutions, 'representing the whole body of the town'.[26] With the exception of Dordrecht and Utrecht, in most northern towns other municipal corporations such as the guilds had no political role of importance in town government.

In the south the situation was different and even more complex.[27] First of all, in contrast with the north, in the course of the fourteenth century the guilds had been able to acquire an important role in town government. Thus, especially in Flanders, a number of aldermen were specifically recruited from the ranks of the guilds and also of the *poorterij*, the well-to-do citizenry. These groups were also present in the larger town council, also a product of fourteenth-century struggles for power, whose authority was comparable to the authority of the northern *vroedschap*. Also in Brabant citizenry and guilds were explicitly present in town government, although the role of the guilds

---

[25] For a historical sketch see R. van Uytven, 'Stadsgeschiedenis in het noorden en zuiden', in *AGN* ii. 187–253.
[26] C. C. Hibben, *Gouda in revolt: particularism and pacifism in the revolt of the Netherlands 1572–1588* (Utrecht, 1983), 26.
[27] See van Uytven, 'Stadsgeschiedenis' and also van Houtte, 'Die Städte der Niederlande', 222–7; W. P. Blockmans, *De volksvertegenwoordiging in Vlaanderen in de overgang van middeleeuwen naar nieuwe tijden (1384–1506)* (Brussels, 1978), 72–87; W. P. Blockmans, 'De representatieve instellingen in het zuiden 1384–1482', in *AGN* iv. 157–60.

here was of less weight than in Flanders. Like the Flemish towns the cities of Brabant had, besides the town magistrate, a 'greater' or 'broad' council, which had three or four collective 'members', the magistrate as first member included. Antwerp's broad council, for example, had four members. The second member comprised all former members of the magistrate. The third included the leaders of the thirteen city quarters and the four chiefs of the citizenry and represented the citizenry as such. The fourth, finally, comprised the deans of twenty-eight guilds. Since such a council included all groups, it was an important vehicle for bargaining processes under the leadership of the town magistrate, which in most instances was the dominant member of town government.

Of growing importance in all towns was the civil service, under the leadership of one or more professional town pensionaries. As university-trained jurists the town pensionaries were the local exponents of the rise of the professional civil servant and, to a certain extent, the response of the towns to the process of professionalization which was taking place at the central level.[28] Town pensionaries soon became key officials in town governments. The town pensionary was the principal political and legal councillor of town magistrates, often acted as their spokesman at the States assemblies and also frequently functioned as the town's 'ambassador'.

For the protection of public order the magistrate had to appeal to the citizen militia, which in social composition was an 'elite of the second rank'.[29] Their role in town politics, apparently not a highly active one, was not without importance, not only because they more or less controlled the town's military means, but also because they united citizens, non-members of town government from diverse professional backgrounds, in a body which was founded primarily on a sense of civic unity and solidarity.

In Dutch towns citizenship was acquired either by birth, by marriage, by having certain qualities or by paying a certain fee. The new citizen then had to swear the citizen oath. Citizenship essentially meant that one had to fulfil certain civic duties, such as serving in office or in the militia, and that one was entitled to certain economic,

---

[28] See J. A. F. de Jongste, 'Hollandse stadspensionarisssen tijdens de Republiek: notities bij een onderzoek', in S. Groenveld, M. E. H. N. Mout and I. Schöffer (eds.), *Bestuurders en geleerden* (Amsterdam, 1985), 85–96.

[29] J. C. Grayson, 'The civic militia in the county of Holland, 1560–1581: politics and public order in the Dutch Revolt', *BMGN* 95 (1981), 39.

social and legal privileges, such as the *jus de non evocando*, which said that a citizen could be put on trial only in his own town.

For the ordinary citizen, throughout the Burgundian–Habsburg era, his town remained the principal point of social and political identification. As the tradition of urban revolts exemplified, the great towns themselves never relinquished their ambition of becoming independent city republics. Although this ambition never materialized, the towns remained, as Smit has put it, 'semi-autonomous corporations with highly developed political lives of their own, for a highly integrative socialization process had found expression in a peculiarly republican political consciousness'.[30]

Cherishing self-government, towns and provinces had extorted a rich variety of written rights and freedoms from their sovereign lords throughout the late medieval period. As elsewhere in Europe, privileges served recipients in many ways. Some privileges conferred certain privileged economic rights or franchises to some town, guild or other corporation. Thus in 1299, Count Jan I of Holland granted the city of Dordrecht staple rights on wine, which made the town the centre of the wine trade. Other privileges were truly *Herrschafts-verträge*; they contained a 'frame of government',[31] dividing power between prince and subjects and thus delimiting the authority of the sovereign to a greater or lesser extent. Examples of this sort of privilege in the Low Countries were the Grand Privilege of 1477, the 1312 Charter of Kortenberg and the famous Joyous Entry of Brabant, to which every Duke of Brabant on the occasion of his inauguration by the States had to take a solemn oath, and which was confirmed by Philip II in 1549.[32]

The 1477 privileges and the Joyous Entry were principal vehicles for formulating political rights and duties. First, some articles were clearly intended to offer the inhabitants protection against arbitrary

---

[30] J. W. Smit, 'The Netherlands revolution', in R. Forster and J. P. Greene (eds), *Preconditions of revolution in early modern Europe* (Baltimore, Md., 1970), 28.

[31] J. P. A. Coopmans, 'Het privilege als vorm van wetgeving in de late middeleeuwen', in Willem Frijhoff and Minke Hiemstra (eds.), *Bewogen en bewegen: de historicus in het spanningsveld tussen economie en cultuur* (Tilburg, 1986), 108.

[32] The first Joyous Entry was granted, or rather extorted, in 1356. Already in its first formulation it was a 'sort of constitution which regulated the relation between prince and subjects in detail' (R. van Uytven, 'De rechtsgeldigheid van de Brabantse Blijde Inkomst van 3 januari 1356', *TvG* 82 (1969), 139). It was confirmed again in 1406, 1427, 1430, 1467, 1477 and 1494, and in 1515 by Charles V. Although the specific articles were open to important modifications from one Entry to another, the basic character of the Joyous Entry remained the same.

and corrupt rule. The Grand Privilege, as well as the other provincial privileges of 1477, in particular sought to ward off corruption. The privilege granted to Flanders had seventeen articles against corruption. Article 3 guaranteed that no one would seek office by means of bribery, article 5 promised a fair and honest administration of justice, prohibiting officers to accept bribes. Secondly, privileges guaranteed certain civic rights. Often these articles concerned the administration of justice. Principal examples were the seventh article of the 1549 Joyous Entry, which guaranteed equality before the law, and the 1477 privileges, which, amongst others, gave the inhabitants of the Low Countries the right to be tried in accordance with their local privileges. Both the Joyous Entry and the 1477 privileges contained a clause of disobedience, which stated that if the prince violated the privileges, the subjects, and, as the Grand Privilege added, 'each of them in particular', had the right to disobey him, to refuse him services, until he had repaired his ways.[33] Third, privileges such as the Grand Privilege and the Joyous Entry contained articles which restricted central power and articulated claims to participation in the decision-making process on behalf of the provinces, towns and inhabitants of the Low Countries. Thus, the 1477 privileges sought to decentralize the administration of justice, to strengthen the grip of the provinces on central policy, to guarantee the respect of all privileges and to strengthen the position of the States General. As such the privileges of 1477 were the expression of 'a conception of a federal state, dominated by the great cities'.[34]

Of course privileges like the Joyous Entry and the Grand Privilege by no means functioned as modern constitutions. They dealt with the problems of the day, and reflected the power relations between the parties involved; their application was never a simple legal matter, but depended primarily on fluctuations in power relations.[35] Flanders, for example, had no constitutional tradition, essentially because there was no need for the towns to back up their *de facto* political dominance with constitutional paper. The first Flemish constitution was granted in 1477, after the towns had suffered from the formidable power of Charles the Bold. Yet, even though the

---

[33] For a number of these clauses see R. van Uytven, '1477 in Brabant', in Blockmans (ed.), *1477*, 282–4.

[34] W. P. Blockmans, 'La signification constitutionnelle des privilèges de Marie de Bourgogne (1477)', in Blockmans (ed.), *1477*, 516.

[35] See R. van Uytven and W. P. Blockmans, 'Constitutions and their application in the Netherlands during the Middle Ages', *Revue Belge de Philologie et d'Histoire*, 47 (1969), 399–424.

political value of late medieval charters was moot, their effect may be called constitutional. Cumulatively, they began to form a normative, 'implicit, constitution',[36] which, in combination with innumerable other written and unwritten customs and rules, restricted the power of the prince, codified participatory claims and guaranteed civic rights. As such the 1477 privileges and the Joyous Entry were the expressions of a long-lasting, powerful ideological current in the Low Countries. Being extorted at moments when the central government lacked the power to resist the demands of the provinces, they reflected the political views of the provinces, and especially of the cities, which often played the leading role.

During the fourteenth and fifteenth centuries the great towns had manifested their civic consciousness in a tradition of urban revolt against the encroaching Burgundian state. The aim of the revolutionary towns, for example during Brabant's revolts of 1312, 1355 and 1420 and the Flemish revolts of 1339, 1482 and 1540, was, in parallel with 1477, not to destroy central power as such. However, in the view of the revolutionary towns and provinces central government was not the patrimony of the ruling dynasty, but a *chose publique*, for which prince, provinces and towns were to share the responsibility. Throughout the Burgundian era revolutionary towns and provinces propagated a 'communal, federative and constitutional model' dominated by the great towns acting as self-governing city republics.[37] Although this ambition never materialized, Guicciardini, writing in 1567, still compared the town government of Antwerp with the republic of Lacedaemon, presenting it as a perfect example of a Polybian republic:

In my judgment this is a way of governing little different, if it is completely observed, from the form which Polybius, the excellent philosopher and historian, gives as the true and happy republic; because he wants a combination of three states, Monarchy, Aristocracy and Democracy, where the prince has his empire, the optimates their authority, and the people the power and weaponry.[38]

The 1477 privileges and the Joyous Entry were amongst the principal means to achieve the ideal of self-governing independence as cherished by towns and provinces, not only in Brabant and

---

[36] Blockmans, 'La signification constitutionnelle de privilèges', 507.
[37] See W. P. Blockmans, 'Alternatives to monarchical centralization: the great tradition of revolt in Flanders and Brabant', in H. G. Koenigsberger (ed.), *Republiken und Republikanismus im Europa der frühen Neuzeit* (Munich, 1988), 145–54, and, for Brabant in particular, P. Avonds, *Brabant tijdens de regering van Hertog Jan III (1312–1356): de grote politieke krisissen* (Brussels, 1984). [38] Guicciardini, *Descrittione di tutti i Paesi Bassi*, 132.

Flanders, but also, for example, in Holland and Friesland.[39] As such the privileges were an important part of the late medieval constitutionalist legacy in the Low Countries.

2.4. THE DUTCH REVOLT: OVERTURES, 1555–1568

In strong contrast with the communal, federative and constitutional model cherished by towns and provinces the Burgundian dukes favoured what Ullmann has labelled the 'theocratic descending' idea of government.[40] With particular emphasis Charles the Bold, for example, had contended that he had received his power directly from God, and from God alone. As such Charles claimed absolute sovereignty, arguing that the subjects were only there to be governed by their sacrosanct lord in complete obedience. Forcefully the duke warned his subjects never to rise against him.[41]

This view of the prince as the _vicarius Dei_ was highly popular in circles around Philip II. It was endorsed, for example, by two of his counsellors on Dutch affairs, the Spanish Augustinian Lorenzo de Villavencio and the Frisian jurist Joachim Hopperus, and of course by his father, Charles V. In the various instructions to his son, including the 1548 political testament, Charles emphasized that the ruler was God's deputy on earth, who should act as a shepherd guarding the well-being of his flock. First and foremost this meant that the prince should administrate justice, enlightened by the virtue of clemency. The prince himself should be a master of virtue, excelling in justice, temperance, fortitude and prudence. For Charles and Villavencio the prince had been chosen and ordained directly by God as the absolute giver of laws and as the protector of the true Catholic religion.[42]

---

[39] For ideas of self-governance in Holland, see James D. Tracy, _Holland under Habsburg rule, 1506–1566: the formation of a body politic_ (Berkeley, Calif., 1990), for Friesland, J. J. Woltjer, _Friesland in hervormingstijd_ (Leiden, 1962).

[40] W. Ullmann, _Medieval political thought_ (Harmondsworth, 1975), _passim_, esp. ch. 5.

[41] For Charles' vision on government see Prevenier and Blockmans, _The Burgundian Netherlands_, 239–40.

[42] For Charles' instructions and Spanish mirror-for-prince studies, see J. A. Fernandez-Santamaria, _The state, war and peace: Spanish political thought in the Renaissance, 1516–1559_ (Cambridge, 1977). For Villavencio's and Hopperus' ideas see Paul David Lagomarsino, 'Court faction and the formulation of Spanish policy towards the Netherlands (1559–1567)', Ph.D. thesis, Cambridge University, 1973, 290–319, and G. Janssens, 'Barmhartig en rechtvaardig: visies van L. de Villavencio en J. Hopperus op de taak van de koning', in W. P. Blockmans and H. van Nuffel (eds.), _Etat et religion aux XVe et XVIe siècles_ (Brussels, 1986), 25–42.

A more refined view of the origins of princely rule was developed in the studies of various members of the School of Salamanca, a group of neo-Thomist scholars whose founding father was Francisco de Victoria. The neo-Thomists emphasized that every legitimate transition to political society required the consent of the community. In an act of alienation the community transferred its power to the prince, who should then use it for the benefit of the community. In spite of this contractual conception, neo-Thomists refrained from characterizing the prince as a minister of lesser standing than the community; the prince was still seen as the true sovereign with *plenitudo potestatis*.[43]

Philip II's mode of ruling perfectly matched with the Burgundian–Habsburg tradition. His 'absolute monarchy' meant that Philip wanted to take important political decisions concerning his empire in person and that, therefore, all major issues from either America, Italy or the Netherlands, were referred back to the court in Castile, where the king resided after he left the Netherlands in 1559. Philip II was a solitary and secretive man. His personality remained an enigma, both to his contemporaries and to his biographers.[44] On the one hand, Philip II has been described as 'the perfect master in the art of ruling', characterized by a great sense of duty and an 'excessive industry' and blessed with an excellent memory.[45] On the other hand, Philip is said to have been an obstinate, intolerant man without great intellectual capacities resulting in a crucial lack of political insight and resolution.[46] All agree that the Spanish king was a deeply religious man, which did not imply, however, that religion pervaded his politics. Philip was a true Catholic monarch, but his policy was often secular in content.[47] Thus Philip II was not 'the scourge of heretics' only because he thought it was his duty as a Catholic monarch to protect the Roman Catholic church, but also,

---

[43] For neo-Thomism, see Fernandez-Santamaria, *The state, war and peace*, and Skinner, *The foundations of modern political thought*, ii. 136–73.

[44] See e.g. the different pictures of Philip II in John Lynch, *Spain under the Habsburgs*, i: *Empire and absolutism 1516–1598*, 2nd edn. (Oxford, 1981), 181–90, and A. W. Lovett, *Early Habsburg Spain 1517–1598* (Oxford, 1986), 119–22.   [45] Lynch, *Spain under the Habsburgs*, 18ff.

[46] Lovett, *Early Habsburg Spain*, 118–19; Lovett's crushing conclusion: 'Emotionally stunted and intellectually limited, only the physical and mental shortcomings of his descendants made Philip appear of kingly timbre' (p. 122).

[47] See Lynch, *Spain under the Habsburgs*, 293 and 253, where he points out that to view Philip's Spain 'as the champion of the Counter-Reformation is to ignore the secular content of her foreign policy, her adverse relations with the papacy, and her own religious development in the sixteenth century'.

and maybe principally, because he thought that maintaining religious unity within the empire was a pre-condition for maintaining the empire itself. This idea also formed the foundation of Philip's religious policy in the Netherlands, and it was one of the policy priorities Philip presented to his new governess, his half-sister Margaret, Duchess of Parma, when he left the Low Countries in 1559. Margaret's appointment stemmed from another basic policy, whose aim was to prevent the Dutch nobility from exercising real power. In this respect Philip's departure substantially altered the character of Dutch politics. It implied that from 1559 Dutch questions ultimately would be decided in Spain, by a Spanish king, who did not speak Dutch, in a Castilian ambience and surrounded by Spanish councils and counsellors.

In the decision-making process these counsellors played a vital role; they made up policy proposals, formulated policy alternatives and advised on and implemented decisions. However, individual counsellors were involved only in limited areas of policy. The king alone had total knowledge. Thus secrecy and intrigues permeated court life and the rivalry of competing factions strongly affected policy-making, also with regard to the Netherlands.[48] Around 1560 the main factions were grouped around the Prince of Eboli and the Duke of Alva. The struggle between the factions was less about policy than about power, although ideological factors played a certain role. The factions, for example, held different views on how the empire should be governed, the Eboli faction favouring a more federalist way of governing and the Alva faction pleading for centralist policy-making.

The Spanish appearance of Philip's policy was a continuous thorn in the side of the Dutch nobility, which itself had formed the inner circle of his father's government. Regardless of the contents of his policy, Philip II was overwhelmingly seen 'as a Spanish king, ruling a Spanish empire in the interests of the Spaniards'.[49]

However, it was Philip's third policy priority which led to the first

---

[48] See Lagomarsino, 'Court faction and the formulation of Spanish policy towards the Netherlands'. The central thesis of this study is that 'Philip's approach to the problem of the Netherlands should be understood in the context of the very intensive faction wars for political predominance and royal favour' (p. 5). I should like to thank Professor Lagomarsino for sending me a copy of his study, which is unique in showing how Dutch politics was affected by the decision-making processes at the Castilian court.

[49] H. G. Koenigsberger, 'Orange, Granvelle and Philip II', *BMGN* 99 (1984), 591. See also A. Duke, 'From king and country to king or country? Loyalty and treason in the Revolt of the Netherlands', *Transactions of the Royal Historical Society*, 32 (1982), 121.

real conflict. As he was decided upon improving his catastrophic financial situation and making the provinces pay for their government, he practically started his reign by proposing a series of new taxes. The proposal implied an attempt to change the system of taxation, as, instead of demanding a lump sum, he proposed to introduce general taxes on movables and immovables. The States of the core provinces vigorously opposed the plan. After long and, for Philip, frustrating negotiations, a normal aid was granted in 1557. The financial situation for the central government was still worsening rapidly, and after his first 'bankruptcy' Philip soon had to request new taxes. As usual, negotiations followed. The final settlement, 'the novennial aid', was an exchange of money for political power. While the central government would receive a huge lump sum, to be spread over nine years, the States General acquired control over collection and expenditure. The attitude of the States was interpreted as an attempt to tilt the balance of power in favour of a sort of parliamentary government. When he left the Low Countries, Philip decided that the States General formed a sincere threat to royal power and that, therefore, it should not be summoned again.

Soon the king was to find out that there were other sources of opposition in the Low Countries. In 1559 the papal bull *Super Universas* decided on a thorough reorganization of the diocesan structure of the Netherlands. It involved the creation of three new archdioceses with a total of eighteen bishoprics. The old dioceses covered territories which bore hardly any relation to contemporary administrative and political reality. Moreover, the old dioceses were huge and therefore had to cope with insurmountable organizational problems.

The plan aroused vigorous opposition. First of all, in order to guarantee them a certain income, new bishops would automatically become abbots of rich abbeys. According to the abbeys involved, this meant a return to the old and reprehensible system whereby rich abbeys were assigned to non-residing protégés of the sovereign. For the cities the reorganization became unacceptable when they found out that in each diocese two papal inquisitors would be appointed. In their view this was a threat to their jurisdictional autonomy and to their commercial relations, which involved many foreign protestants. The high nobility was indignant as the plan had been developed in complete secrecy. The noble members of the Council of State had not been consulted at all. Moreover, the requirement that new bishops had to be educated theologians deprived the nobility of the opportunity to obtain bishop's sees, which had been tradition in the past. Finally, the papal bull gave Philip II the right to appoint the bishops. In most cases, if only because they would become abbots of important abbeys, new bishops would acquire the membership of the provincial States. Thus the reorganization would strengthen Philip's grip on the States. For example, in 1561 Antoine Perrenot, Bishop of Arras and top civil servant, was appointed Archbishop of Malines. Automatically Perrenot became spokesman of the clergy in the important States of Brabant.

The conflict over the ecclesiastical reorganization strongly contributed to a rupture between the leading nobles and Perrenot. Antoine Perrenot, Lord of Granvelle, was the son of Nicolas Perrenot, the influential secretary of Charles V. In the footsteps of his father, Antoine swiftly made a career in the emperor's civil service, and he succeeded his father after the latter's death. In 1559 Philip II decided that Granvelle, who was an influential member of the Alva faction at court, would stay in the Netherlands. Probably this decision was a set-back to Granvelle's career, as it meant that he was removed from the nerve-centre of the empire in Castile to the periphery of the Netherlands. None the less he became part of the governess' inner circle and soon he was seen as the top policy-maker and prime exponent of central policy. As such he was, however wrongly, regarded as the evil genius behind the plan for ecclesiastical reorganization. In the Council of State he became one of the most permanent and most influential members. In the eyes of noble members like Lamoraal, Count of Egmont, and William, Prince of Orange, Granvelle was usurping power – theirs, as a matter of fact. Egmont was a celebrated military commander, second-in-command to the Duke of Alva in Philip II's forces. He had brought Philip the famous victories over the French at St Quentin in 1557 and at Gravelines in 1558. William of Nassau, the eldest son of a German Lutheran noble family, inherited in 1544 the Princedom of Orange together with numerous rich manors in the Netherlands from his uncle René of Chalon. Suddenly William had become one of the principal nobles of the Netherlands. At the explicit order of Charles V, William was brought to the court to receive a proper Catholic education. The young prince prospered in the Netherlands and soon became the emperor's confidant. In 1555 he was at Charles V's right hand during the abdication ceremony.

These high nobles had strong political ambitions. Since Philip's accession these ambitions had been thwarted repeatedly. Not the nobles but Margaret of Parma had been appointed Governor-General. Egmont and Orange had been appointed Stadtholder over Flanders and Holland, but at the same time Philip II strongly curtailed their authority. Finally, within the Council of State they were continuously confronted with the overbearing presence and influence of civil servants, Granvelle above all. As members of the Council of State they officially shared responsibility for central policy. However, so they complained, in matters of important appointments to office and on important political questions, primarily the plan to reorganize the diocesan structure, they were simply ignored.

In 1561 Egmont and Orange started a campaign against the pre-eminence of Granvelle. The ultimate nature of this conflict remains a matter of controversy. On the one hand it has been seen as a traditional Burgundian struggle of patronage between rival patrons who were building up networks of clients so as to increase their political leverage.[50] On the other hand it has been argued that the traditional role of the nobility as power-brokers in integrating regional networks of patronage lapsed after 1530. Gradually the central government sought to pass over the layer of the noble power-brokers and to strengthen its grip on the regions directly, by means of its growing, professional and far more loyal civil service.[51] From this point of view the conflict over Granvelle was symptomatic of a struggle for power between a politically decaying nobility and a rising professional civil service, of which Granvelle was the principal exponent.

In their campaign against Granvelle, Egmont and Orange were soon joined by other high nobles, such as the Count of Hoorne. In 1562 they formed a 'League of the Great'. Continuously threatening to resign they presented a plan which was an unequivocal expression of aristocratic ambitions. In November 1563 the crisis came to a head, when the nobles flatly demanded Granvelle's dismissal and announced their withdrawal from the Council of State.

At the Spanish court the campaign against Granvelle was strongly supported by the latter's old enemy Eraso, a prime member of the Eboli faction and by 1563 one of the most powerful figures at court.

[50] See Koenigsberger, 'Orange, Granvelle and Philip II', 583.
[51] See van Nierop, 'Willem van Oranje', 656–7.

The combined effort of the Dutch nobles and the Eboli faction was successful. In 1564 Philip decided to remove Granvelle. The nobles returned to the Council of State and took up their role as the governess' advisers. They seemed to revel in triumph. However, although Philip II had acceded to their demand for the removal of Granvelle, he had by no means accepted their policy demands.

Most of all, the crucial issue of the persecution of heretics remained unresolved. During the reign of Charles V the harsh policy with regard to heretics had become a highly controversial matter and his religious placard of 1550, nicknamed the 'blood placard', met with mounting opposition.[52] Philip II continued the policy of harsh repression, and the political question of how to deal with heresy came to dominate Dutch politics.[53]

The opposition against the harsh repression of heretics came not only from the rising number of protestants. There were large 'middle groups' of people who themselves were not protestant but who despised the harsh religious persecution for legal, political and humanitarian reasons.[54] The towns considered the growing activity of the inquisitors, the main executors of the policy of repression, an important threat to their autonomy and privileges concerning jurisdiction. The *jus de non evocando* in particular was threatened. In general the legal principles and the methods used to persecute heretics were widely considered to be in conflict with traditional notions of justice.[55] Moreover, the severe persecution of heresy was regarded by the towns as an important threat to the cherished values of public order and civic unity. Town governments found it difficult, if not impossible, to reconcile the religious policy of Charles V and Philip II with the ideals of civic concord.[56] The towns also had

[52] See J. Decavele, *De dageraad van de Reformatie in Vlaanderen (1520–1565)* (Brussels, 1975), 33, and J. Scheerder, 'De werking van de Inquisitie', in *Opstand en pacificatie in de lage landen: bijdrage tot de studie van de pacificatie van Gent* (Ghent, 1976), 161. For Holland see Tracy, *Holland under Habsburg rule*, 170–5.

[53] See J. J. Woltjer, 'De vrede-makers', in S. Groenveld, H. L. P. Leeuwenberg (eds.), *De Unie van Utrecht* (The Hague, 1979), 58, where Professor Woltjer argues that the political problem of heresy was the unifying theme of the period 1560–80.

[54] See, amongst others, J. J. Woltjer, 'Inleiding', in *Opstand en onafhankelijkheid: eerste vrije statenvergadering in Dordrecht 1572* (Dordrecht, 1972), 9.

[55] See A. Duke, 'Salvation by coercion: the controversy surrounding the "Inquisition" in the Low Countries on the eve of the Revolt', in P. N. Brooks (ed.), *Reformation principle and practice: essays in honour of A. G. Dickens* (London, 1986), 143. For example, the idea that even people who renounced their heresy had to be put to death without the possibility of appeal shocked many.

[56] See A. Duke, 'Building heaven in hell's despite: the early history of the Reformation in the towns of the Low Countries', in A. Duke and C. A. Tamse (eds.), *Britain and the Netherlands,*

economic reasons to oppose the Inquisition, as its actions threatened commercial relations with unorthodox foreign merchants. Thus continuously town magistrates sought to frustrate the working of the Inquisition. Bruges was a noted example. In 1563 the town magistrate even forbade assistance to the inquisitor in Flanders, Titelmans.

The religious policy of the central government also encountered opposition amongst the ranks of the lower nobility. The lower nobles were afraid in particular that the Inquisition would undermine their control over jurisdiction at the local level. Moreover, many people, including many town magistrates and lower nobles, morally disapproved of the policy of harsh religious repression. They simply abhorred the idea of executing people only because they happened to give another interpretation to the Christian faith. These moderate Catholics seem to have been inspired by a far more Erasmian attitude towards religion. Many of them probably endorsed the view exposed in a remonstrance published in May 1566 that 'the weapons of the priests ought to be no other then tears, prayers and suchlike things; they are not allowed to use any weapon, nor violence'.[57]

It is very possible that the League of the Great shared these feelings about the king's policy. On New Year's Eve 1564 William of Orange gave a long and famous speech in the Council of State, boldly rejecting religious persecution and favouring freedom of conscience. The nobles, who now dominated the Council of State, sent Egmont on a special mission to Philip II to present a programme which sought to strengthen the position of the Council of State and its noble character and pressed for moderation of the religious persecution. Egmont's mission became a source of fatal misunderstanding. Philip II had no interest in a direct clash with the Dutch nobles. He conferred some personal favours upon his 'loyal vassal' and put up a screen of soothing words. Philip was sure that he had not made any substantial concession.[58] In fact, Philip's informers in the Netherlands continuously presented a highly negative picture of the nobles, who were depicted as greedy people whose only goal in politics was to fill

---

vii: *Church and state since the Reformation* (The Hague, 1981), 50. For Holland, see Tracy, *Holland under Habsburg rule*, 147ff.

[57] Gilles Le Clerq, *Remonstrance ... aen den Coninck van Spaengen* (1566), 12.

[58] On 24 Mar. 1565 Philip wrote to his secretary: 'My intention is, as you will have gathered, neither to resolve these demands of the count, nor to disillusion him about them, for then he would worry us to death and we would never be finished with him.' Quoted in Geoffrey Parker, *Philip II* (London, 1978), 68, and Lagomarsino, 'Court faction and the formulation of Spanish policy towards the Netherlands', 114.

their own pockets. The religious problem was represented as a political problem created by an insignificant number of town magistrates who had neglected to enforce the edicts concerning heresy. Moreover, Egmont's mission practically coincided with the dramatic fall from power of Eraso, the nobles' most important ally at the Castilian court. The subsequent rise of the Alva faction at court meant that more than ever Philip was pressed to follow a tough policy with regard to the Netherlands.

Egmont's perception of his mission strongly differed from Philip's. The count believed, and such was his joyful message when he returned to the Netherlands, that the king had accepted the suggestions of the nobles for a moderate religious policy. His message created high hopes in the Netherlands, hopes which were crushed when the letters of the king arrived. Although these letters were a toned-down version of what the Alva faction had wanted, it was clear that moderation of the religious persecution was out of the question. In the Netherlands Philip's letters were perceived as a blunt rejection of the proposals of the grandees and as a severe blow to their authority and prestige.

The position of the grandees worsened as Reformed Protestantism, now supported and partially led by a group of lower nobles, members of the so-called Compromise, gained momentum. On 5 April 1566 about 300 nobles went to the court of the governess to offer her a petition which demanded moderation of the religious policy and a meeting of the States General to settle the issue.

Pressure on the governess increased. More and more Reformed Protestants came out in the open. Numerous hedge-preachings were held. The towns, often afraid to disturb public order and to provoke riots, practically ceased to enforce the religious placards. Cities like Antwerp sought to retain their independence as far as possible, and carefully avoided any open alignment with any of the factions involved. Meanwhile, the high nobles around Egmont and Orange continued their middle course, aiming at reconciliation and moderation.

In August 1566 the Iconoclastic Fury began to sweep over the Netherlands. The Fury, which started in the Flemish village of Steenvoorde (a centre of the textile industry), rapidly found its way to other villages and cities.[59] In the south, iconoclasm was mainly the

---

[59] For the Iconoclastic Fury, see J. Scheerder, *De beeldenstorm* (Bussum, 1974); Phyllis Mack Crew, *Calvinist preaching and iconoclasm in the Netherlands 1544–1569* (Cambridge, 1978); and for

work of wandering groups; in the north, local townsfolk were responsible for the image-breaking. Often the attitude of the town magistrate and the civic militia was decisive. In some towns the magistrate was powerful enough to prevent image-breaking; in others the civic militia refused to protect the images by force against their fellow citizens.

The governess, terrified by the troubles, finally followed the advice of the nobles around Orange and Egmont and announced a far-reaching moderation of the religious policy. The middle course of Orange and his partisans seemed to have won, but it turned out to be a Pyrrhic victory as public order could only be restored by giving in to many demands of the more radical elements. At the end of the year the governess felt strong enough to take action. Troops were raised and towns like Valenciennes and Tournai, which refused to open their gates for the governmental troops, were besieged. Protestant armies in revolt were defeated.

The attitude of the grandees was highly ambiguous.[60] They still insisted on their policy of moderation and remained in touch with the more radical elements, and at the same time assisted the governess in suppressing violent elements of protestantism. Eventually they were forced to make a choice. When public order was restored, the nobles were asked to swear a new oath of loyalty. The grandees split up, Egmont took the oath, Orange refused. He left the country and returned to his family in Dillenburg.

The Iconoclastic Fury shocked the Spanish court. It provoked ideas of armed intervention, especially as the financial position of the Crown had improved. While the Eboli faction favoured a moderate approach, the Duke of Alva pressed for armed intervention under Philip's personal command. Philip adopted the latter approach but he was forced, mainly for dynastic reasons (above all the growing insanity of his son Don Carlos), to postpone his departure to the Netherlands. It was decided that the army would be led by a commander, whose task was to pave the way for the king. The Duke of Alva reluctantly accepted the appointment, on condition that Philip would soon follow.

Due to many delays the duke did not arrive in the Netherlands

Holland in particular A. Duke and D. H. A. Kolff, 'The time of troubles in the county of Holland, 1566–1567', *TvG* 82 (1969), 316–37.

[60] For Orange's attitude see Woltjer, *De vrede-makers*, 66–7 and K. W. Swart, 'Wat bewoog Willem van Oranje de strijd tegen de Spaanse overheersing aan te binden?' *BMGN* 99 (1984), 557–8.

until the summer of 1567, when public order had already been restored. Embittered, the Duchess of Parma resigned office, and in December Alva was appointed Governor-General. The policy of the Iron Duke was clear-cut. He intended to crush whatever remained of the opposition, and to establish a new order, *un mundo nuevo*, in which there was no place for heresy, privileges and local autonomy, but where the central government had a firm grip on the country. Thus the Iron Duke completed the reorganization of the diocesan structure, placed Spanish garrisons in important towns, strengthened the grip of the central government on the town magistrates and brushed privileges aside without much ado. The opposition was eliminated with the help of a new tribunal, the Council of Troubles, the 'Blood Council'. It is estimated that about 12,000 people were put to trial. Approximately 9,000, including William of Orange, were sentenced by default and their possessions confiscated. Finally, more than 1,000 people, including the Count of Egmont and the Count of Hoorne, were executed.[61]

An armed invasion by William of Orange, who had overcome his scruples and had opted for armed resistance, ended in total disaster for the prince and his partisans. By the end of 1568 the Dutch Revolt seemed to belong to the past.

2.5. RENAISSANCE, 1568–1576

From the very beginning of his Dutch enterprise Alva was beset with financial problems. He was explicitly ordered to raise taxes so that the Dutch Provinces would at last finance their own government. Alva came up with a plan for three taxes: a tax of 1 per cent, the so-called Hundredth Penny, on capital assets to be levied on a one-off basis, a permanent tax of 5 per cent, the so-called Twentieth Penny, on the sale of immovables and a permanent tax of 10 per cent, the Tenth Penny, on the sale of movables.[62]

In spite of his regime of terror Alva left some traditional legal mechanisms intact. Thus he did not directly impose the new taxes on the Netherlands. In March 1569 he proposed, as *dominium politicum et*

---

[61] The estimates are based on A. L. E. Verheyden, *Le conseil des troubles: liste des condamnés (1567–1573)* (Brussels, 1961).

[62] See Ferdinand Grapperhaus, *Alva en de tiende penning* (Deventer, 1982), for a detailed account of the tax proposals and their fortune. See also Jan Craeybeckx, 'La portée fiscale et politique du 100e denier de duc d'Albe', *Acta Historia Bruxellensia: Recherches sur l'Histoire des Finances Publiques*, 1 (1967), 343–74.

regale required, the introduction of the three taxes to the States General. However, in seeking the consent of the States Alva was dragged into exhausting and frustrating bargaining processes, into the quagmire of Dutch politics.

The States accepted the Hundredth Penny quite quickly, but the Twentieth and Tenth Penny aroused vehement opposition. The States realized that the two permanent taxes were meant to make the central government financially independent and that Alva's fiscal policy was an attempt to alter radically the balance of power in favour of the central government, to make Philip II *senor assoluto* in the Low Countries.

At length the States of Holland, Flanders and Brabant argued against the Twentieth and the Tenth Penny, explaining their social and economic disadvantages and claiming they would ruin the economy. The towns of Brussels and Louvain persisted in refusing to approve the new taxes but, by the autumn, Alva, thanks to persuasion, strong pressure and sometimes sheer intimidation, had acquired the consent of the States.[63]

However, at this point Alva hesitated to actually introduce the new taxes. As he desperately needed money and as he recognized some disadvantages of the new taxes, he proposed to postpone their introduction and to have a normal subsidy of 2 million florins per year instead. Again Alva was dragged into lengthy negotiations, a highly frustrating experience for the duke. In 1571 he changed his mind once again; in July Alva ordered the levying and collection of the Twentieth and Tenth Penny. The States were shocked and vigorously but vainly protested. However, although they were unable to reverse Alva's decision, the States and town magistrates surely were in a position to obstruct its implementation. And so they did, with great resourcefulness. Probably nowhere was the Tenth Penny actually collected. The States also decided to send delegations to Spain, to explain their grievances to Philip II. The obstructionism of the States was partly motivated by the popular anger Alva's decision had aroused. Numerous towns were confronted with riots and strikes, and particularly in Brussels, Alva's residence, it was extremely difficult to calm down popular fury.

A dramatic turn of events occurred on 1 April 1572. A fleet of Sea Beggars, ordered by Queen Elizabeth to leave the English harbours,

---

[63] The exception was Utrecht, which persisted, and was condemned for high treason.

was driven by a storm to the coast of Holland and Zeeland. Completely by surprise, and more or less by coincidence, they captured the town of Brill in Holland. The Sea Beggars, often acting like pirates, more or less formed the naval forces of the rebels in exile. During Alva's regime approximately 50,000 people had sought exile, especially in German and English towns like Emden, Wesel, London and Norwich where communities of Dutch refugees already existed. Especially through the channels of the Reformed Protestant church, networks of communication and co-operation developed. The undisputed leader was William of Orange, who adopted the Reformed faith.

Orange succeeded in obtaining foreign aid. In this respect he profited from Alva's foreign policy, which created a lot of resentment abroad. Not only did Alva repeatedly interfere in French internal affairs, he also waged a commercial war with England and was engaged in a Spanish intrigue with regard to the English Crown. Thus when William of Orange started to design a new plan for an armed invasion of the Netherlands, he was able to obtain the support of both England and France, where Orange had aligned with Huguenot leaders. This support enabled him to invade the Netherlands from the south and the east. In the south Mons and Valenciennes were conquered. Alva had to retreat, both militarily and politically. The resurgence of armed resistance strongly contributed to the decision to defer the introduction of the Twentieth and Tenth Penny. Orange's invasion also forced Alva to draw his forces back from the north and from Holland. Soon Holland became the centre of the Revolt. In the summer of 1572 almost all major towns of Holland (Amsterdam was the great exception), for a variety of reasons and with great reluctance, took the momentous decision to support William of Orange.[64] The grim winter, the trade war with the English and the attacks and blockades of the Sea Beggars severely hurt trade and commerce. Growing poverty and massive unemployment contributed to the feelings of dissension, which were also fed

[64] For the uprising of the towns of Holland and their motives to join Orange, see J. C. Boogman, 'De overgang van Gouda, Dordrecht, Leiden en Delft in de zomer van het jaar 1572', *TvG* 51 (1942), 81–109; H. G. Koenigsberger, 'The organization of revolutionary parties in France and the Netherlands during the sixteenth century', in H. G. Koenigsberger, *Estates and revolutions: essays in early modern European history* (Ithaca, NY, 1971), 233–9; and Hibben, *Gouda in revolt: particularism and pacifism in the revolt of the Netherlands 1572–1588*, 29–67, who emphasizes that 'although a number of common factors can be identified in the "change-over" of the Holland towns, each deserves to be treated as a special case as the factors affecting the fall of these towns varied considerably from place to place' (p. 31).

by Alva's unpopular tax policy and his policy of religious repression. The vigorous resentment against the Spanish troops played an important role as well. Although the towns did not particularly like the rough Sea Beggars, they considered them the lesser evil in comparison with the hated Spanish troops. Finally, as in the case of Gouda, town magistrates were often demoralized and could not rely on the willingness of the civic militia to defend the town.

Once the towns had overcome their hesitations and had opened their gates for the Beggars, the revolutionaries, Beggars and Reformed Protestant minorities alike, quickly took the lead. To a large extent the revolution of Holland and Zeeland was the work of organized minorities, which thanks to their organization and determination were able to take the divided and hesitating majority in tow.

In August perspectives changed once again. With the massacre of Huguenot leaders during the night of St Bartholomew the French Crown dramatically altered its policy. As the support for the Dutch rebels was cancelled, it became easier for Alva to regain the military initiative and to start an impressive and ruthless campaign of reconquest. Orange had to draw back to Holland, the only remaining stronghold of the Revolt. In Holland, an important reorganization of the provincial administration was taking place. In July 1572 the first free meeting of the provincial States took place in Dordrecht. Orange was acclaimed Stadtholder; arrangements were made to finance and defend the Revolt; freedom of religion was officially proclaimed; and to implement this policy three new governmental councils were created. These measures witnessed the revolutionary character of Holland's revolt. Under the able leadership of William of Orange the States of Holland abrogated the authority of their sovereign and became self-governing.[65]

At first it seemed that Holland had taken its measures in vain. In the autumn of 1572 the province seemed to collapse under Alva's military campaign. However, Spain's traditional lack of money and subsequent mutinies of Spanish troops undermined the vigour of the duke's campaign. Moreover, Alva did not keep his promises to reconquered cities and violated the rules of medieval warfare, plundering and massacring the inhabitants of towns which did not

---

[65] For an analysis of the States of Holland before and during the Revolt, see J. W. Koopmans, *De Staten van Holland en de Opstand: de ontwikkeling van hun functies en organisatie in de periode 1544–1588* (The Hague, 1990).

offer any form of resistance such as Malines, Zutphen and Naarden.[66] The brutality of the Spanish forces encouraged Haarlem, Alkmaar and Leiden to a firm defence, and Alva was unable to complete his reconquest.

Because of his apparent failure to suppress the Dutch Revolt the duke lost the king's confidence. On 29 November 1573 Alva was replaced by Don Luis de Requesens. The decision to appoint Requesens was marked by vacillation and confusion.[67] Philip II felt perplexed and did not know what course to follow with regard to the Netherlands. The new Governor-General, equally bewildered, arrived in the Netherlands without clear instructions. Moreover, Requesens soon had to cope with military defeats, frequent mutinies and a permanent lack of money, as the war with the Ottomans devoured the Spanish treasury. Soon Requesens reached the conclusion that it was financially impossible to reconquer Holland.

Requesens was also put under pressure by the loyal provinces, who urged him to open negotiations with Holland and Zeeland. As ten years before, a centre group of Roman Catholics rose who felt that a more lenient policy with regard to the Reformed Protestants would be highly beneficial for the country and even for the church.[68] Even Philip II no longer objected to negotiations. The king had grown desperate. Expressing his belief in a sixteenth-century 'domino theory' he wrote: 'I believe that everything is a waste of time, judging by what is happening in the Low Countries; and if they are lost the rest [of the empire] will not last long, even if we have enough money.'[69]

On 3 March 1575 peace negotiations with Holland and Zeeland started in Breda. They had no result. The religious question was insoluble. Philip II was not willing to grant religious tolerance and Holland and Zeeland insisted on freedom of worship for the Reformed Protestants. Politically, the demand of Holland and Zeeland to give the States General broad authority to settle other important issues was equally unacceptable to Requesens, who defended the authority of the king.

---

[66] According to the rules of medieval warfare the besieger had no right of plundering if the town he wanted to besiege surrendered before the besieger had started his activities. See Parker, *The Dutch Revolt*, 152.

[67] See A. W. Lovett, 'A new governor for the Netherlands: the appointment of Don Luis de Requesens, Comendador Mayor de Castilla', *European Studies Review*, 1 (1971), 89–103. For Requesens and his governorship see also A. W. Lovett, 'The governorship of Don Luis de Requesens, 1573–1576: a Spanish view', *European Studies Review*, 2 (1972), 187–99.

[68] See Woltjer, *De vrede-makers*, 71.   [69] See Parker, *Philip II*, 125.

Thus Holland and Zeeland pursued their revolutionary course. They strengthened their co-operation and concluded a political union. Orange became 'head and highest governor' of both provinces. In Leiden a new university was founded, where the new political elite was to be educated. To a large extent this progress was due to the spirit and energy of William of Orange. In his 'finest hour',[70] the prince continually fostered unity and fought against the particularist inclinations of the towns and their unwillingness to provide finances for the struggle against the Spaniards. Gradually Holland and Zeeland steered towards political independence. In the autumn of 1575 the States of Holland started seriously to discuss the possibility of renouncing Philip II.

After the failure of the Breda negotiations war was resumed. However, Philip II's financial situation continued to worsen and the king was faced with a hopeless dilemma. To solve his financial problems – which, as his counsellors argued over and over again, was absolutely essential – Philip had to proclaim a decree of bankruptcy, with the result that financiers would no longer be willing to grant further loans to Spain. Thus it would become impossible to pay the troops in the Netherlands, and the provinces, so Philip feared, would be lost. There was no way out. Bankruptcy was proclaimed and on 1 September 1575 the flow of money from Castile to the Netherlands stopped. Requesens was horrified.[71] As he already owed his troops several years of back pay, he was convinced that the decree would lead to mutiny. He was right. Having reconquered Zierikzee Spanish soldiers rose in mutiny and started to desert.

On 5 March 1576 the unexpected death of the Governor-General further complicated the perplexing situation in the provinces. Suddenly there was an important power vacuum in the government of the Netherlands.

2.6. INDEPENDENCE AND SEGREGATION, 1576–1590

After Requesens' death the Council of State became the interim government. It was immediately put under pressure by those who had already urged Requesens to seek a political solution for the Netherlands, such as the States of Brabant, Flanders and Hainaut. The centre groups had demanded the withdrawal of all foreigners from the Netherlands, the return to the old way of governing with a

[70] K. W. Swart, *William the Silent and the Revolt of the Netherlands* (London, 1978), 20.
[71] Requesens exclaimed that 'those who advised and arranged the Decree have lost these states for the Catholic Church' (Lovett, 'The governorship of Don Luis de Requesens', 198).

prominent place for the States General and some concessions to the protestants.[72] Their main purpose was to get rid of the mutinying and ravaging Spanish troops in particular and of Spanish officials in general. The Dutch Provinces had to be governed by the Dutch themselves.

The Council of State was put in an awkward position. Philip II persisted in forbidding it both to convene the States General and to negotiate with Holland and Zeeland. On 4 September 1576 the Council's tragedy became complete as its members were arrested in Brussels. Although the precise background of this action has remained obscure, the States of Brabant swiftly made use of the situation.[73] They took the revolutionary step, in which they were immediately joined by the States of Hainaut, of inviting the other provinces (with the exception of Holland and Zeeland) for a meeting of the States General, thus brushing aside the principle that only the sovereign lord could convene the States General. None the less, many, especially in the south, accepted the invitation.

Of course this turn of events highly pleased Holland and Zeeland, and William of Orange in particular, especially as Brabant also started to raise troops to fight the ravaging Spanish soldiers. An extension of the Revolt to other provinces naturally suited Holland and Zeeland; it also fitted in with Orange's ideals of unity amongst all Dutch Provinces. Thus, a request of the Flemish States for military assistance against Spanish mutineers and an invitation of the States General to open negotiations were eagerly accepted by Holland. The peace talks started in Ghent on 19 October 1576. Within three weeks a settlement was reached. On 8 November the Pacification of Ghent, the 'firm and unbreakable friendship and peace' amongst all Dutch Provinces, was concluded. Its main purpose was to ward off the Spanish mutineers and to reinstate all privileges.[74]

Having proclaimed a general pardon, the Pacification ordained that from now on the Dutch Provinces would assist each other at all times with counsel and deed, good and blood: 'and especially to expel the Spanish soldiers and other foreigners and strangers from the

---

[72] For the political programme of the centre groups, see, amongst others, M. Baelde and P. van Peteghem, 'De pacificatie van Gent (1576)', in *Opstand en pacificatie*, 14–5.

[73] See, amongst many others, G. Janssens, 'Brabant strijdt voor vrede', in *Opstand en pacificatie*, 68–9.

[74] See *Copie autentyck, Vanden Payse, Verbontenisse ende Unie... besloten ende gheaccordeert tot Ghendt, opten viij, novembris, 1576* (Delft, 1576). For an English version of the Pacification see E. H. Kossmann and A. F. Mellink (eds.), *Texts concerning the revolt of the Netherlands* (Cambridge, 1974), 126–32.

country, and to keep them out'.[75] The provinces agreed that once the foreigners were expelled, the States General would get together to settle all remaining issues including the religious question. In addition the Pacification guaranteed freedom of movement and commerce and suspended the edicts concerning the persecution of heretics, warranting though that the exercise of the Roman Catholic religion would not be hindered.

The Pacification was not the 'firm and unbreakable friendship and peace' it proclaimed itself to be. The most pressing problems, the attitude towards the king and the religious question, remained unresolved. Here positions differed widely. For Holland and Zeeland concessions on the religious problem were out of the question. At the same time the States General intended, as a resolution of 6 October 1576 put it, to bring Holland and Zeeland back under the obedience of Philip II and to protect the observance of the Roman Catholic faith.[76]

In short, the Pacification of Ghent was not a firm but a frail peace. The intolerable situation, the threat of the Spanish mutineers, who ravaged Antwerp just before the Pacification was officially proclaimed, killing 8,000 people and burning down a major part of the pearl of the Low Countries, had motivated the States General to make peace with Holland and Zeeland, so that it would become possible to defeat their common enemy. The States General hoped for political reconciliation but by no means intended to join the Revolt of Holland and Zeeland.

With the arrival of the new Governor-General, Don Juan of Austria, the frail peace was immediately put under pressure. On 12 February 1577 the States General and Don Juan concluded the Eternal Edict. Grudgingly Don Juan acknowledged the Pacification and promised to send away the Spanish troops. The States General accepted Don Juan as Governor-General, and explicitly avowed their loyalty to the Spanish Crown and the Roman Catholic church.

This was unacceptable for Holland and Zeeland, which did not sign the Eternal Edict. The frail alliance was saved by the behaviour of Don Juan. He had a protestant executed and, on 24 July 1577, in a desperate attempt to enlarge his meagre authority, he seized the citadel of Namur. These actions antagonized the States General and

---

[75] *Copie Autentyck*, 3; Kossmann and Mellink, *Texts concerning the revolt of the Netherlands*, 127.

[76] See W. P. Blockmans and P. van Peteghem, 'La pacification de Gand à la lumière d'un siècle de continuité constitutionnelle dans les Pays-Bas: 1477–1576', in Rudolf Vierhaus (ed.), *Herrschaftsverträge, Wahlkapitulationen, Fundamentalgesetze* (Göttingen, 1977), 327.

with the second Union of Brussels of 10 December 1577 unity was ostensibly restored. None the less different factions continued to pursue their contrasting programmes. A powerful group within the States General of southern high nobles and provincial governors[77] wanted to ward off the rise to power of William of Orange, who was hailed in a triumphal procession into Brussels. This group, whose leader was the Duke of Aerschot, did not want to cut the ties with Philip II. Aerschot's partisans thought they could serve both purposes by offering the governorship to Archduke Matthias of Austria, a nephew of Philip II, who belonged to the more moderate Austrian branch of the Habsburg dynasty.

The treaty with Matthias confirmed that the States General had become a leading political power in the country. Custody over the legislature, the financial realm and the defence of the country were entrusted to the States General, which also acquired the right of free assembly. In fact, as Koenigsberger in particular has emphasized, following the example Holland and Zeeland had been setting since 1572, a revolutionary policy brushed the system of *dominium politicum et regale* aside, replacing it with a parliamentary government which had no precedent in sixteenth-century Europe.[78]

The consensus on which the new system was based, however, was too frail to endure. The factions involved had widely divergent views on the main political problems, the attitude towards the king and the religious question. On one side, there were Holland and Zeeland, with which the 'democratic', non-aristocratic population in the towns of most provinces aligned themselves, supporting the Revolt. On the other side, there was the group of mainly southern nobles, clerics and chief magistrates of central and provincial institutions. This group around Aerschot advocated a return to the system of *dominium politicum et regale*, as it had been under Charles V. The privileges were to be reasserted and the States should play an eminent role in the government of the country. In this view, Philip II was to remain sovereign over the Netherlands, although his sovereignty would be far from absolute. Concerning the religious question this group probably wanted the Netherlands to remain as loyal to the Roman Catholic church as possible. Caught in between were middle

[77] For the composition of this group, see Johan Decavele, 'Willem van Oranje, de "vader" van een verscheurd "vaderland" (1577–1584)', *Handelingen der Maatschappij voor Geschiedenis en Oudheidkunde te Gent*, ns 38 (1984), 72.

[78] See Koenigsberger, 'Why did the States General of the Netherlands become revolutionary?' 109.

groups which, trying to strike a deal between both extremes, were forced to make a choice as, due to religious developments in particular, a process of polarization set in.

After 1577 protestantism once again gained momentum in Flanders and Brabant. This was partly the result of the 'democratic policy'[79] William of Orange pursued in 1577. He clearly supported the non-aristocratic groups within the cities of Flanders and Brabant. In many towns revolutionary committees, so-called Committees of XVIII, were formed, first in Brussels and subsequently in Antwerp and Ghent. In Brussels the States of Brabant were forced to appoint William of Orange *ruwaard*, regent of Brabant. In Ghent the Duke of Aerschot and his following were, with the tacit support of Orange, simply arrested by the revolutionaries, who took over town government. All were staunch supporters of the Prince of Orange, all turned out to be Reformed Protestants. The new regime in Ghent, under the leadership of Jan van Hembyze embarked on a truly revolutionary course. The town was to become a Reformed republic, the 'Geneva of Flanders'.[80]

The history of the Ghent republic is the history of a 'rebellious dream', which, on the one hand, longed for the glorious medieval past of the town and, on the other hand, wanted to free Flanders from Spanish tyranny and Catholicism. Thus the new order was based on the restoration of the old privileges, of which the town had been deprived by Charles V after the revolt of 1540, and on Reformed Protestant radicalism. Already in 1577 Ghent's old privileges were returned to the town by the States General. The old town council, the so-called Collation, which comprised the citizenry, the small crafts and the weavers, together with the drapers, was reinstalled and co-operated with the Committee of XVIII. Thus to an important extent the new republic rested on what has been called 'the democratic element', on the guilds and the non-aristocratic parts of the citizenry.[81]

---

[79] The term is Decavele's. See J. Decavele, 'De mislukking van Oranje's "democratische politiek" in Vlaanderen', *BMGN* 99 (1984), 626–50.

[80] For the history of the Ghent republic, see A. Despretz, 'De instauratie der Gentse Calvinistische Republiek (1577–1579)', *Handelingen der Maatschappij voor Geschiedenis en Oudheidkunde te Gent*, NS 17 (1963), 119–229; Decavele, *Willem van Oranje*; Decavele, 'De mislukking van Oranje's "democratische politiek"'; and J. Decavele (ed.), *Het eind van een rebelse droom: Opstellen over het calvinistisch bewind te Gent (1577–1584) en de terugkeer van de stad onder de gehoorzaamheid van de koning van Spanje (17 september 1584)* (Ghent, 1984).

[81] See Decavele, 'De mislukking van Oranje's "democratische politiek"', 640; Decavele, *Het eind van een rebelse droom*, 52.

Systematically the new regime sought to strengthen the position of the Reformed church, at the expense of Roman Catholics, against whom a ruthless campaign was conducted. In this respect Ghent had little regard for the contents of the Pacification. The policy was remarkably successful. With the help of vigilant ministers Ghent soon became the stronghold of Reformed Protestant radicalism. After two years the town proclaimed its independence. In August 1579 Hembyze declared that Philip II's sovereignty had lapsed and was devolved to the town itself and described the political system of the new republic in terms of popular sovereignty.

Ghent pursued a violent policy of expansion. Many towns in Flanders and Brabant, including Bruges and Ypres, installed like-minded revolutionary committees which sought to control town government. Others, such as Malines, were simply conquered before new more radically minded town magistrates could be installed.[82]

The events in Flanders and Brabant strongly contributed to the breakdown of the Pacification. The arrest of Aerschot and his following in 1577, the furious rise of Reformed Protestantism, the oppression of Roman Catholics and the political radicalization of Flanders and Brabant terrified the Catholic leaders in the south, especially in Hainaut and Artois. More and more the Walloon faction of nobles and clergy, which adhered to the policy of loyalty towards Philip II and the Catholic church, came to the fore.

In the meantime, Don Juan, who died in October 1578, was succeeded by Alexander Farnese of Parma. Both an able diplomat and a brilliant general the new Governor-General exploited the tensions amongst the provinces. He stimulated the *rapprochement* between Artois and Hainaut, sealed by the Union of Arras, in which both provinces reaffirmed their loyalty to peace, king and church. Four months later, in April 1579, a treaty of reconciliation with Farnese was concluded. Farnese promised protection of the privileges and a return to the old form of government as it had been under Charles V.

These events were an important set-back to William of Orange's policy. Orange, and with him Holland and Zeeland, more or less found themselves caught between polarizing groups. Although, in the course of the 1570s the Reformed church had become the public church in Holland and Zeeland, the magistrates abhorred the idea of

---

[82] For Malines, see Guido Marnef, *Het Calvinistisch bewind te Mechelen*, Ancien pays et assemblées d'etats', lxxxvii (Kortrijk-Heule, 1987).

a radical Reformed republic. However, the regime Orange himself had helped to establish in Flanders had a dynamic the prince found impossible to control. Orange and his partisans favoured religious peace, which would leave room for both Protestantism and Catholicism. Yet the policy of religious peace failed. It had been a basic principle of the Walloon faction to seek and retain the monopoly for the Catholic church. At the same time, although the religious peace was proclaimed even in Ghent, radical Reformed Protestants mainly used the idea to foster their religion. Thus the religious peace in Ghent only lasted for a few weeks. Radical protestants in Flanders had little respect for Orange's toleration policy.

Even in Holland Orange's policy of unity was not unequivocally followed. In 1578 the idea of forming a closer union between northern provinces, an idea the prince if only for strategic reasons had always promoted, was taken up by his brother John, Count of Nassau, and turned into a programme for a strong Calvinist union that, at least in the count's mind, would eventually co-operate with fellow German Calvinists.[83] In Orange's opinion, however, a closer union had to strengthen his policy of unity and reconciliation and by no means should undermine the Pacification. The ideas for a closer union were also cherished by a number of town magistrates in Holland and Utrecht. The final result, the Union of Utrecht concluded on 23 January 1579, was mainly their work.[84]

The Union proclaimed that the United Provinces 'shall ally, confederate and unite...to hold together eternally in all ways and forms as if they were but one province'. The Union immediately added that 'this is agreed without prejudice to the special and particular privileges, freedoms, exemptions, laws, statutes, laudable and traditional customs, usages and all other rights of each province and of each town, member and inhabitant of those provinces'.[85] The

---

[83] For a reconstruction of the formation of a closer union and the differences in perspective between Orange and his brother, see J. J. Woltjer, 'De wisselende gestalten van de Unie', in Groenveld and Leeuwenberg (eds.), *De Unie van Utrecht*, 88–100, and A. E. M. Janssen, 'Het verdeelde huis: Prins Willem van Oranje en graaf Jan van Nassau bij de totstandkoming van de Unie van Utrecht', in Groenveld and Leeuwenberg (eds.), *De Unie van Utrecht*, 101–35. Also J. C. Boogman, 'The Union of Utrecht: its genesis and consequences', in J. C. Boogman, *Van spel tot spelers: verspreide opstellen* (The Hague, 1982), 53–82.

[84] Published as *Verhandelinghe van de Unie, eeuwigh Verbont ende Eendracht* (Utrecht, 1579). An English version is found in Kossmann and Mellink (eds.), *Texts concerning the Revolt of the Netherlands*, 165–73.

[85] *Verhandelinghe van de Unie*, 2; Kossman and Mellink (eds.), *Texts concerning the Revolt of the Netherlands*, 166.

provinces obliged themselves to assist each other 'with body, good and blood' if one of them, or all at once, were attacked. The provinces agreed that foreign policy and a number of financial matters would be handled by the whole body of provinces, as if they were one, and that this also applied to other matters if necessary. Finally, in article 13, the Union allowed every province to handle the religious question according to its own judgment, on the condition 'that everyone in particular will remain free in his religion, and that no one will be persecuted or questioned because of his religion'.

For the history of the Dutch Republic the Union of Utrecht has been of great importance, as it more or less became the Republic's constitution.[86] Moreover, in guaranteeing the inhabitants of its provinces freedom of conscience, the Union fundamentally acknowledged it as a political right.[87] However, as the Union was mainly the work of a small vanguard from Holland, Zeeland, Utrecht, Guelders and Groningen its immediate political significance was limited. At first Orange kept aloof from the Union as he was desperately trying to save unity amongst the provinces on the basis of the Pacification of Ghent and his policy of religious toleration. The attempt failed; the Unions of Arras and Utrecht were symptomatic of the basic rupture occurring in the Low Countries. The rupture became evident during the last dramatic attempt to reconcile all parties in the peace negotiations at Cologne, which were a complete failure. War was resumed, and increasingly the States General were put under pressure not only because Farnese reconquered some towns, but also because the provinces supporting the States General were unable to organize an effective defence and suffered from internal tensions. Once again particularism reigned in the Netherlands. Not only did Ghent embark on its radical course, but provinces like Overijssel also displayed extreme particularist attitudes, trying to retain their old semi-independence as far as possible.[88] Holland itself also suffered from parochialism. Gouda, to take a notorious example, was extremely reluctant to pay for the defence of the south. Even within Holland it favoured administrative decentralization, arguing for 'minimum government' at the provincial level.[89] As the in-

[86] See Boogman, 'The Union of Utrecht', 64. In the Republic, the union functioned as one of its 'fundamental laws': see A. T. van Deursen, 'Between Unity and independence: the application of the Union as a fundamental law', *LCHY* 14 (1981), 50–65.
[87] See O. J. de Jong, 'Union and religion', *LCHY* 14 (1981), 29–49.
[88] See Rients Reitsma, *Centrifugal and centripetal forces in the early Dutch Republic: the States of Overijssel, 1566–1600* (Amsterdam, 1982), 170ff.   [89] See Hibben, *Gouda in revolt*, 159.

dividual provinces and towns were unwilling to make sacrifices for the common good, the States General continuously had financial problems in raising and paying troops. Orange worked hard to overcome particularism. However, his policy itself was a source of further division. Confronted with confusion, particularism and division the prince more than ever became convinced that foreign aid was needed. In itself this idea was acceptable to his partisans provided foreign assistance came from reliable sources on the right terms. For strategic and pragmatic reasons Orange favoured French aid or, more precisely, the assistance of François de Valois, brother of the French king, Duke of Alençon and from 1576 also Duke of Anjou.[90] The first contacts with Anjou were already made in 1573 and in the following years there were frequent rumours that Anjou was planning to intervene in the Netherlands. In May 1576 Holland and Zeeland had already offered him the lordship over their provinces in turn for military support and constitutional guarantees. Anjou turned down the offer, but remained in touch with the Dutch. In 1577, in spite of the fact that they accepted the Austrian Archduke Matthias as Governor-General, the States General also negotiated with Anjou, who in July 1578 informed his brother Henry III that he could no longer ignore the pleas of assistance from the Low Countries. Anjou and his army left for Mons in Hainaut, and after haggling negotiations in August an agreement was reached. Anjou was proclaimed 'Defender of the liberty of the Netherlands', a title which obliged him to give the States military assistance but which did not bring him any political authority. Anjou did, however, receive the assurance that if the States abjured Philip II, he would be the first choice to succeed him as lord of the Netherlands, albeit with highly limited authority.

Anjou's 1578 mission was not a great success. He lacked the support of his brother the king, his army suffered from the plague and Anjou himself was short of money. Moreover, the towns in Hainaut which, according to the treaty with the States, were awarded to Anjou, were unwilling to open their gates for him, and, as the treaty showed, in 1578 the States were not prepared to yield any political authority of importance to the duke. In fact from the very beginning the negotiations with Anjou were highly controversial in the Netherlands. The Reformed Flemish radicals deeply mistrusted

---

[90] For Anjou and his role in the Dutch Revolt, see M. P. Holt, *The Duke of Anjou and the politique struggle during the wars of religion* (Cambridge, 1986).

Anjou, a French Catholic prince tainted with the blood of St Bartholomew's night and supported by the Walloon nobility. Also in Holland Orange's French policy was not unequivocally supported. The town of Gouda, again a notorious example, systematically obstructed contacts and alliances with Anjou. For Gouda French aid was simply unacceptable. As Catholic princes the Valois could not be trusted.[91]

In January 1579, due to his financial and political troubles, Anjou returned to France. A year later the States General assented to Orange's proposal to reopen negotiations with the duke. The situation in the Netherlands had changed considerably since Anjou's departure. The rupture with the Walloon provinces had become evident and their reconciliation with Philip II had strengthened Farnese's military and political position. The Governor-General and the 'Malcontents', Walloon troops, had become a viable threat especially to Flanders and Brabant. The States General themselves had difficulties in raising troops and organizing an effective defence. They were in great need of financial and military assistance. Finally, during the Cologne peace negotiations the States General openly announced that if the peace talks failed, as they did, Philip II would be renounced.

Although the States General remained divided over the issue, in August 1580 a commission under the leadership of Marnix van St Aldegonde was sent to France to offer Anjou the lordship over the Netherlands. Once again the negotiations were difficult. While Anjou demanded sovereignty, the Dutch deputies, arguing that the word did not exist in Dutch, insisted on the title of 'highest lord'. Other problematic issues were the right of free assembly for the States General, which shocked the Frenchman Anjou, the Dutch demand that Henry III openly had to support Anjou and, finally, the clause of resistance, which in line with the tradition of the Joyous Entry the Dutch deputies proposed to include in the treaty.[92] None the less on 19 September the treaty of Plessis-lès-Tours was concluded. The treaty reaffirmed the parliamentary form of government which was

---

[91] For the history of Gouda's Francophobia, see Hibben, *Gouda in revolt*, 183–91.

[92] As Holt rightly points out, the formulation the Dutch deputies proposed went beyond the Joyous Entry, as it gave the States the right actually to renounce an unfaithful lord (Holt, *The Duke of Anjou*, 138). This step, however, was not as revolutionary as Holt argues: the articles by which Archduke Matthias had been accepted as Governor already gave the States General the right to take up arms in the case of Matthias violating the treaty. In many ways the treaty of Plessis-lés-Tours reformulated articles which were included in the treaty with Matthias.

developing in the Netherlands. The States retained their powerful position. They now expressly elected the lord of the country and had the right to renounce him in case of disloyalty. The logical consequence of the treaty with Anjou followed on 26 July 1581: with the Act of Abjuration the States General formally renounced Philip II.

Anjou's arrival did not solve problems. On the contrary. The duke had little understanding of his constitutional position, which he thought (or at least hoped) gave him real political power and authority. The States, however, never had any such intention. Moreover, Anjou's appointment was highly controversial. For different reasons Overijssel, Utrecht and Guelders rejected the treaty with Anjou, even after its formal ratification in January 1581. In Holland and Zeeland a faction pleaded for English instead of French aid.[93] Both provinces secured their independent position by reaffirming that William of Orange was their 'head and highest governor'. In Flanders, as Anjou was to experience during his Joyous Entries in Flemish towns, the duke was still deeply mistrusted. Finally, Anjou's military assistance was not a great success. This was partly due to the fact that as a military commander the duke was no match for Farnese. The principal reason, however, was Anjou's eternal financial disarray, caused by the States General, which failed to fulfil their financial obligations to the duke. Anjou was shocked. Suffering from a lack of food and a harsh winter, his army deteriorated. The powerless duke felt betrayed. On 17 January 1583 he took the fateful decision to seize Antwerp with his army. The 'French Fury' became a disaster. The attack itself was a complete failure. About 1,000 French soldiers were killed, and Anjou had to flee for his life. Whatever feelings of loyalty the Dutch had had towards him were now crushed. None the less, as he thought French aid was indispensable, William of Orange pushed for a reconciliation with Anjou. Negotiations were opened, but they were of little avail. Anjou left the Netherlands in the autumn. He died in June 1584.

To many in the Netherlands Orange's pro-French policy was incomprehensible. In Holland he was severely criticized by Gouda, and in Flanders he was depicted as the source of all evil. In many respects Orange's French policy had become a fiasco. It had strengthened neither the military position nor the political unity of the provinces. In the end it had only contributed to further divisions

---

[93] For the English and French factions, see A. J. Tjaden, 'De reconquista mislukt: de opstandige gewesten 1579–1588', in *AGN* vi. 251; Groenveld *et al.*, *De kogel door de kerk?*, 145.

amongst the ranks of the opposition and to the disarray of central government. The prestige and popularity of the prince declined spectacularly in Holland, Flanders and all other provinces.

At the same time, Orange's policy in the south had been counter-productive. His 'democratic policy' had released radical forces Orange was unable to bridle; these forces evoked a fierce opposition of the southern nobility and clergy and thus contributed to disrupt the frail unity amongst the provinces, which Orange himself so desperately had sought to preserve.

On 10 July 1584 Orange was assassinated in Delft. His last words, 'My God have pity on my soul and this poor people', bore testimony of the great confusion that afflicted the Netherlands.

This confusion was due not least to the military successes of Alexander Farnese. These successes were not only the result of Farnese's military genius. From about 1579 truces with the Ottoman empire, improving financial perspectives and a growing awareness of the English threat to Spanish interests in the Netherlands as well as in the New World enabled and urged a substantial change of direction in Spanish policy from the Mediterranean 'to the Atlantic and the north'.[94]

Of course Farnese also profited from the growing divisions amongst the Dutch Provinces. The reconciliation with the Walloon provinces and the defection to the Spanish side of Rennenberg, Stadtholder of the northern provinces, offered important strategic advantages. Moreover, due to its internal divisions Farnese's adversary, the States General, suffered from a chaotic and highly ineffective defence policy. Finally, the decision of the Walloon provinces to open their territories for Farnese's Spanish and Italian troops greatly facilitated Farnese's campaign.

Farnese's *reconquista*, especially between 1582 and 1585, was impressive. Flanders and Brabant were almost completely re-conquered. Bruges and Ghent fell in 1584, Brussels and finally Antwerp in 1585. The immediate consequences for the southern provinces were dramatic. Thousands of people left the provinces.[95] About half of the population left Ghent; Antwerp lost about 38,000 people, more than a third of its population. It is estimated that the

---

[94] See Lynch, *Spain under the Habsburgs*, 287ff.
[95] The Dutch historian J. Briels has published a number of studies about this migration. A recent study is J. Briels, *Zuid-Nederlanders 1572–1630: een demografische en cultuur-historische studie* (Sint-Niklaas, 1985).

northern provinces had an immigration of at least 100,000 people from the southern provinces.[96]

The Spanish *reconquista* alarmed Queen Elizabeth of England, who had no interest in an overall dominance of Spain in the Netherlands. Although she declined the sovereignty offered to her by the United Provinces, she did decide to intervene directly in the Netherlands. The treaty of Nonesuch, concluded three days after the fall of Antwerp, pledged military assistance of an English army for the right to put English garrisons in a number of Dutch towns, such as Flushing and Brill. The English army was led by the Earl of Leicester, one of the Queen's confidants.

The treaty of Nonesuch implied *de facto* an English declaration of war to Spain. It strengthened the idea, propagated for a number of years at the Spanish court, that 'the conquest of England held the key to the Dutch problem' and, as a matter of fact also to the defence of America.[97] Philip II consented to the plan for a direct naval attack on England with a huge 'invincible' Armada, which would be joined by an expeditionary force from Flanders. For years the plan devoured Spanish resources. It was a grand design and, as it turned out in the summer of 1588, a dreadful error. A definite plan was never finalized and communications with Farnese were difficult and ambiguous. In fact Farnese never was able to set off, as the Dutch effectively blocked the Flemish coast. The 'invincible' but lumbering ships of the Armada itself were tormented by mobile English vessels and by merciless weather.

The catastrophe of the Armada was a military turning-point in the Netherlands; the Spanish *reconquista* and its seemingly endless string of victories had been stopped. Politically the situation changed as well. In 1586 the Earl of Leicester had been heralded in the United Provinces. On 4 February he was even appointed Governor-General with 'absolute power' by the States General. Leicester, ambitious and Calvinist, supported by Reformed preachers and Flemish and Brabantine refugees, did not hesitate. In April he issued a prohibition on trade with the enemy on penalty of death. A special committee had to control whether the merchants observed the new regulation. Holland, which had already taken precautions to warrant its

---

[96] Briels (*Zuid-Nederlanders 1572–1630*, 213–21) even estimated that at least 124,000 and perhaps 150,000 migrated. For a sound critique of his figures see Woltjer's review of his study (*Nederlands Archief voor Kerkgeschiedenis*, 66 (1986), 264–8).

[97] See e.g. Lovett, *Early Habsburg Spain*, 182. Parma firmly opposed this idea. He pleaded for a strategy which gave priority to a land campaign in the Netherlands to defeat Holland and Zeeland followed by a cross-Channel expedition from the Low Countries to attack England.

independence by appointing Orange's son Maurice of Nassau Stadtholder and John of Oldenbarnevelt pensionary of the province, was furious. The conflict was aggravated when Leicester joined sides with radical groups in Utrecht and dismissed the moderate magistrates.

The conflict between Leicester and Holland touched the essence of the Dutch political system. While Leicester's partisans argued that the Governor-General was the prime authority in the political system, Holland unequivocally asserted provincial sovereignty. Leicester was fighting a losing battle. He was no match for the political genius of Oldenbarnevelt, who systematically undermined his position.[98] Moreover, Leicester's bold performance highly displeased the English queen, who preferred a far more cautious approach. Finally, the sudden betrayal of the towns of Zutphen and Deventer by English commanders to the Spanish in January 1587 led to a rapid fall in popularity for the English.

When it was revealed that Elizabeth was negotiating with Parma, and that Leicester was ordered to push the United Provinces to the negotiation table, the earl's authority received its death-blow. In an Anjou-like fashion Leicester seized a number of towns, thus digging his own political grave. In December 1587 he left the United Provinces; in April 1588 he officially resigned as Governor-General.

Once again the States, and Holland in particular, had asserted their power. Self-confident Oldenbarnevelt accepted the consequences. In the midst of the conflict with Leicester the pensionary worked on a more effective defence policy and pushed through some far-reaching decisions. The States of Holland decided to raise a huge field army of its own and accepted the financial sacrifices involved. Moreover, together with a committee of the States Maurice of Nassau was put in charge of the new army. A year later the threat of the Armada was approached with equal self-confidence and Maurice was appointed Admiral-General of the Union.

In short, 1588 was a turning-point. Under the military leadership of Maurice and the Frisian Stadtholder William Louis of Nassau a revolutionary reorganization of the army began. In 1590, when Farnese was once again ordered to sacrifice his campaign in the Netherlands and to intervene in France to assist the Catholic Holy League in their fight against Henry of Navarre, Maurice seized the opportunity to take the military initiative. The unexpected capture

---

[98] See J. den Tex, *Oldenbarnevelt*, i: *Opgang, 1547–1588* (Haarlem, 1960), 265ff.

of Breda was the start of a *reconquista* by the United Provinces that brought the northern and eastern provinces and a part of Brabant back under their control.

Under Oldenbarnevelt's political leadership the Dutch themselves finally took full control over their government. No longer were foreign princes asked to become governors. The States asserted their power, and more than ever the States General became the centre of their improving co-operation. Haphazardly the United Provinces had found their own way. They were becoming a republic.

2.7. THE NETHERLANDS IN 1590

The Dutch Republic was, as de Schepper has put it, 'a confederation of almost autonomous provinces and towns' with strong federalizing elements which was based on notions of popular sovereignty.[99] The parliamentary government of the Republic was a mixture of aristocracy and democracy, offering large groups of its population opportunities for political participation which were unequalled in most other contemporary European political systems. In this *mixtum compositum* the States General had become the prime vehicle of co-operation. It dealt with foreign policy, matters of war and peace, the defence of the country and diplomatic affairs. Of course essentially the States General was still very much a forum of deliberation for the provincial States. During the Revolt the provincial States greatly augmented their power in central government and affirmed their semi-independence. In all affairs which were not decided in the States General the provinces were in principle autonomous.

Of course the rise to power of the States implied, certainly in the main province, Holland, the rise to power of the towns, as essential participants in the States assemblies. As the decision-making processes in the States were still characterized by long deliberations and travelling deputies who could only decide by order and after due consultation with their constituencies, to a large extent the ruling elite of the Dutch Republic was formed by the town oligarchies. Politics in the Dutch Republic was a politics of negotiations and compromises and in this respect it has doubtless made a lasting contribution to Dutch political culture.

The provinces had two key officials. First each province had a pensionary, normally a full-time professional jurist, who was perma-

---

[99] De Schepper, *Belgium nostrum*, 43.

nently involved in the affairs of the provincial States and often attended the States General. Because of Holland's prominence the pensionary of Holland could become the country's leading politician, as, for example, Oldenbarnevelt and later John de Witt, who were true secretaries of state. Secondly, the provinces usually, though not always, appointed a Stadtholder. Traditionally the Stadtholder was a member of the Orange–Nassau dynasty and he often held the office in a number of provinces. The Stadtholder held the military command, he was admiral of the fleet, he had the authority to grant pardon and in some cases he elected the town aldermen. The constitutional position and precise authority of the Stadtholder remained controversial; the function, in Rowen's words, was 'neither fish nor fowl'.[100]

A further comparison of the institutional make-up of the government of the northern Dutch Provinces of 1555 with the institutional make-up of the Dutch Republic in 1590 shows that the constituting elements of the two frameworks had remained basically the same. There was one crucial difference. The Dutch Republic had no sovereign 'lord of the country'. His authority and power had shifted to the true victors of the Dutch Revolt, the States and the towns.

The destiny of the south was entirely different. The southern provinces, Flanders and Brabant in particular, had been the main theatre of war. Tormented by battles, sieges, mutinies and plundering they were finally almost completely reconquered by Philip II. The segregation of the northern and southern provinces, which had formed a unity not only politically, but also, and maybe first and foremost, economically and culturally, was one of the main consequences of the Dutch Revolt. The disruption was profound.

In the Spanish (later the Austrian) Netherlands the Habsburgs could resume and to some extent complete the process of centralization. The massive emigration to the north, while a highly valuable influx of human capital for the Dutch Republic, was an economic, cultural and intellectual brain drain for the south. It also made it easier for the Catholic church to regain its monopoly position. Whereas the Dutch Republic indulged in its enjoyment and

---

[100] See Herbert H. Rowen, 'Neither fish nor fowl: the stadtholderate in the Dutch Republic', in Herbert H. Rowen and Andrew Lossky (eds.), *Political ideas and institutions in the Dutch Republic* (Los Angeles, 1985), 3–31. For a comprehensive study of the Stadtholders, see Herbert H. Rowen, *The Princes of Orange: the Stadtholders in the Dutch Republic* (Cambridge, 1988).

'embarrassment of riches',[101] Brabant and Flanders were impregnated with the contrasting and certainly much less tolerant riches of the Catholic Counter-Reformation.[102] The Burgundian Netherlands were no more.

[101] See Simon Schama, *The embarrassment of riches: an interpretation of Dutch culture in the Golden Age* (London, 1987). For critical reviews by Price, Haitsma Mulier and van Nierop of this fascinating and controversial interpretation, see *BMGN* 104 (1) (1989), 39–55.

[102] See W. P. Blockmans, *Culturele geschiedenis van Vlaanderen*, ii (Deurne, 1983), 152, and also Soly, 'Le grand essor du capitalisme commercial', and de Schepper, *Belgium nostrum*. In what is certainly the most vivid, brutal and poetic study of the Dutch Revolt, the *Geuzenboek* (Book of Beggars) of Louis Paul Boon, the Belgian author simply concluded: 'And Flanders was vanquished and died, and all Beggars were exterminated. Amen.'

CHAPTER 3

Religion and resistance: the case of Reformed Protestantism

3.1. INTRODUCTION

The purpose of this chapter is to reconstruct how Dutch Reformed Protestants faced the questions concerning the attitude the faithful should take with regard to a hostile, persecuting government and whether they developed a distinct Reformed Protestant approach to the questions of political obedience and resistance which had troubled Protestants throughout Europe from the very beginning of the Reformation.

Luther himself had set the tone for Reformation political thought on these issues, following the basic tenet of texts such as the thirteenth chapter of Paul's letter to the Romans, 1 Peter 2 and the fourth commandment. All of them emphasized that obedience was a divine command. As the earthly powers were ordained by God to protect the good and to punish the wicked, 'he who resists the authorities, resists what God has appointed', as Romans 13:2 put it. However, Luther's emphasis on obedience and non-resistance was by no means unqualified. From the outset he pointed out, again following the scriptures, that one should obey God rather than men, and that therefore the faithful were obliged to disobey worldly authorities whenever these ordered anything that was ungodly. Moreover, from October 1530 Luther started to waver in his support for the idea of absolute non-resistance, with which he had so ferociously condemned the German Peasants' War. As the threat of an Imperial assault upon the protestants was imminent, Luther and several other major German Reformers conceded in the so-called Torgau Declaration that, as several 'doctors of law' had argued, there might be a legal right of resistance on the grounds of imperial and canon law.[1]

---

[1] For the development of Lutheran resistance theory, see Quentin Skinner, *The foundations of modern political thought*, ii: *The age of Reformation* (Cambridge, 1978), 191–206, and W. D. J. Cargill Thompson, *The political thought of Martin Luther* (Brighton, 1984), 91–111.

On the one hand there was a 'private law theory', developed by jurists from Saxony, which maintained that if Charles V wanted to impose his judgment on the spiritual realm, where he had no jurisdiction at all, the emperor acted as an unjust judge, whose violence was like that of any private person. Therefore, in this case the rule that it was justifiable to repel unjust force with force as formulated in Roman law[2] was fully applicable. In the following decades this theory was further elaborated, for example by Melanchthon, who argued that God had implanted 'a natural instinct of self-preservation' in beasts as well as men. Therefore, in the case of manifest injuries nature allowed men to repel unjust force, even if government officials failed to do so.[3]

On the other hand, a constitutionalist theory had been developed by Hessian scholars, who pointed out that the emperor's powers were limited by the imperial constitution, as embodied by Charles' own *Wahlkapitulation* of 1519. The Hessians argued that if the emperor transgressed the limits of his constitutional powers, 'inferior magistrates', and the Electors of the empire in particular, were obliged to defend the constitution and to resist the emperor. In fact Lutherans started to argue that the 'inferior powers' were expressly ordained by God to prevent superior rulers from misbehaviour. This line of argumentation was developed in particular by Martin Bucer, who concluded that if superior powers fell into ungodliness and tyranny, the 'inferior magistrates' had the duty to resist such, if necessary by means of arms. A major restatement of the constitutional resistance theory was published in 1550 when the Lutherans of Magdeburg justified their armed resistance in their famous *Confession and apology*.[4]

The Lutheran church as such made no important headway in the Low Countries, although eventually a flourishing Lutheran community was founded in Antwerp. Lutheran works and doctrines, however, soon found their way into the Dutch Provinces, which were marked by a remarkable degree of intellectual openness. Moreover, religious life, highly influenced by late medieval mysticism and the movement of the Modern Devotion, had not been insensible to critique on the pomp and circumstance of the Roman church. In the earnestness and austerity of its godliness the Modern Devotion was an

---

[2] See Digest, book 43, title 16, para. 1, sentence 27 (*vim vi repellere licere*).
[3] For Melanchthon's analysis of the issue, see Skinner, *The foundations of modern political thought*, ii. 202–4.
[4] For both Bucer and the Magdeburg *Confession*, see Skinner, *The foundations of modern political thought*, ii. 204–9.

important manifestation of a heartfelt longing for the return to the *ecclesia primitiva* in all its profundity and simplicity.[5]

It has been argued that there were links, directly or indirectly, between the Modern Devotion and the prince of the northern Renaissance, Erasmus of Rotterdam.[6] Erasmus, educated at the schools of the Brethren of the Common Life, personified the search for the *vita Christiana*, which typified humanism in the northern countries. For him, but also for scholars like Wessel Gansfort and Rudolph Agricola, in whose footsteps Erasmus trod, the study of the *bonae litterae*, the recovery of the classics, the study of Latin and Greek, and the development and application of new philological methods were ultimately means and tools to deepen Christian ethical and theological studies and to reform Christendom. These northern humanists represented what is generally called biblical or Christian humanism, or, as IJsewijn has favoured, 'humanist Christianity'.[7]

Humanist studies, those of Erasmus in particular, offered powerful incentives for religious debate and reformation. Erasmus' philosophy of Christ denounced the profane and profiteering elements of the Roman church in general and of the monastic orders in particular, and sought to revive the church through a renaissance of its original spiritual qualities. For Christian humanists like Erasmus Christ's message was above all a matter of the heart and an 'attitude of mind'. Its essence was an ethics of Christian love which had overwhelming consequences for practical life. In Erasmus' view the simple and humble ethics of the *philosophia Christi* was of much greater importance than the chimeras of scholastic theologians, described by Folly as 'a remarkably supercilious and touchy lot', full of 'tortuous obscurities'.[8]

In many ways Christian humanism helped to articulate the controversies that marked Dutch religious life in the sixteenth century.[9] One of the main points concerned the relation between

---

[5] See C. C. de Bruin, 'De spiritualiteit van de moderne devotie', in C. C. de Bruin *et al.*, *Geert Grote en de moderne devotie* (Zutphen, 1984), 102.

[6] See e.g. De Bruin, 'De spiritualiteit van de moderne devotie', 142 and Margaret Mann Philips, *Erasmus and the northern Renaissance* (Woodbridge, 1981), 14–16, 41.

[7] Jozef IJsewijn, 'The coming of humanism to the Low Countries', in Heiko A. Oberman and Thomas A. Brady (eds.), *Itinerarium italicum: the profile of the Italian Renaissance in the mirror of its European transformations* (Leiden, 1975), 223–4.

[8] See Desiderius Erasmus, 'Moriae Encomium id est stultitiae laus' (Praise of Folly), in Desiderius Erasmus, *Opera Omnia. Desiderii Erasmi Roterodami*, series 4, vol. iii, ed. Clarence Miller (Amsterdam, 1979), 144ff.

[9] For a lucid analysis of these controversies, see C. Augustijn, 'Godsdienst in de zestiende eeuw', in *Ketters en papen onder Filips II* (The Hague, 1986), 26–40, and J. Decavele, *De dageraad van de Reformatie in Vlaanderen* (Brussels, 1975), 589–606.

man and God, and more specifically the role of indulgences, images, the role and position of the priest, the sacraments and the many church ceremonies and institutions that lacked evident biblical foundation. It was argued that these matters had been pushed between man and God, and that they distorted the fundamental contradistinction between the earthly and the divine. More or less as a consequence of this line of reasoning the controversial idea was propounded that salvation was obtained through Christ alone, and not through human work or merit. The discarding of church ceremonies and institutions and the emphasis on Christ as the sole mediator between God and man also contributed to a growing, and in the Catholic tradition controversial, emphasis on the individuality of religion and on the study of the word of God, which alone could bring Christ into presence. Seen as the sole pure manifestation of God's word, the Bible was placed at the centre of religious life, a tendency that led to a certain degree of biblical legalism, in which under all circumstances the Bible was awarded the decisive word.

The ideas of Christian humanism were widely cherished among the social, political and intellectual elite of the towns in the Low Countries. Bruges, for example, was imbued with Erasmian openness and toleration,[10] as manifested by the works of the Spanish humanist Juan Luis Vives and of Joris Cassander, whose 'Cassandrianism' stood for toleration and reconciliation.

In this sphere of intellectual openness it was often difficult to distinguish Christian humanism from more direct Lutheran influences. For even though Erasmus eventually denounced Luther in public, it was hard for contemporaries to discern the sometimes rather subtle differences between Erasmian and Lutheran ideas. For a number of decades a situation of perplexing questions and slowly proliferating answers persisted. For even if the points of controversy were clear, the answers certainly were not. Religious identities were still very much in the process of formation and formulation. During the first half of the sixteenth century there was simply no instant, clear-cut choice between well-defined versions of traditional Roman Catholicism, Christian humanism, Lutheranism, Anabaptism and Calvinism.[11]

Of course Luther's schism, the development of other reformatory

---

[10] See Decavele, *De dageraad van de Reformatie in Vlaanderen*, 53–68, and L. Vandamme, 'Het calvinisme te Brugge in beweging (1560–1566)', in Dirk van de Bauwhede and Marc Goetinck (eds.), *Brugge in de Geuzentijd* (Bruges, 1982), 103.

[11] This point has been emphatically made in the highly influential studies of the Dutch historian J. J. Woltjer (see Bibliography).

groups and the policy of the central government to repress unortho-
doxy harshly gradually forced critics of the Catholic church to make
choices. Following Erasmus, many opted for religious unity and did
not leave the Catholic church. Some put their hopes for reformation
on the Pope; others, sometimes called 'protestantizing Catholics',
hoped to reform the church from within and, pleading for toleration
and reconciliation, sought to retain in one way or another Erasmus'
'middle way'.

Leaving aside the influential Anabaptist movement, Dutch Reformed Protestants were the first to make the step from dissent to
schism in the Low Countries. The formation of a Reformed counter-
church and identity started largely in exile, particularly in England
and Germany.[12] Dutch Reformed Protestantism was to an important
extent the result of the activities of the various refugee churches, those
of London and Emden in particular.

The refugee churches, partly due to their dispersion, had a great
variety of international contacts. From about 1550 systematic
contacts were also made with Calvin's Geneva, which more and more
became the centre of an international Calvinist movement. During
the 1550s Calvin's teachings gradually penetrated the Low
Countries, first the French – but later also the Dutch-speaking parts,
and after 1559 Calvinism made headway in the Low Countries.
However, Calvin was never the sole reformer to influence Reformed
Protestantism in the Netherlands, and it even seems doubtful whether
before 1571 his influence was predominant.[13] Even though Dutch
Reformed Protestants tended to follow Calvin on such defining issues
as the eucharist, predestination, discipline and church government,
they always had one eye open for the teachings of seminal figures such
as Luther,[14] Zwingli, Bullinger, Bucer, Musculus and, not least, their
own leaders such as Micron and A Lasco. Moreover, as Reformed
Protestants were still groping for their identity, there were believers
and ministers among their ranks who were in fact much closer to
what is called Spiritualism, a catch-all for a great variety of groups

---

[12] For the Dutch refugee churches in general, see A. A. van Schelven, *De Nederduitsche
vluchtelingenkerken der 16e eeuw in Engeland en Duitschland in hunne beteekenis voor de reformatie in de
Nederlanden* (The Hague, 1908), and more recently Heinz Schilling, *Niederländische Exulanten
im 16. Jahrhundert: ihre Stellung im Religiösen Leben Deutscher und Englischer Städte*, Schriften des
Vereins für Reformationsgeschichte, vol. lxxviii–lxxix, no. 187 (Gütersloh, 1972).

[13] It is for this reason that, following Decavele, I prefer to speak in terms of Reformed
Protestantism rather than of Dutch Calvinism. See Decavele, *De dageraad van de Reformatie in
Vlaanderen*, 168.

[14] For the relationship between Lutheranism and Reformed Protestantism, see the essays in
C. Graafland et al. (eds.), *Luther en het gereformeerd protestantisme* (The Hague, 1982).

and sects,[15] which somehow shared the essential idea that man, the fallen Adam, could be regenerated through direct illumination of the spirit into a New Adam, a reborn man who was able to create a New Jerusalem on earth. Thus, in spite of the growing importance of Calvinist doctrines Dutch Reformed Protestantism was undoubtedly pluriform and eclectic in character.[16]

For Calvin the questions of political obedience and resistance were just as pressing as they had been for Luther. Following the Lutherans, Calvin emphasized the text of Romans 13, thus putting great weight on the imperatives of obedience and non-resistance. However, Calvin not only reiterated the view that obedience was limited, as one should obey God rather than man, he also qualified his views on resistance by pointing out that the imperative of 'non-resistance' only applied to 'private men'. This point in the *Institutes of the Christian religion* was followed by a famous passage in which Calvin argued that sometimes 'popular magistrates', such as the ephors in Sparta, the tribunes in Rome and the demarchs in Athens, had 'been appointed to curb the tyranny of kings'. He added that 'perhaps there is something similar to this in the power exercised in each kingdom by the three orders, when they hold their principal assemblies'.[17]

If this was Calvin's variation of Lutheran constitutionalist ideas, it seems that, during the last years of his life, his reflections on the lawfulness of resistance became more radical, going in the direction of private law theory and even beyond.[18] In a predication of 31 July

[15] Braekman, for example, has distinguished six different brands of Spiritualism, the Loists, the Spiritualist libertines, the individualist Spiritualists like Sebastian Franck and Casper Schwenckfeld, the unitarian Spiritualists like Hans Denck and Sebastien Castellio, the mystic Spiritualists like Guillaume Postel and Jacob Böhme and the egocentric prophets like David Joris, Hendrik Niclaes and Barrefelt. See E. M. Braekman, 'Les courants religieux de la reforme au Pays-Bas', in Michel Baelde and Herman van Nuffel (eds.), *The century of Marnix van St. Aldegonde* (Antwerp, 1982), 24. For a sketch of the riches of Dutch Spiritualism see R. P. Zijp, 'Spiritualisme in de 16de eeuw, een schets', in *Ketters en papen*, 75–93.

[16] See esp. W. Nijenhuis, 'Variants within Dutch Calvinism in the sixteenth century', *LCHY* 12 (1979), 51 and A. Duke, 'The ambivalent face of Calvinism in the Netherlands, 1561–1618', in M. Prestwich (ed.), *International Calvinism 1541–1715* (Oxford, 1985), 120. For a lucid comment on the Calvinist character of Dutch culture and society in general, see G. J. Schutte, *Het Calvinistisch Nederland* (Utrecht, 1988) and the fascinating interpretation in Schama, *The embarrassment of riches*.

[17] John Calvin, *Institutes of the Christian religion* (Grand Rapids, Mich., 1983), 675.

[18] See Skinner, *The foundations of modern political thought*, ii. 219ff., and especially W. Nijenhuis, 'De grenzen der burgerlijke ongehoorzaamheid in Calvijns laatstbekende preken: ontwikkeling van zijn opvattingen aangaande het verzetsrecht', in *Historisch bewogen: Opstellen over de radicale reformatie in de 16e en 17e eeuw* (Groningen, 1984), 67–99. For the counterargument, see J. W. Allen, *A history of political thought in the sixteenth century*, rev. edn. (London, 1957), 57.

1562 Calvin is even held to have pleaded, on the basis of Abraham's example, for a duty of resistance for all 'private persons', if such was required to save the poor from a wicked government.[19]

3.2. OBEDIENCE AND RESISTANCE: PRELUDES

In 1562 Calvin's followers in the Low Countries were preoccupied with setting up a network of underground churches. The first Reformed Protestant 'church under the cross' was founded in Antwerp, which, under the guidance of the Emden refugee church, became the main centre of Reformed Protestantism in the Low Countries. It more or less functioned as mother church for the congregations in Flanders, Brabant, Holland and Zeeland. Ministers were sent, for example, to Brussels (1558), Ghent (1562) and Malines (1564).

The town of Tournai was the second centre of Reformed Protestantism. The organization of the congregation was completed in 1559, when Guy de Bray became minister of the Tournai church under the Cross. Tournai functioned as mother church for the French-speaking provinces. Here the influence of Calvin, the events in France and the manifold contacts with French Huguenots were of great importance to the growth and character of Reformed Protestantism.[20]

The third centre of Reformed Protestant growth was the more industrial area of west Flanders. Here the influence of the English refugee churches, those of London and Sandwich in particular, was of tremendous importance.

The Reformed Protestant growth in numbers was accompanied by a growth in organization. In 1561 a *Confession of faith* was published for the Low Countries and in 1562 the first provincial synod met in

[19] See Nijenhuis, 'De grenzen der burgerlijke ongehoorzaamheid in Calvijns laatstbekende preken', 92. Nijenhuis' argument is built on the following passage: 'Ainsi donc, notons bien, que l'Escriture met ces deux motz, pour exprimer que ce n'est point assez de nous governer paisiblement, sans nuire a personne, mais que nous devons nous opposer au mal, tant qu'il nous est possible. Et cela est commandé a tous en général. Ce n'est pas (di ie) seulement aux princes, magistratz et officiers de iustice, que cecy s'addresse, mais a toutes personne privess aussi bien ... [discusses the example of Abraham and concludes] Nous voyons donc, que c'est une reigle commune qui appartient a tous, de faire iugement et iustice, cest ascavoir de se gouverner en equité et droicture avec tout le monde, et qu'on s'oppose au mal et qu'on y resiste, quand il sera question de soulager les poures affligez et leur donner secours quil est requis'.

[20] For the history of the Reformation in Tournai, see Gérard Moreau, *Histoire du protestantisme à Tournai jusqu'à la veille de la Révolution des Pays-Bas* (Paris, 1962).

Antwerp, which submitted its resolutions for approval to Emden, London and Geneva. The unique strength of its organization, and the combative character of its doctrine and its will to power have often been mentioned to explain the apparent success of Reformed Protestantism after 1555.[21] This success was not restricted to specific social groups. Reformed Protestantism flourished in those areas, such as great towns and important industrial centres, where socio-economic changes, the introduction of early forms of capitalism in particular, had cut down traditional social bonds and opened up new social and intellectual horizons.[22] In these areas, however, Reformed Protestantism appealed not only to uprooted artisans and industrial workers, but also to clergymen, lower nobles, members of the middle classes and to the intellectual and social town elites.

Although from the very beginning Reformed Protestants were confronted with the issues of obedience and resistance, the early works of Dutch authors who aligned themselves with Reformed Protestantism treated them with exemplary caution, staying well within the main stream of Reformed political thought.

Dutch authors fully acknowledged that governmental authority had been ordained by God, not only to punish the evil and to protect the rightful, but also ideally as a fosterer of the true religion. The argument was made, for example, in *The layman's guide*, 'a short report on all principal points of the Christian belief' for the 'simple unlearned Christian', published by Jan Gerritsz Versteghe, a former parish priest from Guelders, under the pseudonym Anastasius Veluanus.[23] It was the first work in Dutch that presented an elaborate Reformed Protestant doctrine, although very much along 'Erasmian–Zwinglian' lines.[24]

---

[21] See e.g. J. J. Woltjer, 'De religieuze situatie in de eerste jaren van de republiek', in *Ketters en papen*, 95; J. Decavele, 'Het onstaan van de evangelische beweging en ontwikkeling van de protestantse kerkverbanden in de Nederlanden tot 1580', in *Ketters en papen*, 51, and J. Decavele, 'Reformatie en begin katholieke restauratie 1555–1568', in *AGN* vi. 173.

[22] See Decavele, *De dageraad van de Reformatie in Vlaanderen*, 586, 638, and J. J. Woltjer, 'Stadt und Reformation in den Niederlanden', in Franz Petri (ed.), *Kirche und gesellschaftlicher Wandel in deutschen und niederländischen Städten der werdenden Neuzeit* (Cologne, 1980), 163.

[23] Anastasio Veluano, *Kort bericht in alle principalen punten des christen geloves...* (Strasburg, 1554), repr. in S. Cramer and F. Pijper (eds.), *BRN* iv (The Hague, 1906). Refs. are to the 1906 edn.

[24] See D. Nauta *et al.*, *Biografisch lexicon voor de geschiedenis van het Nederlands protestantisme*, ii. (Kampen, 1983), 436, and also Andrew George Johnson, 'The eclectic reformation: vernacular evangelical pamphlet literature in the Dutch-speaking Low Countries, 1520–1565', Ph.D. thesis, University of Southampton, 1986, 256–8. For a full biography see G. Morsink, *Joannes Anastasius Veluanes* (Kampen, 1986).

Along traditional lines Veluanus argued that the 'office of government' served two principal purposes. First, the government had to serve 'in eternal matters' by fighting idolatry and fostering the true predication of Christ's word. Secondly, 'in temporal matters' the government's task was to protect the subjects 'so that they do not suffer from violence nor injustice to life, honour and good'.[25]

Veluanus acknowledged that the New Testament ordered Christians to be obedient, to 'love, honour [and] serve... their princes and other overlords', not only the righteous but also the persecutors and the evil. Veluanus also pointed out that civic obedience was not without limits and he reiterated the Reformed view that if worldly authorities ordered 'what God forbids', one should 'not be obedient to any emperor or other authority, for one should obey God rather than the prince'.[26] Veluanus emphasized that this principle also applied to those in office. Referring to the policy of religious persecution, he pointed out that 'if Christian stadtholders, bailiffs, judges or other officers are ordered by their princes to catch or kill good people because of Jesus' word, they are obliged to follow God, the highest prince, who orders as follows: See to it that no innocent blood is shed'.[27]

In general early Reformed Protestant works argued that heretics – and Veluanus referred to Anabaptists in particular – should be persuaded by debate instead of persecuted by force. It was, as Veluanus put it, the task of 'the sword of the emperor' to punish 'criminals, who consciously have done violence or injustice to their neighbours' life, good or honour', but not those who were 'unknowingly deluded' or ignorantly bound in their conscience to wrong doctrines.[28]

These views were reiterated by Marten Micron, who served the London refugee church as minister from 1550 to 1553 and later worked in Norden near Emden in Ostfriesland. In 1554 Micron outlined the presbyterian church order, the church ceremonies and liturgy of the London refugee church in *The Christian ordinances of the Dutch community in Christ... in London*.[29] The work offered a blueprint for the organization of Reformed Protestant churches. However, Micron, himself highly influenced by the Zurich reformers Zwingli

---

[25] Veluanus, *Kort bericht in alle principalen punten des christen geloves*, 347.   [26] Ibid.
[27] Ibid. 350.   [28] Ibid. 338.
[29] Marten Micron, *De christlicke ordinancien der Nederlantscher Ghemeinten Christi... te London* (London, 1554: re-ed. W. F. Dankbaar, *Marten Micron: de Christlicke ordinancien der Nederlantscher Ghemeinten te London (1554)* (The Hague, 1956)). Refs. are to the 1956 edn.

and Bullinger, recognized the pluriformity of Reformed Protestantism and expressed his respect for other Reformed Protestant churches
even if they subscribed to somewhat different church ordinances.

Reformed Protestant authors like Micron did not hesitate to
admonish authorities that persecuted the faithful, warning them in
powerful terms of the final judgment. Thus in one of the first Dutch
martyrologies Micron warned public authorities that 'the persecutors
of the truth' would suffer at the Day of Judgment. Instead of painting
'their swords so easily with the innocent blood of Christians', they
should 'shelter and protect' these poor folk 'against all grief and
injustice'.[30]

Stronger words were used in a work of Willem Gnapheus, one of
the earliest evangelicals in the Netherlands. Gnapheus, who had been
rector of the Latin school in The Hague, spent most of his life in exile,
especially in Emden where he served as tutor for the son of Countess
Anna and as elder of the Emden consistory.[31] In *Tobias and Lazarus*,
published in 1557, Gnapheus admonished public officers, particularly the councillors of the courts in Holland, Zeeland and Friesland,
to follow God, who had called them 'to carry the sword to protect the
innocent and to punish the evil and to administer justice to all people,
without any exception'.[32] It was the task of the public authorities to
guard and advocate both tables of Moses, not to oppress the innocent,
for such 'judges', would 'die as the lowest of the people', and 'perish
as it behoves the tyrants'.[33] At the same time Gnapheus argued that
public authorities were ordained by God and were necessary 'for the
maintenance of the common peace and welfare of the countries' and
that the government should be obeyed 'not just to escape her wrath'
but for 'conscience's sake, as our conscience testifies to us that they
are God's servants'. Thus the faithful should bear 'all pressure and
suffering patiently until the end'. Resistance seemed to be out of the

---

[30] Marten Micron, *Een waerachteghe historie van Hoste (gheseyt Jooris) van der Katelyne, te Ghendt om
het vry opentlick straffen der afgodischer leere, ghebrant, ten grooten nutte ende vertroostinghe aller
christenen* (Emden, 1555), fol. 21; repr. in F. Pijper (ed.), *BRN* viii (The Hague, 1911),
187–253.
[31] For Gnapheus, see Johnston, 'The eclectic reformation', 281–4, and J. P. de Bie *et al.*,
Biografisch woordenboek van protestantsche godgeleerden in Nederland, 5 vols. (The Hague,
1907–43), iv. 269–72.
[32] Wilhelmum Gnapheum, *Tobias ende Lazarus mit grooter neersticheyt ghecorrigeert, verbetert, ende in
die Dialogus oft t'samen sprekinghe, underscheydelicken ghedeelt, alle krancken, bedroefden, ende
eenvoudighe menschen seer profytelick om te lesen* (Emden, 1557), fol. A2. This book was a revised
version of Gnapheus' *Troost ende spiegel der siecken*, first pub. 1531. See Johnston, 'The eclectic
reformation', 281.   [33] Gnapheus, *Tobias ende Lazarus*, fol. A4.

question. Instead patience and constancy were presented as principal virtues of the true believers.

Other authors concurred. Martyrdom was regarded as a basic characteristic of the fate of the faithful. In his 1559 *Gospel of the poor*[34] Cornelis Cooltuyn, a former parish priest of Alkmaar and one of the important figures in the breakthrough of Reformed Protestantism in Holland, emphasized the importance of godly chastisement, which affected the faithful 'so very heavily with dearness, pestilence, war, persecution'. Referring to Augustine Cooltuyn argued that this 'fatherly chastisement to salvation' was to teach and instruct the faithful to their betterment. God kept his children 'under the Cross' to strangle the 'old Adam' in his children, to subject the flesh to the spirit. Moreover, chastisement taught the faithful that God alone was the Lord and that salvation and blessedness would only come from him. Another reason for God's chastisement, and therefore for the faithful's suffering, was 'to test faith, to exercise patience and to bring man to full obedience'.[35] Once again patience and constancy were mentioned as principal Christian virtues.

Cooltuyn also explained that the faithful suffered to glorify God's name. The principal end of all suffering, however, so Cooltuyn argued, was to teach the faithful 'to despise this present life, which is full of misery' and to put their 'hope, study and labour to the coming blessed life'.[36] War, poverty or persecution should teach the faithful to despise their transient life on earth and to long for eternal life in heaven.

Even more than Cooltuyn's *Gospel of the poor*, the 1559 martyrology composed by Adriaen van Haemstede[37] emphasized that life on earth was a life of misery and persecution for the faithful, which they had to live through with patience and constancy, in the expectation of the blessed life in the hereafter.

Van Haemstede, who played an important yet controversial role in the history of Reformed Protestantism, opened his martyrology with an 'admonishment to the government of the Dutch provinces'. He pointed out that they were chosen by God to head the people. As

---

[34] Cornelis Cooltuyn, *Dat Evangeli der Armen* (1559); repr. in S. Cramer and F. Pijper (eds.), *BRN* ix (The Hague, 1912), 217–480. Refs. are to the 1912 edn.   [35] Ibid. 383.

[36] Ibid. 453.

[37] Adriaen Cornelis Haemstedium, *De geschiedenisse ende den doodt der vromer martelaren, die om het ghetuyghenisse des Evangeliums haer bloedt ghestort hebben, van den tijden Christi af totten jare 1559 toe, bij een vergadert op het kortste* (1559). A biography of Haemstede and an analysis of his martyrology is offered by Auke Jan Jelsma, *Adriaan van Haemstede en zijn martelaarsboek* (The Hague, 1970).

such they had to follow the law as given to Moses, which required first of all that they had to work with great 'industry and diligence' to sanctify God's name and spread his empire. However, so van Haemstede thundered, 'the overseers' were 'blind' and 'the shepherds' were 'stupid dogs', who ignored 'the book of law' and left the Bible 'lying behind the chest'. And so the righteous were persecuted and innocent blood was shed. According to van Haemstede there was nothing unusual about this situation. On the contrary, the persecution of the faithful was a permanent feature of human history. Martyrdom was a basic characteristic of the true church, which in this respect was the successor of Christ. Once again van Haemstede warned the authorities in strong and frightful terms of the Day of Judgment: 'Verily, those who follow the tyranny of Pharaoh, disobey God's words and violently oppress the people of the Lord, those will drown and perish in the waters of perniciousness by the powerful hand of the Lord.'[38]

In 1557 van Haemstede was engaged in a religious dispute with a certain Jan Daelman, who argued that the Roman Catholic church was still the church of Christ and that the faithful could participate in its ceremonies, although they were full of superstition and idolatry, if only they did not believe such ceremonies were sanctifying. Daelman's account of his dispute with van Haemstede provoked a powerful reaction by Peter Dathenus, whose response to what he regarded as Daelman's corruptions appeared in 1559.[39] In his *Christian account on the dispute held within Oudenaarde* Dathenus, at the time a minister in Germany, not only stressed the satanic character of the Roman Catholic church and argued forcefully against any form of Nicodemite behaviour. He also defended governmental authority against Anabaptist views, arguing that the government was 'a servant of God, who keeps his Reason, and administers the office which is characteristic for him, namely to punish the evil and protect the good'.[40] Referring to Peter's words, Dathenus pointed out that in matters which did not contravene God's word, one should obey not only rightful but also despotic authorities. In Dathenus' view, no private person was allowed to resist the authorities. However, reiterating another well-established idea of Reformed political

---

[38] Haemstede, *De geschiedenisse ende den doodt der vromer martelaren*, preface (unpaginated).

[39] Peter Dathenus, *Een christelijcke verantwoordinghe op die disputatie, ghehouden binnen Oudenaerde, tusschen M. Adriaen Hamstadt, ende Jan Daelman beschreven met onwaerheyt, ende uutghegheven door Jan Daelman voorseyt*, 2nd edn. (Antwerp, 1582).

[40] Ibid., fol. 58.

thought, he pointed out that it was lawful for the *magistratus inferiores* to resist a tyrannical government.[41]

Thus Dathenus was among the first to leave room for lawful resistance against an unlawful persecuting government, a sign that the times were starting to change.

3.3. YEARS OF RADICALIZATION, 1560–1566

From about 1560 Reformed Protestantism went through a rapid process of radicalization. First of all Reformed Protestants came out in the open. Roman Catholic preaching was interrupted and already in 1557 van Haemstede, much to the disdain of his co-religionists, preached in public and participated in public debates in Antwerp and Oudenaarde. During Easter 1562 the first public sermon was held in Flanders, soon followed by the first armed mass meeting at the churchyard of the Flemish village Boeschepe in July 1562.[42] In 1561 psalm-singing crowds walked through the streets of Tournai and Valenciennes in closely concerted 'chantries'. Increasingly the arrests and executions of protestants provoked demonstrations and riots. Successful attempts were made to free imprisoned protestants. On 6 November 1561 the book-hawker Jan Hacke was released from prison in west Flanders, and in April 1562 a rioting crowd in Valenciennes freed two protestants who were about to be executed.

Thus the problem of active resistance had become pressing for Dutch Reformed Protestants.[43] In February 1561 one of the ministers who worked in the provinces, Godfried van Wingen, wrote a letter to the London refugee church confronting it with a number of questions which were under debate by the brethren under the Cross.[44] Van Wingen wanted to know whether a Christian could in good conscience remain silent in the face of his brother's misery and suffering, and whether he should not by all means, including the use

---

[41] Ibid., fol. 6.

[42] See M. F. Backhouse, 'The official start of armed resistance in the Low Countries: Boeschepe 12 July 1562', *Archiv für Reformationsgeschichte*, 71 (1980), 198–212, and Phyllis Mack Crew, *Calvinist preaching and iconoclasm in the Netherlands 1544–1569* (Cambridge, 1978), 67–8.

[43] For what follows, see also A. A. van Schelven, 'Het begin van het gewapend verzet tegen Spanje in de 16e-eeuwsche Nederlanden', *Handelingen en mededelingen van de maatschappij der Nederlandsche Letterkunde te Leiden over het jaar 1914–1915* (Leiden, 1915), 126–56.

[44] For this letter, see J. H. Hessels (ed.), *Ecclesiae Londino Batavae Archivum*, ii: *Epistulae et tractatus* (Cambridge, 1889), 334–7. Hessels was not sure when the letter was written. He put it at 14 Feb. 1570. Van Schelven ('Het begin van het gewapend verzet', 135) argued on the basis of the acts of the London consistory that the letter was written on 14 Feb. 1561.

of force and the breaking of churches, try to release his imprisoned brother, on condition that blood would not be shed. In this respect the question arose whether inquisitors should be recognized as governmental authorities, and whether prisoners were obliged to reveal and confess their faith openly to the inquisitors and public authorities that persecuted them. While the London consistory duly admonished their co-religionists in the Netherlands not to follow the 'rebellious Anabaptists and the scum of Thomas Müntzer',[45] a number of leading Reformed Protestants, like the ministers Herman Moded, Peter Hazaert and Joris Wybo, who were gathered at the 1562 synod of Antwerp, made the fundamental move of deciding that it was allowed to free co-religionists by force from prison.[46] In June 1562 deliberations took place in London between the consistory and 'servants of the community of Antwerp', the ministers Herman Moded, Peter Hazaert, Sebastiaan Matte and two elders. The basic issues were the position of the inquisitors and the legitimacy of the government's power to make Christians suffer.[47] However, the problems remained unresolved, and the London consistory continued to write 'to those of Antwerp to admonish them of their bounden duty to the government and to warn them against what had any appearance of rebellion or resistance'.[48]

An elaborate attempt to clarify the Reformed Protestant position with regard to the questions of political authority and obedience was made in the 1561 *Confession of faith*, published at the instigation of the Walloon minister Guy de Bray and the church of Antwerp. In its printed form the *Confession* not only contained the thirty-seven articles, which became accepted by Dutch Reformed Protestants as their official guide, but also a *Missive to the Royal Majesty* and a *Remonstrance to the magistrates*.[49] Though the *Confession* itself contained

---

[45] A. A. van Schelven (ed.), *Kerkeraads-protocollen der Nederduitsche vluchtelingen-kerk te London 1560–1563* (Amsterdam, 1921), 321. The French church of London also rejected the use of violence. However, it accepted that it was legitimate to liberate imprisoned co-religionists by peaceful means 'comme de contrefaire quelque clefs ou semblable chose sans user de violence'. See Moreau, *Histoire du protestantisme à Tournai*, 159.

[46] For this important synod, see E. M. Braekman, 'Anvers – 1562: le premier synode des Eglises réformées', in *Bulletin de la Société de l'Histoire du Protestantisme Belge*, 102 (1981), 25–37.

[47] See van Schelven (ed.), *Kerkeraads-protocollen*, 322–3.

[48] Ibid. 354. The London community was not unanimous on this issue. The church acts mention the case of Cornelius Riemslager, who defended 'that it was allowed for a private person to use violence against the government for the sake of his innocent brother' (p. 386).

[49] Guy de Bray(?), *Confession de foy. Faicte d'un commun accord par les fideles qui conversent és Pays Bas, lesquels desirent vivre selon la purete de l'Evangile de nostre Seigneur Jesus Christ* (Rouen, 1561). The first Dutch version of the *Confession* appeared in 1562. For a modern edition of the *Confession*,

only one article on political authority, the *Missive* and the *Remonstrance* amply discussed the political problems Reformed Protestants were confronted with. The *Missive* started with an assurance to Philip II. The Reformed pledged that they desired only to live in obedience and would never do anything which disturbed the 'common peace' or hurt the king. For the Reformed 'were taught, both by God's word as by the continuous teachings of our ministers that the kings, princes and authorities are of God's ordinance: and that who resists the government, is resisting God's ordinance, and will receive reprobation'.[50] This principle was reformulated most explicitly in article 36 of the *Confession*.

The *Remonstrance* acknowledged that not only the king but also the other authorities governing the Low Countries were ordained by God for the 'vengeance and fear of the evil and support and comfort of the good'.[51] In fact it distinctly rejected the idea, propounded by 'the majority of ancient doctors', that the 'material sword' of the government should not 'touch man's conscience' and that in religious matters only the spiritual sword of God's word should bring remedy. Thus the task of government with regard to heresy, seen as 'troubles en un Republicque', was recognized. However, this governmental competence with regard to religion should not be abused as a pretext for oppressing innocent people. Once again, the authorities were strongly warned of God's eventual judgment in this respect. Instead the *Remonstrance* called for public debates where, on the basis of God's word, it should be determined which doctrines were truly heretical.

As to the duty of subjects towards authority, article 36 mainly spoke in terms of obedience, seemingly embracing the more cautious position of the London Church. The *Confession* repudiated those who sought 'to reject the authorities and magistrates' and admonished 'each of whatever quality, condition or state he is' that it was his bounden duty to submit himself to the authorities 'in all things that are not against God's word'.[52] As their ends were by no means of the flesh, the faithful, so the *Missive* to Philip II vowed, were more than willing to render to Caesar the things which were Caesar's. Their sole and humble prayer was to be permitted 'to render to God what he demands'. The faithful, it was argued, could not and would not renounce Christ for they had 'God's fear for [their] eyes' and were 'terrified by Jesus Christ's threat, who says that he will belie us for

together with the *Confession* as accepted by the famous synod of Dordrecht, see J. N. Bakhuizen van den Brink, *De Nederlandse belijdenisgeschriften* (Amsterdam, 1976). Refs. are to the original 1561 edn.   [50] *Confession*, fol. D3.   [51] Ibid.   [52] Ibid., fol. D5.

God his Father if we belie him for mankind'. In fact article 28 of the *Confession* explicitly ordered the faithful to separate themselves from those who had no part in the true religion, and to join the true church, even if this implied that they had to defy the magistrate or prince and even if they had to risk 'death and corporal punishment'. For the faithful were willing to 'offer the back to the blows, the tongues to the knives, the mouth to the brindles and the whole body to the fire: knowing that who wants to follow Christ must take up his cross and renounce himself'.[53]

While the *Confession* recognized that it was the duty of the government to fight heresy, dissenting voices pleaded for a fundamental policy of religious toleration. Petrus Bloccius, a minister who had studied in Louvain and Bologna, published in 1562 *A complaint of Jesus Christ* in which Jesus pointed out that he, the 'sovereign authority' invested with all power, had not even persecuted the worst heretics with violence. Bloccius' Jesus admonished the worldly authorities 'to do likewise, for to dispute against the heretics with bags of fire and gallows is nothing but to sow heresy'.[54] Persecution of heresy was not only to little avail, it was also directly against Jesus' command, who, as the 'head of all princes, lords and kings', ordered 'no one to kill heresies'.[55] Grains and weeds should be allowed to grow together, until Jesus himself would come to harvest and clean the floor with his fan.

An even more outspoken message of toleration was expressed by Pieter de Zuttere, in *A short and simple teaching from the divine scripture*, which discussed whether one should 'vilify, judge and scold at the unbelieving sects and blasphemers'.[56]

De Zuttere was a controversial figure in Reformed Protestant circles. Even though his ideas were definitely close to Spiritualism, he served as a Reformed Protestant minister, first in Emden and later also in his home town, Ghent. He had probably received an excellent humanist education, which had brought him a profound knowledge of both classic and theological works.[57]

De Zuttere limited the role of government strictly to earthly

---

[53] Ibid.
[54] Petrus Bloccius, *Een claghe Jesu Christi, tot dat ongehoorsaeme menschelijcke gheslachte, seer profijtelijck ende nuttelick in dese peryckeloose ende vaerlycke tijden voor alle den ghenen die den Heere van Herten begheert na te volghen* (Delft, 1595), fol. C8. The first edn. appeared in 1562.
[55] Ibid.
[56] Pieter de Zuttere, *Eyne korte unde eynvaldige underwisung uut die Goddelicke Schrift, of man oock lasteren, ordeylen und schelten sal tegen die ongeloovige Secten und Gotzlasteren. Item eyne korte Leerung, wie dat Marter geyn Christen maeckt: unde geyn Christen ungemartert is* (1563).
[57] For de Zuttere, see Decavele, *De dageraad van de Reformatie in Vlaanderen*, 93ff.

matters. The purpose of governmental authority was solely to give
'the peace of the flesh', to protect what was called 'the natural
temporal life' against destructive forces challenging 'the temporal
peace of the flesh', which should be 'punished with the temporal
force of the flesh to maintain temporal peace'.[58] However, it was
emphasized that the government could never give 'God's peace in
Christ, which is unknown to the spirit of the world'.[59] Earthly
government should not try to establish the 'eternal peace of God'. In
fact an 'unbelieving government' that showed 'patience' towards
the sects was nearer to God than an impatient 'Christian government'. Faith, de Zuttere underlined, was a gift of God and the
relation between God and the faithful was highly personal in
character. For the Lord had said, 'as I live... all knees will bend to
me. Therefore each will account for himself, so that each will receive
after he has done, be it good or evil.'[60] The 'immortal soul' was
'subject only to the immortal judgment of God' and neither could
nor should be touched by the earthly government's sword or man's
fallible judgment. Man, according to de Zuttere, simply could not
come 'to the true knowledge of our hearts for God, as long as our own
untruthful heart is covered, because of our sin, by the speck of doom
which is lying on the eye of our soul'.[61] Therefore toleration, humility
and neighbourly love should be the principal virtues of the faithful.

Although such a plea for toleration was by no means unexceptional
in the 1560s, de Zuttere's argument that it was preferable to have a
patient, unbelieving government rather than an impatient Christian
government was certainly highly controversial. In line with the 1561
Confession other Reformed Protestant authors gave the government a
much more active role in religious affairs.

The necessity of a wise and godly government was explicitly
recognized in the writings of Guy de Bray, the putative author of the
Confession. Until his execution in 1567, de Bray, as a minister
especially active in Tournai and later in Valenciennes, played a
leading role in Dutch Reformed Protestant circles.[62]

In his publications de Bray unequivocally accepted the necessity
and divine origin of worldly authority. In the chapter on political

---

[58] De Zuttere, *Eyne korte unde eynvaldige underwisung uut die Goddelicke Schrift*, fol. E1.
[59] Ibid.   [60] Ibid., fol. E8.   [61] Ibid., fol. C1.
[62] For a study of the political thought of Guy de Bray see E. M. Braekman, 'La pensée
politique de Guy de Brès', in *Bulletin de la Société de l'Histoire du Protestantisme Français*', 115
(1969), 1–28. For a biography, see L. A. van Langeraad, *Guido de Bray: zijn leven en werken*
(Zierikzee, 1884).

authority of *The root, the origin and the foundation of the Anabaptists or
Rebaptists of our times*, a work written explicitly against the Anabaptists, he reiterated the view that 'the office and state of the kings,
princes and of other lower authorities' was 'ordained and instituted'
by God.[63] The government's task was twofold. First, as man was
inclined to do evil, it had to maintain civil order. The government, as
de Bray put it, 'does not carry the sword in vain, as she is God's
servant, an avenger, to the punishment of those who do evil'.[64]
Against the Anabaptists, de Bray defended the point of view that
Christians were fully entitled to hold office and to carry the sword, for
'as God has ordered that wrongdoers should be punished by death,
this is a holy, sincere and proper thing to do'.[65] He argued that,
although cruelty should be avoided and '*douceur*' and '*mansuetude*'
were the virtues that distinguished the true king from the tyrant, it
was a 'work of faith to execute the wrongdoers and to use the sword
of government against them'.[66] Thus de Bray urged the faithful to
take up governmental offices for otherwise these would fall in the
hands of unfaithful and impious men.

De Bray espoused the view that the government's office was not
confined to civil matters. The second part of its task directly
concerned religion. The worldly authorities, he asserted, ought to be
the 'patrons and protectors of God's children'. Instead of persecuting
the Anabaptists, who according to de Bray were 'poor, simple
people', most of them 'pitifully seduced by their ignorance and
wickedness', the government should follow the example of Hezekiah
and Josiah. It should banish all idolatry and foster the predication of
the 'true Apostolic doctrine'. In promoting the true religion the
government had the task of judging heretics. Heresy should be
recognized on the basis of God's word and through public debates,
which de Bray greatly favoured. Repeatedly he called upon the
authorities to organize public debates, and to give Reformed
Protestants the opportunity to prove that their doctrine was solidly
based on God's word. At the same time, although it was the
government's task to judge heretics, de Bray seemed to reject the use
of violence. He pointed out that 'burning, hanging and killing can

---

[63] Guy de Bray, *De wortel, den oorspronck ende het fundament der wederdooperen oft herdooperen van onse
tijde* (Amsterdam, 1589), fol. 351. This is the Dutch trans. of *La Racine, source et fondement des
anabaptistes ou rebaptisez de nostre temps* (1565). Refs. are to both edns.

[64] De Bray, *De wortel*, fol. 351.

[65] De Bray, *La Racine*, 816–17; de Bray, *De wortel*, fol. 353.

[66] De Bray, *La Racine*, 824; de Bray, *De wortel*, fol. 356.

not help to exterminate heresies, as the pure and powerful truth of the divine word is the sole means to this end'.[67]

With regard to the faithful's role in politics, de Bray not only pointed out that they could hold office, he also paid attention to their role as subjects. The relationship between subjects and authorities was sketched mainly along traditional Reformed lines, in terms of obedience. De Bray feared 'les tumultes du peuple', and did not stop admonishing the faithful to take up their cross with patience. As God's servant the government should be obeyed not merely because of its power but for conscience's sake. In his 1564 prayer *Oraison au seigneur*, de Bray assured Philip II that it was by no means the desire of Reformed Protestants to diminish his power. Their sincere wish was that the king be 'more and more honoured, obeyed and feared'. Their sole demand was 'la liberté & franchise d'esprit & de l'ame'.[68]

A similar position was taken by a 1564 *Request to Madam duchess of Parma, Governess, and others Governors and rulers of these Netherlands*, presented 'by the poor, dispersed and oppressed faithful, who are wrongly defamed, persecuted and afflicted because of their religion'.[69] The *Request* demanded the examination of the Reformed life and doctrine, 'after the sincere and pure word of God', by wise and impartial judges and assured that they did not tend to mutiny or rebellion.

The request was part of a martyrology which dealt primarily with the sensational case of the celebrated Reformed minister Christopher Fabritius, who died at the stake in Antwerp. While Fabritius himself seems to have taken a more radical stand with regard to the authorities,[70] his martyrology reiterated the well-known pledges for patience and constancy on the part of the faithful. With numerous

---

[67] De Bray, *De wortel*, fol. 224. See also Braekman, 'La pensée politique de Guy de Brès', 18.

[68] Guy de Bray, *Oraison au seigneur, contenant les gemissements, et complaints des poures fideles espers pour le pais bas, Flandre, Artois, Hainaut, et autres contrées: affamez du desir de la predication de l'evengile, et pure administration des sacramens du seigneur* (1564), 5–6.

[69] *Requeste aen myn vrouwe d'Hertoghinne van Parme, Plaisance, &c Regente, ende andere gouverneurs ende regeerders deser Nederlanden, ghepresenteert van wegen der armen, verstroeyden ende verdructen gheloovighen...*, in *Historie ende geschiedenisse van de verradelicke ghevangenisse der vromer ende godsaligher mannen, Christophorij Fabritij dienaer des goddelicken woords binnen Antwerpen ende Oliverij Bockij professeur der Latijnsche sprake in de hooghe en vermaerde schole van Heydelberch* (1565), 199–210; repr. in S. Cramer and F. Pijper (eds.), *BRN* viii. 282–460. Refs. are to the original 1565 edn.

[70] See Decavele, *De dageraad van de Reformatie in Vlaanderen*, 347. In 1562, when Fabritius was in London, he was only permitted to participate in the Supper after he had openly endorsed the London view on governmental authority, with specific reference to the point that the use of violence against the government was not allowed under any circumstances. See van Schelven (ed.), *Kerkeraads-protocollen*, 390.

references to Matthew 5:10, it was argued that 'they are blessed, who suffer persecution for Christ's name' and that 'therefore the Christians must willingly accept and carry that cross, knowing that they are called to the cross and to suffering'.[71] Yet once again the persecuting authorities were warned of the consequences of their policy of doom. The martyrology pointed out to the authorities that 'the sword of justice is given to you by God to revenge and punish the evil and to defend and protect the good. But woe, woe to thee if you do not do this.'[72] It added that on the Day of Judgment 'the burning wrath of God' would overtake them 'as a tempest' and they would be thrown 'in the infernal pool burning with pitch and sulphur'.

Both in the martyrology and in the *Request* demands for a more moderate religious policy were formulated. The government was urged to stop 'persecuting the truth and murdering Christians', to mitigate the religious placards and to grant Reformed Protestants freedom of religion and at least proper legal proceedings in accordance with the laws and privileges of the country.

As this martyrology, but also the 1561 *Confession* and the works of de Bray exemplified, the discussions of political authority and obligation in the Reformed Protestant treatises of the early 1560s mainly reiterated views which had been articulated before in the Low Countries and elsewhere. The divine origin of political authority was reasserted and the duty of the faithful to obey political authority in all matters which were not in conflict with God's word re-emphasized. More and more, however, Reformed Protestant authors focused on the persecution of their co-religionists, which was unanimously condemned.

In doing so some fundamental problems were explored which were to dominate the Reformed Protestants for many years to come. First, the issue of toleration had come to the fore. Whereas mainstream Reformed Protestants seemed to accept that heresy should be judged by worldly authorities with every possible caution, others rejected the persecution of heresy straightforwardly, using Spiritualist arguments as developed, for example, by Sebastian Franck and Sebastian Castellio. Secondly, it was clear that the discussion about the legitimacy of resistance had started amongst the ranks of Dutch

---

[71] *Historie ende geschiedenisse...*, preface. Similar arguments are repeated throughout this martyrology. See e.g. pp. 235, 249 and 282. Adriaen van Haemstede and Joris Wybo have been mentioned as possible authors of this martyrology (Decavele, *De dageraad van de Reformatie in Vlaanderen*, 347). [72] *Historie ende geschiedenisse...*, 141.

Reformed Protestants. Even though the treatises of the first half of the
1560s essentially insisted on the imperative of non-resistance,
Pandora's box was opened.

3.4. THE *ANNUS MIRABILIS*, 1566

In the spring of 1566 large-scale hedge-preaching began. It started in
west Flanders but soon spread to other parts of the Low Countries. In
June allegedly 20,000 people attended a meeting outside Antwerp.[73]
The summer of 1566 also brought the public breakthrough of the
protestants in Holland, who until then 'had led a furtive existence'.[74]
In July the congregation in Amsterdam decided to hold hedge-
preachings, and services were held in West-Friesland, near Haarlem,
Alkmaar and Amsterdam itself. In the autumn, consistories were set
up.

   In August the Iconoclastic Fury started to sweep over the Low
Countries, beginning in the Flemish 'Westkwartier' on 10 August
1566. This wave of iconoclasm was not simply an outburst of popular
fury. Certain patterns of planning and organization were involved.[75]
In the Westkwartier iconoclasm was mainly the work of wandering
groups who often started their iconoclastic work after a predication
and sometimes acted under the leadership of radical ministers.
Occasionally they claimed to act at the explicit order of governmental
authority. Further north, in the region along the Scheldt, iconoclasm
was generally organized within the towns, with Antwerp as 'epi-
centre', by small groups that lacked public guidance by Reformed
ministers but sometimes, as in Antwerp and Ghent, seemed to work
according to carefully devised plans. In the north, iconoclasm had a
hybrid character. Some towns in Holland more or less followed the
Antwerp pattern, in other towns churches were stripped carefully
and methodically, sometimes under the leadership of lower nobles or
magistrates.

---

[73] See Guy Wells, *Antwerp and the government of Philip II, 1555–1567* (Ann Arbor, Mich., 1982),
411; R. van Roosbroeck, 'Wunderjahr oder Hungerjahr? Antwerpen 1566', in Petri (ed.),
Kirche und gesellschaftlicher Wandel in deutschen und niederländischen Städten, 183. It is rather
difficult to estimate the precise strength of Reformed Protestantism at this time. In most
places Reformed Protestants formed a minority, though sometimes a substantial one. For
Antwerp, it is estimated that in *c.* 1566 there were about 14,000 Reformed Protestants, 2,000
Anabaptists and 4,000 Lutherans out of a total of 90,000 inhabitants. Tournai and
Valenciennes had protestant majorities and of the population of Hondschoote, in west
Flanders, allegedly only 20% remained faithful to the Catholic church.

[74] See A. Duke and D. H. A. Kolff, 'The times of troubles in the county of Holland,
1566–1567', *TvG* 82 (1969), 337.

[75] See J. Scheerder, *De beeldenstorm* (Bussum, 1974), esp. 100–1.

In the drama of the *Annus mirabilis*, requests for freedom of worship and pleas for religious toleration abounded. In addition to Petrus Bloccius, who combined his demands for religious toleration with a forceful denunciation of Roman Catholicism in his *More than two hundred heresies, blasphemies, and new dogmas that have come out of the mass*,[76] the influential minister Franciscus Junius raised his voice in *A brief discourse sent to King Philip*.[77] Junius was one of the best-educated ministers in the Netherlands. He had studied law at Bourges and theology at Geneva. Later Junius became professor at Leiden University. In 1593 he published his famous treatise *Le paisible chrestien*, an impressive testimony of his eirenic attitude.[78]

Taking a seemingly impartial stand Junius argued that those who adhered to the 'new religion' sincerely believed that they were following God's word and commandment. Moreover, they were convinced 'that above all things one should be obedient to the creator and rather suffer all torments of the world, yes and die, than willingly and knowingly resist his prescribed words and commandments or show him any infidelity'.[79] Such thoughts, Junius argued, could not be banished by means of persecution, 'for how would it be possible to rule over the conscience and the spirit of man through corporeal things?'

As one could not search, judge nor force the spirit of man by corporeal means, only the force of argument counted in the spiritual realm. Therefore, freedom of speech and discussion should be permitted. In fact, Junius argued that it was 'the very mark' of truth that it 'desires to be revealed and examined', for it was 'like the palm tree, which, the more one forces and loads it to suppress it, the higher and straighter it rises'.[80] In short, so Junius concluded, there was simply no sense in persecuting heretics. In fact, he went on to argue, it was preferable to permit the alleged heretics freedom of worship. A policy which prevented them from attending the Reformed services

---

[76] Petrus Bloccius, *Meer dan tweehondert ketterijen, blasphemien, en nieuwe leeringen welcx uut de misse zyn ghecomen* (1566).

[77] Franciscus Junius, *Een corte verhalinge gesonden aen Coninc Philips... tot welvaert ende profijt sijnder Maiesteit, ende sonderlinghe van syne Nederlanden* (1566). The French original is *Brief discours envoyé au roy Philippe nostre sire et souverain Seigneur, pour le bien et profit de sa Maiesté, et singulierement de ses pays bas...* (1566). Part of this discourse was published in Kossmann and Mellink (eds.), *Texts concerning the revolt of the Netherlands*, 56–9. Refs. are to the 1566 Dutch version and, if applicable, to Kossmann and Mellink's edn.

[78] For Junius, see C. de Jonge, *De irenische ecclesiologie van Franciscus Junius (1545–1602): onderzoek naar de plaats van het geschrift 'Le paisible Chrestien' (1593) in zijn denken* (Leiden, 1980), and Nauta, De Groot et al., *Biografisch lexicon voor de geschiedenis van het Nederlands protestantisme*, 275–8.   [79] Junius, *Een corte verhalinge gesonden aen Coninc Philips*, fol. A3.

[80] Ibid., fol. A6. Thus the Tournai church under the cross was called 'l'église de la palme'.

would have highly negative consequences, Junius asserted. Instead of being taught 'to be honest people fearing God and respecting the king and his officers', they would become 'vile atheists and libertines stirring up sedition and disturbing order and peace'.[81] At present, Junius emphasized, Reformed Protestants were loyal and obedient subjects, just as God ordered them to be.

In short Junius advised Philip II that it was in his own interest to permit the new religion in the Low Countries. He pointed out that it was by no means a novelty to tolerate two different religions in a country. Referring to many historical examples of 'wise kings and princes' who had done so before, Junius concluded that 'in all well-ordered city republics' it was sometimes 'necessary [to ward off all rebellion and mutiny] to give the heretics temples', not because they would further 'strew their errors' but rather because, hearing both truth and lie, they might 'quietly be set in the true and right religion'.[82] Thus, at the end of his discourse Junius advised Philip II to forbid the use of violence, to permit and give room to the new religion, so that through predications and debates the true religion could triumph. Such a policy would benefit the unity of the country and foster obedience to the king. Of course such arguments were not specifically Dutch. They had been used especially in France, for example, by the Chancellor Michel de L'Hôpital and in works such as the 1561 *Exhortation aux princes* and the 1562 *Conseil à la France désolée*, written by Castellio. Employing arguments highly similar to Junius they had contended that in order to safeguard the French nation it was necessary to permit the Reformed religion, thus emphasizing the importance of reasons of state.[83]

Putting forward this perspective Junius had presented himself as a rather impartial political analyst pleading for toleration. Most other requests straightforwardly demanded freedom of worship for Reformed Protestants, without giving any indication that such should be part of a policy of more general toleration. An important example of this view was the *Petition*, which, together with an *Oration on the church of Christ* was presented to the German Reichstag at Augsburg in April 1566.[84] The petition and the oration, allegedly written by the

---

[81] Ibid., fol. B2; Junius, in Kossmann and Mellink (eds.), *Texts concerning the revolt of the Netherlands*, 57.　　[82] Junius, *Een corte verhalinge gesonden aen Coninc Philips*, fol. D6.

[83] For the French case, see Joseph Lecler, *Histoire de la tolérance au siècle de la Réforme*, 2 vols. (Paris, 1954), ii. 36–76.

[84] *Libellus supplex* (1566) and Marnix van St Aldegonde, *Oratio ecclesiarum Christi* (1566), in J. J. van Toorenenbergen (ed.), *Eene bladzijde uit de geschiedenis der Nederlandsche geloofsbelijdenis*

distinguished humanist Philips Marnix van St Aldegonde, urged the German emperor to redress and purify the church, which should be stripped of all forms of idolatry. The *Oration* emphasized the task of political authorities, the emperor in particular, as 'guardians and maintainers of the first Table of God's Commandments, that is to say, of the true and pure doctrine of godly service'.[85] In consequence, so it argued, the duty of the emperor was 'to maintain and take care of the furtherance of the true godliness' and to protect virtue and chastity. The 'extermination of all differences and errors, and the re-establishment and purification of the true Religion' had to be of principal concern to the emperor. At length the *Oration* argued that the Roman Catholic church was the main source (together with the devil) of errors such as the teachings on free will, the saints, purgatory and idolatry. The treatise forcefully exhorted the emperor to exterminate idolatry and to foster the preaching of the true and pure doctrine of Christ, in order to achieve the necessary 'reformation of the church'.

As the *Oration* gave expression to the hope that the emperor would act to the benefit of the Netherlands, others presented their demands to local authorities. Antwerp was an obvious centre for such activities, being the heart of Reformed Protestantism and of the printing business. Moreover, amongst the many provincial and local authorities adopting a lenient approach, Antwerp was a principal example. In the face of the Iconoclastic Fury an 'accord' was concluded in September 1566 which granted Reformed Protestants and Lutherans, who also flourished in Antwerp, certain places to hold their services. Later both protestant groups were even allowed to use a number of churches. Protestant requests abounded in this situation; many of them were printed in contemporary accounts such as the *History concerning the fact of religion as happened in Antwerp*, published in 1566.[86] For example, on 23 August 1566, immediately after the outbreak of iconoclasm in Antwerp, the Reformed presented a proposition to the town magistrate, assuring it of their loyalty and offering an oath of obedience.[87] The Reformed asked for temples and

---

(The Hague, 1861). I should like to thank Guido Marnef for bringing these treatises to my attention.

[85] Marnix van St Aldegonde, *Oratio ecclesiarum Christi*, p. cxv (refs. are to the Dutch translation).

[86] *Geschiedenisse aengaende t'feyt der religien, gebeurt t'Antwerpen int'iaer MDLXVI* (1566; also pub. in French, as *Recueil des choses advenues en Anvers, touchant le fait de la Religion, en l'an MDLXVI*, 1566). [87] *Geschiedenisse...*, fol. C1.

demanded a religious peace, promising to 'force no one in his conscience and to our religion'.[88]

In the autumn, negotiations took place in Antwerp for a request that was addressed directly to Philip II. Reformed Protestant ministers such as Peter Dathenus and Laurens Reael were involved in the talks that led to the so-called *Three million request*. As a joint initiative of Reformed Protestants and Lutherans, the *Request* was part of an attempt to create a unified protestant movement.[89] It urged Philip II not to use violence and to grant his protestant subjects in the Low Countries the freedom to profess their faith. It was explained that religion, once 'imprinted in the heart and mind of men', could not be touched by 'threats and external forces'.[90] As the salvation or damnation of the soul were at stake, it would not be 'light' to exterminate the Reformed religion by violence. In fact this would only produce men 'without religion, libertarians and godless'. Moreover, religious persecution, according to the *Request*, would lead to the country's ruin.

The *Request* admitted that despite all precautions some, 'moved by a too arduous and inconsiderate zeal' and joined by 'unorderly persons', had destroyed images but the king was assured that Dutch protestants did not approve of this behaviour and that there was no intrinsic relationship between the Reformed predications and the Iconoclastic Fury. On the contrary, the protestants wished only to serve the king as loyal and obedient subjects and had no intention whatsoever to 'renew the state of policy'. Their sole demand was to have freedom of religion and worship in certain fixed places. To prove their loyalty they offered the king a sum of '30 ton gouts' (30 tons of gold), i.e. 3 million guilders.

It has been a matter of debate whether this offer was sincere or whether it was a shrewd ploy for raising money for armed resistance. Surely the Lutherans had no intention of the latter sort. In fact, together with a controversy around the eucharist, in which Reformed Protestants refused to accept the Lutheran doctrine of consub-

[88] Ibid., fol. C2.

[89] For the history of the *Three million request*, see R. van Roosbroeck, *Het wonderjaar te Antwerpen* (*1566–1567*): *inleiding tot de studie der godsdienstonlusten van den beeldenstorm af (1566) tot aan de inneming der stad door Alexander Farnese (1585)* (Antwerp, 1930), 153ff. The request itself is in *Geschiedenisse...*, fols. F5ff., and in Pieter Christiaansz Bor, *Oorsprongk, begin en vervolgh der Nederlantsche oorlogen, beroerten en borgerlijke oneenigheden*, i (Amsterdam, 1679; first pub. 1595), 122–4.

[90] *Geschiedenisse...*, fol. F7; Bor, *Oorsprongk der Nederlantsche oorlogen*, i. 122.

stantiation,[91] the issue of the legitimacy of armed resistance was responsible for a basic rift between Antwerp Lutherans and Reformed Protestants. The Lutheran position left no room for debate. Unequivocally Lutherans asserted that the authorities were to be obeyed. In a publication which contained two Lutheran supplications from 1561, both denouncing accusations of rebellious heresy, the suppliants explicitly 'acknowledged and professed' that there was and 'ought to be a magistrate and government, instituted by God the Lord', which, 'following the example and teaching of our Lord, Jesus Christ' ought to be obeyed in 'all matters which are not against God and do not militate or conflict with his holy word'.[92]

The suppliants were willing to give Caesar the things that were Caesar's such as honour, reverence, tribute and obedience but pointed out that they had to give God the things which were God's and that they had to obey God rather than men. The authorities were begged to permit them to profess their religion and were warned of God's final judgment.

The argument remained standard in Lutheran circles. In a treatise that was signed by the ministers of the Antwerp Lutheran community, it was pointed out to the Lutheran faithful, with an explicit reference to Matthew 22:21, that it was their principal duty 'to maintain assiduously' and 'in the sincere fear of God' the basic rule of rendering to 'Caesar the things that are Caesar's, and to God the things that are God's'.[93] In *A missive of comfort*, written in November 1567 when the Antwerp Lutherans were again 'under the cross', the faithful were urged not to resort to resistance under any circumstances.[94]

[91] For the Reformed Protestant view, see *Cort bewijs uit de schriften Luteri en Brentij dat het lichaem Christi niet en sy een lichamelijcke maer een gheestelijcke spijse* (1566). Some Reformed Protestants continued to emphasize the need for protestant unity, in spite of differences of dogma. See e.g. Antonio Corro's *Epistre et amiable Remonstrance d'un ministre de l'evangile de nostre Redempteur ... envoyé aux pasteurs de eglise Flamengue d'Anvers, lesquelz se nomment de la Confession d'Augsbourg, les exhortant à concorde et amitié avec les autres ministres de l'evangile* (1567). Corro was a Spanish Reformed Protestant minister working in Antwerp.

[92] *Supplicatien ende requesten uut den name der Christelicker Ghemeynte binnen Antwerpen: Ende van sommigher ghevangenen Broeders ende lidtmaten der selver Ghemeenten wegen ...* (Antwerp, 1567), 1. The point was made several times; see e.g. p. 55.

[93] *Der predicanten des heylighen Evangelij Jesu Christi binnen Antwerpen, der confessien van Ausburg toeghedaen, vermaninghe tot waerachtighe penitentie, ende vierighen ghebede in dese teghenwoodighe nooden ende periculen aen haere toehoorders* (1567), fol. A4.

[94] See C.D.W., *Een troostelicke sendtbrief aen de Christen ghemeynte der reynder bekentenisse, van den edelen wygaert onses Heeren Jesu Christi, doer syn goddelijck woordt gheplantet binnen Antwerpen* (1567), 14.

In these Lutheran treatises suffering and persecution were once
again presented as basic tenets of Christian life, and the faithful were
admonished to live a life of submissiveness, patience and constancy.
Thus, in another *Missive of comfort* the faithful were admonished to
'be constant' and not to 'look at the thunder nor at the billows of the
sea but at Jesus Christ, our keeper who is with us in the ship, and will
not let his ship be wrecked'.[95] The rift between the Antwerp
Lutherans and the Reformed Protestants on the issue of resistance
became permanent in December 1566, when a Reformed Protestant
synod approved a policy of armed resistance and took steps to
organize and finance the raising of troops.[96] The synod discussed the
question 'whether in the Low Countries a part of the vassals with a
part of the subjects may resist by force their magistrate, if it breaks
and does not observe the privileges and commits wrong or open
violence'.[97] After due deliberation the synod made the capital move
of deciding that such was the case in the Low Countries. Undoubtedly
the decision to take up arms was the culmination of the process of
radicalization that Reformed Protestantism had undergone since
about 1560. None the less, ideologically, Reformed Protestants
remained rather cautious in their discussions of the dramatic changes.
The *History concerning the fact of religion as happened in Antwerp*, for
example, described the Iconoclastic Fury in rather apologetic words,
suggesting that iconoclasm in Antwerp had been done 'with such
assurance, diligence and silence' that it looked as if 'a thousand
people' had been appointed 'by express commission of the government to perform and complete such work right away'.[98]

Others were somewhat bolder. A 1566 treatise in German, the
Newe Zeittung, not only forcefully denounced the idolatry of the

---

[95] *Eenen troostelijcken sentbrief, voor alle die om der waerheyt en om Christus naem vervolcht worden*
(1567?), fol. G. For similar arguments, see other Lutheran missives of comfort such as
Johannis Saliger, *Een troostelijcken Seyndtbrief, ghesonden aen die Christelicke gemeente Christi, tot
Antwerpen* (Wesel, 1567); Francoys Alardts, *Een heerlicke troostbrief van des mensen leven ende
wesen* (1567); and, in addition, a work of two other Lutheran ministers who served the
Antwerp community in 1566, Matthias Flacius Illyricus and Balthazar Houwaert, *Corte
verantwoordinghe oft bescherminghe der confessien oft bekentenisse des gheloofs der Christelijcken
ghemeinten van Antwerpen der Ausborcher Confessien toegedaen* (1567).

[96] For the synod, see esp. van Roosbroeck, *Het wonderjaar te Antwerpen*, 211ff. and van
Roosbroeck, 'Wunderjahr oder Hungerjahr?', 187ff.

[97] See van Langeraad, *Guido de Bray*, app. D. p. lxviii, where a report on a meeting of the
consistory of Antwerp in Nov. 1566 is presented.

[98] *Geschiedenisse*... fol. B6. With regard to iconoclasm in Antwerp it was said (fol. B7) that this
was done 'by very few people' and that it occurred 'without any resistance or ban against
it on behalf of his lord and the government', so that 'the common man did not think but that
the aforesaid labourers had instruction and commission of the lords of the town to do so'.

Roman Catholic church, but also responded to the accusations against the iconoclasts in a rhetorical vein, answering the question whether 'they have done right to start this destruction without the government's authority' with the question whether those had 'done right who have worshipped images?'[99]

Referring to the confession of Augsburg, which of course rejected the worship of images, the pamphlet argued that 'if one should kill those who have broken the images and Gods, one should more justly kill those who have killed the living images of Christ, that is the faithful'.[100]

Such radical words, however, were rare. Much more typical were the two justifications published on behalf of Valenciennes as the town was besieged after refusing to open its gates for government troops. Both justifications were probably written by Guy de Bray, at the time one of the Reformed ministers in the city. The *Brief declaration of fact by those of the town of Valenciennes*, probably written two days before the town was declared rebel by the Governess, pledged the loyalty of the town to Philip II. The purpose of the *Declaration* was to expose 'in all humility and truth' what 'constrained' those of Valenciennes 'to maintain and safeguard the town...in order to preserve the entire obedience and service to His Majesty the King, our sovereign Lord'.[101]

After the town had been proclaimed rebel, the *Remonstrance and supplication of those of the Reformed church at the town of Valenciennes* was published. It was a sharp denunciation of the accusations of rebelliousness. The *Remonstrance* pointed out that the Reformed Protestants of Valenciennes knew very well that the Gospel taught them to render obedience, love, honour and reverence to kings, princes and other magistrates. Therefore, they were fully prepared to pay taxes and to obey the government in 'all political matters'.

[99] *Newe Zeittung. In welcher kürtzlich, ordentlich und warhafftiglich, nach aller umstendighkeit erzelet wird, was sich in der berhümbten Kauffstadt Antorff zwischen den 18. und 28. Augusti diese 1566. Jars in Religion Sachen, unnd anderen grossen hendelen zu getragen und verlauffen hat* (1566), fol. C1.

[100] Ibid., fol. C2. The *Newe Zeittung* was not the only treatise in German to deal with the events in the Netherlands. The main requests of the Reformed, for example, were translated and published in German. Two pamphlets, another *Newe Zeittung* and a pamphlet that dealt specifically with the situation in Valenciennes presented the *Three million request* and a supplication of the city of Valenciennes. See *Newe Zeittung, Der Niderlandische Stette, an die Königliche Kron ausz Hispanien ubergeben...* (1567) and *Vallenzin. Die feste Statt, inn den Grentzen Franckreich und Niderland, von wem und warumb dieselbige belegert...* (1567). See Bibliography for other examples.

[101] Guy de Bray, *Declaration sommaire de faict de ceux de la ville de Valencienne* (1566), 2.

However, the *Remonstrance* asserted that the obedience to the government had a specific limit, arguing 'that if the magistrate commands things against God's word, and, consequently, against conscience and the welfare of the soul, we confess that we are bound, as practised and protested by the disciples of Jesus Christ, to obey God rather than men'.[102] The decision to close the gates against the government troops was presented as a decision taken in self-defence, as taught by 'nature and reason', against a threat of plunder and murder.

The *Remonstrance* also pointed out that it was not only extremely difficult to 'tear from the hearts, by means of arms, the religion which is imprinted in it', but that the Reformed of Valenciennes were not willing to let this happen and would rather die than surrender the true faith. Some of them, like Guy de Bray and Peregrin de La Grange, another Valenciennes minister, did so. The story of their imprisonment, trial and execution was told in the *Procedures observed with regard to those of the religion from the Netherlands* published in 1568. It described how de Bray and de La Grange, 'faithful ministers at Valenciennes' had 'signed with their blood... the doctrine of the Gospel' and had joined the ranks of Reformed martyrs. In a letter to his mother de Bray himself indicated the intrinsic connection between the true faith and martyrdom: 'I go the way through which have passed all prophets and Apostles, even the true son of God, our Lord Jesus Christ, and many thousands of Martyrs, who have shed their blood for the testimony of the Gospel.'[103]

Along familiar lines de Bray admonished his Reformed brethren to remain virtuous and constant in their faith. The faithful should not, as a 'reed, swing with all winds', but should sustain 'constantly the trial and ordeal of the Lord'. For if they walked in fear of God, their reward would be tremendous, as God would 'turn his face and deliver you, reversing your enemies (who are his), and will give you, more than ever, liberty to serve him'.[104]

De Bray's words, written shortly before his execution, testify most dramatically how, even in circumstances of extreme duress, Re-

---

[102] Guy de Bray(?), *Remonstrance et supplication de ceus de l'eglise reformée de la ville de Valenciennes, sur le mandement de son Altesse, fait contre eus le 14. jour de Decembre 1566, a messeigneurs les chevaliers de l'ordre* (1567) (unpaginated).

[103] *Procedures tenues à l'endroit de ceux de la religion du Pais Bas ... Ausquelles est amplement deduit comme Guy du Bres et Peregrin de la Grange fideles ministres à Valenciennes, ont signe par leur sang non seulement la doctrine de l'evangile par eux purement annoncee: mais aussi les derniers assauts, et disputes soustenues contre certains apostats et ennemis de la croix et verité du fils de Dieu* (1568), 367.

[104] Ibid. 40.

formed Protestant authors tended to refrain from elaborate discussions of the legitimacy of armed resistance, emphasizing the virtues of patience and constancy, and the value of martyrdom instead. There was, however, one apparent exception. In the autumn of 1566 it was probably the Reformed Protestant minister Johannes Michaellam who wrote the *Declaration of the church or community of God*.[105] The treatise, published anonymously in order to foster an impartial judgment on the part of the reader, contained an extensive discussion of the authority of the government and of the church. The power of the church was said to be not 'earthly nor external, but heavenly and spiritual'.[106] As such it needed to be sharply distinguished from the authority and power of the political government, which primarily concerned 'external civic justice'. This did not imply that the realms of authority were unconnected. On the contrary, along familiar lines, the *Declaration* argued that the office of the government concerned both Tables of Moses' law. Therefore, the government had to foster and guard God's honour. Thus the 'external government' should not only take care of 'civic justice' and 'feed common peace and quietness', it should also protect religious practice and 'shelter the true doctrine and godliness'.[107]

The *Declaration* fully acknowledged that 'external government' was as necessary as 'bread, water, sun and air' because of men's evil nature, predominantly inclined to do evil. With explicit references to Paul's letter to the Romans and Calvin's *Institutes*, the *Declaration* pointed out that the external government was ordained by God and as such had the specific obligation not to let 'the freedom for whose protection they are instituted be curtailed and even less violated in any part'. If government officials were 'indolent and careless' in this respect, they should be regarded as 'perfidious in their office and traitors of their own country'.[108]

With regard to the subjects the book pointed out that their principal duty was to obey the authorities God had ordained. They were not allowed to undertake political action at their own will and

---

[105] *Uutsprake van der Kercke of Ghemeynte Godes: welcke, wat ende hoedanich sy sy* (1567). This book, signed 30 Nov. 1566, is found together with a collection of public statements by French and Dutch protestants concerning the office of the government and its subjects: Johannes Michaellam, *De collecteur des nieuwen boeckskens. Geintituleert uutsprake van der kerkcken etc. gedruckt anno 1567* (1567). That Johannes Michaellam, a Reformed Protestant minister of whom little is known, was the author of the volume can be inferred from a kind of puzzle poem. It is unclear whether he is also the author of the *Uutsprake*, although the subtitle of *De collecteur...* seems to suggest so.

[106] *Uutsprake van der Kercke of Ghemeynte Godes*, fol. B1.   [107] Ibid., fol. C7.

[108] Ibid., fol. D3.

under no circumstances was the 'common man' allowed to resort to rebellion at his own initiative. As the *Declaration* put it, 'not the common man but the government alone is charged to do the public political reformation and to avert and punish all inconvenience, idolatry and other godlessness'.[109] In an explicit comment on the 'mutiny and rebellion in the Netherlands', the *Declaration* reaffirmed that in general the common man had the strict duty to obey the authorities even if these were godless and tyrannical. The book argued that 'if the upper or high authority together with her inferior magistrates are all godless and... oppress their subjects heavily', the subjects should still remember that they were 'ordered to do nothing else but to be obedient, to endure, to pray to God and call for help'.[110]

However, the duty of the subjects to obey tyrannical authorities was not without qualification. On the basis of the biblical text that one should obey God rather than man, the *Declaration* pointed out that the subjects should not obey an authority acting and ordering against God's word. In fact, according to the book, the authority of a king, who was but a Stadtholder of God, was annulled if he ordered against God.

Likewise, the rule that governmental authority should not be resisted was not without qualification. First of all, the *Declaration* argued that inferior magistrates had an important responsibility in this respect. They had been instituted to bridle the 'evil lust' of kings, and in this sense the *Declaration*, quoting Calvin's *Institutes*, put them on equal terms with 'the ephors, who were set against the Lacedaemon kings, or... the protectors of the people who were set against the Roman mayors, or the lords called demarchs who were set against the Athenian council'.[111] Possibly, and again Calvin was quoted, the three states had to fulfil the role of such inferior magistrates, which had the explicit duty to resist tyrannical kings. According to the *Declaration* the inferior magistrates had been ordained by God to 'bridle and silence the evil kings' and if they forsook this duty they would be 'unfaithful impostors and traitors of the freedom of the people', which they were supposed to protect.[112]

With regard to tyrants it was also possible, according to the author, that God himself showed his Almighty power and, as a clear sign of his loving-kindness, called for a providential tyrannicide. Even without their being aware of it, God could use individuals or groups to exterminate tyranny.

---

[109] Ibid., fol. N6.   [110] Ibid., fol. N7.   [111] Ibid., fol. E4.   [112] Ibid., fol. P1.

In commenting on the situation in the Netherlands the book appealed to the ideas on resistance it had just articulated. It condemned the behaviour of those who had risen to iconoclasm and to 'mutiny and rebellion'. According to the *Declaration* these people had gravely misunderstood the meaning of Christian freedom, which was 'solely spiritual and of the conscience'.[113] They were wrong in thinking that they were robbed of their Christian freedom if they had to submit themselves to an unchristian government. They were also wrong in assuming that as private persons they had the right to exterminate idolatry and thus by consequence to resist the government at their own discretion.

However, not everyone remained as cautious as the *Declaration*, whose analysis remained within the confines of protestant constitutionalist thought, emphasizing the role of 'inferior magistrates' and denouncing rebellious citizens. A much more urgent call to resistance was presented by the *Conseil sacré*, published in 1567.[114] In sharp terms it denounced Philip II, as 'le chef et le protecteur' of the Roman Catholic cause. The treatise warned that, as with all princes, it was engraved in Philip's heart to revenge himself with arms on those whom he perceived to have acted against him. No prince would tolerate subjects which had united against him in a league. By conclusion the Dutch could only expect to be condemned by Philip II as 'seditious, rebels and criminals of lese-majesty'.[115]

The *Conseil sacré* asserted that to resist the forces of the king was not an act of rebellion, but a mere act of self-defence in accordance with nature. The condition of the Dutch was compared to that of a slave, who could hardly be blamed 'for closing the door of his room if he sees his master coming to cut of his throat and can not save himself by any other way', for 'nature' had 'imprinted in all creatures the immortal desire to preserve their life'.[116]

However, to resist the king's threat was not just a matter of self-defence. It was also a religious duty, a fight for God's cause and the truth, which, the *Conseil sacré* argued, should be defended until death. Moreover, the Spanish feigned in arguing that they were arming themselves only to act against what they called 'the seditious and

---

[113] Ibid., fol. N3.
[114] Gervais Barbier(?), *Conseil sacré d'un Gentilhomme François aux Englises de Flandre, qui peut servir d'un humble exhortation a l'excellence des tresillustres Princes Protestans du Sainct Empire: et d'advertissement certain aux seigneurs des Pais Bas* (Antwerp, 1567). As Professor Woltjer has pointed out to me, it is more than likely that this treatise was written in the first months of 1567, before the defeat of the protestant forces.
[115] *Conseil sacré d'un Gentilhomme François aux Eglises de Flandre*, 40.   [116] Ibid. 46.

heretics'. In reality they were threatening all inhabitants of the Dutch Provinces, and therefore it was also a matter of civic duty, of defending 'l'ancienne liberté', to resist this threat. Thus the Dutch, in spite of religious differences, should unite. As the *Conseil sacré* put it, 'it is the duty of a virtuous man to have a total zeal for his religion, but it is prudence and good advice to govern himself in such a way that his affection does not damage his fatherland'.[117]

The *Conseil sacré*, allegedly written by Gervais Barbier, also called for international co-operation. The Dutch Reformed were urged to set aside the traditional animosities with the French and to co-operate with their French co-religionists. Co-operation was also required with the princes of the 'holy empire' who were called to intervene in the Netherlands. The *Conseil sacré* pointed out that if 'the laws, customs, or civil government' were at stake, foreign princes should not interfere, for these matters were the unique competence of 'chiefs of state'. However, if religion was at stake then it should be remembered that the kingdom of Christ had no earthly frontiers and that therefore 'each member is obliged to help another, in accordance with Christian charity and God's commandment'.[118]

In short, the *Conseil sacré* asserted that resistance against Philip II was a matter of religious and civic duty for all inhabitants of the Low Countries, and it called for co-operation amongst European protestants to form a united front against Philip II. Like those of Valenciennes it appealed to the natural law of self-defence in legitimizing Dutch resistance.

By contrast the *Declaration* essentially followed the constitutionalist line of thought, and it is clear that Calvin's analysis in the *Institutes* had been a major influence. This adoption of the constitutionalist defence of resistance seemed entirely in line with the debates at the 1566 synod of Antwerp, which led to the momentous decision to approve armed resistance. In the dream of the *Annus mirabilis*, Reformed Protestants overcame their scruples. However, the synod's decision was not based on any religious argument, but on a constitutionalist one. Significantly, it approved of resistance only because it was permitted by the privileges of the country.

---

[117] Ibid. 72.   [118] Ibid. 107.

3.5. RETURN TO EXILE

For many Reformed Protestants more fortunate than de Bray and de La Grange, the *Annus mirabilis* eventually led to exile. Many succeeded in escaping from the hands of the central government and Alva's Blood Council and had the opportunity of defending themselves, while in exile, through the printing press. Herman Moded was amongst them. Throughout the 1560s Moded had been one of the leading and more radical ministers. While serving the Antwerp church under the cross he had been involved in the dispute with the London refugee church over the resistance issue, and had taken the more radical stand as approved by the 1562 Antwerp synod. In 1567 he published the *Apology or account of Herman Moded against the calumniations and false accusations strewed, to the vilification of the holy Gospel, and his person by the enemies of the Christian religion*.[119] At various places in his apology Moded discussed the Iconoclastic Fury, the armed resistance and his own involvement. Commenting on his role in iconoclasm Moded acknowledged that after the 'expressed will and truth' of God's word, he had admonished 'all godly and pious lords' to purify 'the temple of the Lord...of all idolatry, and human superstition', because it was 'expressly incompatible, as a horrible calumniation and blasphemy, with the second and third command of God our Lord'.[120] In fact he seemed to suggest that eventually the purification of the church had been forced and commanded by God and as such was a work of providence.[121]

Moded denied, however, any participation in 'rebellion or commotion', nor did he accept any responsibility in these matters. Likewise he denounced any accusation of 'having acted against God or against the government, or also against the tranquillity of the country and republic'. He admitted that he had preached in the open and had done everything to glorify God and to serve the community of the faithful. If it was argued that such had been against the government and its mandates, Moded answered that in this matter the response of the Apostles sufficed 'that in the matters of God and of conscience one should obey God rather than man'.[122] The office of government, according to Moded, should not be against God's word.

---

[119] Hermanni Moded, *Apologie ofte verantwoordinghe Hermanni Modedt teghens de calumnien ende valsche beschuldinghen ghestroeyet, tot lasteringhe des H. Evangelij, ende zijnen persoon door de vianden der christelijcker religie* (1567), repr. in G. J. Brutel de la Rivière (ed.), *Het leeven van Hermannus Moded, een der eerste Calvinistische predikers in ons vaderland* (Haarlem, 1879).

[120] Moded, *Apologie*, 37.   [121] Ibid. 38.   [122] Ibid. 57.

A Christian government was instituted by God to administer justice in 'political or civic affairs', 'so that rebellion and difficulties are avoided'. If there arose any problem or conflict with regard to religion, however, its task was not to tyrannize or to use violence in favour of one specific party but 'as this concerns conscience' to help organize a 'legal meeting' to resolve such conflict on its proper 'foundation, which is God's word'.[123] Forcefully Moded denounced 'the yoke of the Inquisition, the tyranny and murderous servitude of popery', and once again the authorities, who in Moded's view were 'the cause of all malignities and atrocities' were warned of the Day of Judgment.

Another fundamental discussion of Reformed Protestant involvement in public preaching, armed hedge-preachings and iconoclasm was written by Marnix van St Aldegonde, a Brabant noble who had studied in Geneva and who became one of the main protagonists and publicists of the Dutch Revolt. In 1569 he published *The beehive of the Holy Roman church*, a work of great literary value and the highlight of Dutch sixteenth-century protestant literature. Above all, however, it was a sharp attack on the Roman Catholic church. By means of satire, rarely used by Reformed authors, Aldegonde denounced its idolatrous ceremonies and its insatiable lust for power.

The beehive, however, did not comment on the issues of obedience and resistance. With regard to politics it mainly proposed the thesis that the popes had always sought to dominate the ecclesiastical and political affairs in the world. In 1567 Aldegonde published his main political work of the 1560s, the *True narration and apology of the events taken place in the Netherlands concerning the issue of religion in the year 1566*, which was claimed to be written 'by those who do profession of the Reformed religion in this country'.[124]

With regard to the public preaching Aldegonde strongly rebutted the charges of rebellion and argued that, in fact, this had been the 'true and unique means' to achieve what all placards and ordinances had failed to do, 'namely to hinder the drift of malicious and profane sects, to bring the people in peace and tranquillity and to a true recognition of the duty they have to magistrate and king'.[125] Thus Reformed public preaching had contributed to the peace and

---

[123] Ibid. 72.
[124] Marnix van St Aldegonde, *Vraye Narration et apologie des choses passees au Pays-Bas, touchant le fait de la religion en l'an MDLXVI* (1567), repr. in *Philips van Marnix van St. Aldegonde*, ed. J. J. van Toorenbergen, i (The Hague, 1871), 35–133. Refs. are to the 1871 edn.
[125] Marnix van St Aldegonde, *Vraye Narration*, 88.

tranquillity of the country and had fostered proper obedience to the magistrates and the king. Moreover, the preachers had, above all, followed God's explicit commandment to the apostles and to all who had commission to preach the Gospel 'to go and preach in public at all crossroads like a clarion and trumpet'. With regard to the remark that the apostles had never borne arms while preaching the Gospel, Aldegonde retorted that the Reformed had only done so to defend themselves against 'illegitimate violence', to deter vagabonds and brigands, which was in correspondence with 'natural law and confirmed by the common sense of all nations'. In other words, weapons had only been borne 'to avert all force and violence, not to commit it'.[126] Thus at this point Aldegonde seemed to espouse the 'private law' argument, based on the Roman law rule of *vim vi repellere*, that it was legitimate to resist unjust force.

With regard to the Iconoclastic Fury, Aldegonde denounced the claim that this was merely 'a manifest perturbation of all political order'. He argued that it was 'impudent' to blame the Reformed ministers, elders and consistories in general for the Iconoclastic Fury, as it was known to be part of Reformed Protestant teaching that private persons had no authority to break the images which had been erected by 'public authority', but that such was the proper office and duty of the magistrate. Aldegonde admitted that a number of Reformed Protestants had been engaged in iconoclastic activities. He conceded they had been wrong to do so without the authority of the magistrate. Yet Aldegonde noticed that in some towns the churches had been purified by women and children while in others the magistrates had assisted in stripping the churches. The Iconoclastic Fury had been an amazing event, and, taking all circumstances into consideration, Aldegonde could only conclude that it had been a work of God's providence, to show how much he detested the idolatry of the images.

Thus, although Aldegonde admitted that some Reformed Protestants had made mistakes and had forsaken their proper duty to the government, he asserted they had had no intention of rebelling against their prince. As he put it in another treatise (probably unpublished during the sixteenth century), these people 'had never intended to despise the government, but through an untamed and fiery zeal only [wanted] to express to all people how deep their grief

[126] Ibid. 94–7.

was because of idolatry'.[127] They were, however, 'good and loyal subjects' of the king, as God and their conscience ordained them to be, and as such were willing to obey in all matters that were not against God.

Like Moded, the *True narration and apology* strongly warned the king against those counsellors who advised him to introduce the yoke of the Inquisition in the Dutch Provinces, as this would turn the Dutch into 'perpetual slaves of the Inquisitors'. It was not only illusory, Aldegonde argued, to think that one could exterminate the Reformed religion by force. It was also clear that any attempt in this direction would lead to the ruin of the country. Therefore, Aldegonde urged Philip II to grant his faithful subjects freedom of conscience and not to follow those counsellors who advised him 'to wage war against God, and to pull Christ from his chair by force of arms'.[128] Such counsellors sought to serve not the common good but their own private benefit and Aldegonde invoked the image of a conspiracy to bring the Low Countries, and the king as well, under the tyranny of the Inquisition.

Pamphleteers of the 1560s seemed to be keen on such conspiracy theories. Pamphlets were published with titles such as *The subtle means invented by the Cardinal Granvelle with his accomplices to institute the abominable Inquisition with the cruel maintenance of the placards against those of the religion*, while another pamphlet revealed, as its title put it, *The articles and decisions of the Inquisition of Spain, to attack and hinder those of the Netherlands*.[129] According to these pamphlets there was a 'threefold papacy', consisting of the pope of Rome, the pope of France (the Duke of Guise) and the pope of the Netherlands (Granvelle), whose plain and simple purpose was to subject all 'lords of the country, nobles and worldly authorities' in order to achieve dominance over Europe. In this view Philip II, a 'simple and ignorant' man, had been cruelly misled and had fallen victim to the ambitions of the 'threefold papery'. Of course such an interpretation made it possible to depict the armed resistance of the Dutch as a proper defence of the

---

[127] Marnix van St Aldegonde, *Van de Beelden afgheworpen in de Nederlanden in Augosto 1566*, in *Philips van Marnix van St Aldegonde*, ed. J. J. van Toorenenbergen, 29.

[128] Ibid. 127.

[129] Another example was the *Verclaringhe van die menichvuldighe loose practijcken en listen so van d'Inquisitie, observantie en onderhoudinghe van die Placcaten en andersins, dye de Cardinael Grandvelle, met zyn adherenten, gheinventeert en ghebruyckt hebben om de vervloecte en Tyrannighe Spaensche Inquisitie in dese vermaerde Eedele Nederlanden in te voeren* (1566). This pamphlet was also translated in German, where it appeared under the title *Drey Bapstumb*.

king's authority and thereby to avoid further discussion about its legitimacy.

For this issue still loomed large over Reformed Protestantism. The London refugee community in particular became the centre of a long-lasting conflict over the legitimacy of resistance. The London minister Godfried van Wingen played a central role in this conflict. After he had been appointed in 1563 the London refugee church fell victim to a number of disputes between a group within the London consistory centred round van Wingen and another group centred round a number of deacons.[130] At first these disputes focused on the church ordinances concerning baptism and the position of the church government in the election of church officials. In 1566, however, van Wingen publicly denounced image-breaking as an act which was 'against God and the government'.[131] His position, which probably represented a minority view in the London community, caused great disturbance and gave rise to another controversy. In March the van Wingen group devised a number of theses[132] which dealt with key questions of the conflict. A delegation was sent to Geneva, Berne, Lausanne, Zurich, Heidelberg and Emden, in short to the main centres of protestantism, to ask for comments on the theses.

In his *Advice concerning the dispute in the Dutch church of London in England*[133] Marnix van St Aldegonde commented on the London theses. The *Advice* started with a discussion of the meaning of Christian freedom. The London theses held that Christian freedom was 'a mercifully given right, obtained by the death of the Lord Christ', through which the faithful were 'liberated from the rule of sin and death', and might 'live safely and secure in God's justice'.[134] As such, Christian freedom was a 'purely spiritual and inner matter' which therefore submitted 'itself readily to all human ordinance and to the church authorities'. Aldegonde, who strongly condemned the discord within the London community, responded that Christian

---

[130] For the so-called Wingean disputes, see van Schelven, *De Nederduitsche vluchtelingenkerken*, 152–78. See also J. Lindeboom, *Austin Friars: geschiedenis van de Nederlandse hervormde gemeente te London, 1550–1950* (The Hague, 1950), 46–51.

[131] Van Schelven, *De Nederduitsche vluchtelingenkerken*, 166. See also Symeon Ruystinck *et al.*, *Gheschiedenissen ende handelingen die voornemelick aengaen de Nederduytsche Natie ende Gemeynten wonende in Engelant ende int bysonder tot London*, ed. J. J. van Toorenenbergen, Werken der Marnix-vereeniging, series 3, vol. i, part 1 (Utrecht, 1873), 67.

[132] See *Philips van Marnix van St Aldegonde*, ed. van Toorenenbergen, 547–54.

[133] Marnix van St Aldegonde, *Advys aengaende den twist in de Nederduytsche kercke tot London in Engellandt* (1568), in *Philips van Marnix van St Aldegonde*, ed. van Toorenenbergen, 135–82. This letter was addressed to Pieter Carpentier, a former elder of the London refugee church. [134] *Philips van Marnix van St Aldegonde*, ed. van Toorenenbergen, 547.

freedom meant the redemption of conscience not only from the 'ceremonies of the law' but also from all 'human yoke'. No institution, ecclesiastical or governmental, should attempt to force man's conscience, significantly defined as 'the agreement with what one thinks is God's word and will'.[135] As this meant that 'each specific member of the community' had 'the freedom to judge the doctrine, which is expounded to him',[136] freedom of conscience seemed to be the essence of Aldegonde's plea.

A substantial part of the London theses was devoted to the authority of government and the lawfulness of resistance. The government was recognized as ordained by God to protect the good, restrain the evil and maintain religion, virtue and peace. According to thesis 23 those who did not want to rise against God's authority should obey the government. It was added that a devout and faithful government had to be seen as a blessing of God whilst a tyrannical government was 'a scourge and punishment over the sin and wickedness of the subjects'.[137]

Theses 26 and 27 dealt with the issue of resistance. Thesis 26 propounded that 'if someone, in contravention of the laws and privileges of the country, makes himself lord and master, or if the existing government unjustly deprives its subjects of their privileges and freedom, which are sworn to them, or oppresses them with tyranny, then this should be resisted by the ordinary magistrates, who are obliged after God and their duty to protect their subordinates as much against the internal as against the external tyrant'.[138] Two years later van Wingen added that the 'ordinary magistrates' should fulfil their duty of resistance in a lawful manner, without giving rise to any form of sedition or rebellion.

Thesis 27, which seemed to refer to the situation in the Low Countries, maintained that if he who was by the laws and rights of the country its lord committed an offence, 'such may only be remedied by the government and the States of the country'. Only the 'superior powers or the States of the country', as van Wingen put it in 1570, had the right to correct an impious, ambitious, cruel or impudent ruler. Private persons and inferior magistrates, van Wingen argued, should rather suffer than disobey, for against an 'impious magistrate' only spiritual weapons were to be used by the subjects.[139]

---

[135] Ibid. 144.   [136] Ibid. 153.   [137] Ibid. 552.   [138] Ibid.
[139] See A. Kuyper, *Kerkeraadsprotocollen der Hollandsche gemeente te London, 1569–1571*, Werken der Marnix-vereeniging, series 1, vol. i (Utrecht, 1870), 343.

The London theses can be regarded as a substantial attempt to redefine the constitutionalist ideas as used in Reformed circles to circumscribe the legitimacy of resistance. Above all the theses wanted to specify the precise rights and duties of the 'inferior magistrates' who featured so prominently in Reformed constitutionalism. Thus the right of resistance was strictly limited to 'superior powers', such as the States. 'Ordinary magistrates' were only allowed to resist with peaceful and lawful means a foreign invader or a tyrannical government seeking to destroy the privileges and liberty of its subjects.

Aldegonde, though basically agreeing with the theses on political authority, condemned both theses on the issue of resistance as too general. He argued, offering another interpretation of the constitutionalist theme, that whether one was allowed to resist tyranny depended on the 'laws and rights of the country'. For example, one should sharply distinguish – and Aldegonde referred to the history of Babylon and Rome – the situation of countries that were conquered by the sword from countries, such as the Dutch Provinces, that had accepted their governments 'with certain contracts and mutual obligations... and had established and inaugurated them with the duty sworn by oath to maintain the privileges'.[140] Further criticism came from Geneva. Its spiritual leader Theodore Beza, who was to publish one of the major Huguenot treatises on resistance theory in 1574, condemned the London theses as 'too dark, too uncareful'. Beza had particular problems with thesis 26, which he felt was too dangerous.[141]

The London group around van Wingen continued to have problems with any form of active resistance in the Netherlands. When in 1568 William of Orange, wholeheartedly supported by Aldegonde, appealed to the London consistory to support his plans for the liberation of the Netherlands, a number of Londoners responded that it was 'incredible' that Orange had 'the opinion to thrust the king out of his country and to make himself lord and master of it with violence'.[142] It was argued that Orange had no authority whatsoever to act as he intended. It would only 'defame' him and would bring the country to ruin.

---

[140] *Philips van Marnix van St Aldegonde*, ed. van Toorenbergen, 155–6.

[141] See Ibid. 553; *Nederduitsche vluchtelingenkerken*, 171, and Ruystinck *et al.*, *Gheschiedenissen*, 67–77, for the Swiss response to the London theses.

[142] Hessels, *Ecclesiae Londino Batavae Archivum*, ii. 304.

Moreover, in the summer of 1570 van Wingen, who still had some support in the London refugee church,[143] once again condemned those as 'seditious and rebels' who had released persons imprisoned by the magistrate, had opposed arrests by the magistrate or had participated in iconoclastic activities, and later he decidedly turned down a resolution of compromise, proposed by the consistory, which suggested that the iconoclasts might have acted on divine command.[144]

The 'Wingean disputes' showed that in 1568, and even in 1570, armed resistance was still a highly controversial issue amongst Reformed Protestants. Thus when William of Orange took up arms in 1568 for an invasion that was intended to liberate the Low Countries from Alva's tyranny, he mounted a carefully orchestrated propaganda campaign to justify this act of armed resistance. Most of his arguments were predominantly political in character, but one work, written by Orange's army chaplain Adrianus Saravia, had a distinctly religious character. The *Heartfelt desire of the noble, long-suffering and high-born Prince of Orange*[145] was mainly directed against the 'bloodthirsty tyranny' of the Duke of Alva. If the Iron Duke succeeded in ruining the Netherlands, 'justice, the servant of God' would 'no longer be used in these countries'.[146] Instead force and violence would torment the Low Countries. Again Philip II was portrayed as a king cruelly misled by his ambitious counsellors. Thus, Orange's armed intervention was not presented as armed resistance but as an act of bounden duty to both God and king.

Above all, however, Saravia's treatise was a dramatic 'call to prayer and conversion'.[147] Orange's intervention was presented as a religious enterprise which was divinely inspired, and the faithful were admonished to pray for its success so that Alva's tyranny would be ousted without too much bloodshed.

---

[143] See e.g. Kuyper, *Kerkeraadsprotocollen*, 179–81, and the letter in Hessels, *Ecclesiae Londino Batavae Archivum*, 352–64, in which 'certain members of the Dutch church' asked the superintendent of the church, the Bishop of London, to intervene in the conflict on behalf of van Wingen. The final sentence of the bishop was in fact largely in favour of van Wingen. See Kuyper, *Kerkeraadsprotocollen*, 257–9.

[144] See Kuyper, *Kerkeraadsprotocollen*, 176.

[145] Adrianus Saravia, *Een hertgrondighe begheerte van den edelen, lanckmoedighen hoochgeboren Prince van Oraengien* (1568), repr. in M. G. Schenk (ed.), *Prins Willem van Oranje, geschriften van 1568* (Amsterdam, 1933), 129–55. Refs. are to the 1933 edn. On Saravia, see Willem Nijenhuis, *Adrianus Saravia* (c. *1532–1613*), *Dutch Calvinist, first reformed defender of the English episcopal church on the basis of the ius divinum*, Studies in the history of Christian thought, i (Leiden, 1980), which also discusses the *Hertgrondighe begheerte* (pp. 27–31).

[146] Schenk (ed.), *Prins Willem van Oranje*, 139.   [147] Nijenhuis, *Adrianus Saravia*, 28.

Whereas Saravia remained rather cautious in his argumentation, the *Admonition to the common captains and soldiers in the Netherlands*, written by another Reformed minister, Pneumenander, was much more vehement.[148]

In discussing the proper 'office' of captains and soldiers Pneumenander pointed out that God had not created men as 'irrational animals in the field' but as 'reasonable creatures, bestowed with an immortal soul'. As such they had to render account for their deeds and Pneumenander emphasized the great responsibility that captains and soldiers in the Netherlands had taken upon themselves by serving tyrants. With an elaborate analysis, based on both biblical texts and Roman law,[149] the minister demonstrated that not only the authors were responsible for the evil they ordered, but that their counsellors and servants, who executed such orders, also shared full responsibility.

Pneumenander acknowledged that the Lord had ordained the faithful 'to render Caesar the things that are Caesar's and to render God what is God's,[150] which meant that a Christian should give 'life and good to the worldly government' if he could do so 'without polluting his conscience'. Thus those who suffered from tyranny and persecution were urged to accept 'the bitter suffering of Christ', and to await God's mercy. By contrast, the 'papist servants' were warned that they were serving the Antichrist, which would bring them 'hell and eternal damnation'. In this respect Pneumenander referred to the elementary rule that 'you may serve or please no man to do what is against God'. The word, according to the minister, 'must remain unchanged: one should obey God rather than man'.[151]

According to Pneumenander the 'bloody and murderous Inquisition of papists and monks' were not only acting against God's word, but also violating all laws, privileges and immunities of the country. Thus the captains and soldiers in the Netherlands were helping 'to destroy the freedom and liberties of their dear fatherland to bring it under the eternal servitude and slavery of the Spanish Inquisition'.[152] This meant that the captains and soldiers in the Netherlands were also acting against the welfare of their fatherland,

---

[148] Pneumenander, *Vermaninghe aen die gemeyne Capiteynen ende Krijchsknechten in Nederlandt* (printed 'outside Doesborgh', 1568). The treatise was signed 1 Apr. 1568. I have not been able to trace who Pneumenander was.

[149] For Pneumenander's eclectic use of a great variety of Roman-law rules, many of them dealing with criminal acts of complicity, see fols. 37–41.   [150] Ibid., fol. 27.

[151] Ibid., fol. 44.   [152] Ibid., fol. 61. See also fols. 25, 29, 35, 42, 43 and 55.

thus forsaking their civic duty. For, as Pneumenander pointed out, with references to Cicero and Plutarch, it was 'the rule and law of nature' to set one's 'life and private welfare' aside in favour of the 'life and welfare of the common fatherland'.[153]

In this respect the captains and soldiers who served Alva were admonished not to take regard of the oath they had sworn to the 'tyrants in the Netherlands'. As Pneumenander put it, with reference to sources in canon law, 'if someone swears to do something that is against God's will and the welfare of his neighbour, he shall not keep it, as it is of no value'.[154] Moreover, Alva himself had strongly violated the oath he had taken to maintain 'the right, liberty and privileges' of the Netherlands and thereby had become a tyrant to whom obedience was not due. To strengthen his argument Pneumenander quoted the Joyous Entry of Brabant, arguing it was the explicit duty of the king's officers to uphold the charter, and pointing out that, if the king violated the Joyous Entry, his subjects were entitled to suspend their services to him. Moreover, all rules and regulations that were against the Joyous Entry were to be held of no value, and the same applied to officers that were appointed in contravention of the privileges.

Pneumenander urged the captains and soldiers who served Alva to 'cast off the works of darkness ... and to take up the weapons of the light'.[155] In this respect the Reformed minister defended the armed resistance of the 'Beggars', as he called the resistance forces in general, arguing 'that the Beggars had rightly taken up the weapons to advocate the privileges and freedoms after the king's oath and promise, and to render the king the things that are the king's and God the things that are God's'.[156]

In general, Reformed Protestant authors had played down the political role of the individual subject considerably. With the exception of providential tyrannicide, when God made use of individual subjects, private persons were not entitled to resort to resistance at their own initiative. Pneumenander, however, did not speak so much about rights as about duties. From this perspective it was possible to argue that 'private persons' had the civic and religious duty to refuse to assist tyrants, and to help the forces of light, which rightfully resisted tyranny.

---

[153] Ibid., fols. 46–7.   [154] Ibid., fol. 59.   [155] Ibid., fol. 30.   [156] Ibid., fol. 77.

3.6. CONCLUSIONS

Having returned to exile, Reformed Protestants attempted to strengthen the co-operation among the dispersed refugee churches and to work out a more uniform church organization. The convent of Wesel which met in November 1568 was a first step in the process leading to the synod of Emden, held in October 1571.[157] The synod affirmed the presbyterian character of the Reformed Protestant church. Local churches had to be governed by a consistory made up of ministers, elders and deacons. The synod ordered the co-operation of the various congregations in a regional 'classis' and in provincial and general synods. This co-operation was based on the anti-hierarchical principle, which had marked Reformed Protestantism from the outset, that no church should exercise dominion over other churches and that no ecclesiastical office-bearer should rule over other officials.[158]

The Emden synod subscribed to the 1561 *Confession of faith* and also, to bear witness to the bonds with the French protestant churches, to the French confession. As far as catechisms were concerned, the synod preferred, although other valuable catechisms were not banned, the use of the Heidelberg Catechism in Dutch-speaking congregations and the use of the Geneva Catechism in French-speaking communities. In addition the synod stressed the importance of church discipline, whose contents were laid down in ten articles.

The synod of Emden has been seen as 'the triumph of the Calvinist church-order among the Reformed in the Low Countries'.[159] A

---

[157] For the convent of Wesel, see J. P. van Dooren, 'Der Weseler Konvent 1568: neue Forschungsergebnisse', *Monatshefte für die Evangelische Kirchengeschichte des Rheinlandes*, 31 (1982), 41–55. For the synod of Emden, see D. Nauta, J. P. van Dooren and Otto J. de Jong (eds.), *De synode van Emden Oktober 1571* (Kampen, 1971); W. Nijenhuis, 'De synode te Emden 1571', *Kerk en Theologie*, 23 (1972), 34–54; and D. Nauta, 'Les Réformés aux Pays-Bas et les huguenots spécialement à propos du synode d'Emden (1571)', in *Actes du Colloque: l'amiral de Coligny et son temps* (Paris, 1974), 577–600; also D. Nauta, 'De synode van Emden (1571) en de Hugenoten', *Gereformeerd Theologisch Tijdschrift*, 73 (1973), 76–98. The Wesel articles and the *Acta* (in Latin and Dutch) of the Emden synod are found in F. L. Rutgers (ed.), *Acta van de Nederlandsche synoden der zestiende eeuw*, 2nd edn. (Dordrecht, 1980), 1–119.

[158] See Rutgers (ed.), *Acta van de Nederlandsche synoden*, 54–5. For an analysis of the decisions on church order, see J. Plomp, 'De kerkorde van Emden', in Nauta *et al.* (eds.), *De synode van Emden*, 88–121, and Nauta, 'Les Réformés aux Pays-Bas', 584ff.

[159] Duke, 'The ambivalent face of Calvinism in the Netherlands', 127. For a balanced analysis of this conflict, see W. Nijenhuis, 'De synode te Emden', 41–8, and J. J. Woltjer, 'De

minority, mainly refugees from Holland, however, had some strong doubts. While the main stream of the synod favoured a clear-cut separation of political and ecclesiastical polity, the Hollanders were willing to leave room for political authorities in the ecclesiastical polity. In this respect the Hollanders urged that nothing should be done that could harm the plans of Prince William of Orange. Moreover, like William of Orange, the Hollanders favoured, for religious and political reasons, an ecumenical co-operation with the Lutherans. The majority of the synod did not follow this line. Although, in accepting the Heidelberg Catechism, the synod may have left some opening to the Lutherans, on the whole at the beginning of the 1570s Calvinist influences got the upper hand in Dutch Reformed Protestantism.

In their treatises dealing with the issues of political obedience and resistance Dutch authors adopted the ecumenical approach so typical of early Reformed Protestantism. The discussion remained well within the main stream of Reformed political thought, from Luther to Calvin. Thus, at least until the *Annus mirabilis*, most Reformed Protestant authors were at great pains to emphasize the imperative of obedience and non-resistance. All Reformed Protestant authors acknowledged that political authority had been ordained by God to protect the good and to punish the evil. The government was, as Romans 13:4 put it, 'the servant of God to execute his wrath on the wrongdoer'. Thus the task of the government was to ensure external peace and order.

In many, but not all, Reformed Protestant treatises it was argued that the government, as the protector of both tables of Moses' law, had a second principal task, which was to fight idolatry and to foster the true predication of God's word. This argument, already presented by Veluanus and later also by de Bray, Moded, Aldegonde and others, was incorporated in the 1561 *Confession of faith* and therefore seemed to represent the view of the mainstream of Dutch Reformed Protestantism. An important consequence of this view was that the government had a duty to fight heresy. However, almost unequivocally Reformed Protestant authors rejected any use of physical violence and persecution in this matter. The fight against heresy had to be purely spiritual in character. In particular the promotion of public debates was favoured. This argument implied that the

politieke betekenis van de Emdense synode', in Nauta *et al.* (eds.), *De synode van Emden*, 22–49.

government had to make room for debate and that at least to a certain extent freedom of speech and worship had to be granted. However, Reformed Protestant authors generally gave no indication of how far such freedom should go. An exception was Junius, who seemed to favour a general freedom of speech and worship, as under such circumstances the truth would prevail.

Following mainstream Reformed political thought Dutch authors never doubted that subjects had to pay tribute and tolls and had to honour, revere and obey the worldly authorities which God had set over them, even if these were godless, cruel and tyrannic. At length it was explained to the faithful that human suffering and persecution, and therefore martyrdom, was their lot and an ethics was developed which presented patience and constancy as principal Christian virtues. Only when worldly authorities ordered against God did subjects have the duty to disobey. Especially after 1560 this precept was readily applied. With apostolic zeal Reformed Protestant authors called upon 'loyal subjects' to join the true church, and, thereby to defy the government. In addition the martyrologies showed that Reformed Protestant authors almost sanctified individuals who disobeyed the orders of worldly authorities to denounce their religion. Thus, in spite of the recurrent emphasis on the duty of obedience, Reformed Protestants willy-nilly encouraged acts of civil disobedience.

With this stunning exception Reformed Protestant authors remained rather elusive about when, under which circumstances, the subjects actually had a duty to disobey worldly authority. Perhaps this was out of embarrassment. Perhaps Reformed Protestant authors simply saw no need to explicate when governments acted ungodly, as in their perception the word of God itself provided the faithful with full answers. Whatever the true explanation may be, eventually the decision to disobey and defy the government was often an individual one.

With regard to individuals who resorted to active resistance Reformed Protestant authors, once again following the main stream of Reformed political thought, remained adamant. Private persons had no private authority to resist the government. However, in exceptional circumstances private persons could be providential instruments, used by God to rectify blasphemy or tyranny. Some authors seemed to make the controversial claim, forcefully denounced by van Wingen, that the Iconoclastic Fury, other resistance activities of Dutch Reformed Protestants and indeed the 1568 armed invasion led by William of Orange could be interpreted, and thereby justified, in this sense.

So far Dutch Lutherans went hand in hand with Reformed Protestants. The issue of resistance, however, caused a fundamental break between the two groups. Whereas Lutherans continued to emphasize the absolute imperative of non-resistance, Reformed Protestants espoused and elaborated the main theories of resistance as developed by continental Calvinists and indeed Lutherans up to 1560.

A number of Dutch authors adopted the 'private law' theory. The natural right of self-defence and the maxim that it was permitted to repel unjust force by force, featured in a number of Dutch treatises. In general, however, Reformed Protestants seemed more inclined to the constitutionalist line of thought. Dutch authors accepted, again on the basis of Romans 13, that, as with superior magistrates, such as kings and princes, inferior magistrates had been instituted by God to protect the good and to punish the evil. Putting them, following Calvin, on equal terms with the famous ephors of Lacedaemon, it was argued that it was the specific office of inferior magistrates to 'bridle and silence the evil kings', as the author of the 1566 *Declaration* put it. As early as 1559 this idea had been articulated by the Dutch Reformed Protestant Dathenus. In the following decade it aroused strong debate. At issue was not the principle as such but its precise formulation and its implications for the situation in the Netherlands. The more cautious approach held that 'ordinary magistrates' were only allowed to resist with peaceful and lawful means a tyrant who either acquired power in violating the laws and privileges of the country or who as a ruler deprived the people of their liberty and privileges. If a lawfully constituted ruler turned to tyranny, only a superior power such as the States of the country had the right of resistance. The alternative approach, exemplified by Aldegonde, maintained that the legitimacy of resistance depended on the laws and privileges of the country. The Antwerp synod of 1566 must have inclined to a similar view, as the discussion of the question whether in the Dutch situation it was legitimate to resist a government that had broken the privileges was decisive for its attitude to armed resistance. Although in this discussion the role and significance of inferior magistrates was certainly not ignored, it was essentially built on interpretations of the Dutch political order. What was at stake were questions regarding the significance of the privileges, the character of Dutch customs and liberties and the meaning of the oath of inauguration for the relationship between government and subjects.

The answers to such questions, of course, had no typical Reformed Protestant character. Essentially, in close resemblance to the Lutheran move of the 1530s, the debate was transferred from the religious to the constitutional and therefore political realm. As such there was no typical Reformed Protestant theory of resistance.

Although the discussion on the legitimacy of resistance transcended the religious character of the Reformed Protestant approach to politics, the conclusion that in certain respects there was a distinct Reformed Protestant approach to the issues of political authority and obedience still seems warranted. This, however, did not amount to a unified political doctrine. Although Reformed Protestant authors agreed on a number of basic principles, the precise articulation and application of these principles to the situation in the Netherlands aroused strong debate. At least until 1571 there was, so to speak, diversity in unity, which once again exemplified the pluriformity of Dutch Reformed Protestantism in the sixteenth century.

CHAPTER 4

Politics and resistance: the political justification of the Dutch Revolt

4.1. INTRODUCTION

As was indicated by the momentous decision of the Antwerp synod in 1566 to approve armed resistance against the government, the vehemence of the Wingean disputes, the repudiation of the 1568 London theses by Marnix van St Aldegonde and Pneumenander's appeal to the Joyous Entry of Brabant, in the justification of the resistance against the government of Philip II arguments based on the rights and privileges of the Low Countries began to play an eminent role in the 1560s.

This chapter reconstructs the political justification of the Dutch Revolt. The focus is on the articulation of the political right of resistance against Philip II, which finally led to his abjuration as lord of the Dutch Provinces.[1]

4.2. THE EARLY PROTESTS OF THE 1560S

On 5 April 1566 about 300 nobles marched through the streets of Brussels. The impressive procession was heading for the court of Margaret of Parma, where they offered the famous *Petition* to the governess. The *Petition* was an initiative of the so-called Compromise, a group of nobles whose main objective was to save the Low Countries from falling under the yoke of the Inquisition. As the constitutive document of the Compromise argued, a number of foreigners, driven by private avarice and ambition, had misled the

---

[1] Parts of the argument of this chapter are based on the following articles: Martin van Gelderen, 'A political theory of the Dutch Revolt and the *Vindiciae contra tyrannos*', *Il Pensiero Politico*, 19 (1986), 163–82; Martin van Gelderen, 'The position of the States in the political thought of the Dutch Revolt', *Parliaments, Estates and Representation*, 7 (1987), 163–76; Martin van Gelderen, 'Conceptions of liberty during the Dutch Revolt (1555–1590)', *Parliaments, Estates and Representation*, 9 (1989), 137–53.

king and, under the pretension of protecting the Roman Catholic religion, had introduced the Inquisition. This form of 'barbarism' exceeded the worst acts of tyranny. It would 'destroy all old privileges, freedoms and immunities' and it 'would make the citizens and inhabitants of these Countries eternal and miserable slaves of the Inquisition'.[2] Depriving them of their liberty, it would lead to the ruin of the Netherlands. Therefore, the confederated nobles solemnly swore to do all in their power 'to extirpate and eradicate' the Inquisition entirely as 'the mother and cause of all disorder and iniquity'.[3]

In the *Petition* the nobles, presenting themselves as most loyal servants of Philip II, asked the governess to suspend the Inquisition and the execution of the placards concerning the persecution of heretics. They urged moderation and implored Philip II 'very humbly... to seek the advice and consent of the assembled States General for new ordinances and other more suitable and appropriate ways to put matters right without causing such apparent dangers'.[4]

Dutch nobles were certainly not alone in arguing that there was a distinct policy of introducing the Inquisition in the Netherlands, which inevitably would lead to the ruin of the country. The same argument was propounded, for example, in a request to the town government of Antwerp, 'presented by the common citizenry'. Again the protest centred round the privileges. It was pointed out that the religious policy of the government was 'directly' against the privileges of the country of Brabant, an allegation which was supported by specific references to the Joyous Entry.[5]

Extensive appeals to the privileges were also expressed by the numerous protests of the Four Members of Flanders and of the four capital towns of Brabant, Louvain, Brussels, Antwerp and Bois-le-Duc, which formed the powerful third estate of Brabant's provincial States. From 1564 the Members of Flanders presented four requests

[2] 'Compromise' (1565), in Jacob van Wesembeeke, *De beschriivinge van den geschiedenissen in der Religien saken toegedraghen in den Nederlanden* (1569), 348. Part of the Compromise is published in E. F. Kossmann and A. F. Mellink (eds.), *Texts concerning the revolt of the Netherlands* (Cambridge, 1974), 59–62.

[3] Van Wesembeeke, *De beschriivinge*, 349; Kossmann and Mellink (eds.), *Texts concerning the revolt of the Netherlands*, 61.

[4] *Propositie ende requeste opt stuck van de Inquisitie* (Vianen, 1566), fol. A3. For a modern edn. of the *Petition* in English, see Kossmann and Mellink (eds.), *Texts concerning the revolt of the Netherlands*, 62–6.

[5] *Requeste aen de Eerweerdighe, Wijse en seer voorsienighe heeren, Borghemeesteren en Raet der vermaerder Coopstadt Antwerpen, gepresenteert byde gemeyne Borgerschap der selver Stadt* (1565).

to Philip II containing powerful protests against the actions of the inquisitor Titelmans. They argued that Titelmans' actions continuously contravened the 'customs, liberties, immunities and privileges' by which Flanders had been traditionally governed and 'held in good policy'. Philip was urged to maintain 'the old liberties and freedoms' as he had sworn to do.[6]

Likewise the Brabant towns pointed out with great vigour that the religious policy of the government was 'in diverse respects, concerning the introduction of the clerical Inquisition as well as diverse points of the Concilium [of Trent], explicitly and directly against the Joyous Entry of our Lord the King and the old rights, usages, customs and privileges of the country of Brabant, as diverse good documents show'.[7] In particular the article of the Joyous Entry forbidding the clergy to administer justice in Brabant was violated by the government's plans. Moreover, the introduction of a clerical Inquisition would reduce the authority of the public authorities and, in fact, of the king himself. As the towns emphasized, in Brabant a prince was not allowed to reduce his authority without the consent of the States.

In a number of pamphlets the protest against the alleged violation of the privileges and liberties of the country was combined with a more active call for resistance, which itself was again based on the privileges. A *Remonstrance* to the king, signed 28 May 1566 and allegedly[8] written by Gilles le Clerq, an elder of the Antwerp Reformed Protestant community, vehemently attacked the placards against heresy. They were said to endanger 'the prosperity and common weal of the country', to be against 'the privileges of the Low Countries' and therefore to 'cause a general destruction and spoliation'.[9] With references to the Joyous Entry and to fifteenth-century ordinances of Philip the Good, le Clerq sought to prove that, especially in its manner of proceeding and of punishing, the placards and the actions of the Inquisition were in direct conflict with the privileges. Le Clerq explicitly endorsed the view the nobles had presented in the *Petition* and called for moderation of the religious policy. As he put it, 'the weapons of the priests ought to be no other

---

[6] Van Wesembeeke, *De beschriivinge*, 366. Both the requests of the Members of Flanders and the requests and protests of the Brabant towns were published by van Wesembeeke.

[7] Ibid. 327.

[8] See P. A. M. Geurts, *De Nederlandse Opstand in de pamfletten 1566–1584* (Utrecht, 1983; first pub. 1956), 17.

[9] Gilles le Clerq, *Remonstrantie ofte vertoogh aen den grootmachtigen Coninck van Spaengen etc. op de Requeste byden Edeldom der Co. M. erfnederlanden den 5. april 1565 aen mijn Vrouwe de Hertoginne van Parme gepresenteert* (Antwerp, 1566), 5.

than tears, prayers and suchlike things'; priests should not be 'allowed to use any rifle nor violence'.[10] Pleading for freedom of conscience le Clerq argued that as the placards against heresy defied the privileges, they were to be held of no value and in an implied threat he alluded to the clause of disobedience in the Joyous Entry.

According to Jacob van Wesembeeke it was quite common amongst the pamphleteers of 1566 to follow this line of argument. As Wesembeeke pointed out in his comprehensive account of the events of the *Annus mirabilis*, many treatises propounded the view that the placards against heresy were 'annulled by the privileges'.[11] Some treatises, however, not only declared the religious policy of the government of no legal value whatsoever, they also demanded active resistance. Thus a *Remonstrance* published in March 1566 asserted that the placards were of no value and that 'in conformity with the Joyous Entry... one ought not tolerate them or the Inquisition, but resist them in deed'.[12]

This was also the position of the anonymous author of the *Third warning and admonition to the good, faithful rulers and community of the country of Brabant*. At length he warned of the calumnious actions of Cardinal Granvelle and other adherents of the Inquisition, reiterating the view that the actions of the 'cardinalists' would lead to the 'irreparable ruin and spoliation of His Majesty, of this country of Brabant and to the complete destruction of the Joyous Entry, old sworn rights, freedoms and privileges of the country'.[13] The religious placards of the cardinalists and their 'seditious publications', which allegedly propounded intolerable punishments, were presented as a 'notorious novelty' against the 'sworn old rights, customs and provenances of the country of Brabant' as contained in the Joyous Entry. Therefore, they were 'null', of no validity.

The *Third warning* asserted that each and every Brabanter had the duty to resist the placards and ordinances of the cardinalists. Such resistance was 'for each and everyone of the subjects of Brabant and all her descendants in general and in particular' not only 'permitted', but also 'expressly ordained and commanded' by the Joyous Entry, on which both lord and subjects had sworn a solemn oath. As was specifically added, this principle applied to all, even to the 'lowest subjects'.[14]

---

[10] Ibid. 12. [11] Van Wesembeeke, *De beschriivinge*, 138. [12] Ibid. 111.
[13] *Derde waerschouwinge ende vermaninghe aende goede, getrouwe regeerders en gemeinte vanden lande van Brabant teghen de calumnien vanden Cardinael van Granvel, nieu Bisschoppen, Viglius, Morillon, theologiennen van Loeven, dekens, prochianen, monniken, Alonso Delcanto ende andere Inquisiteurs haren aenhangers* (1566), fol. A2. [14] Ibid., fol. A5.

The Joyous Entry was also central to the argument of the *Advertisement by the good and loyal subjects and inhabitants of the Royal Majesty's patrimonial Netherlands.*[15] Like the *Third warning* the *Advertisement* endorsed the protest of the April *Petition*. It demanded the immediate cessation of all placards and ordinances concerning heresy and urged the strict maintenance of the Joyous Entry, depicted as a contract between the inhabitants of Brabant and Philip as Duke of Brabant.

Again like the *Third Warning*, the *Advertisement* followed the *Petition* in urging Philip II to convene the States General in order to resolve the problems 'without prejudice to anyone's privileges, freedoms, rights and customs'.[16] A new religious policy had to be formulated by the king 'on the advice and consent of the States General', as the nobles themselves put it in their second admonition.

The suggestion to convene the States General was not original. During the political crisis of 1563 the high nobles, Orange, Egmont and Hoorne, demanding the retirement of Cardinal Granvelle and the reform of the governmental apparatus, sent Philip II a letter in which they announced their intention to suspend their activities in the Council of State. In this letter, published by Wesembeeke, the nobles already asserted that they could 'find no better means to get out of these anxieties than through the assistance and help of the States General'.[17]

In short, to the manifold protests of 1565 and 1566 the privileges and freedoms of the Netherlands were of central importance. They repeatedly emphasized that the government's religious policy violated the privileges and old freedoms. Such allegations were supported with detailed references to the privileges, the Joyous Entry of Brabant in particular. The violation of privileges and liberties was seen as a grave and intolerable offence, especially since Philip II had taken a solemn oath, sealing a contract between prince and subjects, to uphold and maintain the very privileges which were so ruthlessly diminished. Thus frequent reference was made to the clause of disobedience of the Joyous Entry, which gave the subjects the right to

---

[15] *Advertissement bijde goede ende ghetrauwe ondersaten ende inwoonderen der CM. Erfnederlanden gedaen aende gouverneurs en Staten derselver landen van, tghene dat sijlieden verstaen ende versuecken geordonneert te worden opt stuck van der religie* (1566). Franciscus Junius, Gilles le Clercq and Gaspard van der Noot have been mentioned as authors of this treatise. See A. A. van Schelven, 'De opkomst van de idee der politieke tolerantie in de 16e eeuwsche Nederlanden', *TvG* 46 (1931), 340.   [16] *Advertissement*, fol. A3.

[17] Jacob van Wesembeeke, *Bewijsinghe vande onschult van mijn heere Philip Baenreheere van Montmorency, Grave van Hoorne etc.* (1568), fol. C2.

disobey a prince if he violated the articles of the Joyous Entry and to refuse him their services until the prince repaired his ways. Some treatises, such as the *Third warning*, went beyond this formulation in arguing that the subjects, and each in particular, had the civic duty to resist a policy which so gravely offended the privileges, liberties and rights of the country.

4.3. THE APOLOGIES OF THE *ANNUS MIRABILIS*: JACOB VAN WESEMBEEKE AND THE DEFENCE OF LIBERTY

The arguments of the early 1560s were reiterated and elaborated by the authors of the apologies dealing with the events of the *Annus mirabilis*. One of the most extensive apologies was of course Aldegonde's *True narration*. Aldegonde felt as well that there was a grand design drawn up by Granvelle to deprive the Low Countries of their privileges in order to bring them into servitude of the Inquisition. In fact Aldegonde claimed that the objective was to turn the Netherlands *en pays de conqueste*, and subsequently, by abolishing the privileges, into a kingdom.[18]

However, so Aldegonde believed, the inhabitants of the Low Countries were not willing to suffer the yoke of the Inquisition. They would rather choose 'a brief death, with the hope of leaving the ancient liberty to their children than to await a servitude more miserable than a thousand deaths'.[19]

In line with the protests of 1565 and 1566 Aldegonde's *True narration* suggested there was some sort of intrinsic relationship between the ancient liberty and the privileges. This relationship was fully articulated by Jacob van Wesembeeke, probably the most productive publicist of the late 1560s. Wesembeeke, born in Brussels, was a member of Brabant's social and political elite. In 1556 he succeeded his father as pensionary of Antwerp and as such he had an important part in the events of 1566, when he was a mediator between the protestants and the town government. Soon after William of Orange was appointed Governor of Antwerp Wesembeeke became his secretary. In 1567 he followed Orange into exile.[20] In 1568 and 1569 Wesembeeke produced his main political works. In

[18] Marnix van St Aldegonde, *Vraye narration et apologie des choses passees au Pays-Bas touchant le fait de la religion en l'an MDLXVI* (1567), 46. [19] Ibid. 128.

[20] For biographical details on van Wesembeeke see C. Rahlenbeck (ed.), *Mémoires de Jacques de Wesenbeke* (Brussels, 1859), pp. v–xx.

1568 he published apologies on behalf of the beheaded Count of Hoorne[21] and for the Count of Hoochstraten,[22] and was probably involved in Orange's 1568 *Justification*. In January 1569 Wesembeeke published his own justification[23] and in the same year he published a defence on behalf of the former Antwerp burgomaster van Stralen.[24] In August 1569 the famous *Description of the history in the matter of religion as happened in the Netherlands* appeared.[25]

In many respects Wesembeeke's apologies and defences had a highly personal character. Their aim was to defend and justify the actions, and thereby the honour and name, of the persons involved. His *Description* was of major importance as a historical work and has been widely acknowledged as one of the most authoritative accounts of the events of the *Annus mirabilis*.

In addition Wesembeeke's works were of principal importance to the development of the political thought of the Dutch Revolt. For although Wesembeeke echoed the protests of 1565 and 1566 in arguing that the policy of the central government was in violation of the privileges and liberties of the country, the former pensionary of Antwerp was among the first to put such arguments into a broader perspective by expounding a more comprehensive interpretation of the fundamentals of Dutch politics.

Wesembeeke endorsed the common view that the objective of the cardinalists was to bring the Netherlands into servitude. Thus the liberty of the provinces and their inhabitants was at stake. Wesembeeke presented liberty as the political value *par excellence* as he spoke of the 'natural, inborn freedom, which man above all esteems and values and will not allow to be taken away'.[26] According to Wesembeeke, the Dutch people in particular had esteemed and cherished liberty throughout the centuries. This became particularly manifest when attempts were made to take away the 'old liberty', of

---

[21] Van Wesembeeke, *De Bewijsinghe vande onschult van mijn heere Philip van Baenreheere Montmorency, Grave van Hoorne.*

[22] Jacob van Wesembeeke, *La defense de messire Antoine de Lalaing, comte de Hoochstrate* (Mons, 1838; first pub. 1568).

[23] Jacob van Wesembeeke, *La defence de Jacques de Wesenbeke jadis conseiller et pensionnaire de la ville d'Anvers, contre les indevës et iniques citations contre luy décrétées* (1569), in Rahlenbeck (ed.), *Mémoires de Jacques de Wesenbeke*, 1–45.

[24] Jacob van Wesembeeke, *Corte Vermaninghe aen alle christenen oft vonnisse oft advis, met grooter wreetheit the wercke ghestelt teghen Heer Anthonis van Stralen, Borghemeester van Antwerpen ende commissaris generael vanden Staten der Nederlanden* (1569).

[25] Jacob van Wesembeeke, *De beschriivinge*. The French edn. of this work was re-edited by Rahlenbeck (ed.), *Mémoires de Jacques de Wesenbeke*, 47–392.

[26] Van Wesembeeke, *De beschriivinge*, 10.

which the Dutch 'with an exceptional and extremely powerful assiduity, had always been very great lovers, supporters and advocates'.[27] Wesembeeke argued that the prosperity of the Low Countries was closely linked to the eager protection of Dutch liberty. The distracted policy of the government was not only an outright attack on the freedom of the Netherlands, making the Dutch 'the most oppressed slaves in the world'. In addition it would lead 'to the complete ruination of the whole country, which was standing solely on its liberty and freedom (and the trade, merchandise and the multitude of goods and persons, which had followed from this)'.[28]

Wesembeeke was not alone in emphasizing the intrinsic connection between the liberty and the prosperity of the Netherlands. The idea had been familiar to town magistrates for a long time and had been used frequently in debates with encroaching central institutions. It was highly popular in the political literature of the Revolt. The general feeling seemed to be, as the 1568 *Complaint of the sorrowful land of the Netherlands* put it with a nice sense of rhetoric, that *Marchandise*, *Manufacture* and *Negotiations* were the sisters of *Liberté*, the daughter of the Netherlands.[29]

According to Wesembeeke there was an inseparable connection between the protection of the freedom of the country and the maintenance of the privileges. The privileges were the embodiment of liberty. As Wesembeeke pointed out, 'with regard to the state of the Netherlands' it was 'clear to everyone that the inhabitants more than other people of all old times have been particular lovers and upholders of their freedoms and franchises'. Therefore, the Dutch had provided themselves 'through emperors, kings and princes with fine privileges, to whose maintenance they have always made their princes swear and promise solemnly before they have wanted to accept them'.[30] To protest against the infringements of the privileges was to fight for the liberty of the Netherlands, and Wesembeeke pointed out that in view of their 'honour and oath' the Dutch were obliged to resist such infringements. This was, so Wesembeeke explained, the leitmotif of the protest against governmental policy. Time and again it had been pointed out that this policy was 'against the notorious freedom and privileges of the country'.[31]

[27] Ibid. 12.   [28] Ibid. 39.   [29] *Complainte de la desolée terre du Pais Bas* (1568), 3.
[30] Van Wesembeeke, *De bewijsinghe vande onschult van mijn heere Philip Baenreheere van Montmorency*, 373.
[31] Van Wesembeeke, *De beschriivinge*, 59.

The violation of the privileges was also a dominant theme in Wesembeeke's apologies. As a trained lawyer Wesembeeke was fully equipped to expound in detail how in each personal case privileges had been violated, paying special attention to the privileges of the Order of the Golden Fleece, of which both Hoochstraten and Hoorne were members, and the Joyous Entry of Brabant. In this respect Wesembeeke repeatedly invoked the Joyous Entry's clause of disobedience. In Hoochstraten's defence it was explicitly argued that as Brabant's privileges had been offended against, 'following the clause of the Joyous Entry, law and condition of the duchy of Brabant', Hoochstraten was no longer held to render obedience to Philip II, until the latter had repaired his ways. In his *Proof of the innocence of... the Count of Hoorne* Wesembeeke was even more radical with regard to the right to disobey and resist a prince who violated the privileges. He pointed out that although it had never been the intention of the nobles to keep Philip II out of the country or to resist his armies by force, they were in fact entitled to do so, 'after the clear privileges of the country – through the first and last article of the Joyous Entry of Duke John of the years 1421 and 1422 – and the commitment which they had in maintaining these'.[32]

In his treatises Wesembeeke endorsed the call for a meeting of the States General. As he pointed out, a convocation of the States General was generally recognized to be the only way out of the disastrous situation. In his apology for Hoorne, Wesembeeke argued that 'it was a general principle of politics' to regard the meeting of the States as 'a sound resort and secure remedy in all anxieties'.[33] This principle applied especially to the Low Countries, where it was 'normal, yes, according to the privileges of the country, proper and necessary (following the third article of the Joyous Entry)' that the princes made use of 'the discretion and consent of their States, especially in matters of general placards which so much touch the inhabitants, yes, committing their freedom and conscience'.[34]

With these arguments Wesembeeke made a number of important ideological moves. The first was to articulate a view, lumbering in the earlier protests, that liberty was and should be considered the highest political value and the 'daughter of the Netherlands'. It should be

---

[32] Van Wesembeeke, *De bewijsinghe vande onschult van Philip van Montmorency*, 142. Although Wesembeeke spoke of the Joyous Entry of Duke John, the agreements of 1421 and 1422 are (and were) usually called the 'New Regiment'.

[33] Ibid. 148.   [34] Ibid. 151.

noted that Wesembeeke and others explicitly used the words freedom and liberty in the singular. This indicates, that although notions of liberty were closely related to late medieval liberties, franchises and privileges, different conceptions of liberty were in development.

Next, Wesembeeke made the important move of arguing that the prosperity of the country and the personal freedom of the inhabitants rested upon the country's old liberty. The loss of liberty would be catastrophic: the country would be ruined and the people turned into slaves. As Wesembeeke emphasized, there was an inseparable connection between upholding the liberty of the country and protecting the personal liberty of the inhabitants. In fact it would become standard to argue that, if Granvelle, Alva and their henchmen succeeded in depriving the country of its liberties and privileges, the inhabitants would become 'the most oppressed slaves in the world'.

Wesembeeke's third move was to argue that liberty was embodied in the privileges of the country, which should be regarded as the constitutional guarantees of liberty, which a prince was not allowed to violate or to change. If, in spite of all, he did so, the privileges, and more particularly the Joyous Entry of Brabant, stipulated that the subjects had the right to disobey a prince violating the privileges until he mended his ways. In this respect Wesembeeke joined those who had argued that the subjects had the civic duty to resist violations of the privileges and he even pointed out that the inhabitants had the right to actually resist the forces Philip had sent to the Netherlands.

Wesembeeke's final ideological move concerned the role of the States in the political order of the Netherlands. Whereas earlier treatises had advocated the convocation of the States as a practical solution to what they considered a catastrophic situation, Wesembeeke claimed it was imperative for the prince to seek, in matters of weight, the advice and consent of the States, as ordained by the privileges. From a practical solution for a specific political problem Wesembeeke elevated this imperative to a principle of politics and of Dutch politics in particular.

The result of Wesembeeke's ideological innovations was the articulation of a conception of the Dutch political order as built upon liberty, privileges and States, forming an inseparable trinity.

4.4. FROM JUSTIFICATION TO REVOLT, 1568–1572

Wesembeeke's views were echoed in the treatises published in the name of William of Orange on the occasion of his 1568 invasion of the Netherlands. In April 1568 an apology on behalf of Orange was printed, which, as the title of the 1575 English translation indicated, was *A justification or cleering of the Prince of Orendge agaynst the false slaunders, wherwith his ilwillers goe about to charge him wrongfully.*[35] In July 1568 the *Declaration and document of the illustrious, highborn Prince and Lord, William, Prince of Orange*[36] was published, soon followed by a manifesto from the prince to 'all faithful subjects of the Royal Majesty in the Netherlands', signed 31 August 1568. In September the *Warning of the Prince of Orange to the inhabitants and subjects of the Netherlands*[37] and a manifesto to *All captains, men of arms and faithful soldiers of the Netherlands* appeared.

Amongst Orange's 1568 writings, the *Justification* was probably the most personal in character. It was written by Orange himself in consultation with the Huguenot publicist Hubert Languet and with Wesembeeke, who was also involved in Orange's other treatises.[38] In its structure and argument the *Justification* strongly resembled Wesembeeke's apologies. It sought systematically to undermine the accusations raised against Orange by the summons Alva had issued against him. Its main point was to refute any allegation of ambition on Orange's behalf to usurp the authority of Philip II.

Time and again Orange's 1568 treatises reiterated the view that Granvelle and Alva were trampling on the privileges and thereby violating the 'old traditional freedom'.[39] Under the pretence of religion and the service to the king both tried to destroy the prosperity of the Netherlands and to bring 'the inhabitants who before had had good freedom, in pitiable slavery with oppression and extermination of all the privileges and franchises of the country'.[40]

---

[35] *Verantwoordinghe des Princen van Oraengien* (1568), repr. in Schenk (ed.), *Prins Willem van Oranje*, 23–98. The English trans. was printed in London by John Day. The 1568 publication in French was the work of Theodore Beza.

[36] *Verklaringhe ende uutschrift des Duerluchtighsten, Hoochgeborenen Vorsten ende Heeren... Willem, Prince van Oranien...* (1568), repr. in Schenk (ed.), *Prins Willem van Oranje*, 99–116.

[37] *Waerschouwinghe des Princen van Oraengien aende inghesetenen ende ondersaten van den Nederlanden* (1568), repr. in Schenk (ed.), *Prins Willem van Oranje*, 117–28.

[38] See Geurts, *De Nederlandse Opstand*, 27–30, and Helmut Cellarius, 'Die Propagandatätigkeit Wilhelms von Oranien in Dillenburg 1568 im Dienste des niederländischen Aufstandes', *Nassauische Annale*, 76 (1968), 128–9.

[39] See e.g. Schenk (ed.), *Prins Willem van Oranje*, 122–3.

[40] *Allen ende elckerlicken Capiteynen, volck van wapenen ende ghetrovven Crijchsluyden van Nederlant* (1568), 3.

In his *Warning* Orange reminded the inhabitants of the Netherlands of their traditional form of government. He pointed out, in a
language almost identical to Wesembeeke's, that the Low Countries
had been governed by their princes 'in all sweetness, right and
reason' and 'in accordance with their freedoms, rights, customs and
privileges', which the inhabitants, 'as exceptional lovers and
advocates of their liberty and enemies of all violence and oppression',
had acquired from their princes.[41] To uphold these freedoms and
privileges, which had brought the fatherland great wealth and
prosperity, so it was added, the subjects had concluded a contract
with their princes, confirmed and sealed by solemn oath, which
bound the inhabitants to obedience only if their privileges were
indeed maintained.

Thus Orange too referred to the clause of obedience of the Joyous
Entry of Brabant and argued (passing over the question whether this
charter applied to other Dutch provinces as well) that the inhabitants
of the Netherlands had the right to disobey a prince who offended the
privileges and freedoms. Moreover, Orange's treatises went beyond
the mere formulation of a right of disobedience in asserting that 'all
men in the world' had the duty to resist a 'gruesome tyranny', which
violated 'all divine, natural and written rights, yes... all freedoms,
oaths, contracts and privileges of the country'.[42] The Dutch were
therefore urged to 'remember their usual freedom and prosperity', to
'meet the commitment and promise' they had to their 'fatherland'
and to do everything to 'restore themselves with violence and power
in their old usual liberty'.[43]

From Orange's perspective his own military campaign against
Alva should be seen as a proper act of 'necessary, reasonable,
Christian, permitted and inevitable defence and self-defence'[44]
against a most sanguinary tyranny. The objectives in exterminating
this tyranny were to further God's honour and 'to re-establish the
poor, expelled, persecuted, imprisoned Christians in their liberty'.
Orange promised to restore the country to its old state, to re-establish
the privileges, freedoms and contracts and to solve all further
problems with the advice of the States General.

The essential difference between Orange's treatises and Wesembeeke's work was of course that while Wesembeeke invoked his
interpretation of the Dutch political order as based on liberty,

---

[41] Schenk (ed.), *Prins Willem van Oranje*, 120.
[43] Ibid. 125. See also p. 126.
[42] Ibid. 124.
[44] Ibid. 101-2.

privileges and the States to justify the protest against the policy of the
central government, Orange's treatises did so to justify an armed
invasion. However, this interpretation of the Dutch political order
was not yet elaborated into an ideology that justified armed resistance
against Philip II himself. For although Orange argued that Philip's
decisions were among the principal causes of the troubles, he retained
the image of the Spanish king as a man misled by false informers,
whose authority in fact was said to be defended by Orange and his
supporters.

Another important difference from Wesembeeke's other treatises
was that Orange's writings not only appealed to the laws and
privileges of the Netherlands but also referred extensively to notions
of natural and divine law.

These evolutions in political thought were echoed in other treatises
published in 1568. The *Faithful exhortation to the inhabitants of the
Netherlands against the vain and false hopes with which their oppressors amuse
them* warned the inhabitants of the Netherlands that the Spaniards
were not 'merely persecutors of God's word', but also 'enemies,
oppressors and extirpators of the privileges, liberties and franchises of
the country' and 'bloodsuckers, murderers and insatiable ravishers
of your persons and goods, however innocent and from whatever
religion you may be'.[45]

Resolutely the *Faithful exhortation* called for resistance to restore the
old freedom. It pointed out that, according to the Joyous Entry, the
subjects had the right to disobey a prince if he violated the promises
and conditions on which the inhabitants had accepted and received
him. Explicitly the *Faithful exhortation* asserted that in such cases the
inhabitants had the right to resist the prince by force. For according
to the privileges granted by Duke John IV in 1421 and 1422, the
inhabitants were 'permitted to close the gates of their towns and to
resist by force not only the servants of their prince, but also the prince
himself' if he proceeded 'by force of arms'.[46] In fact, according to the
Faithful exhortation all inhabitants were bound by their 'duty,
obligation and oath' to resist the 'oppression' of their 'liberties' and
the 'killing' of their 'persons'. It was their civic duty 'to chase away
those strangers and tyrannic invaders and common enemies of God,
the king, the fatherland and of all inhabitants'.[47]

In the summer of 1568, however, such calls for resistance were to

---

[45] *Fidelle exhortation aux inhabitants du pais bas contre les vains et faux espoirs dont leurs oppresseurs les
font amuser* (1568), 7.   [46] Ibid. 14.   [47] Ibid.

little avail. The populace of the Dutch Provinces did not rise *en masse* to join and assist William of Orange. The prince was forced to withdraw his troops from the Netherlands. Again in exile, he renewed his efforts to set up a more effective resistance movement and to organize another military campaign for what was in his view the liberation of the Netherlands. Foreign aid was crucial to the success of such plans. Thus Orange sought to consolidate his contacts with French Huguenot leaders and with German princes.

One of the attempts to enlist German support was a petition presented on 26 October 1570 to the Reichstag at Spiers, the *Libellus supplex Imperatoriae Maiestati*. The English translation, *A Defence and true Declaration of the things lately done in the lowe Countrey*, was published in 1571 by the office of John Day in London.[48] Until recently it has been assumed that the Reformed Protestant minister Peter Dathenus was the author of the *Defence*.[49] New research, however, has argued that Marnix van St Aldegonde was its author.[50]

The *Defence* offered both an account of the origins and causes of the troubles in the Netherlands and a defence of the Dutch exiles and their activities. It asserted that Europe was afflicted by the conspiracies of 'certain idle men', who under the cloak of religion tried as inquisitors to usurp civil government. For more than fifty years the inhabitants of the Netherlands had patiently endured their attempts to frustrate hope for religious freedom and to introduce 'a far more grievous tyranny', which would deprive the Dutch 'of all the residue of their right and liberty'.[51] In fact the goal was to turn the country into a kingdom, to have it, as the *Defence* put it, 'reduced into one body, and made subject to one form of laws and jurisdiction and brought to the name and title of a kingdom'. In abrogating 'the power of popular magistrates and laws' the plan was to govern the Low Countries at will 'with new laws' like 'the kingdom of Sicily and Naples, which have been acquired by conquest'.[52]

With great eagerness the conspirators sought to destroy the

---

[48] *A Defence and true Declaration of the things lately done in the lowe Countrey whereby may easily be seen to whom all the beginning and cause of the late troubles and calamities is to be imputed* (London, 1571). For a modern edn. of this treatise, see Martin van Gelderen (ed.), *The Dutch Revolt*, Cambridge texts in the history of political thought (Cambridge, 1992).

[49] See e.g. T. Ruys, *Petrus Dathenus* (Utrecht, 1919), 265–7.

[50] See D. Nauta, 'Marnix auteur van de *Libellus supplex* aan de rijksdag van Spiers (1570)', *Nederlands Archief voor Kerkgeschiedenis*, 55 (1975), 151–70. See also van Gelderen, *The Dutch Revolt*, introduction. The *Libellus supplex* was translated by Elias Newcomen (1550–1614).

[51] *Defence*, fol. xxii.   [52] Ibid., fol. A7.

privileges of the Netherlands. They had realized that the flourishing country was not only well defended militarily 'with strong towns and castles', but also with 'good laws and ordinances, and with large privileges, prerogatives, immunities and other liberties'.[53] In other words, the conspirators had acknowledged that the privileges were fundamental constitutional arrangements, whose purpose was to guarantee the country's liberty and thereby to protect and foster its prosperity.

The role of the conspirators, Granvelle being a principal exponent, was unravelled in detail in the *Defence*. Their main focus, it argued, was on the position of the States. Continuously, according to the treatise, they tried to undermine the authority of the States assemblies, for in their view 'the ancient liberty of assembly of the estates in parliaments' was a serious threat to 'the power of the prince'.[54] Following Wesembeeke, the *Defence* pointed out that in accordance with the 'most ancient usage of their forefathers' and 'the promises and covenants of the princes themselves confirmed with their oaths', the prince had no authority to undertake any action affecting the liberty of the people and the authority of the laws without 'the will and assent of the estates of the whole country'.[55] Thus, like in Orange's and Wesembeeke's treatises, the importance of the States in the political order of the Netherlands was emphasized as being 'the only stay and remedy of all mischief and public calamities'.

Given the prominence of the States, the prince was far from dominant. In fact, according to the *Defence*, the inhabitants 'more regarded the acts of the estates than the king's proclamations'; they 'esteemed the king not as a king but as some common duke or earl', who should be a 'guardian of their right and laws', and who should 'govern the commonwealth not by his own authority but after a prescribed form of laws and the ordinances of the estates'. The *Defence* asserted that 'the princes' had always 'from time to time been subject to the power of the general Parliaments' by which they were elected and confirmed and 'without whose assent and authority they never would decree anything'. This fundamental principle was enshrined in 'the privileges of Brabant and the customs of Flanders'.[56]

---

[53] Ibid., fol. A6.   [54] Ibid., fol. A7.   [55] Ibid.

[56] Ibid. At this point the Latin original referred (in the margin) to articles 3, 18 and 25 of the Joyous Entry (*Libellus supplex*, fol. 39). Article 3 of the Joyous Entry obliged the Duke of Brabant not to wage war or impose taxes without the advice and consent of the 'towns and country of Brabant', and never to harm the rights, liberties and privileges of the country and its inhabitants. Article 18 ordered the same with regard to mintage. Article 25 assured that

In underpinning the claim that the prince was bound by his contractual obligations, as laid down in the privileges, the original Latin version of the *Defence* referred to the works of the fourteenth-century commentators Bartolus of Sassoferrato and Baldus de Ubaldis. For example, reference was made to Bartolus' comment on Ulpian's rule that the conditions on which an office has been accepted must be respected,[57] and to his comment on the famous *lex omnes populi*.[58] In so doing the *Defence* made one of the first attempts to connect Dutch arguments with the European framework of Roman law.

As the *Defence* pointed out, the attack on the authority of the States had been a leading theme in the protests against the policy of the conspirators. The treatise rejected the accusations that these protests had been unlawful. It reiterated the view that the Joyous Entry granted the inhabitants of Brabant a right of petition and referred to its clause of disobedience. As the *Defence* acknowledged, in spite of their great patience and humility, eventually the inhabitants, seeing 'neither public liberty, nor their wives' chastity, nor their consciences' tranquillity, nor their own lives safely defended from violence',[59] had resorted to armed resistance and as such could be accused of rebellion.

However, so the *Defence* argued, any accusation of this sort should take the horrors of the new tyranny into account. At this point the blame was put directly on the shoulders of Philip II. For even if those who had resorted to armed resistance were rebels, the treatise asked, was it therefore 'lawful for the king to violate his faithful promise, to pervert the laws of both God and man, and to pollute all things both holy and profane with this unaccustomed tyranny?'.[60]

The *Defence* was a powerful reformulation of views which had been articulated during the 1560s, claiming that the foundation of the Dutch political order was a trinity of liberty as the crucial political value, with privileges as the constitutional guarantees of liberty, and the States as the guardians of the privileges.

In comparison with the treatises of the 1560s the analysis of the authority of the States and the relationship between States and prince was expanded radically, leading to the conclusion that in

someone who had harmed the country and its inhabitants, or had assisted their enemy, could not be pardoned without the consent of Brabant's estates.
[57] Digest, book 50, title 6, para. 2.   [58] Digest, book 1, title 1, para. 9.
[59] *Defence*, fol. E8.   [60] Ibid., fol. G2.

general, and therefore by implication also in the political order of the Netherlands, the prince should be regarded as 'subject' to the power of the States.

The account of the motives to resort to armed resistance was also novel. Although the importance of religion was not played down and the *Defence* presented an urgent call for freedom of conscience and religion,[61] the armed resistance was primarily presented as a defence of the liberty of the country and its inhabitants against the attempts to turn the Netherlands into a kingdom, depriving it of privileges and freedom. From this perspective the Dutch Revolt was above all a fight for liberty.

Finally, the *Defence* was among the first openly to hold Philip II himself responsible for the troubles and tyranny afflicting the Netherlands. Others still hesitated greatly to express such views in public. Thus another treatise, published in 1571, presented Alva's tyranny as a deliberate attempt by the Pope 'to subtly rob the king of the Netherlands and to bring them under his slavery'.[62] It was 'unbelievable' that the king had consciously commissioned Alva 'to murder his good and faithful vassals and subjects', which the king had called 'my faithful Flemings'.[63] After all, Philip himself had called the Low Countries 'Tierra de Libertad'.

4.5. THE REVOLT OF HOLLAND AND ZEELAND, 1572–1576

In 1572 the provinces of Holland and Zeeland unexpectedly, and to a certain extent reluctantly, became the centre of the Revolt, especially after Orange was forced to withdraw to Holland, thinking he was to find his grave in the province of water, dikes and towns. Yet part of Holland was retained as a stronghold of the Revolt and in the summer of 1572, with Orange acclaimed Stadtholder, a policy for the new course was set out by the provincial States. In the instructions for Marnix van St Aldegonde, who attended the first 'free' meeting of the States of Holland in July 1572 as Orange's deputy, a programme for political action was articulated. One of the principal objectives was to re-establish 'in their old form and full vigour all the old privileges, rights and usages' and to restore 'the power, authority

---

[61] Ibid., fol. H5.
[62] *Bewijsinghe dat die commissie die Ducq Dalve als Capiteyn Generael over de Nederlanden heeft laten uutgaen, By den Paus met zijn tyrannighe adherenten op den naem vanden Coninck onwetelijcken versiert, gedicht ende hem verleden is* (1571), fol. A4.   [63] Ibid., fol. B3.

and reputation of the States to their former condition in accordance with the privileges and rights which the king has sworn to maintain'.[64]

In two missives, both published at the end of 1573, the States of Holland addressed themselves to the States General of the provinces still under Alva's authority, which had been convoked by the duke. Unequivocally the States of Holland urged the necessity for concord between the provinces. Taking the history of Rome as an example, they argued that the provinces should unite to 'resist the common enemies', in order 'to chase them away...and to re-establish the Countries in their old flower, prosperity and power, in which because of good concord they have stood so long'.[65]

The States of the provinces under Alva's control were urged to accept their special responsibility in this respect. In expressing their point of view on this point the States of Holland extensively circumscribed the position and authority of the States, and the States General in particular. It was pointed out that in the Netherlands a prince only became lord of the country after the States General, 'in the name of the towns and the whole community', had accepted him on the condition that he would observe and maintain the privileges of the country. The States of Holland asserted that the States General were elected to see to this and to guard the country's liberty and privileges against anyone who tried to violate them. As the States of Holland put it to the States General: 'You are the States of the country; which is to say, the upholders and protectors of its liberty and of its privileges; it is your bounden duty by God and all people to defend and to maintain them.'[66]

In another missive Orange and the States of Holland and Zeeland pointed out to Philip II himself that the maintenance of the freedoms, rights and privileges had always been the essence of the government of the Low Countries. Before the prince was 'accepted' and 'acknowledged' as 'overlord of the Countries' he had to take a solemn oath to maintain the Countries in 'their rights and freedoms'. This oath of inauguration, Orange and the States asserted, was the

---

[64] 'Instructions and advice for the honourable Philip Marnix, lord of St. Aldegonde...', in Kossmann and Mellink (eds.), *Texts concerning the revolt of the Netherlands*, 99.

[65] *Copie eens sendtbriefs der Ridderschap, Edelen, ende Steden van Hollandt...aen...die Staten vanden Landen van Herwaerts overe. Hen vermanende, om eendrachtelick ten dienste vande Coninklicke Maiesteyt, die Landen te helpen brenghen in haren ghewoonlicken voorspoet ende vryheyt* (Dordrecht, 1573), fol. A2.   [66] Ibid.

'sole and right foundation on which both the power and authority of the prince as the loyalty and obedience of the subjects is grounded'.[67]

This form of government had brought the Netherlands concord and prosperity and had greatly contributed to the honour of their princes. However, due to the 'hate and envy' of a number of people around the king, who themselves aspired to 'highness', the countries recently suffered from aggravating troubles. Under the pretext of religion and by means of the Inquisition these ambitious men had sought to bring the Netherlands under their 'rule and dominance'. This of course was a highly familiar claim in the treatises of those who urged resistance. The missives supported this claim with yet another historical account of the mischief committed by the villains and the tyranny as set up by the Duke of Alva. Never before, it was argued, had such 'atrocious injustices, great outrages and wilful wantonness' been committed. Therefore, Orange and the States asserted, they had 'been forced from sheer necessity to take up arms to try with all possible means to free our poor oppressed fatherland from such a gruesome tyranny'.[68] Orange and the States preferred 'to die an honest death for the liberty and the welfare of our fatherland' rather than become 'the soles of some wilful strangers'. Thus once again the fight for liberty, both religious and civil, was presented as the heart and soul of the resistance against Alva's audacious tyranny.[69] As Orange and the States put it, 'we fight for freedom of conscience, for the freedom of our wives and children, of our good and blood'.

The missives of the States closely followed, both in their language and the structure of their arguments and in the arguments themselves, the set of ideas as developed previously in the protests of 1566, in Orange's and Wesembeeke's treatises of 1568 and in the 1570 *Defence*. Rather striking was the strong emphasis on the representative character of the States, now claimed to be elected by the towns and the community they represented to uphold and maintain liberty and supervise the maintenance of the privileges and freedoms by the prince, as promised and solemnly sworn in the oath of inauguration. Moreover, it was now explicitly argued that the States accepted the prince as ruler in the name of the community they represented, on condition that he would observe the privileges. This condition

---

[67] *Sendbrief in forme van supplicatie aen de Conincklijcke Maiesteyt van Spaengien: van wegen des Princen van Oraengien, der Staten van Holland ende Zeeland, mitsgaders alle andere zijne getrouwe ondersaten van desen Nederlanden...* (Delft, 1573), fol. A3.   **[68]** Ibid.

[69] For a similar conclusion see A. C. J. de Vrankrijker, *De motiveering van onzen opstand* (Nijmegen, 1933), 92.

formed the essence of his oath of inauguration, the formal sealing of the acceptance of a prince by the States and the sole foundation on which both the authority of the ruler and the obedience of the subjects was based. Thus substance was given to the contract between prince and subjects; a contractual conception was elaborated whose beginnings can be discerned in the political writings of 1566.

With regard to the justification of the resistance against Alva's tyranny the 1573 missives did not make innovative moves. They reiterated the familiar view that there was a right of disobedience based on the privileges. More radical, though still familiar, views on this point were expressed by Willem Bardesius, an Amsterdam exile, when he tried to persuade an admiral to choose the side of the revolt. Bardesius reaffirmed, on the basis of the Joyous Entry of Brabant, the notion of a civic duty of resistance. He argued that, once the mutual covenant between prince and subjects had been broken by the prince, the subjects were released from the contractual obligation to obey. In fact every subject was 'obliged, everyone in his own quality, to oppose himself against this, until such a misleading and abusing king and prince does his proper duty and office again'.[70] In a similar vein a treatise published in 1573 called upon all citizens to take 'good courage' to 'stand for the fatherland until the very end'. In expressing this call the treatise reaffirmed that there was an intrinsic connection between the liberty of the country and the personal welfare of its inhabitants. It urged the citizens 'to boldly protect and defend' their 'wives and children' against the 'blood-sucking enemies' and to restore 'all concord' so that the 'liberty and privileges' as 'received from our ancestors' could be left 'to our children and our children's children'.[71]

The conception of the Dutch political order as based on the trinity of liberty, privileges and States was further elaborated in 1574 on the occasion of the peace negotiations between Holland and Zeeland and the new Spanish governor Requesens. The principal demands of Holland and Zeeland during the negotiations at Breda were the withdrawal of all foreigners from the country and the convocation of the States General. The States should be allowed 'to advise and decide freely' on the proper policy for 'the conservation of a sound

---

[70] Pieter Christiansz Bor (ed.), *Oorsprongk, begin en vervolgh der Nederlantsche oorlogen, beroerten en borgerlijke oneenigheden*, i (Amsterdam, 1679; first pub. 1595), 405.

[71] *Antwoorde ende waerachtighe onderrichtinghe op eenen brief nu onlancx onder den name des Hertoghen van Alba, by forme van pardoen aen die van Aemstelredamme gheschreven...* (Delft, 1573), unpaginated.

peace, quiet and unity of the provinces', leading to 'the reinstatement of the trampled privileges, justices and laudable customs',[72] as it was formulated in one of the treatises published in response to the negotiations.

As the Breda negotiations failed, a powerful justification of Holland and Zeeland was published in a collection of documents called *Certaine letters wherein is set forth a Discourse of the peace that was attempted and sought to have bin put in effecte by the Lords and States of Holland and Zelande in ... 1574.*[73]

The main part of this collection was the *Discourse* written by Johan Junius de Jonghe. Junius was Governor of Veere in Zeeland and a counsellor to William of Orange. In 1579 he became mayor and alderman of Antwerp. During the 1580s he was a member of the Council of State and fulfilled a number of diplomatic missions for the United Provinces. Junius travelled widely through Europe and was acquainted with leading German and French protestants. It has been argued that he was the author of the *Vindiciae contra tyrannos*, traditionally regarded as the highlight of Huguenot political thought.[74]

The *Discourse* contained a radical analysis of the position of the prince in the political order. Junius boldly suggested that a prince was 'made' by the people, for, as he put it, 'a prince without his subjects is no prince'.[75] Reiterating a familiar view, Junius claimed that the task of the prince was to administer justice in accordance with the sworn contracts and bound by the liberties and privileges of the country. He pointed out that in this respect the prince was checked by the States. It was the 'oath and duty' of the States to seek 'by all industry ... the maintenance of the good and lawful rights, contracts and liberties'.[76] In discussing the position and authority of the States, Junius asserted that these assemblies were more than mere guardians of the liberties and privileges of the country. They were

---

[72] *Cort ende warachtich verhael, van het gene dat op de handelinge vanden Vrede nu coreelinghe tusschen den Prince van Oranegien, met die Staten van Hollandt ande Zeelandt ... aen de eene zyde: Ende die Spaensche Gouverneure der Nederlanden met den synen aen de andere zijde, to Breda geschiet is* (1575), 23.

[73] The original Dutch version was *Sekere brieven waer inne den aenghevanghen vredehandel deses Jaers LXXIIII vervaetet is* (Delft, 1574). The Dutch version also included the *Discourse* of Junius. Refs. are to the 1576 English trans.

[74] See D. Visser, 'Junius: the author of the *Vindiciae contra tyrannos*', *TvG* 84 (1971), 510–25. Visser contends that Junius is 'the most likely candidate' for the authorship of the *Vindiciae*. He does not, however, give any clear or final proof; his argument is more suggestive and hypothetical in character.   [75] Junius, *Discourse*, in *Certaine letters*, 49.

[76] Ibid. 8.

'the chief and principal heads of the people, representing the body of the multitude'[77] upon which both the legitimate authority of the prince and the prosperity of the country rested. As the governor of Veere explained, the 'true and legitimate power and dignity of all kings, monarchies and emperors, and the greatest unity of all people and provinces' did 'especially consist and principally depend upon the assembly of estates'.[78] The assembly of the States was comparable to an ecclesiastical Concilium as it was 'certain, that where as many assemble together and consult (whether it be for the affairs of the commonwealth or of the church of God) ordinarily God himself is president', sending 'his good spirit, lightening most commonly the eyes of a number in such cases, as peradventure one alone or a few cannot discern a whit'.[79] Therefore, as the ancestors had ordained, the prince should be 'very straightly bound and united with the estates of the country'. He should not do 'anything of importance without communicating the matter unto them first'.[80]

Junius espoused the idea that the Revolt had been caused by the attempts of some who were 'most studious of their own particular profit' to 'make themselves masters of His Majesty's country and subjects'.[81] A supplication of the States of Holland, also included in the collection, pointed out to Philip II that the 'poor subjects' had been 'forced against their will' to resort to armed resistance in order to preserve their 'privileges, rights, ancient customs, and allowed liberties'.[82]

As Junius explained, following traditional argumentation, the States had been fully entitled to take up arms against Alva's tyranny. Junius too referred to the Joyous Entry, pointing out that its clause of disobedience relieved everyone of his duty of obedience if the prince no longer observed the privileges. Moreover, at his entry and acceptance the king had declared that officers should be taken 'for ciphers, and of no validity' if they violated the articles of the Joyous Entry. Therefore, the king himself put weapons into the 'hands' of his subjects to resist the tyranny of Alva and his followers.

Though in a less systematic way, other treatises published in 1574 expressed views very close to the interpretation of the Dutch political order and the ideas concerning political resistance as expounded in Junius' *Discourse*. The *Truthful warning against the absolute grace and general pardon by Don Loys de Requesens*, for example, also emphasized

[77] Ibid. 62.   [78] Ibid. 78.   [79] Ibid.   [80] Ibid. 63.   [81] Ibid. 20.
[82] Ibid. 26.

the political importance of the States. Like Junius' *Discourse* it claimed that in the Netherlands the prince could take no decision without the advice and consent of the States. As Wesembeeke had already argued in 1568, the *Truthful warning* claimed that this principle was enshrined in the privileges. It referred explicitly to the oath of Philip II and to the Joyous Entry, where the king had promised 'not to do anything which might affect the country, but by advice, will and consent of the States'.[83]

In this context the *Truthful warning* pointed out how crucial it was to maintain privileges like the Joyous Entry, for, and here again a familiar point was made, they were the guarantees of the country's liberty and just government. According to the treatise the 'ancestors' should be praised 'highly' for 'having maintained these laudable customs and laws'. The Dutch should 'do the utmost' to keep the privileges maintained henceforward if they wanted 'to be free, and no slaves', 'to be governed with right and justice' instead of with 'violence and tyranny'.[84]

Thus once again the intrinsic connection between the maintenance of the privileges and the preservation of liberty was underlined. On this point the 1574 treatises mainly reiterated familiar arguments presenting the privileges as the constitutional guarantees for freedom and just government. In their analysis of the role and authority of the States, too, the 1574 treatises were on familiar ground. The States were once again depicted as the guardians of the liberties and privileges and it was argued that for this reason they were entitled to disobey a prince who violated the privileges and liberties and, in fact, were obliged to take up arms against Alva and Requesens, who, according to the very privileges they trampled, should be held as nothing but 'ciphers'. With this move Alva and his followers were deprived of any legitimate authority. By implication it seemed to suggest that to resist their tyranny was to resist barbarous private persons. At this point the legitimization of resistance as based on Roman-law notions of private law was probably influential.

In line with the arguments of Wesembeeke, the *Defence* and the 1573 missives of the States of Holland and Zeeland, the 1574 treatises argued that all political matters touching the country had to be settled by the prince in co-operation with the States. This claim was

---

[83] *Warachtighe waerschouwinghe teghens de absolute gratie ende generael pardoen by Don Loys de Requesens* (Dordrecht, 1574), fol. B5, with specific reference to articles 3, 17 and 25 of the Joyous Entry.
[84] Ibid.

built upon a familiar appeal to the constitutional framework of the Low Countries, and again specific reference was made to the Joyous Entry of Brabant. In itself this was remarkable. Whereas up to 1572 the literature of the Revolt concentrated strongly on Brabant, now, reflecting the changes in the political situation, Holland had become the centre of ideological activity. None the less, the arguments continued to be Brabantine in spirit.[85]

In addition, the defence of the authority of the States was based on a more general reflection on the character of politics, exemplified by Junius' *Discourse*. Elaborating the ideas of the *Defence*, Junius asserted that the legitimate authority, the unity and prosperity of a country, consisted in and depended on the assembly of the States. In short, next only to the maintenance of the privileges and liberties, the assemblies of the States were essential for the liberty, prosperity and just government of the country.

4.6. FROM REVOLT TO ABJURATION, 1576–1581

The views on the role of the States, as articulated by Junius and the States of Holland, were unacceptable for Requesens, which partly explained the failure of the Breda negotiations.

The sudden death of the governor in 1576, however, created room for political initiatives and change. With eagerness these opportunities were seized by the States of Brabant and Hainaut. At their initiative the States General were convened and negotiations were opened with Holland and Zeeland.

In this situation the *Address and opening to make a good, blessed and general peace in the Netherlands* was written.[86] The purpose of the author was to persuade the States General to open negotiations with Holland and Zeeland, in order to re-establish peace, privileges and (therefore) prosperity. This appeal was followed by an elaborate

---

[85] If not in letter. Junius, for example, came from Brabant. None the less, it was remarkable that arguments based on Brabant's Joyous Entry were, without discussion, applied to other provinces. Apparently the principles counted, not their provincial origins.

[86] *Vertoog ende openinghe om een goede, salighe ende generale vrede te maken in dese Nederlanden ...* (1576). As the treatise referred to the ongoing siege of Zierikzee, it must have been written between 5 Mar. 1576 (the death of Requesens) and 2 July 1576 (the day Zierikzee surrendered). For a modern edn. of the *Address*, see van Gelderen, *The Dutch Revolt*. Van Schelven, 'De opkomst van de idee der politieke tolerantie', 361, mentions (without giving any evidence) Philippe Duplessis-Mornay as the author of this treatise. I have not been able to check this proposition. Considering the detailed knowledge of the privileges of Brabant as displayed by the author of the *Address*, it seems at least unlikely that the Frenchman Duplessis-Mornay was the (sole) author.

exposition of the nature of politics, and of Dutch politics in particular, which put full emphasis on the position of the States within the political order.

In line with previous views, the *Address* asserted that the lord of the country had received his 'highness' on certain conditions, limiting his power. This was in accordance with divine ordination, for not only did all power come from God, God had also 'enclosed all power within limits and decided and willed that everyone remains within the limits of the vocation to which he was called'.[87]

So far the *Address* essentially reformulated the familiar conception of the political order as based on liberty, privileges and States. Moving beyond previous formulations, the *Address* asserted that, as the privileges and the contracts between prince and States and indeed God's word itself clarified, the Netherlands had 'never been governed by way of an absolute monarchy or kingdom, where the lord of the country would have been allowed to steer the matters of the country at will, without minding its laws or rights'. The Low Countries had 'always been steered and upheld, with right and justice, by way of a Republic or civil policy'.[88]

In this republic, so the treatise asserted, the prince, though present, was no more but 'a servant and professor of the rights and laws', who only became lord of the country after he had been accepted by the States. Being 'elected from the whole generality... to represent the entire corps', the States had the right and principal duty of protecting and upholding the liberties and privileges of the country and the common peace and unity with 'power and force' against anyone who tried to violate them, even if it was the lord of the country himself.

In supporting this claim the *Address* offered a detailed analysis of a long list of late medieval charters and alliances amongst the towns of Brabant, such as the first main alliance between the Brabant towns in 1261, the 1312 Charter of Kortenberg, the 1339 treaty affirming the unity between Brabant and Flanders, the Joyous Entry of 1356 and the 1421 New Regiment. The main purpose was to make clear that at crucial historical moments the towns, those of Brabant in particular, had shaped the political order and were fully entitled to do so. In this way a powerful constitutional argument was made for the political power and the right of resistance of the States. On the basis of 'all authentic and credible accounts, letters and charters' the *Address* concluded that it was the 'office and bounden duty of the

---

[87] *Vertoog*, fol. A5.   [88] Ibid.

States to use their authority, name and power in the public questions and matters affecting the country and community in order to bring the country peace and concord and to ordain, decide and do what serves the country's common good'.[89]

Thus if a prince had violated the limits of his power as indicated by the privileges and liberties, as Philip II clearly had done, the States were entitled to disobey and to replace him by a so-called *ruwaard*, a regent, until the prince repaired his ways.[90]

The *Address* not only elaborated the constitutional argument for the States' power and right of resistance. It also went beyond previous formulations by offering a more general reflection on the nature of the political order, resulting in the conclusion that, as a general political principle as well, it was fundamentally mistaken to discard any right of resistance.

Princes, the *Address* asserted, 'ought to stand under the laws'. They had been established to govern in accordance with the laws and rights of the community, whose 'welfare and bliss' was the 'supreme law' of politics. The community, so the treatise emphasized with a classic formulation, was not created for the sake of the princes, 'but they for the sake of the community'.[91] Therefore, if the prince forsook his duty and oath and sought to govern the country at will, it was 'better to fall into disgrace with a prince' who acted as a tyrant than to 'spoil, against right and reason, his own fatherland and to incur the curse of the oppressed community and the wrath of God'.[92] In the case of tyranny the higher cause of the common good simply commanded resistance.

In short, the *Address* not only offered a refined example of the constitutional argument that the Dutch political order was built on liberty, privileges and the States, carrying it to the conclusion that the Netherlands were no monarchy, but a republic. In addition, the treatise made the important move of defending the right of resistance on behalf of the States as a fundamental principle of the art of politics, whose principal aim was to serve the common good of the *res publica*. For these reasons the *Address* should be regarded as an important moment in the development of the political thought of the Dutch Revolt.

The *Address* was certainly not the only treatise to urge the provinces which had been under Alva's and Requesens' rule to conclude peace

---

[89] Ibid., fol. B3.
[90] As usual the last claim was made with reference to the 1421 New Regiment.
[91] *Vertoog*, fol. C4.　　　　　　　　　　[92] Ibid.

with Holland and Zeeland. For the purpose William of Orange and the States of Holland themselves put up a campaign of letters and pamphlets. Missives were addressed, for example, to the States of Guelders, to Utrecht and to Amsterdam.

Unequivocally these treatises urged the addressees to change sides in order 'to release the country of the foreign Spanish tyranny and to bring it again in its old liberty, trade and prosperity',[93] as it was formulated in a missive of the States of Holland to the government and civic militia of Amsterdam. Orange and the States of Holland emphasized that everyone had the duty to free the country from tyranny and to restore the privileges. As Orange put it in an address to the States of Guelders, everyone who wanted 'to be taken for a truthful lover of his fatherland and for an upholder of the legal freedoms of our ancestors, should, because of his bounden duty... use all possible diligence, labour and industry', for the liberation of the 'dear fatherland... from this unbearable Spanish yoke'.[94]

In the missive to Amsterdam the States likewise asserted that the protection of freedom, trade and welfare 'ought to be observed with diligence by each one in accordance with his profession and possibilities'.[95]

In this missive the States acknowledged 'that in religion there may be some diversity and distinction' between themselves and those of Amsterdam, who had remained loyal to Philip and Roman Catholicism. This was, however, 'no reason to remain in discord and difference in the common sake of the country regarding the policy, freedom, justice and welfare of the Countries'. At this point the States denied having taken up arms for religious reasons. In fact the States gave assurance that they had resorted to armed resistance not because of religion, but because the freedom and welfare of the fatherland were at stake.[96]

Thus while reasserting the familiar view that it was a civic duty to uphold and protect the countries' freedoms and to fight for their liberty, justice and welfare, the States made the important move of explicitly denying having resorted to arms out of religious motivations. Unequivocally the Dutch Revolt was presented as a political fight for justice, welfare and liberty.

Of course 1576 was not just a year of ideological innovation. The

---

[93] *Sendtbrieven bijde Ridderschappen, Edelen ende Steden van Hollandt, representerende den Staten vanden selven Lande, laestgheschreven ende ghesonden aenden burghermeesteren en regeerders van Amsterdam...* (Delft, 1577), fol. A3.   [94] Bor, *Oorsprongk der Nederlantsche oorlogen*, i. 702.
[95] *Sendtbrieven bijde Ridderschappen*, fol. A3.   [96] Ibid.

intellectual developments in the political thought on resistance, and on the character of the Dutch political order in general, coincided with major political events. With the Pacification of Ghent essential elements of the political programme as presented in the *Address* and the missives of Orange and the States seemed to be realized. All foreigners should be expelled from the country, the privileges were to be reinstated and all other problems, including the religious issue, should be settled by the States General.

Although the temporary reconciliation between the States General and Don Juan bore evidence of the fragility of the Pacification, Don Juan's misconduct restored, at least for the time being, the unity amongst the provinces. War was resumed. This time Holland and Zeeland were not alone in taking up arms. The States General as a whole resorted to armed resistance.

In the autumn of 1577, at the instigation of the States General, Marnix van St Aldegonde published a *Short discourse* to explain why the States were forced and entitled to do so.[97] In this important treatise, Aldegonde elaborated the constitutional arguments as developed by the *Defence*, Junius' *Discourse* and the *Address*. Just as Granvelle and Alva had been, Don Juan was accused of having violated the privileges and his agreement with the States General, of trying to sow discord and of having intended from the very start to wage war in the Netherlands to 'purify' the country. Therefore, the States had been forced to take up arms against him. For the States were 'called by God and men to be the protectors of the privileges, rights and liberties of the common people', of whom they represented 'the body by the three estates of clergy, nobles and towns'.[98] As such, the States had taken an oath to protect 'the common people'. By the same token, having received the king's and also Don Juan's oath, it was their duty to see that these were not broken. If the prince abused his power and violated the privileges, the States, according to Aldegonde, were 'bound to oppose him with force'. Restating on behalf of the States the by now familiar claim to the right of resistance, Aldegonde asserted that they were entitled to refuse the prince 'every obedience and to choose a new governor in government until the committed faults had been repaired', and Aldegonde too referred to 'the privileges of the country and the examples set by the forefathers in conformity with written law'.[99]

---

[97] Marnix van St Aldegonde, *Cort Verhael vande rechte oorsaecken ende redenen die de Generale Staten ghedwongen hebben, hen te versiene tot hunder beschermenisse, teghen den Heer Don Jehan van Oostenrijck,* (Antwerp, 1577).   [98] Ibid. 55.   [99] Ibid. 56.

And so the States did. On 8 December 1577 Archduke Matthias of Austria, a member of the Austrian wing of the Habsburg dynasty, was accepted by the States General as Governor. The articles of the acceptance largely corresponded with the ideas as formulated by those treatises which had characterized the Dutch political order as based on the constitutional trinity of liberty, privileges and States. Thus Matthias was to govern the country in co-operation with a Council of State, nominated by the States General. Moreover, in accordance with what was held to be a key principle of Dutch politics, Governor and councillors could not take 'any decision on important matters concerning public affairs such as requests for or levying of money, declaration of war or conclusion of peace, alliances and confederacies with foreign princes or Countries and other such matters without the permission and approval of the States General'.[100]

The last article contained a revolutionary radicalization of the Joyous Entry clause of disobedience. The States declared that if Matthias, having accepted the articles of acceptance, 'came to infringe any of these conditions', they were 'entitled, if after admonition he should not want to correct the infringement, to take up arms for their lawful protection against the lord Archduke or others'.[101]

At his Joyous Entry into Brussels, which, as the Brussels poet Jean Baptist Houwaert wrote in his account of the event, followed Roman traditions, Matthias was welcomed as the Roman hero Scipio, whose task was to protect the Netherlands 'and free [it] from that highly unjust and unbearable oppression of Don Juan and his adherents and also to maintain us in our liberties, rights and privileges, which we have received from our ancestors'.[102] For the occasion twenty-four stages had been erected devoted to the presentation of classical virtues such as truth, justice, diligence, constancy, faithfulness, temperance, liberality, clemency and modesty. Matthias and Orange, who was appointed Stadtholder-General, took the oath which included the reformulated clause of disobedience. The right of resistance was now enshrined in the Joyous Entry.

---

[100] Bor, *Oorsprongk der Nederlantsche oorlogen*, 927. See also *Articulen ende puncten, geconcipieert bij die generale Staten, waer op ... Matthias ... van Oostenrijck aengenomen is voor Gouverneur over dese Nederlanden* (Leeuwarden, 1578) and Kossmann and Mellink (eds.), *Texts concerning the revolt of the Netherlands*, 141–5.   [101] Bor, *Oorsprongk der Nederlantsche oorlogen*, 929.
[102] Jean Baptist Houwaert, *Sommaire bechrijvinghe van de triumpelijcke incomst vanden ... Aerts-hertoge Matthias binnen ... Brussel* (Antwerp, 1578), 7.

The appointment of Matthias, a gross subversion of the authority of Philip II, was defended by Marnix van St Aldegonde in a *Oration* for the Reichstag at Worms on 7 May 1578, published in the same year.[103] Plantin also printed a rhetorical version of the *Oration*, composed by Houwaert.[104]

An important part of the *Oration* was devoted to yet another historical account which presented the Dutch as most faithful subjects, who out of loyalty to Philip II had endured the mischief committed by his governors with 'exceptional patience and moderation'. Once again the picture was invoked of Alva's horrifying tyranny and Aldegonde expounded how Don Juan had sought nothing but the ruin of the country, how he had trampled the privileges, had forsaken his oath and finally had brought the country back to war. Aldegonde argued that such had constrained the States to take up arms. This time, however, he invoked the 'law of nature', which had 'imprinted in the hearts of all animals the charge and care of their survival and health'.[105] It was remarkable that at this point the rhetorical translation of Houwaert, diverging from the original oration, explicitly connected the law of nature with the maintenance of the privileges, as it pointed out that the States had 'found in the law of nature that they should not let their privileges be diminished nor their land or good be hindered'[106] and had therefore taken up arms.

Not that Aldegonde neglected the privileges. On the contrary, in defending the revolutionary appointment of Matthias, Aldegonde argued that the States were fully entitled to take such measures. The privileges of Brabant gave the States (and every individual citizen) the right to disobey not only a governor, 'but also the prince himself' if he violated the privileges. Moreover, if someone such as Don Juan, being appointed 'in the government of the country in the name of the prince', violated the 'aforesaid privileges', he was, so Aldegonde explained, 'because of that fact declared abrogated of his government and dignity'.[107] Aldegonde pointed out, and he was one of the few to do so, that this right not only pertained to Brabant but, and here

[103] Marnix van St Aldegonde, *Oraison des ambassadeurs du serenissime prince Matthias archiduc d'austriche &c. Gouverneur des pais bas: & des Estats generaux desdits pais* (Antwerp, 1578).

[104] Jean Baptist Houwaert, *Oratie der Ambassadeuren vanden doorluchtighen Prince Matthias Aertshertoge van Oostenrijck, etc. Gouverneur van die Nederlanden* (Antwerp, 1578).

[105] Aldegonde, *Oraison*, fol. E1.   [106] Houwaert, *Oratie*, 53.

[107] Aldegonde, *Oraison*, fol. E3.

Aldegonde referred to the 1477 Grand Privilege, 'by public treaty and covenant was made common and universal to all the Netherlands' during the reign of 'la Serenissime Marie'.[108]

As the *Oration* made perfectly clear, the States General were not willing to return to the situation as it had been under Charles V, a proposal which had made upheaval amongst those pleading for a reconciliation with Philip II and which eventually would be accepted by Hainaut and Artois. For although, as Aldegonde acknowledged, 'the *res publica* had been governed well during the time of Charles V', the times had changed dramatically.

This view was endorsed by Elbertus Leoninus, the author of the *True answer to the open letters and treacherous persuasions of Don Juan of Austria*,[109] a treatise which responded to certain letters of Philip II's governor, portraying him as a harsh exponent of Spanish tyranny. Leoninus, a professor of law at the University of Louvain, explained it had never been the intention of the States General to bring the country back to the situation as it had been under Charles V. Between the Pacification of Ghent, still cherished as the basis for peace and concord, and the government of Charles V the difference was great, and in this context Leoninus pointed in particular to Charles V's placards concerning heresy, which were suspended by the Pacification.

The Pacification was also central to the argument of the *Discourse containing a true understanding of the Pacification of Ghent, of the union of the States and other treaties with regard to religion*, which presented another meticulous defence of the actions of the States General. This important treatise reasserted the view that the protection of the 'common liberty' was the principal objective of the States. The principal aim of the armed resistance had been 'no other but to defend the liberty of the fatherland, to free oneself of servitude, to reform all the abuses and orders which, under the shadow of the religion and the authority of His Majesty, held the States and the whole country in bridles, in sum to redress everything that is against liberty, under whatever title it may have been introduced, be it religion, the authority of His Majesty or whatever else'.[110]

---

[108] Ibid.

[109] Elbertus Leoninus, *Waerachtighe antwoorde op de opene brieven ende bedrieghelicke persuasien van don Jan van Oostenryck...* (Antwerp, 1578). On Leoninus' authorship see Geurts, *De Nederlandse Opstand in de pamfletten*, 74.

[110] *Discours contenant le vray entendement de la Pacification de Gand, de l'union des Estats & aultres traictez y enzuyviz touchant le fait de la Religion* (1579), 23.

This popular view was also propounded by the *Short narration on some facts of the States General of the Netherlands*, which reasserted that the States always had sought to preserve the 'liberty, rights and privileges of the country'.[111] In this treatise the States, and the States General in particular, were once again characterized as representative institutions. The States were the 'deputies' of the 'clergy, nobles and the countries and towns', 'being sent and authorized by them after the power which each...has pleased to yield'.[112] Following this definition, the States General did not have 'full power to order and attend to the affairs of the country, as necessity demands'. As deputies the States General could only act after the 'order and ordained power' they had received from the countries, towns, clergy and nobles they represented.

The protection of liberty and the position and authority of the States were dominant themes in the literature commenting on the 1579 Cologne peace negotiations. In particular, the articles proposed by the mediating party, the commissioners of the German emperor, gave rise to strong debate.[113] Essentially the peace proposals promised a return to the old state of government, with Philip II respecting the privileges and liberties of the country and accepting the Pacification of Ghent and the Eternal Edict, and with the States making restitution of the proper authority and obedience to Philip. With regard to the religious issue the proposals contained few concessions to the protestants, who at most were offered some sanctuaries in Holland and Zeeland. In general the maintenance of the Roman Catholic religion was stressed.

The great majority of the treatises commenting on the peace proposals adopted a strongly negative attitude.[114] A principal

---

[111] *Cort Verhael, op eenighe feyten, der generale Staten van den Nederlanden* (1579), fol. 4.

[112] Ibid., fol. 3.

[113] The peace proposals were published in 1579. See *Artikelen des pays vanden Nederlanden, by den Eerwerdichsten, Doorluchtichsten, Doorluchtighen, ende Welgeboren heeren Commissarizzen der Keyserlicke Mayesteyt geconcipeert, ende beyde partyen den 18. Julij gecommuniceert* (Cologne, 1579). In the same year a collection of documents was published under the title *Brieven der Keurvorsten, die te Cuelen versamelt zijn om den Peys vande Nederlanden te maken* (Antwerp, 1579). In 1580 Aggaeus van Albada, the principal spokesman of the States General, published the complete acts of the peace negotiations, followed in 1581 by a richly annotated version (see 153–7).

[114] See e.g. *Protest van de christelijcke ghemeynte binnen Antwerpen, toeghedaen der Confessien van Ausborch op de articulen vande pacificatie van Nederlant, ghemaeckt tot Cuelen der xviij. Julij* (Antwerp, 1579) and *Sommiere verclaringhe vande sware perikelen en miserien die den inghesetenen van dese Nederlanden te verwachten soude hebben soo verre het concept vande artikelen ende conditien van de pacificatie tot Coelen uytgegeven, ende voorts al omme in dese landen gestroyt, gevolcht ende aengenomen worde* (Leiden, 1579). An exception was the *Grondelycke onderrichtinghe aen de gemeene*

example was the *Clear presentation and report on the articles and conditions recently proposed by the electors, princes and other imperial deputies in the peace negotiations at Cologne*, which argued that the peace proposals were nothing but an attempt to sow discord amongst the provinces and to disarm them so that they could be brought 'under the yoke, slavery and absolute tyrannic government of the Spaniards'.[115] The treatise plainly rejected the proposal to re-establish Philip II as lord of the Dutch Provinces in agreement with the 'accords and treaties' by which he had been accepted as 'lord and protector'. Referring to the abuses of the recent past, which had violated the contracts of inauguration and the privileges of the country and had made the government more like 'a tyranny than a lawful government', the treatise concluded that the country should not be re-established in its old state of government, as it had been under Charles V.

According to the *Clear presentation* the peace proposals formed a direct threat to the personal liberty and welfare of the inhabitants as they proposed to put 'their body and good, wives and children' at the mercy of the Spaniards, as if the country had been conquered. With references to the massacres in South America and the fate of Naples and Milan, the treatise stated such could only lead to a state of utter deprivation.

Strongly the *Clear presentation* urged the inhabitants to resistance. The individual citizen should prefer to 'die an honest death to the defence of his fatherland and preservation of his good, wife, children and offspring than to wait all days and from hour to hour to be led to death as a sheep'.[116]

The interpretation of the political order of the Netherlands as expounded in the *Clear presentation* contained many elements of the vision of the Netherlands based on the constitutional trinity of liberty, privileges and States, as developed by Wesembeeke, the *Defence*, Junius, the *Address* and Aldegonde. In this respect the *Clear presentation* was no exception amongst the treatises rejecting the peace proposals. Another fine example was the *Good warning for the citizens and especially those of the members of Antwerp*, which also argued that the

---

inghesetenen van Nederlandt (Cologne, 1579), whose putative author Gaspar Schetz, Lord of Grobbendock, strongly urged the inhabitants of the Netherlands to accept the peace proposals. For this treatise see most recently Craig E. Harline, *Pamphlets, printing, and political culture in the early Dutch Republic* (Dordrecht, 1987), 191–9.

[115] *Clare vertoninge ende bericht der articulen ende conditien nu onlancx tot Cuelen inde vredehandel byden Churfursten, Fursten ende andere Keyserlycke Maiesteyts Ghesanten, gheproponeert* (1579), fol. B1.

[116] Ibid., fol. C4.

sole intention of the peace proposals was 'to bring us in eternal slavery' so that the Dutch would 'remain in continuous war for liberty'.[117] In strong terms the treatise denounced the person and policy of Philip II, arguing that 'either the king must be tyrannic by nature or so bad that he does not understand his affairs, or at least he must be in somebody's power so that he can neither do nor deal with us as he would want to'.[118] In either situation, the *Good warning* concluded, 'nothing good was to be expected from such a prince'. In this context the treatise rejected any suggestion of re-establishing the country in its old state of government as it had been under Charles V. Demolishing the myth of the former emperor, it argued that Charles had paved the way for the tyranny of his son.

Systematically the *Good warning* denounced the peace proposals of the German mediators. With regard to the idea of re-establishing the authority and obedience to Philip II, the treatise pointed out that the States had always sought to 'preserve the proper authority of His Majesty' in accordance with divine and natural law and with the privileges and customs of the country. In this respect the Joyous Entry of Brabant was again invoked as the sole basis of the prince's legitimate authority, and it was added that the divine and worldly rights 'do not permit tyranny', but in fact 'absolve the subjects of obedience as far as they are tyrannized, as also the privileges of the country do'.[119]

Full emphasis was put again on the role of the States in the Dutch political order. The *Good warning* argued that the 'assurance' of the Netherlands could only be guaranteed by a system of self-government, with the States in a leading role and the prince tied hand and foot to States and privileges. The 'States and the country' should remain 'masters of the weapons and of their purse'. No one should be 'in government without their consent' and 'the direction of policy' should be 'in the power of the States and the members of the country'.[120] Obviously the maintenance of the rights and privileges should be assured, and the prince should accept that in case of violation the Countries were 'allowed to take up arms to their just protection...in accordance with the privileges of the country'.[121]

Although according to the *Good warning* the authority of the States

---

[117] *Goede waerschouwinghe voor den borgheren ende besonder dien vanden leden van Antwerpen, dat sy hen niet en souden laten verlocken met het soet aengheven vande bedriechlijcke artijckelen van peyse onlancx ghecomen van Cuelen* (1579), fol. 3.　　[118] Ibid., fol. 3.　　[119] Ibid., fol. 22.
[120] Ibid., fol. 24.　　[121] Ibid.

was pivotal in Dutch politics, the treatise reasserted that it was not without limits. The States could not make a 'general regulation', especially concerning the religious issue which affected the bliss of each individual inhabitant, 'without the consent of the members of the towns'.

Perhaps the most radical and elaborate rejection of the peace proposals was the *Brief discourse on the peace negotiations now taking place at Cologne*,[122] which combined a strong condemnation of Philip II's policy and person with a staunch defence of the political authority of the States and their right of resistance.

The *Brief discourse* also rejected the very possibility of reconciliation with Philip, thundering that princes in general and the Spanish king in particular were full of injustice and could hardly be trusted. Philip's one and only goal, so the treatise claimed, was to deprive the Low Countries of their liberty, to bring them into eternal servitude. Thus, although the wording of the treatise was particularly strong, it basically reiterated the familiar claim that the States had only resorted to armed resistance in order to preserve liberty and that they were fully entitled to do so.

In legitimizing the State's right of resistance, however, the *Brief discourse* made a remarkable move. It still presented the privileges as an important part of the Dutch political order, circumscribing the division of power between prince and States. The 'privileges, the laws and constitutions of the country' had tied the prince hand and foot to the States. As the treatise pointed out, the States had always had 'so much authority and respect' that the 'dukes and princes have not been able to make any alterations in the matter of sovereignty or been able to levy duties or other taxes, to have new money minted, or to make peace or war without the express consent of the States'.[123]

According to the *Brief discourse* the political dependence of the prince on the States had important ramifications for the issue of sovereignty. Endorsing the revolutionary view that the States were the leading sovereign powers in the Netherlands, the treatise contended that the States had 'reserved the power to decide on all matters concerning the sovereignty to themselves'.[124]

---

[122] *Brief discours sur la negotiation de la paix, qui se tracte presentement à Coloigne entre le Roy d'Espaigne, & les Estats du Pays Bas* (Leiden, 1579). The same text was published as the *Petit traicté servant d'instruction à messieurs les estatz et touts bons patriots* (Ghent, 1579). I have not been able to retrace the precise background of this double publication. For a modern edn. see van Gelderen, *The Dutch Revolt*.

[123] *Brief discours*, fol. B1.   [124] Ibid., fol. B2.

As leading sovereign powers the principal duty of the States was to maintain the rights and liberties of the people. In doing so the States were entitled to take up arms against the prince. Indeed, the *Brief discourse* not only argued that the States had the authority to resist a prince by force, it also asserted that, if necessary, for the sake of the country, the States were entitled to 'take another prince for lord instead of suffering such a barbarous resolution'.[125]

Like the *Good warning*, the *Brief discourse* emphasized the representative character of the States, which 'of old and within the memory of man' had 'represented the people to defend their rights and to maintain them in peace and tranquillity, and to guard them from all injuries, violence and oppression against every one, even their princes'.[126] Thus the States never acted of their own accord. Defending the States' demand for freedom of religion, the *Brief discourse* argued that as the States represented 'the whole people and all the inhabitants of the country', it was 'reasonable' for them to 'conform themselves' to the 'disposition and desires' of the inhabitants 'in just and proper matters for the common good of the country'.[127]

In short, just like the *Clear presentation* and the *Good warning*, the *Brief discourse* presented a normative interpretation of the political order of the Netherlands as based again on the key elements of liberty, privileges and States. The preservation and maintenance of liberty was still regarded as a major political value and the chief motivation of armed resistance. The privileges were still seen as the constitutional guarantees of liberty; the States, as the representatives of the people, were again presented as the central institution of Dutch politics.

The *Brief discourse* made the important move of taking the continual emphasis on the political authority of the States to its ultimate conclusion, by arguing that the States were indeed the leading sovereign powers within the Dutch political order, which had the right to abjure and replace a prince. The States' right of resistance was said to be implied in this sovereign role. Thus with the *Brief discourse* Dutch resistance theory in a way started to transcend the concrete constitutional foundation, on which it had been based since the beginning of the Revolt.

---

[125] Ibid., fol. B3. [126] Ibid. [127] Ibid., fol. B1.

4.7. THE DEFENCE OF THE ABJURATION

The *Brief discourse*'s line of argumentation to articulate a right of resistance on behalf of the States along constitutional lines, yet transcending the specificities of privileges, was taken up by a number of treatises published in 1580 and 1581. A fine example was *Emanuel–Erneste*, a 'dialogue of two persons on the state of the Netherlands', allegedly written by Gerard Prouninck alias van Deventer, a former secretary of Bois-le-Duc, one of the four capital towns in Brabant.[128] Addressing the question whether it was legitimate for the Dutch Provinces to take another prince, the dialogue exploited all possibilities the constitutional arguments of the Revolt offered.

Thus, first of all, the dialogue restated the constitutional argument as based on specific articles of Brabant privileges in particular. It referred to the well-known Brabant 'New Regiment' of 1421, in which Duke John granted that, if he or his successors violated the rights and privileges of the country, the subjects were not only absolved of their oath of obedience but the States were also allowed 'to choose a regent or protector of the country whom the inhabitants are bound to obey as the prince himself, until and in so far as the mistakes and infractions are properly redressed'.[129] This rule, as the dialogue recognized, did not entitle the States to appoint another prince, yet, according to *Emanuel–Erneste*, rather than see the subjects and the liberty of the country ruined, it was preferable to take another prince if the present one persisted in forsaking his duty. Otherwise, Emanuel argued, 'it would be in the power of the prince to make fruitless what the ancestors had so carefully conditioned'.[130] In other words, Emanuel argued, in line with the 1576 *Address*, the importance of the liberty and common good of the country should overrule any hesitation to oppose a prince who forsook his duty. When Erneste pointed out that princes, both good and bad, were ordained by God and asked whether to resist a bad prince was not to resist divine ordination, Emanuel seized the opportunity to discuss the authority of the prince and his relationship to the States in the Netherlands. He asserted that there was a crucial difference between a sovereign monarch and a 'sovereign prince to whom the people

---

[128] See Louisa Raus, 'De dialoog Emanuel–Erneste en zijn auteur', *De Gulden Passer*, 10 (1932), 25–39. According to Raus, the dialogue was not published before Mar. 1581.

[129] Gerard Prouninck van Deventer, *Emanuel–Erneste. Dialogue de deux personnages sur l'Estat du Pais Bas* (Antwerp, 1580), 28.   [130] Ibid. 29.

themselves give jurisdiction', and he repeated the maxim that it was 'the people who make the princes and not they the people'.[131] If the people had transferred all power, without retaining anything, they had neither right nor authority to complain in case of oppression. However, if, as Emanuel put it, 'the people have retained the right to give jurisdiction to the princes, the princes cannot overrule this jurisdiction and usurp sovereign rights and power'.[132] The people had no obligation to the prince beyond the limits of the power they had rendered to him. Such a situation had always been characteristic of the Dutch, who were so proud of their liberty. In Brabant, the principal province, the duke was obliged to maintain the inhabitants in 'all their rights, franchises, liberties and privileges'. He was not allowed to do violence to them or to decree rules which hurt 'the good, repose and prosperity of the country'. He could neither levy taxes, nor take military decisions without the consent of the States. Emanuel added that if the duke violated these and many other 'sworn conditions', the subjects were absolved from duty of service and obedience, which meant in practice that the duke was 'no longer their prince, nor they his subjects'.[133] Thus the celebrated clause of disobedience was interpreted in such a way that violation of the conditions on which the prince had been accepted made him lose his office and thereby dissolved the prince–subject relationship and the principality as such, which meant the people were free to do what suited them best.

Erneste readily accepted this view and concluded that, as 'it seems that most of the sovereignty remains with the States', there was a close resemblance between the Republic of Venice and Brabant. Thus, like the *Brief discourse*, the *Emanuel–Erneste* dialogue acknowledged the States as the leading sovereign powers. In addition, it articulated a right of resistance which, though still referring to the privileges, was more and more based on a general reflection of the relationship between prince and subjects, as it acknowledged the limits of the constitutionalist argument based on the specificities of privileges.[134]

---

[131] Ibid. 30.   [132] Ibid. 32.   [133] Ibid. 33.

[134] The States themselves were bolder on this point. In the negotiations with the Duke of Anjou on his election as successor to Philip II, they explicitly claimed the right of abjuration. The list of articles proposed to the duke included an article which said that if he violated the treaty, 'it will be in the power of the States to take another prince, following the contents of the Joyous Entry of Brabant'. See *Articulen gheraemt en ghestelt by myn Heere den Prince van Oraengnen en de ghedeputeerde Heeren van de Generale Staten, op den welcken men zoude moghen handelen met mijn Heere den Hertoghe van Anjou* (1580), article 27.

Even stronger than the *Emanuel–Erneste* dialogue, the *True warning to the good men of Antwerp*, probably published in 1581, recognized that the privileges of Brabant included merely a right of disobedience and in fact did not speak at all about resisting or abjuring a prince. However, the *True warning* denounced the suggestion that therefore it was forbidden to renounce the prince, even if he had turned into a tyrant and oppressor of the country. With reference to Greek, Roman and more contemporary history, the *True warning* asserted that 'all other provinces, all kingdoms, all nations in the world' had always had the 'power and liberty by God, by nature and by themselves' to depose a prince who had become a tyrant, 'persecuting the devout and trampling justice', and to choose another prince'.[135]

As the *True warning* argued, God had created men free; it was his wish that they were governed with right and justice, not with tyranny. No one, therefore, had been given absolute authority. The 'king or lord of the country' was 'merely a servant of justice, a stadtholder of God, a shepherd of the people, a father of the country to administer righteousness and justice to everyone'.[136] The 'power and authority' the prince could claim was 'granted and given to him by the Countries, that is, by the States of the Countries (who represent the whole body of the community)'. They had done so on certain conditions in accordance with the rights of the country. If the prince exceeded the limits of his authority, as demarcated by the people, and turned into a tyrant, the people were entitled to resume the power and authority they had given to him and to 'elect, as their ancestors have done in the beginning, such protector and lord of the country and propose to him such conditions as they judge best for the preservation of the country and the welfare of the community'.[137]

As the *True warning* acknowledged, this right of resistance and abjuration was not expressed 'in the conditions of investiture'. However, as the treatise put it, 'nature and human intellect' convey this fundamental principle 'of themselves'; it was 'planted and imprinted in the hearts of all men that, because men have been created free by God, they cannot become slaves by the will of him who has no power over them save that they themselves have granted and given to him'.[138]

The privileges should be seen to complement these natural principles of the politics. Privileges indicated particular conditions

---

[135] *Een trouwe waerschouwinghe aen de goede mannen van Antwerpen* (*Antwerp*, 1581), fol. A1.
[136] Ibid., fol. A2.   [137] Ibid.   [138] Ibid.

the prince had to respect, on penalty that he was no longer obeyed if he violated them. These particular arrangements, however, did not imply that 'the ancestors would have agreed to deprive themselves or their descendants of the power and the right, which they have by God and by right, to be allowed to punish their lords of the country with weapons, yes, with eternal abjuration, if they see that they had become oppressors of the country and tyrants'.[139]

This, according to the *True warning*, was the case in the Low Countries. The cause of the war was not some 'particular violation of the privileges of the Countries but a public, general, cruel and inhuman tyranny', where the prince had 'completely overthrown the right of nature and had acted with his subjects as with slaves and insensible animals'.[140] To abjure the prince in this situation was, as the *True warning* concluded, in line with the spirit of the privileges, 'for our privileges have been made and given to uphold our freedom, and not to oppress us'.[141]

Of course the *True warning* rearticulated many familiar views. Its sketch of the political order, the office of the prince and the relationship between prince and States was highly similar to the constitutional argument which said the Dutch political order was based on liberty, privileges and States. However, with regard to the issue of resistance the analysis of the *True warning* moved beyond previous formulations. Acknowledging that the privileges contained no right of resistance or abjuration, the treatise argued, even more explicitly than the *Brief discourse* and *Emanuel–Erneste*, that the States had the natural right to oppose and abjure a prince who violated the terms of the contract upon which he was accepted as lord of the country.

A similar argument was developed by the preamble of the Act of Abjuration of 26 July 1581.[142] The Act was the outcome of a decision-making process which had formally started on 6 June 1581 with a

---

[139] Ibid., fol. A3.   [140] Ibid., fol. A4.   [141] Ibid.

[142] *Placcaet van verlatinghe* (Leiden, 1581). The most comprehensive study on the Act of Abjuration is M. E. H. N. Mout, *Plakkaat van verlatinge 1581 : inleiding, transcriptie en vertaling in hedendaags Nederlands* (The Hague, 1979), which includes a facsimile of the 1581 Act and a modern Dutch trans. An edn. in modern English is included in Kossmann and Mellink (eds.), *Texts concerning the revolt of the Netherlands*, 216–28. Refs. are to this edn. For information on the historical background and political ideas of the Act of Abjuration see, in addition to Mout's study: W. P. Blockmans, 'Du contrat féodal à la souveraineté du peuple: les précédents de la déchéance de Philippe II dans les Pays Bas (1581)', in *Assemblee di Stati e istituzioni rappresentative nella storia del pensiero politico moderno* (Rimini, 1983), 135–50; J. P. A. Coopmans, 'De herkomst van het plakkaat van verlatinge', in G. van Dievoet and G. Marcours (eds.), *Justicie ende gerechticheyt* (Antwerp, 1983), 36–52.

request of the States General to the provinces to give their opinion on the plan to abjure Philip II. To integrate the provincial opinions a committee of conciliation was formed under the presidency of Andries Hessels, member and clerk of the States of Brabant. There is some debate about the final authorship of the Act of Abjuration. Doubts have been cast on the traditional view that the final editing work, including writing the preamble, was done by Jan van Asseliers, the 'Audiencier' of the States General and former secretary to the Council of State.[143]

As to the expression of political thought, the Act was a sober, prudent and not highly original document. Essentially the preamble reiterated views which had become commonplace in the political literature of the Revolt. In sketching the authority and position of the prince, the preamble espoused the view that he had been ordained by God for the sake of the subjects, to protect and govern them in accordance with right and reason. If a prince, so the Act asserted, instead of protecting his subjects endeavoured 'to oppress and molest them and to deprive them of their ancient liberty, privileges and customs and to command and use them like slaves',[144] he should be regarded as a tyrant. In such a case the subjects should no longer acknowledge him as a prince, but in accordance with right and reason should renounce him and choose another lord instead. The Act added that this rule applied in particular to those countries which had been 'governed (as they should be) in accordance with the oath taken by the prince at his inauguration and in conformity with the privileges, customs and old traditions of these countries which he swears to maintain'.[145] At this point the Act referred explicitly to the contracts containing the conditions on which the prince had been accepted. One of these conditions – and here the well-known clause of disobedience was invoked – was said to prescribe that, if the prince broke the contracts, he legally forfeited his sovereignty.

After this preamble, the Act of Abjuration presented a long and familiar list of grievances to demonstrate that from the very beginning of his reign 'the king has been trying to deprive these Countries of their ancient freedom and to bring them under Spanish rule'.[146] Thus the story of the reorganization of the diocesan structure, Alva's

---

[143] See Mout, *Plakkaat van verlatinge 1581*, 58, 65, and especially Coopmans, 'De herkomst van het plakkaat van Verlatinge', *passim*. The 'Audiencier' was the official who codified the decisions and had responsibility for the implementation of decisions with regard to requests.

[144] Kossmann and Mellink (eds.), *Texts concerning the revolt of the Netherlands*, 217.

[145] Ibid.   [146] Ibid. 218.

dreadful tyranny, the calamities of Spanish mutineers and the misbehaviour of Don Juan was rehearsed, leading to the conclusion that, 'despairing of all means of reconciliation and left without any other remedies and help', the States had been forced – 'in conformity with the law of nature and for the protection of our own rights and those of our fellow countrymen, of the privileges, traditional customs and liberties of the fatherland, the life and honour of our wives, children and descendants so that they should not fall into Spanish slavery – to abandon the king of Spain and to pursue such means as we think likely to secure our rights, privileges and liberties'.[147]

In its presentation of the Revolt as a fight for the privileges and liberties of the country and the life and honour of the inhabitants, in its description of the position of the prince and his relationship to the States and in its conclusion that the States had the natural right to resist and abjure a prince-turned-tyrant, the Act of Abjuration was of course espousing the argument which essentially held that the Dutch political order was designed to preserve liberty by means of a constitutional framework whose fundamental components were the privileges and the States.

A similar argument can be made with regard to what is undoubtedly one of the classics of the political literature of the Dutch Revolt, William of Orange's *Apology*.[148] The *Apology*, immediately published in four languages, was written under Orange's direct supervision by Loyseleur de Villiers, the court chaplain of the prince.[149] Villiers, born in Rijssel, had studied law in Orléans and theology in Geneva. He had many contacts with Huguenots and had been minister of the French refugee church in London. In 1577 Villiers entered the service of Orange and soon became one of the prince's most influential advisers. Villiers wrote the *Apology* in close consultation with two important Huguenots, Hubert Languet and Philippe Duplessis-Mornay.

The *Apology*, the direct answer to Philip II's ban declaring William of Orange an outlaw, was principally a highly passionate and

---

[147] Ibid. 225.
[148] *Apologie, ofte verantwoordinghe des doerluchtighen ende hooghgeborenen Vorsts ende Heeren, Heeren Wilhelms van Godes ghenade prince van Orangien* (Leiden, 1581; originally in French, 1581). In the same year English and Latin edns. also appeared. For the English trans., see *The Apologie of Prince William of Orange against the proclamation of the king of Spaine*, ed. H. Wansink (Leiden, 1969). Refs. are to this edn.
[149] For Villiers, see C. Boer, *Hofpredikers van Prins Willem van Oranje. Jean Taffin en Pierre Loyseleur de Villiers* (The Hague, 1952).

personal justification and a vehement attack on the person and policy of Philip II. In addition, it offered an elaborate justification of the Dutch Revolt and of Orange's role in particular.

The *Apology*, addressed and offered to the States General, presented Orange as 'lawfully elected and chosen' by the States, his 'superiors', and the people 'to be the claimer and challenger of their liberty'.[150] The life and work of the prince were devoted, as pointed out in the opening sentences of the *Apology*, to the recovery of liberty, and the safety of 'persons, goods and consciences'.[151]

Liberty, of course, had been defended against the ambitions of the Spaniards and Philip II in particular. The Spaniards, the *Apology* asserted, had always sought to deprive the Netherlands of their ancient liberty and their rights and privileges in order to bring them into Spanish slavery. In this respect Philip II was held personally responsible for the troubles afflicting the Netherlands. The fiction of the misled, yet basically virtuous, prince was definitely turned upside-down. Now Philip II was portrayed as 'an incestuous king, the slayer of his son, and the murderer of his wife',[152] to mention but a few of the fierce accusations addressed against the King of Spain.

The *Apology* stressed that in the Netherlands Philip II was not king but merely duke and count, whose powers were strongly curtailed by the privileges. At length the *Apology* reiterated the view that, as the privileges ordained, the prince could take no decision of importance as far as legal, financial and military matters were concerned without the consent of the country. Again emphasis was put on the authority of the States, which, according to the *Apology*, was 'indeed the true foundation of an Estate, the assurance of the commonwealth, and the only peace and quietness of princes'.[153]

As the guardians of liberty, the States had the duty to maintain and uphold the privileges. The constitutional trinity of liberty, privileges and States was explicitly recognized in the *Apology*, which said the policy of the Spaniards 'to hinder the calling' of the States was meant 'to cut off by the foot the tree of your privileges, and utterly to dry up the spring of your liberty'.[154]

The *Apology* had no doubts about the legitimacy of the Revolt. It too referred to the clause of disobedience of the Joyous Entry and reiterated the view that if the prince violated the privileges the subjects were 'no longer bound to him' in service and obedience and

[150] *Apologie*, 120.   [151] Ibid. 12.   [152] Ibid. 44.   [153] Ibid. 58.
[154] Ibid. 97.

that therefore the prince–subject relationship was dissolved. The *Apology* seemed to suggest, following the 'private law' theory of resistance, that in such a situation taking up arms did not amount to armed resistance against a prince, as the latter had lost office and become a private person. In addition, the *Apology* restated the view that, on the basis of the privileges of Brabant, the States had the duty to protect and maintain the common good and as such had to check and control the prince. The States were compared with the Spartan ephors, following Calvin's *Institutes*. As the *Apology* acknowledged, the privileges only freed the subjects from their oath to the king until he had mended his ways, but it left no doubt that Philip II would never do so. Moreover, as Philip II had been relieved by the Pope from his oath, the States were definitely no longer bound to him.

In purporting an interpretation of the Dutch political order as based on liberty, privileges and States, the *Apology*, like the Act of Abjuration, essentially restated ideas which had become common-place in the Netherlands. Neither of these politically eminent documents were of principal intellectual importance to the development of political thought. In this respect another 1581 publication undoubtedly surpassed them. The annotated edition of *Acts of the peace negotiations which took place in Cologne* was one of the highlights of the political literature of the Dutch Revolt. The *Acts* were the work of Aggaeus van Albada, the principal spokesman for the States General at the negotiations.[155] Albada was a highly gifted Frisian lawyer who had received a thorough humanist education in Paris, Orléans, Bourges and Italy.

Albada was a convinced Spiritualist, deeply influenced by the teachings of Caspar Schwenckfeld, whose works he translated and propagated.[156] Thus Albada abhorred any form of religious coercion and favoured a sober broad church, without sacraments and rituals but fully recognizing that the spirit of God was free and could not be tied to any outward ceremony.

His elaborate annotations to the *Acts of the peace negotiations* were primarily meant to justify the policy of the States General. As such the *Acts* were a not too systematic defence of the Dutch Revolt. None the less they are of great importance for the history of the

---

[155] For a recent biography of Albada, see Wiebe Bergsma, *Aggaeus van Albada (c. 1525–1587), schwenckfeldiaan, staatsman en strijder voor verdraagzaamheid* (Meppel, 1985).
[156] For a lucid discussion of Albada's religious convictions, see ibid., 74–110.

political thought of the Revolt, not only because of the aptitude and originality of Albada's thoughts but also because he was one of the few to link his arguments explicitly to intellectual developments in the rest of Europe. While most of the treatises justifying the armed resistance against Philip II did not, with the apparent exception of Dutch constitutional documents, reveal their intellectual sources and only occasionally referred to other texts, Albada quoted extensively from a large body of classical, late medieval and contemporary texts to underpin his arguments.

Albada's political thought was based on the premise – for which he referred not only to the Spanish Dominican Fernando Vasquez, a member of the famous neo-Thomist school of Salamanca, but also to Plato, Aristotle, Cicero's *De officiis* and Bartolus' *De regimine civitatis* – that the essence of political authority was to foster and protect the common good of the community.[157] Dwelling on the study of the Italian jurist Mario Salomonio *De principatu*, which successfully connected the study of Roman law with the republican traditions of the Italian Renaissance,[158] Albada argued that God had created men 'free and equal'. The sole purpose for the creation of princes had been to profit the people, to enlighten the maintenance of 'human and civil society or citizenhood' and to make it easier for people to help each other with 'mutual benefactions'.[159] In short, what the republican authors of the Italian Renaissance had called a *vivere civile* was the ultimate aim of politics.

Albada emphasized that princes had been made by the people, and not the people by princes. Referring to the highlight of Huguenot political thought, the 1579 *Vindiciae contra tyrannos*, and again to Salomonio, Albada held that it was impossible to argue that all men had been created for the sake of a hundred princes and he pointed out that many nations lived without a prince, but no prince could be without a people. Thus Albada wondered who, 'since a king is made by the people and because of the people, and without the people could not remain king, will be surprised that we conclude that the people is above the king?'[160]

Albada also maintained that this idea did not only apply to the prince. It applied to all magistrates, amongst whom the prince held but 'the first place'. Again the argument was that 'there had been

---

[157] Aggaeus van Albada, *Acten van den Vredehandel geschiet te Colen* (Antwerp, 1581), 166.
[158] See Quentin Skinner, *The foundations of modern political thought* (Cambridge, 1978), i. 148–52, and ii. 132–4. Also J. W. Allen, *A history of political thought in the sixteenth century* (London, 1957), 332–6.   [159] Albada, *Acten*, 166.   [160] Ibid. 101.

common people before there ever was any magistrate'. Moreover, the magistrates had been created 'because of the will of the people and not... the people because of the magistrates'. Therefore, as Albada concluded, 'the authority of all magistrates, no matter how high and powerful', rested 'completely on the common authority of those who have raised and brought them to this highness'.[161]

This suggested that ultimately the people were sovereign, and, indeed, Albada cited with approval Salomonio's conclusion that 'the right of ruling' was 'nothing but a right of the common people'.[162] The authority of all magistrates, including both prince and States, rested on the 'supreme rule of the common people'.[163]

These fundamental principles were employed to offer an elaborate analysis of the position and authority of the prince and the States. Realizing that the position of the prince was, as Albada himself pointed out during the negotiations, next to religion, the principal point of difference with the Spaniards, the Frisian humanist emphasized that the prince was but a 'custodian, servant and executor' of the law, 'a servant of the ship' who differed 'from the others not in general but in species'. In the ship of the community the prince held the place of the steersman, while the people were the masters of the ship.[164]

The States had been created for the same purpose as the prince: it was their bounden duty, and here Albada referred to both Cicero and Roman law, to serve the 'fatherland', 'to foster the common welfare and good, yes, to consider their own welfare inferior to the common'.[165] The States were the representatives of the community. As such they were elected officers of the community, not of the prince. As a matter of fact, in the Netherlands the prince had received his authority and power by way of contract out of the hands of the States. In this context the Joyous Entry of Brabant was once again presented as the main contract of the provinces. However, and here Albada was indebted to Aldegonde's 1578 *Oration*, to which he referred, the 1477 Grand Privilege had declared this 'law of privilege' universal for all the Netherlands. In Albada's view the Joyous Entry made it absolutely clear that in the Netherlands 'the king had not received

---

[161] Ibid. 144.   [162] Ibid. 64.

[163] Ibid. 26. Here Albada was quoting the *Vindiciae*.

[164] Ibid. 101, with reference to another main text of Huguenot literature, Hotman's *Francogallia*, and again to Salomonio.

[165] Albada, *Acten*, 123. Amongst others Albada referred to the law *ut vim atque iniuriam* (Digest, book 1, title 1, para. 3). This was the law dealing with the 'right to repel violent injuries', and as such played an important role in Reformed political thought.

supreme rule', for 'in almost all common affairs' he could 'not act without consent and approbation of the people'.[166]

Reiterating one of the fundamental principles of the constitutional defence of the Revolt, Albada asserted that from the beginning the dutiful protection of liberty and of the privileges of the country had been the motivating force of the States' policy. Thus the States had two main objectives. First, they wished to maintain 'complete, unbroken and unharmed the liberty, rights and privileges, persons and goods, of themselves as of their people'.[167] In addition the States demanded full recognition of the freedom of conscience.

Albada left little doubt about whether the States had been entitled, as he put it, to 'take up arms in the defence of their life and freedom'. His argument on this issue was threefold. To begin with he referred to the Joyous Entry's clause on disobedience, which, in Albada's formulation, gave the States the right to disobey a prince who broke the laws and rights of the Countries. Moreover, Albada argued, in 'inaugurating' their duke, the Brabanters 'publicly and expressly' declared that if he broke the Joyous Entry, they would be 'allowed to choose another one at their own discretion'.[168]

Following a basic tenet of Reformed political thought, the second part of Albada's argument emphasized the right of resistance of inferior magistrates, which must have appealed to the German mediators at the peace negotiations. Referring to the work of the German Roman Catholic jurist Fickler, Albada took up the view that if a prince who had been appointed on certain conditions openly broke them, the 'inferior magistrates, yes, also the Countries and towns' which had established him in his authority were not only 'lawfully dismissed of their oath', but were also entitled to 'openly' resist 'the oppression of the empire or province whose maintenance and protection each of them, after his office, had accepted under oath'.[169]

Finally, Albada concluded, on the basis of the principle of popular sovereignty he had formulated, that those who had established a prince in his authority retained the power to take the latter's authority back, if he violated the conditions on which he was appointed.[170]

Of course Albada's views on the nature of politics, the position of the prince, the authority of the States, the importance of liberty and

---

[166] Albada, *Acten*, 78.   [167] Ibid. 128.   [168] Ibid. 24.   [169] Ibid. 143.
[170] Ibid. 144.

privileges, and the right of resistance, were first of all a major restatement of the constitutional defence of the Revolt, based on the key elements of liberty, privileges and States. However, at least on two points Albada's *Acts* were a work of important ideological innovation.

First, although other treatises moved in this direction, Albada was the first author to give a full account of popular sovereignty, making it the fourth key element in the legitimization of the Revolt. Secondly, the *Acts* exemplified that the political literature of the Dutch Revolt was not an isolated stream of treatises. Albada's annotations can be seen as a deliberate attempt to align the political justification of the Revolt with the Renaissance appropriation of classical texts and with late medieval and sixteenth-century studies of Roman law. In doing so, Albada connected the political thought of the Dutch Revolt with major contemporary intellectual developments in Europe.

In this respect Albada's work was followed by the anonymous *Political education*, a treatise published in 1582, whose comments on the abjuration of Philip II were likewise attended with numerous references to biblical, classical, late medieval and contemporary authorities.

Like Albada, *Political education* emphasized, quoting Seneca, that the purpose of government, said to be an 'office, not an empire', solely 'consists in the welfare and prosperity of the community and subjects'.[171] To hold a governmental office was not a matter of glory or liberty, but a burdensome duty of public service. Being 'instituted to do justice', as Cicero had put it, a prince should excel in 'the knowledge of warfare' and, above all, in virtue. Along traditional Ciceronian lines *Political education* argued that persistence in duty, fortitude and of course prudence were amongst the main virtues needed.[172]

Recognizing that the prince was ordained by God and accepted by the people to serve the common good, which primarily existed in the administration of civic justice and care for a strong external defence, *Political education* made a point of arguing that princes and governments in general, as 'guardians, servants and advocates of the laws', should themselves be subject to the law. The argument was based on famous Roman-law sources, such as the rule of the emperors

[171] *Politicq onderwijs* (Political education) (Malines, 1582), fol. B3. For a modern English edn. of this treatise, see van Gelderen, *The Dutch Revolt*.
[172] *Political education*, fol. B3.

Theodosius and Valentine, that it was 'worthy of the majesty of a reigning prince for him to profess to be subject to the laws'[173] and on classical examples such as Pausanius' saying that 'laws ought to have authority over men, not men over laws'.[174]

If princely rule or any other 'state of government' started to serve its own 'profit' and 'unbridled passions', suppressing 'what is right with force and violence', it should be considered tyrannical. This claim was substantiated by a lengthy analysis of the most famous late medieval treatise on the subject, Bartolus' *De tyranno*. On the basis of Bartolus' work three distinguishing characteristics of tyranny were defined. Essentially a tyrant was a ruler who maintained his subjects in discord, who impoverished them and who persecuted their person and good.[175]

According to *Political education* there was no doubt that Philip II fitted Bartolus' definition. With lengthy historical illustrations the treatise showed how Philip had 'sought by all means to take away the ancient freedom from these Countries and to bring them into a miserable slavery under the government of the Spanish blood-hounds'.[176]

Boldly *Political education* asserted that the 'pious and godly citizen and subject can not have community with the tyrant'. Paraphrasing Cicero it pointed out that 'as one should amputate a rotten limb for the conservation of the body', so the tyrant should be 'destroyed'.[177] In order to support this general claim the treatise not only referred to the famous words of Aquinas that, as *Political education* put it, 'there is merit in killing such a tyrant',[178] but also to contemporary authors such as the Italian jurists Ludovicus Carrerius and Cataldinus de Boncompagnis de Visso and the Spanish neo-Thomists Alfonsus de Castro (who had dedicated the work which was quoted to Philip II)

---

[173] Ibid., fol. B4. The reference is to the Codex Justinianus, book 1, ch. 14, no. 4. Throughout the medieval period this text, a constitution of Theodosius II in 429, played a major role in the discussion on the limits of princely rule, being primarily used to sustain the idea of limited, 'constitutional' rule.

[174] This was a quote from Plutarch, *The sayings of Spartans*, 230f. See Plutarch, *Moralia*, vol. iii (172a–263c), Loeb edn. (Cambridge, Mass., 1968), 383. Pausanias was King of Sparta between 408 and 394 BC.

[175] For the description of the marks of tyranny, see Bartolus of Sassoferrato, *De tyranno*, in Diego Quaglioni (ed.), *Politica e diritto nel trecento Italiano: il 'De tyranno' di Bartolo da Sassoferrato (1314–1357)* (Florence, 1983), 196–9, where Bartolus referred to Aristotle's views on tyranny as outlined in *The politics*, book 5, ch. 10.   [176] *Political education*, fol. D2.

[177] Ibid., fol. B3. The reference is to Cicero, *De officiis*, 3. 6. 32.

[178] *Political education*, fol. C1. See Thomas Aquinas, *Summa theologiae*, IIa–IIae, question 42, 2, article 2, where Aquinas says that 'those who liberate the multitude from the power of a tyrant are praised'.

and Domingo de Soto. De Soto's argument that, if the tyrant was a 'legal prince' due to succession or election, he should not be killed by any 'private person' was said to imply that in such cases 'the States of the country and those who represent the subjects' had as 'public persons' the right and duty to resist and kill the tyrant.[179]

However, *Political education* itself did not restrict the right of resistance to the States. It claimed 'all pious nobles and faithful subjects' were 'permitted' to resist and curb tyranny.[180] This radical claim was further supported by an elaborate appeal to the idea, celebrated in the *Vindiciae contra tyrannos*, of a double covenant binding the prince to both God and the people.

The covenant with God obliged the prince to govern 'body and goods' in accordance with God's law. If princes such as Philip, who had intruded God's own realm with his attempt to rule the soul and conscience of his subjects, broke this covenant, they forfeited 'in God's eyes their empire and supreme power'. Of course it was permitted, as the famous Roman law *ut vim* from the Digest had clearly shown, to defend oneself against the violence of such a tyrant.[181]

According to *Political education* the idea of the covenant between prince and people was especially applicable to the Low Countries, where in most parts the prince was received 'on conditions, by contract and agreements', stipulating that the prince should govern the countries in accordance with the 'privileges, customs and old habits'. In such circumstances absolute rule was out of the question. Even Ulpian's famous rule '*Princeps legibus solitus est*',[182] often said to celebrate the absolute lawgiving power of the prince, recognized, as *Political education* argued, that 'all princes are subject to the laws they have given, conditions they have sworn to, contracts they have made, and agreements they have concluded'.[183] To substantiate this claim the treatise referred to the great Glossator Accursius, to late medieval Commentators such as Guido de Suzaria, Cynus de Pistoia and Paulus de Castro, to the famous canon lawyer Panormitanus and to sixteenth-century authors such as Restaurus Castaldus[184] and

---

[179] *Political education*, fol. C1. See Domingo de Soto, *Libri decem de Iustitia et Iura* (Lyons, 1569), fols. 138b–139b. For an analysis of de Soto's political thought see Skinner, *The foundations of modern political thought*, ii. 136ff. [180] *Political education*, fols. B3 and D3.

[181] See *Political education*, fol. C3, where Digest, book 1, title 1, para. 3, the rule about the 'right to repel violent injuries' was explicitly invoked.

[182] Digest, book 1, title 3, para. 31. [183] *Political education*, fol. D1.

[184] The reference was to Restaurus Castaldus, 'De imperatore', in *Duodecimum Volumen Tractatuum e variis iuris interpretibus collectorum* (Lyons, 1549). Castaldus came from Perugia

Andreas Alciatus.[185] Following these, and many other comments, *Political education* argued that, to a prince, such as Philip, who had broken his promises, the fundamental rule 'to whom breaks faith, faith will be broken' fully applied.[186] In short, in regard to specific Dutch contracts also, one could only conclude, as the author of *Political education* did with full reference to the Act of Abjuration, that it had been perfectly legitimate to abjure Philip II.

4.8. CONCLUSIONS

Political education offered a delicate synthesis of the ultimate political justification of the Dutch Revolt. After 1581 the issue of resistance lost its pre-eminence in the political debate. One of the rare treatises to address the issue was a 1586 study by Frans Coornhert, the brother of the famous Dirck Volckertsz Coornhert. Summarizing the arguments of the *Vindiciae contra tyrannos* Frans Coornhert confined the actual right of resistance to the States, though emphasizing the general civic duty to assist in the preservation of liberty, without which life was hardly worth while.[187] Another exception was *A clear answer from God's word*, which addressed the question 'whether a Christian inferior magistrate' had the right to resist a tyrannizing 'higher government'.[188] Its author, Eusebius Montanus, went as far as to praise tyrannicide, his final conclusion being that, since tyrants

and taught in his home town and in Bologna. He died in 1564. 'De imperatore' was a comment on the title 'De institutionibus' of the Codex Justinianus.

[185] Alciatus (1492–1550) was a principal exponent of legal humanism, which he exported from Italy to France. He contributed greatly to the introduction of humanist techniques in legal interpretation, abandoning the more traditional scholastic methods. Alciatus used these techniques, for example, to formulate a theory of popular sovereignty, taking traditional views, such as Bartolus had offered as a starting-point. One of his pupils during his stay at the University of Bourges was John Calvin.

[186] See *Political education*, fol. D1. Here reference was made, for example, to Bartolus' comment on the title 'De pactis' of the Codex, which started with this proverb. See Bartolus, *In primam Codicis partem* (Augustae Taurinorum, 1589), fol. 59.

[187] See Frans Coornhert, *Cort Onderwijs eens Liefhebbers des welstandts deser Nederlanden, waerinne allen Christenen goede ghemeenten en Patriotten claerlijck bewesen wort: Dat het wel gheoorloft is tegen te staen een Coning ofte Here vande landen, die Godt ende zijn heylich woort onderstaet te verdrijven ende...de selve Landen onderstaet te berooven van hare gherechticheyden, Privilegien, ende Vrijheyden* (Amsterdam, 1586).

[188] Eusebius Montanus, *Een clare beantwoordinge wt Gods Woort op dese vraghe oft een Christelicke Onder-overheyt, haerder hoogher-overheyt, dewelcke om der oeffeninghe der warer religie, over haer Ondersaten, met confiscatie aller Privilegien, lijfs ende goets, tyranniseert, met vrijer conscientie wederstaen mach* (Middelburg, 1588). It is possible that this treatise was written in 1568 as it is signed 17 May 1568 and refers to Philip II as lord of the country. It is also possible that this was a rhetorical twist. A minister by the name of Eusebius Montanus active around 1568 (or later) is unknown (see also Skinner, *The foundations of modern political thought*, ii. 215).

were 'enemies and destroyers of all God had ordained', the 'inferior magistrates' should 'rightfully resist' them.[189]

Neither Frans Coornhert nor Eusebius Montanus presented new arguments. By the beginning of 1582 the political justification of the Dutch Revolt was well established. Since 1565 a constitutionalist ideology had been developed which conceived of the Dutch political order as based on the key elements of liberty, privileges, States and eventually popular sovereignty.

This ideology started from the familiar assumption that the purpose of any form of political authority was to protect and foster the common good of the community it served. For the political treatises justifying the Revolt, the common good of the community was inseparably linked to liberty. Liberty was seen as the political value *par excellence*, the 'daughter of the Netherlands', the source of prosperity and justice, and the intrinsic connection between liberty of the country and the personal liberty and welfare of the inhabitants was emphasized repeatedly.

The Dutch Revolt itself was essentially interpreted as the defence of liberty, threatened by the lust for power and the tyrannical ambitions of Philip II's government. This is not to ignore religion as a motivating force of the Revolt.[190] Nevertheless, there was a gradual shift to present the resistance against Philip II more and more as a fight for liberty. In 1576 the States of Holland even went as far as to deny explicitly having taken arms because of religion.

The political order was said to have been deliberately created with the purpose of safeguarding liberty. It tried to achieve this goal by means of a constitutional framework consisting of a set of fundamental laws, the privileges, charters and customs of the provinces, and a number of crucial institutions such as the States, whose functioning and flourishing, it should be added, required acts of civic virtue at all levels of society.

In articulating these arguments Dutch treatises abounded in references to the great constitutional documents and traditions of the late medieval period, particularly those of the province of Brabant. Unanimously the charters were regarded as constitutional guarantees which no prince was allowed to violate or change; they were the

---

[189] Ibid. 36.
[190] See ch. 6 for a more detailed analysis of the conceptions of liberty as developed during the Dutch Revolt, showing that for some authors freedom of conscience and religion was in fact the essence of liberty.

bridles of the prince and they contained the conditions on which the prince had been accepted by the States on behalf of the people.

None the less, from the very beginning the political ideas of the protesting and rebelling Dutch moved beyond the ideological legacy of their constitutional past. In 1566 it was already argued, still on the basis of the privileges, that ordinations and decrees, such as the religious placards, which violated the privileges, were to be held of no value and should indeed be actively resisted. This was the start of a continuous reinterpretation of the privileges and their clauses of disobedience, time and again leading to more radical conclusions. A major step in this evolution was the appeal, made as early as 1568, to the so-called New Regiment of 1421 and 1422, which was claimed to grant the right (and duty) to resist the Duke of Brabant and his armies by force, if he violated the privileges. In addition it was argued on basis of the New Regiment that the States were entitled to replace a duke who violated the privileges by a regent, until the prince repaired his ways.

In short, the reaffirmation of the right of disobedience as contained in constitutional documents such as the Joyous Entry[191] soon evolved into the articulation of a political right of resistance, which allowed the inhabitants to disobey and oppose by force a prince who violated the privileges, and, by means of their representatives, the States, to replace him by a regent.

In the ultimate defence of the abjuration, the specificities and constitutional limits of the privileges were transcended and absorbed into the articulation of the right of resistance as a fundamental principle of politics. While endorsing Dutch constitutional traditions, treatises such as the 1576 *Address*, the 1579 *Brief discourse*, the 1580 dialogue *Emanuel–Erneste*, the 1581 *True warning*, Albada's 1581 *Acts*, the 1582 *Political education* and also Orange's *Apology* and the Act of Abjuration developed what might be labelled a natural right of resistance. Essentially the argument was twofold.

First, the contractual conception already emphasized in the constitutional arguments was enriched with notions of popular sovereignty. Central to the covenant between prince and people were the ideas that the prince was made by the people and that the States were the leading sovereign powers in Dutch politics. Since the States

---

[191] On the relationship between the Joyous Entry and the political thought of the Dutch Revolt, see also H. de la Fontaine Verwey, 'De Blijde Inkomste en de Opstand tegen Filips II', in H. de la Fontaine Verwey, *Uit de wereld van het boek I: humanisten, dwepers en rebellen in de zestiende eeuw* (Amsterdam, 1970), 113–32.

were unequivocally presented as representative institutions, created and elected by the community to represent it, the suggestion of popular sovereignty was reinforced. Repeatedly authors pointed out that the States could only make decisions after due consultation with, and on the orders of, its constitutive elements, the nobles and the towns. In 1581 Albada embedded this analysis of the States as representative institutions in a powerful vision of popular sovereignty.

The combination of contractual and constitutionalist ideas with notions of popular sovereignty resulted in the argument that if the prince, the minor power, exceeded the limits of his authority as demarcated by nature and covenant, the people were fully entitled to resume the power and authority they had given to the prince. In its final argumentation this move made use of both the rules of Roman law and late medieval comments emphasizing the duty of the prince to uphold his contracts, oaths and promises and of contemporary authors such as the French Monarchomachs, and also of the Spanish neo-Thomists and some Italian authors who, as in the case of Salomonio, seemed to combine the study of Roman law with the republican ideas of the Italian Renaissance.

Secondly, some treatises formulated a right of resistance starting from the notion that the common good of the community was the supreme law of politics. If a choice had to be made between loyalty to a prince who had become a tyrant and the preservation of the common good, the former should be sacrificed for the sake of the supreme value of the common good.

In addition, at times Dutch authors reiterated the argument based in particular on the rule of Roman law *vim vi repellere* that there was a natural right of self-defence against a prince-turned-tyrant. In this respect there was a clear link with the political thought of the Reformation.

It was not always clear whether the right of resistance should be confined to the States or was extended to all citizens. It seems there was no unanimity on this point. On the one hand there was a strong tendency during the 1570s to confine the right of resistance and abjuration to the States. The States were presented as the principal guardians of liberty, created to appoint and accept the lord of the country, to check and bridle him, to see to the maintenance of the privileges and, finally, to take the important political decisions. The authority of the prince and the liberty and welfare of the country were said to depend on the States. At the same time, in urging people to join the resistance against Philip II, many treatises spoke in terms of

a civic duty, which applied even to the 'lowest subjects', as the 1566
Third warning put it. Even in these treatises, however, it is not always
clear whether the citizens should join the resistance because they
were entitled and obliged to do so at their own initiative or because
they had been summoned by the States.

In short, the articulation of the right of resistance was enshrined in
the gradual formation of a strongly constitutional conception of
Dutch politics, presenting the political order as celebrating liberty,
protected by a political framework based on the notion of popular
sovereignty and functioning through fundamental constitutional
guarantees and political institutions which were the guardians of
liberty. Of course the development of this conception was not a
uniform, linear process. Each treatise had its own individual
characteristics and there was certainly diversity of opinion. None the
less, in sharing a highly similar normative vocabulary, structure of
argument and crucial set of arguments, the authors of the political
treatises justifying the Dutch Revolt developed an impressive
ideology of political resistance in particular and of Dutch politics in
general.

The development of this ideology coincided with the main political
developments of the Revolt. Political arguments were never developed in splendid philosophical isolation but in a continuous
confrontation with political practice. In fact treatises such as the
Defence and Orange's *Apology* were important political actions
themselves. The political developments of the Revolt challenged the
authors of political treatises to formulate their arguments in more
and more detail, whereby each extension of argument conditioned
political action and further political argumentation. It was no
coincidence that the centres of ideological activity were also the
centres of political activity. From the titles, arguments and authors it
can be inferred that up to 1572 Brabant was the centre of ideological
activity *par excellence*, as the incessant emphasis on the Joyous Entry
witnessed.[192] Between 1572 and 1576, Holland became not only the
stronghold of the Revolt, but also the centre of ideological activity.
After 1576 the situation was again reversed, bringing Brabant and
also Flanders to the forefront of ideological activity.

In responding to the dramatic political challenges of their time

---

[192] It is at least remarkable that, for example, the 'Stichtse Landbrief', the charter of the
province of Utrecht, whose clause of disobedience was stronger than the formulation in the
Joyous Entry, was completely ignored in the political literature of the Revolt.

Dutch authors first of all returned to the indigenous traditions of constitutionalism and civic consciousness. However, as Albada's *Acts* and *Political education* exemplified, the political thought of the Dutch Revolt was not an isolated phenomenon, but was aligned with the sixteenth-century appropriation of classic and late medieval texts and made part of contemporary intellectual developments in Europe.

CHAPTER 5

From revolt to republic: the quest for the best state of the commonwealth (1578–1590)

5.1. INTRODUCTION

In June 1575 Holland and Zeeland concluded a closer union, which not only strengthened the co-operation between the two provinces but also enlarged the authority of William of Orange. In retrospect the 1575 union should be regarded as an important step on the road to independence. In October 1575 the States of Holland were already discussing a proposition to abjure Philip II. Although the idea was certainly not supported unequivocally, offers of sovereignty in return for military support were made to Queen Elizabeth in November 1575 and to the Duke of Anjou in May 1576.[1] Eventually the contacts with Anjou led to the treaty of 13 August 1578, which awarded the duke the title of 'Defender of liberty against the tyranny of the Spanish and their allies' and which promised that, if the States should abjure Philip II, Anjou was their first choice as successor. The threat to deprive Philip II of his political authority was expressed in public during the Cologne peace negotiations. On 4 July 1579 the States' deputies announced that if Philip II did not accede to the demands of the States, the latter would 'proceed to the act of privation, by which they will declare that the king is fallen out of all rule, authority and seigniory'.[2] With the Act of Abjuration, this was effected.

From about 1578 political treatises started to comment on the political course the provinces should adopt. They discussed whether it was wise to ally with Anjou, they sought to come up with a

---

[1] See M. P. Holt, *The Duke of Anjou and the politique struggle during the wars of religion* (Cambridge, 1986), 73. In the offer to Anjou, the States pointed out they no longer considered themselves to be 'bounded and obliged in any manner whatsoever to the King of Spain, because he has violated his oath, assaulted their liberty and had sought to subject them to the barbarous tyranny of a foreign nation, to ruin and to wreck them' (quoted in A. C. J. Vrankrijker, *De motiveering van onzen opstand* (Nijmegen, 1933; repr. 1979), 125).

[2] Aggaeus van Albada, *Acten van den Vredehandel gheschiet te Colen* (Antwerp, 1581), 142.

diagnosis of the bewildering political problems of increasing discord and war, and above all they addressed the question of what sort of government was best to promote the common good and the welfare of the Netherlands.

Of course these questions were highly characteristic of Renaissance political thought. Essentially this chapter can be said to reconstruct the search of late sixteenth-century Dutch political treatises for 'the best state of the commonwealth', as Sir Thomas More and many other Renaissance theorists put it.

5.2. PLEAS FOR PRINCELY RULE: THE PROBLEM OF FRANÇOIS, DUKE OF ANJOU

In 1579 a *Remonstrance* to the States General was published on behalf of the inhabitants and community of Antwerp. The treatise was written 'in form of complaint' to indicate the 'causes and origin' of the 'confusion' and 'pitiable desolation of the fatherland' and 'the mistakes and abuses in the government'.[3] The problems were great, the *Remonstrance* assured, but 'the remedies are clear and sure'. First, the Dutch had to turn to God, and secondly, they had to 'remould' their government.

The *Remonstrance* fully recognized the authority of the States General. It propounded the familiar view that the States General had been chosen by the community 'in the name of God, to represent her right'. The 'office' of the States General was 'to set good order in all policies and governments of the country, to make laws and just ordinances, choosing a head and governor as superintendent'.[4] In addition, as this superintendent could not govern alone, a set of councils should be set up, consisting of a Council of State, a Privy Council and a Council of Finances. Thus the office of the States General was twofold. It should set up a proper governmental structure along the lines indicated and it should decide on the most important matters that affected 'the general state of the country' such as matters of war, foreign treaties and coinage.

In this conception of the political order the governor should rule 'under the name and authority of the States General'. None the less the *Remonstrance* asserted that the States General had delegated full

---

[3] *Remonstrantie oft vertooch in maniere van beclach aen mijne Heeren, de gedeputeerde vande generale Staten, ende vanden gheunieerden Provincien, by den inwoonderen ende ghemeynte der Stadt van Antwerpen, met advijs om te voorsiene tot de quade orde van desen lande* (1579), 3, 5. [4] Ibid. 6.

power and authority to the governor to decide 'absolutely' in matters of his concern. The big problem was the continual interference by the States General in the affairs of the governor. In addition, the towns were haunted by particularism, seeking more their 'particular profit' than the general. This led to incorrect decision-making and to inefficient government. The States were urged to redress this situation, and to appoint a governor with full power to decide. For 'as nature shows that the body must have a head, and expediency shows that all assemblies need a leader', the *Remonstrance* concluded, 'it is the duty of the States to choose a Governor-General who, being head of the community, has the same power and authority as the aforesaid States, which is to govern completely on his own, to conduct policy, and to deal with the necessities of the countries in the place of the aforesaid States'.[5] This did not mean the governor could rule at will. As he had received his authority and power from the States, the governor was always bound to 'the laws and conditions', following their instruction and orders. If he forsook his office, if he did not administer justice properly or did not maintain the 'rights, laws, privileges and freedoms', the States General were fully entitled to 'dismiss him and constitute another in his place'.[6]

The *Remonstrance* was of the opinion that the Prince of Orange was the best choice for the position of Governor-General. Others, however, urged the appointment of François, Duke of Anjou, to the position. In 1578 a 'German noble' published a letter of advice on the state of the Netherlands, which was addressed to Marnix van St Aldegonde. His intention was to show which policy the States should adopt for the 'conservation and health' of the provinces. For this purpose, the German noble argued, the books of political doctrine were of little help. Their traditional categorization of governments in 'gouvernmens populaire, de peu, et royal' bore no relation to the rich variety of political reality, where the diversity of 'laws and privileges' and 'the customs of people' evaded political doctrine.[7]

According to the treatise, the state of the Netherlands could best be described as 'mixed'. Authority was divided between the lord and the 'popular force' with the accent clearly on the latter. This was particularly due to the importance of commerce, and, consequently,

---

[5] Ibid. 13.   [6] Ibid. 14.

[7] *Lettre contenant un avis de l'estate auquel sont les affaires des Pais-bas, tant pour le regard des principales provinces & villes en particulier, comme de toutes ensemble en general, avecq la recherche due party, le plus promt plus asseuré, que les Estats puissent prendre contre l'Espagnol, pour leur conservation & salut* (Reims, 1578), p. iiii.

of the towns, especially in Flanders, Brabant, Holland and Zeeland. The Dutch, recognizing that powerful lords had strong ambitions, 'were so envious of their liberty, that they did not desire the augmentation of their lord'.[8]

Acknowledging the importance of the States in actual government, the treatise pointed out that, despite the evident merits such had in peacetime, the inefficiency of the States, with their endless deliberations, was a hazard in wartime. Now the provinces were at war they needed a 'chef', a powerful, rich and virtuous prince, who was 'strong enough to suffer and repair numerous losses with constancy and assurance'.[9] To prevent an outburst of rivalry amongst Dutch nobles, it was advisable to take a foreign prince, who, not only by virtue and experience, but also by 'his dignity and illustrious birth', stood above them. Considering all alternatives, the German noble opted for Anjou, not only because he was of 'a gentle nature and a tempered power' but also because he was French and therefore much closer to the Dutch nature than a German. Moreover, 'Monsieur' had the necessary means at his disposal and had no intention of becoming 'master' of the provinces.

Such was also the opinion of the *Letter of a noble from Hainaut*. It recognized that there was no hope for a fruitful reconciliation with Philip II, who, 'blinded by an envy of revenge', had become a 'cruel and mortal enemy'.[10] Reconciliation could only lead to the 'subversion' of all ancient laws, privileges and customs and would bring the Dutch into 'extreme servitude and oppression'. This was unacceptable to 'all brave nations', the Hainaut noble asserted, for there could be nothing 'good, agreeable, lovely, glorious or honest … without temperate liberty'.[11] It was only too natural that in this situation the state was changed, and at this point the *Letter* referred to the change of the Roman Empire into a republic, to show that even the 'most holy magistracy in the world' had to subordinate itself to the course of nature, due to which like the human body, the state was liable to change.

According to the *Letter* it would in fact be a 'great crime' to deny that the Netherlands should undergo a change of state, 'for the state is no longer what it was'.[12] The tyrant had already been deprived of

[8] Ibid., p. xiii.   [9] Ibid., p. xii.
[10] *Lettre d'un gentilhomme de Haynault, a monsieur de la Mothe, Gouverneur de Gravelines* (1578), 26.
[11] Ibid. 39.   [12] Ibid. 16.

his power, which had been 'attributed' to the States General, and it would be a matter of treason to abandon those who had done everything 'for the defence of the common liberty'. In the view of the *Letter* the most viable option for the Dutch was to accept Anjou; it would be a disgrace to refuse the favour of 'a great prince, full of the will to do good, full of courage, full of temperance and prudence'.[13]

A 1579 pamphlet addressed to all 'honourable men' fully agreed. It was high time to discard the Spanish yoke and accept Anjou as lord. For France was the only country which could cut off Spanish logistics and Anjou had both the power and the position to achieve this. The argument that the duke could not be trusted was countered with the advice to 'accept him on such conditions that he cannot cheat you'.[14] Thus the Dutch should allow no foreign garrisons to enter their towns, they should retain control over the elections of governors and magistrates and, finally, they should take care that 'the helm' remained in the hands of people they themselves had freely chosen.

A similar view was propounded by a *Short admonition to the further United Provinces and towns of the Netherlands*, the written version of a speech William of Orange made in January 1580,[15] published in the same year. The *Short admonition* argued that, since reconciliation with Philip II would only lead to the ruin of the country and its commerce, war should be continued and in fact intensified. As the Dutch themselves lacked the means to do so, the assistance of a foreign 'king or potentate' was required. The choice should fall on Anjou, the treatise argued, for not only was there no foreign prince to equal him in sympathy for the Netherlands, but, coming from France, the duke had also the possibility of striking where it was most necessary, namely at the southern border of the Netherlands. Moreover, he was in fact the only one amongst the kings or potentates who would not hesitate to assist the Netherlands.

Orange, emphasized, too, that in accepting Anjou the 'legal government' should not be endangered. In this respect three points in particular, touching the essence of the Revolt, were at stake. First, the Netherlands should have 'a rightful, just and legal govern-ment...under the policy and administration of the inhabitants

---

[13] Ibid. 11.

[14] *Eersame goede mannen, het is nu hooch tijt dat ghy lieden eenmael besluyt oft ghy het Spaensch iock wilt teenemael afleggen ofte niet* (1579), fol. A2.

[15] See P. A. M. Geurts, *De Nederlandse Opstand in de pamfletten 1566–1584* (Utrecht, 1983; first pub. 1956), 109.

themselves'. Secondly, the 're-establishment and unbreakable main-tenance of the rights, laws, charters, statutes, privileges and freedoms of the country'[16] should be guaranteed. Finally, religious persecution should be abolished and free exercise of the Reformed religion should be permitted. In short, Anjou was not to govern 'absolutely' in the Netherlands, but in accordance with proper conditions guaranteeing the 'liberty and welfare of the country'.[17]

The choice of Anjou was also defended by *Emanuel–Erneste : dialogue of two persons on the state of the Netherlands*, which offered an elaborate analysis of the alternative policies the United Provinces could adopt.[18] The dialogue dealt with the question whether the state of the Netherlands should be transformed into a 'popular republic' or whether the Low Countries should appoint another prince. The dialogue plainly rejected the idea of a republic. First, it argued that the Dutch were accustomed to be governed by others, 'so they don't know what is bad and what is common good'.[19] Secondly, it pointed out that the Netherlands consisted of diverse provinces, each with their own privileges and liberties and all keen to promote their own interests. For a self-governing republic this rivalry and lack of unity should be considered a grave and essential disadvantage. Thirdly, according to the dialogue, it was characteristic of small republics that 'they don't resolve this [disadvantage], and do no good but from necessity'.[20]

Having rejected the general case for a republic, the dialogue continued to denounce the proposal that the Netherlands should adopt the model of the Swiss Republic. Like the Netherlands, so Emanuel argued, the Swiss Republic consisted of a number of provinces, with a high level of self-government, co-operating in the resolution of affairs which regarded them all, such as the defence of the country. Erneste, however, answered that if one considered 'the habits, courage and discipline' of both nations, one should conclude that 'the state of the one will be the ruin of the other'.[21] According to Erneste there was a decisive difference in mentality between the Swiss and the Dutch. The Swiss were a hard-working people, uncorrupted by the pleasures of life and full of love for liberty, which they valued

---

[16] William of Orange, *Corte vermaninghe aende naerdere gheunierde Provincien ende Steden der Nederlanden* (1580), fol. B.   [17] Ibid., fols. C3–C4.

[18] See also Paul Geurts, *Overzicht van Nederlandsche politieke geschriften tot in de eerste helft der 17e eeuw*, (Maastricht, 1942), 104ff., and Geurts, *De Nederlandse Opstand*, 199ff.

[19] Gerard Prouninck van Deventer, *Emanuel–Erneste. Dialogue de deux personnages sur l'Estat du Pais Bas* (Antwerp, 1580), 6.   [20] Ibid.   [21] Ibid. 11.

higher than their own goods and life. In addition, they were unique
amongst the Christian nations in maintaining 'the ancient military
discipline'. Thus the Swiss possessed the virtues necessary to uphold
a popular republic, which 'requires a constant, virtuous, united
people, who do not care for riches, who, with regard to both the
choice of magistrates and the administration of justice, obey neither
lords nor relatives, nor to some favours'.[22] In addition the people of
a popular state should 'govern themselves voluntarily in obedience to
the laws and military discipline'. The Dutch, Erneste asserted,
lacked any of these virtues. They abounded in riches and indulged in
the pleasures of life, which had made them 'effeminate and corrupt'.
Although they boasted of their liberties and franchises, they were
unwilling to sacrifice some of their abundance for the sake of liberty.
As Erneste pointed out with unconcealed repugnance, 'there are
those amongst them who have sworn to the living God not to sacrifice
any blood or good for the defence of their fatherland, who storm,
curse and threat, and are even on the point of revolting if one asks
them but a small portion of their annual revenues'.[23] Moreover, the
Dutch suffered from great inconstancy and lacked a proper and
disciplined army. Finally, unlike the Swiss Republic, the Dutch had
to reckon with a considerable nobility, which would be unwilling to
render their prerogatives and powers to the people. To ignore the
aristocrats, great enemies of democracy, would only lead to bloodshed. In short, a popular republic was not a viable option for the
Netherlands.

With regard to the proposal of an aristocratic republic Erneste
arrived at an identical conclusion. He pointed out that the nobles of
the Netherlands were 'too corrupt, envious, partial and forlorn of the
virtue which in former times had been the true source of the status
of their ancestors'.[24] Moreover, the differences in power and riches
amongst them were too great and they were so accustomed to being
governed by a prince that 'their habits and conditions, disposed to a
principality, are completely incapable of aristocracy'. Therefore, the
dialogue concluded that the problems of the Netherlands could only
be 'surmounted by the virtuousness of a new prince'. The dialogue
opted for Anjou, arguing that the duke could dispose of the necessary
power to resist Philip II. However, in line with previous pleas for
Anjou, the dialogue demanded certain guarantees from the duke.
First, he should above all 'love, cherish and follow the advice of the

<hr />

[22] Ibid. 21.   [23] Ibid. 12.   [24] Ibid. 27.

Prince of Orange'.[25] Secondly, he should respect the authority of the States and maintain the privileges of the country, confining himself mainly to military affairs.[26] Finally, he should leave the religious question entirely in the hands of the States General.

On grounds also regarding the virtuousness of the Dutch, the *Advice of a lover of the common good to the citizenry of Antwerp*, published in July 1580, likewise favoured the Anjou option. According to this treatise, allegedly written by Marnix van St Aldegonde[27] the situation had deteriorated to such an extent that the welfare of the country, indeed the sheer existence of the state, was threatened. In the view of the 'lover of the common good' the principal cause of this *grand mal* was the neglect of the common good. Instead of regarding the common good, most men let themselves be ruled by passion. The *Advice* argued that to resist the tyranny of Philip II it was necessary to create concord and co-operation amongst the provinces and towns, and to obtain the support of a foreign prince. Therefore, the *Advice* favoured Anjou, who was described as a peaceful man, without passion and full of virtue.

Anjou's virtuousness was also praised by other treatises. The 1578 *Letter containing the clarification of the actions and behaviour of…the Duke of Anjou* did its best to present the duke as a most virtuous prince. He was said to be a peaceful man, who possessed the three virtues of 'generosity', namely 'fidele amitié, moderation et prudence'.[28] Following the example of the Romans, who re-established the Greeks in their liberty by chasing away their oppressors, Anjou would consider it a most honourable victory to liberate the Dutch and to maintain them in their old privileges and franchises.

In 1579 Anjou was even presented as a gift of God. According to the anonymous *Advice from a lover of the Netherlands* the welfare of the community depended to a large extent on the virtue of its prince. As the *Advice* put it, 'a prince is the torch which illuminates the people, and leads them to good works. If he is good and virtuous, so will be the people; if he is evil, the people will be likewise; for each seeks to follow him in order to please him.[29]

---

[25] Ibid. 59.

[26] Ibid. 59, 61. The dialogue assumed also the continuation of the clause of disobedience, as it pointed out that if the new prince violated 'the laws and sworn conditions', the States and people were obliged not to obey him any more (p. 63).

[27] Geurts, *De Nederlandse Opstand*, 109.

[28] *Lettre contenant l'eclaircissement des actions et deportemens de Monsieur, filz & frere de Roy Duc d'Anjou, D'Alençon &c.* (Rouen, 1578), p. x.

[29] *Advijs van eenen liefhebber des Nederlandts* (1579), fol. A2.

Therefore, the choice of a good and virtuous prince was the key to the solution of the Dutch troubles. Anjou, described in terms of the heavenly manna, was seen as the perfect choice. Of course Anjou's activities in the Netherlands turned out to be at least as controversial as the treaties concluded with him. Thus the debate on his virtuousness continued. The importance of virtue was stressed, for example in the duke's own Joyous Entry into Antwerp in 1582. When he entered the town a still life was presented to him symbolizing the alliance between Antwerp and himself; the scene featured, amongst others, Justice surrounded by Concord, Prudence and Fortitude'.[30] In other still lifes Anjou was compared to David beating Saul, with the province of Brabant itself in the role of Jonathan. At the same time it was emphasized that the duke, as ordained by God and elected by the people, was to govern in accordance with the privileges and laws of the country.

As if all previous praise was not enough the *Principal apology for 'monseigneur' and the States of the Netherlands* presented Anjou as Hercules chasing the tyrant and fighting his battle against fortune with great virtue.[31] Anjou, however, was no Hercules. His fateful attack on Antwerp crushed every feeling of sympathy and loyalty towards him. The 'French Fury' refuelled the discussion on Anjou, and thereby on the necessity of a prince. Some of the treatises, arguing in favour of princely rule, still defended Anjou; others searched for alternative solutions.

One of the first treatises to assess the situation and weigh a number of alternatives was the 1583 *Warning to all good inhabitants of the Netherlands*. The treatise sought to establish how the freedom of the Reformed religion and the liberty and security of the country, on which, as it added, the 'particular welfare of each depended', could best be protected. The authors, presenting themselves as true 'lovers' of the Reformed religion and the liberty and security of the country, took three proposals into consideration.

First, the idea was discussed to reunite with the 'Malcontents', the Walloon provinces which had reconciled themselves with Philip II. According to the *Warning* this was impossible as both clergy, nobility and towns of the reconciled provinces would be unwilling to do anything against Spain. In fact to negotiate with the 'Mal-

---

[30] See *De blijden ende heerlijcke Incomste van mijnheer Franssois van Vranckrijck ... in sijne zeer vermaerde stadt van Antwerpen* (Antwerp, 1582), 40, 41.
[31] *Premiere apologie pour monseigneur, et les estats des Pays-Bas* (1582), 37.

contents' was to negotiate with the Spaniards themselves, who had full control over the reconciled areas. The proposal of reconciliation with Philip II himself was rapidly rejected as such could only lead to 'eternal slavery'.

Secondly, the *Warning* addressed the proposal of turning the country into a republic, and of adopting either an aristocratic or a democratic government 'after the example of Venice, and the cantons of Switzerland and after the example of Holland and Zeeland'.[32] The examples invoked were highly significant. They not only confirmed that both Venice and Switzerland were considered as model governments, but also indicated that Holland and Zeeland were considered, at least by the authors of this treatise, to have adopted a republican form of government. The *Warning* felt that although it would be 'very good' to make a republic of the United Provinces, this was not a feasible option. In contrast with Venice and Switzerland the geographic location made the provinces vulnerable to attacks from powerful neighbouring princes. Moreover, the provinces were afflicted by particularism and a very slow and inefficient process of decision-making.

For these reasons the provinces could not do without a prince who was able to prevent discord and internal rivalry, the traditional causes of the fall of republics. However, the *Warning* did not want unbridled princely rule. According to the treatise, 'in matters of state the best, most assured and most stable policy and government' was a 'monarchy' which was 'so cut and bridled with conditions' that the monarch was 'not allowed to use tyranny or improper and unlawful violence against his subjects'.[33] Such was assured, according to the treatise, by the Joyous Entry of Brabant and by the treaty with Anjou (which in line with the Joyous Entry curtailed the duke's political powers). As military and financial help of a foreign prince was indispensable, the provinces were forced to reunite themselves with Anjou, who should be accepted on the conditions of the treaty concluded with him.

Similar conclusions were formulated by *A humble address and simple explanation of the sole means, through which from now on one will preserve these Netherlands from further destruction.* In the view of this treatise the Dutch

---

[32] *Waerschouwinghe aen alle goede inghesetenen vanden Nederlanden, die tot beschermenisse vande vrijheydt van hunne Religie, persoonen, Previlegien, ende oude hercomen, teghens die tyrannie vande Spaingnaerden ende heuren aenhanck, t'samen verbonden en vereenicht sijn* (1583), fol. A3.

[33] Ibid., fol. B3.

Provinces suffered from two principal problems. The first regarded
the decision-making by the States, which was far too slow, whereas in
matters of war 'diligence' was demanded. The second problem
considered the people occupying governmental posts. According to *A
humble address* the government was run by people who lacked
experience and it urged a revision of this situation. The 'affairs of
state and war' should be handled by nobles and 'old experienced
officers' loyal to the Reformed religion, together with 'the highest
and most experienced men of the towns (being richer of reason than
of goods)'.[34]

The *Humble address* denounced the idea of a reconciliation with
Philip II with the familiar argument that this could only turn the
Dutch into 'poor slaves of the Inquisition for eternity'. The only
feasible option was a reconciliation with Anjou on the terms of the
treaty of Bordeaux. One of the principal conditions was that Anjou
should not try to introduce Frenchmen into the government of the
country. The treatise added that if the duke was unwilling to meet
these demands, another 'head', preferably the Prince of Orange,
should be appointed, for 'these countries cannot exist without a
head'.[35]

The demands for a reconciliation with Anjou were to little effect.
The duke retired to France, where he died in 1584. The Dutch were
forced to find other ways to preserve their country from the ever-
growing threat of the Spaniards, who by that time had reconquered
the greater part of Flanders. The 1584 *Discourse of a sincere, impartial
and unfeigned patriot on the present state of these Dutch Provinces* still looked
in the direction of France for help. It reasserted that in the present
state of affairs, the true patriot, 'who without any partiality of
religion or otherwise, does not seek but the welfare of the country',[36]
had to search for the liberation of the country from foreign tyranny,
for freedom of conscience and for the freedom to ply his trade, all in
accordance with the old freedom and privileges. Such could only be
achieved, according to the *Discourse*, by means of war, for the sole
purpose of the King of Spain was to bring the Netherlands into
'eternal slavery'. The *Discourse* rejected the proposal to adopt a
republican form of government. In fact the government 'by many
heads, chosen from the state of the community, who have not had

---

[34] *Een ootmoedich vertooch ende eenvoudighe verclaringhe vanden eenighe middel, waer deur men voordaen dese
arme Nederlanden sal behoeden van voorder verwoestinghe* (1583), fol. A4.   [35] Ibid., fol. C.

[36] *Discours van eenen oprechten, onpartijdighen ende ongheveynsden Patriot opden teghenwoordighen staet van
dese Nederlantsche Provincien* (1584), fol. A2.

absolute authority to govern and command' and 'the small power which the United Provinces now have' were the main causes of all problems.[37] To be successful an army required the absolute command of a prince. Therefore, the *Discourse* favoured the acceptance of the King of France as lord and prince over the Netherlands. It recognized that this was a controversial proposal and argued that, if the proposal contributed to discord, the idea should be dropped in order to maintain unity amongst the provinces. Then, the *Discourse* argued, 'it would be best for the provinces and towns to remain united ... as they now are and to make good and steady policy both on the issue of government and of war'.[38] The *Discourse* suggested that in this situation a Council of State should be formed of 'experienced and excellent persons who will have the authority to command absolutely'.

A similar preference for French aid was formulated by Dirck Volckertsz Coornhert in his 1584 *Consideration of the present situation of the Dutch affair*. Coornhert, repudiating any suggestion of reconciliation with Philip II, argued that, due to religious differences and strife, discord was the main problem of the Netherlands. He reiterated the view that the provinces were in desperate need of foreign aid. Thus it was necessary to obtain a 'head', which was 'powerful enough to protect these countries and to maintain it in concord'.[39] For Coornhert the King of France was the obvious choice; he had the necessary means at his disposal, he allowed the Reformed to worship according to their religion and he had a common interest in fighting the Spanish threat. Coornhert acknowledged that the French king could also employ his power to the disadvantage of the Netherlands. However, indicating that his plea for the King of France was a highly practical one, he retorted, 'we are in such a bad state, that we are in no position to choose between good and evil, even less between good and better. We have to choose between bad and worse.'[40] To minimize the risks Coornhert proposed accepting the King of France under certain conditions which should guarantee the freedoms and privileges of the Netherlands.

In the meantime, other treatises had begun to speak in even more pessimistic tones, concluding that there was no viable alternative but to reconcile with Spain. A principal example of this attitude was

---

[37] Ibid., fol. A3.   [38] Ibid., fol. A4.
[39] Dirck Volckertsz Coornhert, 'Overweginghe van de teghenwoordighe gelegentheyt der Nederlantsche saken', in Dirck Volckertsz Coornhert, *Wercken*, 3 vols. (Amsterdam, 1630), vol. i, fol. 551. For Coornhert, see 243–56.   [40] Ibid., fol. 553.

the 1583 *Friendly address*, discussing 'which means these depressed countries may employ to their conservation and maintenance of the religion, liberty and privileges'. Assuming that the free worship of the Reformed religion and the maintenance of the freedoms and privileges of the countries were the two principal objectives of the war, the treatise analysed a number of alternative policies.

It repudiated any form of foreign aid and intervention, for every foreigner merely sought 'to enrich himself with our poverty and to fanaticize his violence and rule, keeping us in slavery'.[41] Foreigners, the main message was, simply could not be trusted.

Likewise the *Friendly address* rejected the idea that the Netherlands should 'remain by themselves' and try to defend the country by means of civic militia. It deplored the state of the Netherlands, lamenting that the government was 'disgraceful, weak, negligent and effeminate'.[42]

The treatise rejected also any proposal to change the form of government in a republican direction, arguing that every violent change of 'the state of government' distorted 'liberty and freedom', which formed the essence of 'justice and good policy'. Therefore, each country should seek to maintain its traditional form of government, be it monarchy, aristocracy or democracy.

The *Friendly address* praised the traditional form of government of the Netherlands, which of 'time immemorial had been governed under the power of an overlord, who left the nobility and communities the use of their proper liberty'.[43] It was described as the 'most perfect and free' government, unsurpassed in bringing the people 'to honour and virtue'. In this respect the Venetian and Swiss models were bluntly set aside. Venice was depicted as governed by only thirty or forty families, which had absolute power, suppressed the rest of the community and abused their power as they liked. Switzerland was said to be a country of great confusion, tormented by faction and unbridled corruption.

The treatise concluded that it would be best to seek a reconciliation with the 'Malcontents' and with Philip II himself. It was argued that a prince, having done his duty to maintain what he could not allow to be hurt without losing his good reputation, would be willing

---

[41] *Vriendelick Vertooch. Daerby ghediscoureert werdt wat middelen dese bedruckte Landen te wercke moghen legghen tot haerlieder conservatie en onderhout van de Religie, Liberteyt ende Privilegien* (Friendly address) (1583), fol. B.

[42] Ibid., fol. B3.　　　　[43] Ibid., fol. B4.

to comply with the demands of his people, rather than see it extirpated.[44]

The *Friendly address* and other treatises putting forward similar arguments gave expression to the feeling of desperation that was taking root in some Dutch circles. It certainly stood in line with the treatises which argued that princely rule was the only solution to the Dutch troubles, although most abhorred the idea of reconciling with the King of Spain.

Some of them pleaded for princely rule because such was in accordance with nature. Just as the human body could not do without a head, so the body politic needed a prince. To protect the common good of the body politic a prince was indispensable. The prince was regarded as a necessary warrant against discord, confusion and particularism, the main problems afflicting the Netherlands. In this respect a principal element for the argument in favour of princely rule was the rejection of a republican form of government. Some treatises identified the republic with discord and confusion; others referred to the geographic location of the Netherlands, which made the provinces, in contrast to the models of Switzerland and Venice, vulnerable to attacks from powerful princes who surrounded them; *Emanuel–Erneste* argued that the Dutch simply lacked the virtue necessary to uphold a republic. In short, to preserve the common good, threatened by discord, corruption and inefficient decision-making, a virtuous prince was needed, who, above all in the role of military leader, could provide justice, concord, prudence and fortitude. In effect this was a rearticulation of standard Renaissance arguments.[45]

Of course the choice of princely rule and of Anjou in particular was also based on highly practical reasons, especially on the recognition that the Netherlands were helpless without foreign aid, and that Anjou possessed both the financial and military means to come to their aid. In this respect it should be underlined that to argue for the necessity of a prince was almost never to argue in favour of absolute

---

[44] Ibid., fol. D3. A similar argument was presented in the *Middelen ende conditien door de welcke d'Inghesetenen der gheunieerde Provincien, met der Maijesteyt vanden Coninck van Spaignen, haren matuerlicken Heere, met goeder conscientie, mits behoorlicke versekertheyt zouden moghen accorderen* (1584). It praised the Swiss Republic but claimed the Swiss model was not applicable in the Netherlands. In line with the *Friendly address* it stressed the dangers inherent to any change of the form of government and it saw good possibilities for a reconciliation with Philip II.

[45] For a recent overview see Skinner, *The foundations of modern political thought*, i. 113–28 and, for the northern Renaissance in particular, pp. 213–44. For a lucid summary, see Quentin Skinner, 'Political philosophy', in Charles B. Schmitt and Quentin Skinner (eds.), *The Cambridge history of Renaissance philosophy* (Cambridge, 1988), 389–452.

princely rule. The advocates of a prince in general favoured a 'bridled monarchy' along traditional Dutch lines. Thus the authority of the States was recognized; it was demanded that the actual government over the provinces should remain in the hands of the inhabitants. Anjou was only to be accepted if he was prepared to submit himself to the laws and privileges of the country. Likewise, some urged guarantees for the freedom of the Reformed religion.

These demands were in accordance with the policy of the States. Both in the 1578 treaty which gave him the title of 'Defender of the liberty of the Netherlands' and in the 1580 treaty of Plessis-lès-Tours, which made him lord of the Netherlands, Anjou's powers were strongly curtailed. The 1578 treaty, for example, explicitly ordered the duke not to interfere with matters which concerned 'the policy and the government of the country'.[46] In the negotiations at Plessis-lès-Tours, the States deputies under the leadership of Marnix van St Aldegonde refused to include the word 'sovereign' in Anjou's title, arguing that the word did not exist in the Dutch language (which was complete nonsense). The true reason of this refusal was probably that the use of the word sovereign, given the interpretation of Anjou's adviser Jean Bodin, might create the impression that the duke could rule freely in the Netherlands.[47] Aldegonde, however, used the Lacedaemon republic as a leading example during the negotiations.

5.3. JUSTUS LIPSIUS AND THE RISE OF POLITICAL NEOSTOICISM

The traditional Dutch emphasis on the limits of monarchy and the authority of the States was completely missing in the most elaborate and eloquent plea for princely rule to appear during the Dutch Revolt, the 1589 *Six bookes of politickes or civile doctrine*, written by Justus Lipsius, 'professor historiarum et iuris' at the recently founded

---

[46] See *Accord ende verbondt ghemaeckt tusschen mijn Heere de Hertoghe van Anjou...ende de Prelaten, Edelen ende ghedeputeerde vande Landen ende Steden, representerende de generale Staten van de Nederlanden* (Antwerp, 1578), fol. A4; see also Holt, *The Duke of Anjou*, 104–5.

[47] See Gordon Griffiths, 'Humanists and representative government in the sixteenth century: Bodin, Marnix, and the invitation to the Duke of Anjou to become ruler of the Low Countries', in *Representative institutions in theory and practice: historical papers read at Bryn Mawr College, 1968: studies presented to the International Commission for the History of Representative and Parliamentary Institutions* (Brussels, 1970), 61–83. Griffiths presents the negotiations as a clash between the political ideas of Bodin and of Marnix van St Aldegonde, describing the latter as a 'civic humanist' (p. 67) propounding a republican view. For the negotiations, see also Holt, *The Duke of Anjou*, 134–40, who presents the treaty as a highly revolutionary document.

University of Leiden.[48] The *Politics* were meant to instruct people in government, and princes in particular, on how, employing the precepts of the classical authors, they should 'set forward in the way of civil life (*vita civilis*), and finish their journey without wandering'[49] and without being carried away by the whims of fortune.

Completely in line with the humanist fashions of his time Lipsius argued that, to attain a *vita civilis*, the life 'we lead in the society of men, one with another, to mutual commodity and profit, and common use of all',[50] man had to be guided by prudence and virtue.

In the Lipsian analysis, government was crucial in attaining the *vita civilis*. Quoting Seneca and Livy, Lipsius described government as 'the chain, by which the commonwealth is linked together... the vital spirit, which so many millions of men do breathe'.[51] Government was the 'rod of Circes, which tames both men, and beasts' and which brought everyone 'in awe and due obedience, where before they were all fierce and unruly'.[52]

Lipsius left no doubt that among the possible forms of government princely rule was to be preferred. The principality, defined as 'the government of one, imposed according to custom, and laws, undertaken and executed for the good of the subjects',[53] was not only the most 'ancient kind of commanding', and 'most agreeable to nature', it was also consonant with reason.

As Lipsius' definition explicitly stated, the prince ruled for the benefit of his subjects. The ultimate purpose of the principality was to serve the *bonum publicum*. Quoting Cicero, Lipsius argued that 'a governor of a state, ought to propose, and set before him, the happy life of his citizens' which should be 'strengthened in wealth, abundant in riches, renowned and magnificent in glory, honest and venerable through virtue'.[54] To accomplish his task, and thus to achieve greatness, a prince needed prudence in his actions and virtue in his life. Above all a virtuous prince needed the sun of justice, 'the foundation of eternal fame', and the moon of clemency, 'a virtue of the mind, which with judgment, inclines from punishment, or revenge, to lenity'.[55] Justice had to be complemented by *fides*, and, since the prince 'is but a man, though he rules over men', clemency needed the company of 'modesty'.

---

[48] Justus Lipsius, *Politicorum sive civile doctrinae libri sex* (Leiden, 1589). In 1590 a Dutch trans. was published. The English trans., which appeared in 1594, was reprinted in the series The English experience, no. 287 (Amsterdam, 1970). Refs. are to this edn.; the spelling has been modernized.   [49] Lipsius, *Six bookes of politickes*, 1.   [50] Ibid.
[51] Ibid. 16–17.   [52] Ibid. 17.   [53] Ibid. 19.   [54] Ibid. 23.   [55] Ibid. 31.

In the first book of his *Politics* Lipsius had already argued that virtue was to be accompanied by prudence, especially because 'all virtue consists in election and means to bring things to pass, which we cannot purchase without prudence'. Thus without prudence, 'virtue is not obtained'.[56]

In the third book Lipsius argued that a prince was first of all in need of 'foreign prudence', of good counsel, as it was impossible for him to acquire perfect knowledge. More specifically the prince needed two sorts of assistant: counsellors, who assisted 'with their opinion and speech', and ministers, like 'governors, presidents, officers of the exchequer, judges', who assisted 'with action, and handy work'. The sort of counsellors and ministers a prince needed, and how their work should be organized, was described at length.

In discussing the 'proper prudence' of the prince himself, Lipsius emphasized the need of what he called civil and military prudence. In his analysis of civil prudence Lipsius put forward his controversial claims concerning the use of religion and the necessity of punishing public acts of heresy.[57] Equally controversial, if not more so, was his plea for 'mixed prudence', which held that occasionally it was necessary to intermingle prudence with a 'few drops of deceit'. In a rhetorical vein Lipsius asked whether, 'having to deal with a fox', the prince should not sometimes 'play the fox, especially if the good and public profit, which are always conjoined to the benefit, and profit of the prince, does require it?'[58] The ultimate criterion here was 'the good of the commonwealth'. In other words Lipsius judged it prudent for the prince to employ 'light' and 'middle' deceit – and he took great pains to explain these concepts – if the *bonum publicum* was at stake.

Next to civil prudence Lipsius stressed the importance of military prudence. In the fifth book of the *Politics* he developed a detailed blueprint for a disciplined, virtuous standing army. The soldiers for this army should be 'elected', as Lipsius put it, out of the proper subjects. Strangers not only were 'treacherous' and 'rebellious', they also lacked the affection for prince and country which was 'ingrafted' in the subjects by nature.

Lipsius' analysis of how, and on the basis of what criteria, these soldiers had to be elected out of the subjects, offered one of the few

---

[56] Ibid. 11.
[57] See 251, 254–6 for Lipsius' views and his conflict with Coornhert over this issue.
[58] Lipsius, *Six bookes of politickes*, 113.

instances of the *Politics* where the citizens were brought to the fore. Lipsius had discussed the role of the citizen in politics in a previous book, the celebrated *De constantia*, published in 1584.

The work intended to offer a word of comfort 'in publicis malis'. *De constantia* urged the reader to endure the times of trouble with constancy, defined as the 'sincere and immovable strength of the mind which is neither elated nor downcast by outward or fortuitous circumstances'.[59] Strength in this context referred to what Lipsius called 'a firmness implanted in the heart, not by any delusion or opinion, but by judgment and right reason'. Guided by reason one should patiently endure the whims of fortune and fate without lamenting. As Lipsius emphasized, such an attitude did not amount to defeatism. It was the result of calculation on the scale of reason, which taught the wise to act or to acquiesce, each at the proper moment.

De constantia warned against a too strong affection for the fatherland. It reminded the reader that the Patria had been founded by the ancestors out of private interests, because they realized it would contribute to their own welfare. It was proper for the citizen to love and defend his country, even to die for it. However, he should not lament it. Ultimately only heaven was man's one and true fatherland. The earthly fatherland was submitted to the laws of growth and decline. And Providence could not be resisted. In the fortunes and misfortunes of life the greatest virtue of man was to be constant, to follow reason and to quell passion.

These ideas were reflected in the final book of the *Politics*, dealing with civil war. According to Lipsius, nothing was more 'miserable' and 'dishonourable' than civil war, 'the very sea of calamities', and he urged princes to prevent it. The citizens were warned never to cause a civil war, or to participate in it, not even in the case of tyranny: 'Let them endure things present, in hope of amendment.'[60]

Lipsius was not alone in underlining the importance of 'constancy'. For example, in 1569 the Antwerp poet and painter Joris Hoefnaghel wrote, on commission of a well-to-do Dutch merchant, a *Treatise of patience*, which in twenty-four emblems stressed the importance of patience for all aspects of human life.[61] In 1583 Jean

---

[59] J. Lipsius, *Twee boecken van de Stantvasticheyt* (Leiden, 1584), 21.

[60] Lipsius, *Six bookes of politickes*, 202.

[61] *Traité de la Patience*, in *Patientia. 24 politieke emblemata door Joris Hoefnaghel*, ed. R. van Roosbroeck (Antwerp, 1935). For Hoefnaghel and the *Patientia* see N. Mout, 'The Family

Baptist Houwaert published his book on ethics, which, as the subtitle indicated, taught man 'how to live properly and virtuously, to die blessed and to come in eternal glory'.[62] One of the virtues Houwaert emphasized was constancy. The purpose of his book was to stimulate man to 'remain constant in faith, hope and love until the end and obtain the desired eternal glory'.[63]

Both Lipsius and Hoefnaghel, and perhaps Houwaert as well, were members of the Family of Love, a distinguished Spiritualist sect whose other members included famous scholars and humanists such as the Antwerp printer Plantin and the geographer and cartographer Ortelius.[64] As the doctrines of the Familists, in which constancy played an important role, contained many elements perfectly in line with Lipsius' views, it has been suggested that Lipsius' books on ethics and politics were inspired by Familism and perhaps should be seen as an articulation of the ethical and political ideas dominating the Family of Love.[65]

As the seminal studies of Gerhard Oestreich have shown, Lipsius was one of the principal protagonists in the revival and actualization of Stoic teachings, which had been so characteristic of Renaissance humanism. Many concepts and principal ideas of Renaissance political thought were derived from Roman Stoic sources.[66] However, according to Oestreich, Neostoicism, as a distinct and coherent moral and political philosophy, was developed in the Netherlands; indeed Oestreich did not hesitate to speak in terms of the 'Netherlands movement'.[67]

In its conception and argumentation Lipsius' Neostoicism stood squarely within the tradition of Renaissance political thought, employing its political language and organizing categories. His analysis of princely rule in the *Politics* elaborated on the humanist mirror-for-princes tradition. Thus the prince was presented as the *vir*

of Love (Huis der Liefde) and the Dutch Revolt', in A. Duke and C. Tamse (eds.), *Britain and the Netherlands*, vii: *Church and state since the Reformation* (The Hague, 1981), 89.

[62] Jean Baptist Houwaert, *De Vier Uuterste, van de doot, van het oordeel, van d'eeuwich leven, van de pyne der hellen* (Antwerp, 1583), front page.   [63] Ibid., p. xix.

[64] For the Family of Love, see Alistair Hamilton, *The Family of Love* (Cambridge, 1981).

[65] See Mout, 'The Family of Love', and M. E. H. N. Mout, 'Heilige Lipsius, bid voor ons', *TvG* 97 (1984), 195–206, esp. 202–4.

[66] See Skinner, *The foundations of modern political thought*, vol. i, p. xiv, and W. J. Bouwsma, 'The two faces of humanism: Stoicism and Augustinianism in the Renaissance', in W. J. Bouwsma, *A usable past: essays in European cultural history* (Berkeley, Calif., 1990), 19–73.

[67] See in particular Gerhard Oestreich, *Neostoicism and the early modern state* (Cambridge, 1982), and Gerhard Oestreich, *Antiker Geist und moderner Staat bei Justus Lipsius (1547–1606)* (Göttingen, 1989), with a fine introduction by Nicolette Mout.

virtutis, who, with virtuous and prudent acts, had to fight capricious fortune in order to achieve glory and greatness. The qualities the prince needed to do so were scrupulously outlined in the *Politics*, which contained thorough humanist analyses of classical virtues such as justice, clemency, modesty and prudence.

At the same time Lipsius, following Machiavelli's analysis in *The Prince*, discarded the humanist mirror-for-princes tradition at crucial points.[68] First, following the Machiavellian lead, Lipsius argued that the traditionally overarching virtues of justice and honesty should be set aside if the supreme value of the common good was at stake. Secondly, like Machiavelli, Lipsius had a much keener eye for the realities of power politics than most other humanist theorists of princely rule. Both Machiavelli and Lipsius emphasized the importance of a strong and disciplined army, Machiavelli arguing for a disciplined civic militia and Lipsius arguing for a disciplined standing army, largely elected out of the proper subjects.

Likewise, *De constantia* elaborated on the humanist debate on what should be regarded as the noblest way of civil life. Reviving the classical ideals of Livy, Sallust and above all Cicero's *De officiis*, many humanists had argued that the highest earthly duty of man was to put his talents in the service of his fatherland. A life of *negotium*, of virtuous acts of public service, was the supreme road to glory and happiness. In contrast, other humanists such as Petrarch and the fifteenth-century Italian Platonists repudiated the active life, celebrating a life of *otium* instead. Only through a life of contemplation could man raise his mind above the accidental whirls of history in order to reach the eternal realm of wisdom and truth. Instead of getting involved in the corruption of politics it was best to leave the burdens of the community to a virtuous prince.

In *De constantia* Lipsius apparently celebrated a life of *otium*, urging his readers to distance themselves from the caprices of life and to cultivate constancy in order to bring 'in subjection this broken and distressed mind of mine to right reason and God and subdue all human and earthly things to my mind'. This should not lead to a complete withdrawal from politics; Lipsius' thought featured the characteristic Stoic emphasis on self-sufficiency combined with a

---

[68] On the relationship between Machiavelli and Lipsius, see Martin van Gelderen, 'The Machiavellian moment and the Dutch Revolt: the rise of Neostoicism and Dutch republicanism', in Gisela Bock *et al.* (eds.), *Machiavelli and republicanism* (Cambridge, 1990), 205–23. For a different interpretation, see Oestreich, *Antiker Geist*, 166ff.

detached concern for others. However, whereas humanists pleading for a life of *negotium* had argued that creative and active participation was the principal duty of the citizen, Lipsius emphasized dutiful obedience under the guidance of a virtuous prince as the outstanding virtue.

As such, Neostoicism demanded, to quote Oestreich, 'self-discipline and the extension of the duties of the ruler and the moral education of the army, the officials, and indeed of the whole people, to a life of work, frugality, dutifulness and obedience'.[69] In the course of the seventeenth century the Lipsian appropriation of Stoic ideas turned out to be highly influential in the development of absolutist theories, especially in the German Empire.[70] In Oestreich's view Neostoicism provided the philosophical and moral foundation for the modern state. The Lipsian view of man and the world 'entailed rationalization of the state and its apparatus of government, autocratic rule by the prince, the imposition of discipline on his subjects, and strong military defence'.[71] In addition Lipsius' Neo-stoic ideology offered the first blueprint for 'the qualities and duties of a modern bureaucracy'.[72]

Unlike modern bureaucracies, however, the counsellors and ministers from the third book of Lipsius' *Politics* did not represent a relatively autonomous apparatus of government, a rationalized power structure which would exist independently of those in charge of government. They were still very much the personal advisers of the prince, appointed by him to enhance his prudence.[73] The Lipsian governmental apparatus, though occasionally described as a state, still seemed to be very much the patrimony of the prince, and in this sense Lipsius' analysis should be seen as an important elaboration of widespread Renaissance ideas on the role of the political counsellor. Therefore, it seems much more appropriate to value Lipsius as one of the last Renaissance philosophers, paving the way for absolutist theories on prince and citizens.[74]

---

[69] Oestreich, *Neostoicism and the early modern state*, 7.
[70] See ibid. and Oestreich, *Antiker Geist*, 188–212.
[71] Oestreich, *Neostoicism and the early modern state*, 30. See also Gunter Abel, *Stoizismus und frühe Neuzeit: zur Entstehungsgeschichte des modernen Denkens im Felde von Ethik und Politik* (Berlin, 1978), 70, who regards the *Six bookes of politickes* as a political theory of the early modern state, presenting the state as an 'independent order of morality based on command and obedience which demands military power, power of government and power of admini-stration'.   [72] Oestreich, *Neostoicism and the early modern state*, 45.
[73] As Oestreich himself has emphasized, not the state as organization but the prince as acting statesman was at the heart of the *Sixe bookes of politickes*. Oestreich, *Antiker Geist*, 148, 172.
[74] See Oestreich, *Antiker Geist*, 186, where Lipsius is labelled the 'last Renaissance philosopher'.

In the context of the Dutch Revolt Lipsius' work was above all the most distinguished plea for princely rule and a powerful repudiation of some of the main arguments employed by Dutch authors to support the Revolt. For example, whereas various legitimizations of the Revolt had celebrated the fatherland in the highest terms and had emphasized the civic duty of active resistance against tyranny, Lipsius strongly tempered the importance of the fatherland and denounced any form of resistance. Moreover, the role of the provincial States and the States General, so prominent in actual Dutch politics and in the political literature of the Revolt, did not enter the Lipsian analysis of politics at all. The silence was significant. Lipsius, who was in touch with the leading politicians of his day, favoured a more centralized princely rule for the Netherlands. In his view the States' government of the 1580s was a catastrophe.[75] Lipsius' principal argument that the *vita civilis* could only be attained in a political order marked by unified, virtuous princely rule, was a plain rejection both of the reality of Dutch politics and of those treatises which felt princely rule was not the solution to the Dutch troubles.

5.4. FOLLOWING THE SWISS AND THE PLEA FOR DEMOCRACY

In strong contrast with those advocating princely rule, some authors started to contemplate republican options. One of the options was the model of the Swiss confederacy, denounced by many of those pleading for princely rule.[76]

One of the first treatises to praise the Swiss model was *The true patriot to the good patriots*, probably written by Petrus Beutterich, both a Reformed minister and counsellor to the Count of the Palatinate, Johann Casimir, and a distinguished advocate of the latter's republican policy.[77] The *True patriot*, published in 1578, offered a lengthy defence of Ghent's demeanour, just after the town had embarked on a more radical course. It intended to show that Ghent's

---

[75] For this point in particular, see M. E. H. N. Mout, 'In het schip: Justus Lipsius en de Nederlandse Opstand tot 1591', in S. Groenveld, M. E. H. N. Mout and I. Schöffer (eds.), *Bestuurders en geleerden* (Amsterdam, 1985), 55–64.

[76] See A. A. van Schelven, 'De staatsvorm van het Zwitsersch Eedgenootschap den Nederlanden ter navolging aanbevolen', in *Miscellanea historica in honorem Leonis van der Essen*, ii (Brussels, 1947), 747–56.

[77] Ibid. 754. In 1578 Beutterich stayed in Ghent, where he accompanied Casimir during an unsuccessful campaign in the Netherlands.

sole aim was 'complete liberation from servitude, the assurance of liberty and the establishment of good repose'.[78] Liberty, said to consist of 'liberty of conscience and political or civic liberty', was once again presented as a principal objective of good policy.

In defending Ghent the *True patriot* strongly denounced the 1578 treaty with Anjou, arguing that the duke was totally unqualified to function as 'Defender of liberty'. Anjou was an ordinary mercenary driven by his own ambitions. His role with regard to the Huguenots was severely criticized; the 'oppressor of Gallic liberty' could never be the 'defender of Belgian liberty'.[79] Yet the *True patriot* did not embrace Switzerland unequivocally as a model for the Dutch Provinces. It accepted the Swiss metaphor in so far as it meant that the towns and provinces promised 'to help and assist each other and to oppose with all their means and power those who wanted to introduce the same tyranny as that of the Spaniards'.[80] Whether this actually meant that the Dutch provinces should adopt the Swiss form of government remains unclear in the treatise. In this respect the attitude to Switzerland of the leader of the new Reformed Republic of Ghent, Jan van Hembyze, was certainly more positive. Though the precise character of the 'new order' he had in mind for Ghent remained rather obscure, Hembyze surely took Switzerland as a leading example, seeing Ghent in the role of Geneva.[81]

Hembyze seemed to favour a more democratic form of government, based on a notion of popular sovereignty. In 1579 he declared that Philip II had forfeited his sovereignty, which was now 'devolved' on the town magistracy. This idea was also expressed in an *Opening to the three members of Ghent*, which dealt with the possible visit of William of Orange to Ghent. One of the conditions put to Orange was that 'he should promise and assure not to prejudice those of Ghent in their privileges, rights and freedoms and in particular not in the highness, pre-eminence and sovereignty recently devolved on them'.[82] According to another treatise the visit of Orange to Ghent was 'not advisable' as the prince would 'rob the community of the sovereignty

---

[78] Petrus Beutterich, *Le vray patriot aux bons patriots* (1578), fol. A1.
[79] Ibid., fol. A4. Belgium here, as elsewhere, was synonymous with the Netherlands.
[80] Ibid., fol. C2.
[81] See Decavele, 'De mislukking van Oranje's "democratische politiek" in Vlaanderen', *BMGN* 99 (1984), 636, Decavele, 'Willem van Oranje, de "vader" van een verscheurd "vaderland"' (1577–1584)', *Handelingen der Maatschappij voor Geschiedenis en Oudheidkunde te Gent*, NS 38 (1984), 81, and Decavele, *Het eind van een rebelse droom* (Ghent, 1984), 37.
[82] *Openinghe ghedaen den drie leden der Stede van Ghendt, Augustus 1579* (Ghent, 1579).

and highest liberty which has fallen in its bosom and which belongs there rightfully'.[83]

A much more explicit condemnation of Orange's attitude to the Flemish radicals was enunciated by the *Advertisement and counsel to the people of the Low Countries*, also published in 1579. The treatise presented a detailed political programme to the people for the conservation of 'your liberty and sovereign authority, which you have acquired today'.[84] As it made clear, due to the fact that Philip II had not acceded to the demands put forward to him during the Cologne peace negotiations he had forfeited his sovereignty, which thereby was 'devolved' on each of the provinces. In fact in the first article of its political programme, the *Advertisement* urged each province to take a solemn oath on the acquired sovereignty. Discarding Orange's policy, the treatise urged the provinces to league. Probably invoking the Swiss model the *Advertisement* proposed the provinces 'each being sovereign' to enter 'in a very tight league and confederation, as between sovereigns', for the common defence.[85] The 'body of this league' should stand under the leadership of a council, to which each province was to appoint two members. Office would be held for six months, after which new members should be appointed. Thus the form of government as proposed by the *Advertisement* was obviously republican in character, although the treatise did not indicate a specific preference for either aristocracy, democracy or a mixed constitution.

One of the first of the treatises to present an outright argument in favour of democracy was a *Discourse* commenting on the optimal government for the Netherlands. Its title-page featured quotes from Livy and the Bible praising liberty as the main value in life.[86] The *Discourse* argued that 'in the beginning of the world' men had lived with each other in all freedom. After some time they had chosen some amongst them as 'governors' and 'regents' in order to protect and foster 'chastity, virtue and justice'. Thus, as the *Discourse* pointed out, men had not been created for the sake of political authorities, but 'by

---

[83] *Een corte openinghe der causen, waerome het niet raedsam zy, dat de Prince van Oraignen nu ter tijt commen soude binnen der Stede van Ghendt* (Ghent, 1579), fol. A1.

[84] *Advertissement et conseil au peuple des Pays-Bas* (Roucelle, 1579), fol. B2.

[85] Ibid., fol. B3.

[86] The quote from the Bible was 1 Cor. 7:21: 'Were you a slave when you were called? Never mind. But if you can gain your freedom, avail yourself of the opportunity.' The quote from Livy featured Brutus: 'When Brutus chased away the tyrant Tarquinius from Rome, he spoke: Amongst two things we have to choose this one: an honest life in liberty, or a manly death for our freedom.'

godly inspiration' governments had 'been ordained and instituted for the service and welfare of man'.[87] As history showed, government had assumed several forms. There was monarchy, the absolute rule of one person, aristocracy, the rule of the nobles who had acquired their title because of the virtue of their parents or their own service to fatherland and justice, and democracy, the rule of the 'most honest and wisest citizens', elected by their fellow citizens on certain laws and conditions.

The *Discourse* had little confidence in monarchy, as it easily, if not always, decayed to tyranny. Aristocracy, it was pointed out, in itself was praiseworthy, but the Netherlands lacked virtuous nobles. Moreover, a pure aristocracy more or less implied the oppression of the citizens.

The best form of government, according to the *Discourse*, was a mixture of aristocracy and democracy, 'the government of the best nobles and the wisest citizens in which the most competent and able inhabitants and citizens are elected to the government by their fellow citizens for a certain period and on certain conditions'.[88] The most important condition was that the citizens retained the 'power and liberty' to dispose of the elected government if it turned out to be incompetent or forsook its duty. Principal examples of this form of government were the republics of Rome and especially Switzerland.

The author of the *Discourse* urged his fellow countrymen to follow the Swiss example. In his view the Dutch possessed the necessary virtue to do so. In this context the treatise explicitly rejected the argument of the 1580 dialogue *Emanuel–Erneste*, thundering that its author should be ashamed 'to despise all inhabitants of our fatherland as drunkards and misers'.[89] In fact an aristocratic–democratic regime fitted well in the Netherlands, for, although a 'monarch or head' had governed the country for some time, 'the marks of our old liberty' had always been the States. The States were the 'relics' of the aristocratic–democratic government the Netherlands had had 'of old times'.[90]

The *Discourse* rejected all pleas for foreign aid, arguing that it was high time 'to open up our eyes and to use our own hands and people for our liberation and protection'.[91] In particular, the treatise denounced the use of foreign mercenaries (quite wrongly presented as

---

[87] *Discours verclaerende wat forme ende manier van regieringhe dat die Nederlanden voor die alderbeste ende zekerste tot desen tyden aenstellen mochten* (1583), fol. A2.　　　　[88] Ibid., fol. B2.

[89] Ibid.　　　　[90] Ibid., fol. C4.　　　　[91] Ibid., fol. B2.

Machiavelli's preference) and pleaded in favour of a form of national army. It argued that, since the welfare of the inhabitants directly depended on the liberty of the fatherland, they were the best defenders of the country's liberty.

The call for a republic was sometimes motivated by the failure of the Anjou experiment. This was exemplified by *A Christian warning and refutation*, which denounced the arguments in favour of Anjou's rule as formulated in the 1583 *Warning*. The French Fury was presented as clear proof of Anjou's disgraceful tyranny, which was said to be worse than Philip II's. The alliance with Anjou should not be renewed, as it was against God's word to ally with the godless. Anjou was simply part of a Machiavellian conspiracy together with the Pope and Philip II.

The 1583 *Discourse* was undoubtedly the most distinct plea for a change of government in a democratic direction along Swiss lines. The call for a republican turn was expressed in other treatises as well, but none of them took great pains to delineate the precise republican form of government they preferred. The new order of Ghent was, as far as is known, not based on a fundamental constitutive treatise or document. Its character and frequent references to Geneva indicate the importance of notions of city republicanism. This was also suggested by Ghent's conception of sovereignty, which was said to be devolved on the town community. Thus the Ghent notion of popular sovereignty was primarily a notion of town sovereignty (including territorial control over surrounding regions). In this respect Ghent republican ideas were probably inspired by long-standing political traditions, as the rebellious town had always favoured a city-state system, based on the superiority of the great towns.

5.5. THE CALL FOR CIVIC VIRTUE

However, even in Ghent there was a feeling that to reform what was regarded as the traditional Dutch political order, with the States supreme, would not solve Dutch troubles. Thus Peter Dathenus, a principal Dutch Reformed minister who was one of Ghent's spiritual and most radical leaders, discarded in his 1578 *Cry of the watchman*[92] any suggestion of changing the form of government, which the

---

[92] According to his biographer, Dathenus was only the translator of the treatise. The author is unknown. See T. Ruys, *Petrus Dathenus* (Utrecht, 1919), 283.

'laudable ancestors have ordained and instituted so carefully and wisely'.[93] Together with the privileges, described again as contracts between prince and people, the old form of government had been instituted 'to eschew all tyranny'. The true problem of the Netherlands, according to the *Cry*, concerned the virtuousness of those in office. Fierce accusations were addressed to town magistrates, to those responsible for the country's financial affairs and who were in charge of the 'principal affairs' of the country.[94] They were depicted as hidden agents of the members of the Spanish tyranny with the principal aim of suppressing 'the liberty of the fatherland'.

The *Cry* concluded that 'the cause of the present pitiful state' did not 'stem from the old way of government, which is natural and convenient for this country', but had 'to be sought in the persons who, being in government, misuse the aforesaid way of government'.[95] The treatise urged the people to 'seize the matter' and to renew the government in accordance with the privileges and freedoms of the country with 'devout, capable persons', 'lovers of freedom and of the fatherland'.

Very much in line with the *Cry of the watchman* was the call for virtuous leaders by a *Short discourse on the means to preserve and maintain the true Christian religion, and to safeguard and assure the United Provinces.* The treatise, doubtlessly written by a Reformed Protestant, reiterated the view that the purpose of political authority was 'to seek the glory of God' and to 'procure the temporal good of those of whom they are in charge'.[96] It stressed the importance of virtuous leaders for a republic, arguing that the first essential step towards a 'well-ordered republic' was to choose and elect men in office who were devoted to the fatherland and, above all, to the glory and word of God.

The call for virtuous acts of public service was not limited to the *Cry of the watchman* and the *Short discourse.* In many other treatises references were made to the importance of civic virtue. Of course this was well in line with the main stream of Renaissance political thought. In particular, pre-humanist and civic humanist defenders of republican government had emphasized the necessity of civic

---

[93] *Wachtgeschrey. Allen liefhebbers der eeren Gods des Vaderlandts en der privilegien ende Vryheden des selven tot waerschouwinghe ghestelt* (1578), fols. B3–B4.

[94] An exception was made for Orange, who was compared with the classic hero Trasibulus, the saviour of Athens. See fol. B.　　　　　[95] Ibid., fol. B4.

[96] *Sommaire discours sur le moyen de conserver, et maintenir la vraye religion christiene, & garder & assuerer les provinces unies* (1581), fol. A2. The title-page featured a quote from Sallust: 'C'est chose belle, que de bien faire à la Republique.'

virtue.[97] Moreover, it was commonplace, both in scholastic and in humanist political thought, to argue that, for the preservation of peace, for the promotion of the common good, and, as civic humanists were fond of emphasizing, for the defence of liberty, concord was the absolute prerequisite. Dutch authors agreed: concord and unity were seen as indispensable for the preservation of liberty and the common good of the fatherland, the supreme political values. For example, in its attempts to preserve unity with the Walloon provinces, Artois and Hainaut, who were on the verge of reconciliation with Philip II, the town magistrate of Brussels argued that the maintenance of unity was of the highest importance for 'le bien de la patrie'.[98]

The principal analysis of the importance of civic virtue was propounded by the author of *Political education*, offering a defence of the demand by the States General to swear a new oath of loyalty after the 1581 abjuration. The main purpose of *Political education* was to show the rightfulness of this demand by means of articulating a view on citizenship along republican, Ciceronian lines. With elaborate references to biblical and classical examples, the treatise emphasized that the dutiful patriot could attain true honour and perfect glory only through a life of virtuous acts of public service. The primary duty of a good patriot was to put himself in the service of the fatherland and to fight for liberty. Quoting Cicero's *De officiis*, *Political education* argued that 'one, for the sake of liberty, and to maintain it, should not consider anything too arduous, and that one should rather die than to bow to any slavery'.[99] The dutiful citizen would not hesitate to give his life for the fatherland, if by his death he could render it a service.[100]

The treatise emphasized that the main virtue needed was concord. With references to numerous classical examples, derived from Cicero, Sallust, Livy and Seneca in particular, the treatise attempted to show

---

[97] For the background and development of civic humanist ideas on this point, see most recently Quentin Skinner, 'Machiavelli's *Discorsi* and the pre-humanist origins of republican ideas', in Bock *et al.* (eds.), *Machiavelli and republicanism*, 121–41. For a distinction between scholastic and humanist ideas on this point, see Skinner, 'Political philosophy', 414–15, and Quentin Skinner, 'Ambrogio Lorenzetti: the artist as political philosopher', *Proceedings of the British Academy*, 72 (1986), 7.

[98] *Rapport faict par le Seigneur Guillaume vanden Hecke...à messieurs du Magistrat d'icelle ville...reiteré...en l'assemblee des Estats generaux en Anvers* (Antwerp, 1579), 6.

[99] *Politicq onderwijs* (Political education) (Mechelen, 1582), fol. B1. This was a reference to both Cicero, *De officiis*, 1. 13. 81, where it is argued that one should prefer death to slavery and disgrace, and to *De officiis*, 1. 20. 69, where Cicero argues that 'in defence of liberty a high-souled man should stake everything'.

[100] *Political education*, fol. A4, where reference is made to Cicero, *De officiis*, 1. 17. 57.

that concord was 'the foundation of all republics, or states of government', as Cicero had put it.[101] The chief motto, derived from Sallust and Seneca, was simple: 'Concord makes small commonwealths great, discord disrupts the greatest ones.'[102] In this respect the oath as required by the States General was presented as the 'best bond' amongst men and the best means to promote concord in the United Provinces. As *Political education* concluded, 'both from the reason of God's Law and the Pagan and Christian authors', it had become clear that in order to attain 'public concord' and to prevent faction and discord 'we should reassure each other by oath'.[103]

Along similar lines the necessity of concord was underscored by *A clear address of the secret deliberations and practices which the common enemies use to subject these Netherlands again to the Spanish tyranny and Inquisition.* The treatise, addressed to the 'good patriots of the town of Ghent and all other lovers of the fatherland', urged the Dutch to follow the example of the Roman Republic and beware of the 'children of Brutus', of traitors who sought to subvert the republic. The *Clear address*, published in 1583 when Flanders was surrendering to Farnese, felt that it was possible to find the proper means against 'treachery and conspiracy', 'if we follow in the footsteps of the Romans, who teach us to love our fatherland more than our own children'.[104] Instead of appointing another prince, the Dutch should unite and fight against Spain. The treatise, praising the leader of Ghent, Hembyze, 'as another Brutus', argued that the 'ship of the Flemish welfare' could only survive the storm if all in good concord came to its help. Concord was the foundation of a proper defence against tyranny and the *Clear address* reiterated the 'truthful proverb', as derived from Sallust and Seneca, that 'great kingdoms are destroyed by indigenous misunderstanding and discord, and that, on the contrary, small, poor and tiny governments are strengthened and augmented by their concord'.[105] Thus the treatise, probably written by a supporter of Ghent's radical course, urged the United Provinces to set aside all forms of discord and follow the example of the 'pious captains from Athens, Themistocles and Aristides', who, though

---

[101] *Political education*, fol. B1. The reference was to *De officiis*, 2. 22. 78.
[102] See Sallust, *Bellum Jugurthinum*, 10. 6, and Seneca, *Epistolae morales*, book 14, letter 94, sect. 46. This proverb also played a major role in Italian republicanism. See Skinner, 'Machiavelli's *Discorsi* and the pre-humanist origins of republican ideas', 129, and Skinner, 'Ambrogio Lorenzetti', 6ff.   [103] *Political education*, fol. E3.
[104] *Een claer vertooch der heymelijcke raetslaghen ende practijcken die de ghemeyne vyanden ghebruycken om dese Nederlanden wederomme der Spaensche tyrannie ende Inquisitie te onderworpen* (1583), fol. A2.
[105] Ibid., fol. A3.

'mutual enemies', made peace if the 'common liberty and welfare of their town and country' was in peril, and, thanks to their piety and concord were able to obtain a 'wonderful victory' over the 'common enemy'.[106]

That the loss of concord, that is to say the dissolution of the union between the provinces, would have disastrous effects, was also recognized by a 1583 treatise commenting *On the state of the present Dutch government*. It joined those who had argued that the problems of the provinces were not due to their form of government. On the contrary, it asserted, the 'foundation and certainty of our liberty and privileges is the power and authority of the States General and of the States of each province'.[107] Thus the position of the States, 'the guardians and protectors of the common liberty', was reaffirmed. The treatise argued that the 'high or (as one now says) sovereign authority is with the States of each province'.[108] These independent provinces had been brought together because of the war in a 'common union' and it was the task of the States General to handle the affairs of the 'community of the common union'. The basic problem of the Netherlands was that no one respected the authority of another and that everyone meddled in each other's affairs. Therefore, concord, a proper division of labour amongst the diverse political institutions and the recognition of the civic duty to risk 'body and life' for the sake of the fatherland were keys to the solution of the Dutch problems. Thus the treatise featured on its front page Sallust's popular proverb on the merits of concord.

Having emphasized the necessity of concord some treatises started to address the question which particular virtues would promote concord. A *Fraternal warning* admonished those responsible for the election of magistrates not to pay attention to the social background of candidates. In fact it urged them to appoint not only nobles but also 'good and God-fearing citizens' without regard to their profession. Appealing to Cicero's *De officiis*, the *Fraternal warning* argued that civic equality was the foundation of civic society.[109] It asserted 'that the equality of the citizens underlies civic society, and

---

[106] Ibid., fol. C4.
[107] *Van den staet der tegenwoordiger Nederlandtsche regierung* (1583), fol. A2.
[108] Ibid., fol. A4.
[109] Gordon Griffiths has argued that, although the *Fraternal warning* suggested that crucial passages on the importance of civic equality were direct quotes from Cicero's *De officiis*, this was not exactly true. See Gordon Griffiths, 'Democratic ideas in the revolt of the Netherlands', *Archiv für Reformationsgeschichte*, 50 (1959), 52. However, the point that, in addition to concord, civic equity is the foundation of the commonwealth was made in *De officiis*, 2. 22. 78. See also 2. 23. 83.

that civic unity flourishes most if all affairs are handled with equal rights, which is the case if one elects from all levels of citizens, both amongst the rich and the poor, the most useful and competent, to the office of government'.[110]

The author of the *Fraternal warning* preferred a proper mixture of virtuous artisans and notables. At any price, the treatise asserted, the election of mischievous magistrates should be avoided, for the 'ambition and zeal for state and highness', was a disaster to any political community. In this respect, and again Cicero's *De officiis* guided the analysis, the treatise warned against the danger that such ambitions could lead to partiality, which as a cancer would infect the citizenry.[111] To avoid faction, the treatise argued, the maintenance of civic equality was essential, as it permitted no man to rise above the others.

While ambitious magistrates were a cancer in civic society virtuous ones, on the contrary, formed the key to its 'abundance and prosperity'. Therefore, a 'state of government' could only exist if it was dominated by 'virtue and good laws', which had to be based on 'piety and justice'. This meant that one should only elect to office men who were virtuous, God-fearing, truthful and faithful and who 'seek the common more than their own profit'.[112]

One of the most forceful pleas for virtue was William of Orange's epitaph, published in 1584 under the title *Remonstrance in form of a discourse to each and all countries, provinces, towns and communities, containing the epitaph on the death of the Prince of Orange*. The main message of the epitaph was that in addition to concord the virtues of wisdom and prudence were absolutely essential to the maintenance of liberty. Presenting Orange himself as a shining example, the Dutch were urged to follow the ants in their concord, prudence and wisdom to preserve the common good, and the birds in their desire for liberty.[113] As the treatise emphasized, prudence and wisdom were the keys to concord.

The epitaph asked the inhabitants to obey and assist the States and magistrates in promoting the 'welfare of the common country', stressing that both people and States were completely dependent on

---

[110] *Broederlijcke waerschouwinghe : aen allen Christen broeders, die van God verordent sijn tot de verkiesinghe der Overicheyt ende Magistraten inde Steden der gheunieerde Provincien* (Fraternal warning) (Antwerp, 1581), fol. A3.

[111] Ibid., fol. A4. The reference was to Cicero, *De officiis*, 1. 25. 87.

[112] *Fraternal warning*, fol. C2.

[113] *Remonstrantie by forme van discours aen allen en eenen yeghelijcken Landen, Provintien, Steden en Ghemeenten, inhoudende t'Epitaphium op de doot des ... Prince van Oraingien* (Delft, 1584), fol. B3.

each other. As it asserted, if the citizens loved their 'life and liberty, preservation of goods, wife and children' more than anything else in the world, they would 'pray and desire to give as much for the common good as one will order each after his wealth, quality or benignancy'.[114]

The epitaph also underscored the importance of a good military defence. The emphasis was not uncommon. Next to concord, some Dutch authors argued, a virtuous army was necessary for the preservation of liberty. Marnix van St Aldegonde compared the Dutch Provinces with a country which was under threat of flooding due to a heavy storm. To safeguard the country from a catastrophe the 'sea dike' needed to remain intact and such could only be achieved if the inhabitants of the country worked together to strengthen the dike, for one or two holes sufficed to put the country under water. The moral was clear. To protect the country against the Spaniards a proper defence was needed, which not only required sacrifices from the inhabitants but also good concord amongst them.[115]

In this respect the Dutch were urged to rely on their own strength. The 1584 *Story of the true means to preserve both the state of the common good and the religion in the Netherlands* reiterated the view that both 'good laws' and virtue were essential for the welfare of the community, emphasizing the necessity of concord. Sallust's saying that 'concord makes matters grow, but discord makes them deteriorate' was argued to contain more wisdom than many other 'great books'.[116] Although the treatise deplored the loss of main parts of the provinces to the enemy, it argued that on condition of concord there was still a good possibility of preserving the remaining parts. The common religion was seen as the proper means to promote such concord. For the author of the treatise religion and the maintenance of free worship of the Reformed religion in particular was the heart and soul of the war. He argued that, as no prince was willing to permit such free worship, the provinces should, with good constancy, be prepared to rely on their own strength (and of course on God's help). Thus the treatise had little regard for either Philip II or the Duke of Anjou. Only in case of absolute necessity, if the 'true religion and the liberty of the fatherland' were at stake, alliances with Anjou should be taken

[114] Ibid., fol. C2.

[115] Marnix van St Aldegonde, *Ernstighe vermaninghe vanden standt ende ghelegentheyt der Christenheyt, ende vande middelen haerder behoudenisse ende welvaren* (1583), fol. A2.

[116] *Verhael vande rechte middelen om so wel den standt van de ghemeynse saecke als de Religie in den Nederlanden to moghen behouden* (1584), fol. A2.

into consideration, for the preservation of the true religion and the liberty of the fatherland were of overriding importance.

Likewise a 1584 *Address to my lords the States General on the resurrection and maintenance of the State of the Netherlands*, even though it did not reject French aid, argued that the provinces should be prepared to resurrect their 'State' on their own. Above all, this required financial sacrifices to build up a 'right and good army'. The *Address* complained that the short-sightedness of the provinces, unwilling to make sacrifices for the common good, was one of the main problems of the Netherlands. The refusal to offer money in the short term would have lasting, devastating consequences. The *Address* compared the provinces with a patient who, having cancer in his arm, refused to follow the surgeon's advice of offering up the arm in order to survive, the ultimate result being the death of the patient.[117]

The second cause of Dutch 'reprehension and irresolution', the *Address* asserted, was the unwillingness to set up a proper and disciplined army. The treatise strongly blamed the provinces for their irresolution on this point, referring to Tacitus' saying that 'war is much more secure than a doubtful peace'.[118] In order to correct these defects the *Address* argued in favour of the formation of a Council of State 'of honourable and God-fearing persons, with an understanding of affairs of politics and State as well as of war'.[119] In addition, it pleaded for the formation of a Council of War, to which 'all power and sovereign authority' with regard to the affairs of war should be recommended.

Most authors pleading for civic virtue presented themselves as dutiful patriots and great lovers of the fatherland. In his preface, the author of *Political education* explained that he had written the treatise because, as he put it, 'a man is created for the sake of others, so that we should not only live for ourselves but also for the fatherland and our descendants'.[120] It was not uncommon for political authors to present their writings as acts of civic virtue. In 1582, to give another example, Jan van den Kiele published his pamphlet *Redene exhortatyf* under the motto that '(as Cicero teaches in *De officiis*) each good subject (after the gifts conferred unto him by the Lord, and after his quality) is bound to foster his fatherland and to render service'.[121]

[117] *Vertooch aen mijn Heeren de Staten Generael op de wederoprichtinghe ende behoudenisse vanden Staet der Nederlanden* (1584), fol. B3. Here the *Address* was probably paraphrasing Cicero, *De officiis*, 3. 6. 32.   [118] *Vertooch*, fol. C1.   [119] Ibid., fol. C3.
[120] *Political education*, fol. A1.
[121] Jan van den Kiele, *Redene exhortatyf* (Antwerp, 1582), 1.

Thus the idea that a life of *negotium*, of virtuous acts of public service, was conducive to both individual happiness and common good was central to the call for virtue as articulated in the Low Countries between 1578 and 1590. The Dutch call for virtuous political leaders and virtuous citizens followed the essential lines of Renaissance political thought on the topic, with Cicero and Sallust, as in the Italian case, being the main classical sources of inspiration. Thus the Dutch call for virtue was the expression of the idea that the willingness to serve, even to die for, the fatherland was essential to the maintenance of liberty. It was also the expression of the recognition that concord would make small commonwealths great, while discord would destroy the greatest ones, as Sallust's popular proverb put it. In addition, it was the expression of the acknowledgment that political and military action should be based on wisdom, prudence, constancy and the willingness to make sacrifices for the sake of the common good in order to make the old laudable form of government work. Finally, it was the expression of the conviction that neither the form of government nor the lack of a prince and not even foreign aid were the key to the solution of the problems confronting the Dutch Provinces, but that civic virtue was the heart of the matter.

5.6. THE FINAL COUNTDOWN: HOLLAND, THE EARL OF LEICESTER AND THE DEBATE ON SOVEREIGNTY

After the Anjou deception the idea that some form of princely rule was beneficial for the United Provinces probably contributed, next to the necessity for foreign aid, to the appointment of Robert Dudley, the Earl of Leicester, to the position of 'Governor and Captain General' in January 1586. Leicester was awarded broad powers. As the States General declared, the earl should order 'completely and absolutely' on matters of war and would have 'full and absolute power in matters of policy and justice'.[122] Yet his government was not to hurt the 'rights, privileges, liberties, treaties, contracts, statutes, ordinances, decrees and customs of the provinces in general and of each province, town and member in particular'.

The position of Leicester was compared with that of a governor under Charles V. In comparison with the treaties concluded before with Matthias and Anjou, the States seemed to recede dramatically,

---

[122] Pieter Christiaansz Bor, *Oorsprongk, begin en vervolgh der Nederlantsche oorlogen, beroerten en borgerlijke oneeningheden*, ii (Amsterdam, 1679; first pub. 1595), 685.

having invested the earl with 'full and absolute power'. There is little
doubt that his supporters in the provinces intended it this way. For
them Leicester was the virtuous prince the Dutch had been waiting
for so long. The States of Holland had a different perspective. When
Leicester actually started to behave as an absolute ruler the conflict
with Holland was both inevitable and desperate for the earl.

The conflict between Holland and the Leicester party gave rise to
a stream of passionate publications. Central to the debate were the
questions concerning the best government for the United Provinces
and the issue of sovereignty.

Gerard Prouninck van Deventer, the author of *Emanuel–Erneste*,
was one of the staunchest supporters of the earl. He was appointed
burgomaster of Utrecht, the centre of the Leicester party. In March
1587, in the heat of the battle, Prouninck published his *Answer to
diverse evil accusations falsely imputed to him by some persons of the present
government*. In this apology Prouninck gave expression to the feeling
that the United Provinces needed a 'sovereign head'. Defending
Utrecht's offer of sovereignty to the English queen, Prouninck
asserted that without a sovereign the provinces were not able to resist
their formidable enemy. Making this point he referred to the
'perversity of our nature' and to the fact 'that we of old are used to
the rule of a supreme head'. Instead of being equal to the enemy on
the most important point, the 'best form of government', the
provinces were weakened by 'the government of many', which had
caused mistrust and discord amongst them.[123] Having appointed a
prince, because, as Prouninck argued, the government did not
suffice, the 'supreme authority' should not reside with many but with
one. Sovereign power should remain undivided. As Prouninck put it,
'navigation teaches us that a ship, in a thunderstorm at sea, should be
steered only by the command of the senior steersman'.[124]

Prouninck condemned the continuous appeals to privileges by his
adversaries. Although there was no 'man under the sky' who loved
the 'rights, freedoms and privileges of the fatherland' more than
himself, Prouninck asserted that many privileges, 'profitable in times
of peace', were rather harmful in times of war. Therefore, such
privileges should be set aside. For, as Prouninck put it, 'the supreme
law is the repose and welfare of the community'. If this was hurt, 'the

---

[123] Gerard Prouninck van Deventer, *Antwoorde teghens verscheyde quade opspraken die hem by
sommige persoonen van de teghenwoordighe regeringhe onwaerachtelijck zijn nagehouden* (Utrecht,
1587), fol. B1.   [124] Ibid., fol. B2.

privileges should stand still'. The privileges were there 'for the sake of the community, not the community for the sake of the privileges'.[125]

Prouninck's views probably expressed the feeling of a dominant group in Utrecht. In November 1587, when the conflict with Holland was practically lost, Utrecht sent a *Missive to the States of the country of Holland* which reiterated to a large extent Prouninck's arguments. The missive reasserted that the provinces could not be governed 'without a head of supreme authority'.[126] It fully defended the authority of Leicester, arguing that the dispute over sovereignty was futile, as all provinces had sworn to obey the earl. It was simply 'impossible and incompatible to retain sovereign power and to be bound to humble obedience' at the same time.[127] According to Utrecht Leicester in fact was more than a governor had been under Charles V, for the commission of the States General gave the earl 'supreme command and sovereign power in affairs of war, which has never been given to any Governor-General in the times of the Emperor Charles'. Only as far as the earl's political power was concerned, his position, Utrecht recognized, was comparable with previous Governor-Generals. As far as Utrecht was concerned, however, the provinces had given the 'use of the sovereign power' to the earl, as Prouninck put it in another treatise.[128]

Utrecht pressed the provinces, who were wont to take the 'most powerful nations and republics' as examples, to follow the people of Rome, who, in spite of their own impressive power and discipline, used the creation of an 'extraordinary authority' as a 'last resort' for their preservation. According to Utrecht, the Roman dictator had full power to do as he liked, regardless of any privileges or liberties and regardless of the people's sovereignty. Such was the position Utrecht favoured with regard to the Earl of Leicester.

Another defence of Leicester, and in fact an outright attack on the States of Holland, was presented by Thomas Wilkes, one of the English members of the Council of State.[129] Wilkes' line of argument,

---

[125] Ibid., fol. B3.

[126] *Seyndtbrief…aen de Staten slandts van Holland* (Utrecht, 1587), fol. B4.

[127] Ibid., fol. C.

[128] Gerard Prouninck van Deventer, *Een corte errinneringhe ende waerschouwinghe opt schandelyck verraedt daer mit de Colonnel Stanle ende Hopman Jorck de Stadt Deventer ende de schanse teghens Zutphen, den Spaengiaerden om gelt verraden ende ghelevert hebben* (Utrecht, 1587), fol. A3.

[129] With the treaty of Nonesuch it had been decided that the Council of State would have a number of English members.

however, differed from Prouninck's. While the latter presented mainly a defence of the authority of Leicester, Wilkes questioned the authority of the States of Holland. In his *Remonstrance* addressed to the States General and the States of Holland on 16 March 1587,[130] Wilkes accused the States of Holland of 'reducing' the authority of Leicester and of 'resisting and derogating' the Council of State. Wilkes reasserted the view that Leicester had been awarded, by the commission of the States General, 'the supreme command and absolute authority' both in military and political affairs 'as the Governor-Generals had in the time of Charles V'.[131] This authority had been continuously undermined by the States of Holland, and Wilkes presented a long list of concrete accusations.

Most of all Wilkes questioned the States' claim to sovereignty in asserting that 'by default of a legal prince' sovereignty belonged 'with the community', not with the States, who were 'but servants, ministers and deputies of the aforesaid community'.[132] As Wilkes pointed out, the community continuously limited the authority of the States, setting conditions to their functioning and decisions. Therefore, their authority was as different from sovereignty as 'heaven is different from hell', for, as Wilkes put it, 'sovereignty is limited neither in power, nor in command, nor in time'.[133] Still less, Wilkes added, the States represented sovereignty, for such was precisely the role of the Governor-General, described 'as a *dispositarius* or guardian of sovereignty until it pleases the prince or the people to revoke it'.[134]

It has been argued that Wilkes' *Remonstrance* was the expression of a leaning to democracy that allegedly prevailed in Utrecht.[135] The argument was indeed based on a notion of popular sovereignty, interpreted in a highly specific way. For to Wilkes 'popular' primarily referred to the community, which the English councillor distinguished from the States. The distinction was not without precedent. It had been commonplace in the United Provinces to present the States as representative institutions, and the idea of popular sovereignty, underscoring the authority of the community, was a key element in the ideological justification of the Revolt. Albada's *Acts*, for example, had emphatically presented the political

---

[130] Thomas Wilkes, *Remonstrance* (1587), in Bor, *Oorsprongk der Nederlantsche oorlogen*, ii. 918–21.   [131] Bor (ed.), *Oorsprongk der Nederlantsche oorlogen*, ii. 918–19.
[132] Ibid. 921.   [133] Ibid.   [134] Ibid.
[135] This would mean that Prouninck had dramatically changed his mind, for in his 1580 dialogue he plainly rejected democracy.

authority of the States, as of all magistrates, as being 'raised and brought to his highness' by the community.

Wilkes, however, employed the idea of the States as delegates acting on order and instruction, to arrive at a radical political conclusion. Combined with the notion, probably derived from Bodin, that it was the essence of sovereignty not to be limited, either in power or in time, Wilkes reduced the importance of the States, whose claims to political dominance, let alone sovereignty, were subtly rejected. As such, Wilkes' analysis was a devastating attack on the interpretation of the States as leading sovereign powers, as articulated during the 1570s.

This interpretation had retained a pre-eminent position and was undoubtedly cherished by the States of Holland. In August 1587 a *Remonstrance* was published on their behalf which asserted that 'by default of a prince of the country, the sovereignty of the country returned to them'.[136] The authority of Leicester, the *Remonstrance* argued, was 'conferred' and by no means sovereign. The States declared themselves willing to obey the earl and to maintain his authority, 'as long as His Excellency is using the aforesaid authority lawfully'.[137] Leicester himself responded angrily to such declarations, arguing that they reduced his authority and were against his Act of commission.[138]

However, Holland not only retained the view of the States as leading sovereign powers, but extended it radically. The *Answer of the knighthood, nobles and most towns of Holland and Westvriesland on the declaration and remonstrance of His Excellency* pointed out that the provinces had concluded a treaty with England because they were in need of foreign aid to 'resist the violence of their enemies'. As such Leicester had been sent to 'promote' the affairs of war and to give the States 'good advice on the government and defence of the provinces'.[139] This view on Leicester's position was reiterated in a *Further declaration of the States of Holland*. The States reasserted that they should be regarded as sovereign powers, for otherwise it would have been 'unjust' to declare 'the King of Spain forfeited of the

---

[136] *Remonstrantie by de Ridderschap, Eedelen ende Steden van Hollandt ende West-Vrieslandt, ghepresenteert aen syne Excellentie binnen der Stadt Dordrecht in Augusto, xvᵉ zevenentachtich* (Delft, 1587), fol. A2.

[137] Ibid., fol. A3.

[138] See *Vertooch ende Remonstrantie by...Robert Grave van Leycester...ghedaen aen den Staten Generael...den vij. September anno 1587 stilo novo* (Dordrecht, 1587), fol. A4.

[139] *Antwoorde vande Ridderschap, Edelen ende meeste Steden van Hollandt ende Westvrieslandt op de verclaringhe ende Remonstrantie van syne Excell.* (Delft, 1587), fol. A2.

administration of sovereignty',[140] which implied that all subsequent actions of the States, including the treaty with England, were highly 'doubtful'. The States acknowledged having conferred on Leicester 'the supreme command in matters of war' and the political power 'equal to that which the governors of the Netherlands had in the times of the Emperor Charles'.[141] However, so they emphasized, this formulation implied that the States were in the position of the former emperor. Thus it was 'reserved' to the States to decide on the matters 'which concern the countries the highest'.

Thus, to rebuff the accusations of having reduced the authority of the Earl of Leicester, the States of Holland first of all came up with a shrewd description of the earl's authority, based on a comparison with the Governor-Generals of Charles V. Of course this argument did not rebut Thomas Wilkes' forceful attack on the States, and Oldenbarnevelt recognized the necessity of responding to Wilkes' *Remonstrance*. The town pensionary of Gouda, François Vranck was asked to write a defence of the authority of the States. Originally a declaration of the States of Holland, Vranck's work was published, in a slightly revised version, as the *Short exposition of the right exercised from old times by the knighthood, nobles and towns of Holland and Westvriesland for the maintenance of the liberties, rights, privileges and laudable customs of the country*,[142] which has been celebrated as the Magna Carta of the Dutch Republic.[143]

Vranck pointed out that for 800 years Holland had been governed by counts in close co-operation with the States of the country. The counts had never taken major political decisions without 'the advice and consent of the nobles and towns of the country', for they simply had no power in their own right. They were completely dependent on the States. If a count, having received his authority 'with the approval and consent of the inhabitants', acted against the 'liberty and welfare' and became a tyrant, the inhabitants could oppose him lawfully by means of the States, whose main task was to 'maintain the

---

[140] *Naerder verclaringhe van de Staten van Hollandt waerby int corte verthoont wort dat de poincten aen zijne Excie, binnen Dordrecht versocht, zijn nootelick voor de welstant der Landen, en dat sonder het onderhout der selver, de Landen daerinnen niet gheconserveert en moghen worden* (Delft, 1587), fol. A2. This formulation seemed to suggest that Philip II had never been sovereign but had only administered sovereign power.   [141] Ibid.

[142] References are to the original declaration of the States, as printed in Bor (ed.), *Oorsprongk der Nederlantsche oorlogen*, ii. 921–4. For modern edns. of the *Short exposition* see van Gelderen (ed.), *The Dutch Revolt*, and Kossmann and Mellink (eds.), *Texts concerning the revolt of the Netherlands*, 274–81.   [143] See J. den Tex, *Oldenbarnevelt*, i (Haarlem, 1960), 402.

rights, freedoms and privileges of the country and to avert and resist all infraction'.[144]

Thus the political authority of the States was reaffirmed. As Vranck emphasized, this authority did 'not consist in the policy, authority or power' of the 'thirty or forty persons' who appeared at its meetings.[145] In order to be able to oppose tyrannical rule and abuse of princely authority, the inhabitants were divided into two 'estates', the nobles and the towns. The towns were described as independent, self-governing political entities, governed by a college of town councillors. According to Vranck the 'colleges of magistrates and town councils, together with the corporation of the nobles', represented 'the whole state and the entire body of the inhabitants'.[146] The persons forming the States assembly were not 'the States in person or on their own authority', but the deputies of nobles and towns. Their representative work had to be seen in terms of delegation. A delegate, participating in the States, could only act 'in conformity with his instruction and commission'. Therefore, 'Wilkes and everybody else' should understand that in arguing that 'the sovereignty of the country is with the States', one was not referring to the individual delegates, but to 'their principals, whom they represent by virtue of their commission'.[147]

Thus Vranck accepted the notion of popular sovereignty, and argued that the term 'popular' could only refer to the 'nobles and towns' of the country. Like Wilkes he interpreted the representative character of the States in terms of delegation, accepting that the States only acted on order and instruction of their 'principals'. This did not, however, diminish the importance of the States. For, although sovereignty resided with the people, it was administered by their delegates, the States. Thus, developing a crucial distinction between the residence and the administration of sovereignty, Vranck was able to reassert that the authority of the States was 'the foundation on which the common state of the country is resting, which cannot be offended without ruining the common good' and to conclude 'that the sovereignty of the country is with the States in all matters'.[148]

---

[144] Bor (ed.), *Oorsprongk der Nederlantsche oorlogen*, 922.   [145] Ibid.   [146] Ibid. 923.
[147] Ibid.
[148] Ibid. 924. My analysis of Vranck's declaration is greatly indebted to Pieter Geyl's 'An interpretation of Vrancken's deduction of 1587 on the nature of the States of Holland's power', in Charles H. Carter (ed.), *From the Renaissance to the Counter-Reformation* (London,

Appealing to the normative force of age and tradition Vranck self-consciously asserted that the political order based on the authority of the States and their principals, the nobles and town magistrates, had brought Holland honour, prosperity and 800 years of liberty. As such, Vranck claimed, Holland was only equalled by the Republic of Venice.

However historically wrong this assertion might have been, it was by no means exceptional. In his *Necessary considerations which all good lovers of the fatherland should consider with regard to the proposed treaty of peace with the Spaniards* William Verheyden warned his fellow countrymen to mistrust the attitude of appeasement of Philip II's government and of his Governor Farnese in particular, who, according to Verheyden, merely applied the teachings of Machiavelli's *Prince*.[149] Verheyden urged his fellow countrymen to uphold the 'exceptional freedom which we have inherited from our ancestors'. Concord was to be retained and measures were to be taken to protect 'a freedom which, I say, during the time of 1,500 years, has never been burdened with slavery by foreign nations'.[150]

It became a political dogma, and an important part of what has been called the Batavian myth,[151] to argue that the liberty of the United Provinces, and of Holland in particular, had been raised by the Batavians, the classical and direct ancestors of the Dutch, and that it had been vigorously maintained ever since. The highlight in this respect was doubtless Grotius' *Treatise of the antiquity of the Batavian now Hollandish Republic*. Grotius set out to prove that the supervision of the Batavian and Hollandish common good had

1966), 230–46, which stresses the lasting influence of Vranck's ideas of representation on Dutch political thought.

[149] W. Verheyden, *Nootelijcke consideratien die alle goede liefhebbers des Vaderlandts behooren rijpelijck te overweghen opten voorgeslaghen Tractate van Peys met den Spaengiaerden* (1587), fol. B.

[150] Ibid., fol. C3. In the French version of this pamphlet Verheyden said that this liberty had existed 'depuis le temps de Iule Caesar'. See *Considerations necessaires sur un traicté avec l'espagnol* (1587), fol. C3.

[151] See I. Schöffer, 'The Batavian myth during the sixteenth and seventeenth centuries', in J. S. Bromley and E. H. Kossmann (eds.), *Britain and the Netherlands*, v: *Some political mythologies* (The Hague, 1975), 78–101. Schöffer points out that the idea of Batavian freedom had come up at the end of the 15th century. The Batavian myth gained momentum through 16th-century humanism, largely due to the rediscovery of Tacitus' *Germania*. In the 1580s a number of studies focusing on the history of the Batavians were published. Thus, during the Revolt this became a fashionable topic. For example, in Latin, Leiden, whose university soon became famous because of its Tacitus studies, was baptized 'Lugdunum Batavorum'. See also Schama, *The embarrassment of riches*, 75–85, who also discusses Grotius but fails to acknowledge that the political ideas about the Dutch political order as contained in the Batavian myth were to a great degree an extension of arguments developed during the Revolt.

always resided with the States, whose power was described as 'the foundation of the republic, the resort of equal justice, the bridle of princely highness'.[152] As such, the States had been respected and obeyed by military commanders, kings and counts. They had protected the holy and unbreakable privileges and they had carried the Hollandish freedom through heavy tempests. Grotius took great pains to show the antiquity of the free Hollandish republic and of its form of government, which was aristocratic in character. The republic had always been governed by the *ottimati*, representing the two *ordines* of Holland, in the States. Grotius argued that 'for more than seventeen hundred years the Batavians, now called Hollanders, have used the same government, of which the highest power has been and still is with the States'.[153] The States had always sought to preserve freedom, deeply cherished by the Batavians. Already during the times of the Roman Empire they had been respected as 'authors of freedom',[154] as a free, self-governing people willing to do the utmost to retain its liberty.

Thus in a truly humanist fashion Grotius' treatise on the republic of Holland, which was published in 1610, in many ways epitomized a pattern of ideas, developed in the previous decades, which presented the Dutch Republic as built upon liberty, privileges, the States and popular sovereignty.

5.7. CONCLUSIONS

The ideological quest for the best state of government in the United Provinces between 1578 and 1590 started from a number of assumptions which had been the starting-point for political reflection throughout European late medieval and Renaissance political thought. Late sixteenth-century Dutch authors in general seemed to share the Renaissance assumption that the principal purpose of the art of politics was to create and protect what Renaissance authors used to call the *vivere civile* or, as in the case of Simon Stevin, the *vita politica*, which in his view was characterized by the rule of law and the

---

[152] Hugo Grotius, *Tractaet vande Oudtheyt vande Batavische nu Hollandsghe Republique* (The Hague, 1610), fol. ij.

[153] Ibid. 46–7. Grotius explained that in the republic there also had been an element of princely rule. However, the Batavian military commanders, the Counts of Holland and the present Governors had always been the minor power.

[154] Ibid. 19. According to Grotius the Batavians later were called Frisians, because this word was so close to the word freedom. See p. 22.

'greatest peace and welfare of the community'.[155] The first essential step towards this goal was, as almost every late medieval and Renaissance theorist had emphasized, the preservation of external and internal peace. All agreed that within the community the forces of discord were the principal enemy of civic tranquillity. Discord should be overcome, and concord should triumph. This victory could only be achieved if factional interests were set aside in the pursuit for the common good, the *bonum commune*. Thus the community should be governed with virtue, with prudence, justice, fortitude and temperance, as Cicero's classical analysis had argued.[156] Like their late medieval and Renaissance predecessors, Dutch authors addressed the question which state of government was suited best to promote virtue and thereby the common good.

At this point opinions diverged. To an important extent the debate centred round the necessity for a prince. The most fundamental and eloquent plea for princely rule was undoubtedly Lipsius' *Politics*, which presented princely rule as the most ancient, the most natural and the most rational form of government. Other treatises used the metaphor of the body to argue that the body politic needed a head. In general, princely rule was favoured because the virtuous prince was seen as the best possible guarantee against discord and confusion, for some authors synonymous with republican government.

In addition, authors favoured princely rule on practical grounds. For them the calculation that the provinces were in desperate need of foreign financial and military aid was the overriding argument. These authors were in general against 'absolute power' for a prince. Although the inefficiency of the States was at times deplored, their authority was respected. What these authors favoured was a mixed constitution which assured the provinces of their privileges and liberties by adding some form of princely rule to the political rule of the States.

After two unfortunate experiments the United Provinces finally embarked on a republican course. The stream of political treatises in favour of princely rule makes clear that this republican policy was not without fundamental critics. It is important to conclude that during the Dutch Revolt a series of arguments was developed which considered some form of princely element necessary for the maintenance and furtherance of the common good of the Dutch Provinces.

[155] Simon Stevin, *Het Burgherlick Leven* (Leiden, 1590; repr. Amsterdam, 1939), 26.
[156] Cicero, *De officiis*, 1. 5. 15ff.

In fact in some pleas for princely rule the rejection of republican alternatives was an essential element of the argument. In particular, authors sought to demolish the alleged proposals of adopting the model of the Swiss confederacy or the Venetian Republic. It is uncertain whether the support of such proposals was as widespread as the treatises which rejected them sometimes suggested, if only because very few explicit defences of either the Swiss or the Venetian model have survived the centuries.

Most treatises which did not opt for princely rule merely wanted to retain what was seen as the old form of government, with the States in a pre-eminent position. Perhaps these treatises did not call for the creation of a republic because, in their view, the republic was already there. Like those favouring princely rule, this group of treatises saw discord, the inefficiency of the government and the lack of a proper and disciplined army as the fundamental problems. The essence of their solution was not a revision of the constitutional and institutional framework which the ancestors had set up to safeguard liberty and to foster the common good, but a call for civic virtue.

The pledge for civic virtue was greatly inspired by an appeal to Cicero and Sallust, whose works had influenced authors throughout the late medieval and Renaissance period.[157] As such the Dutch appropriation of these classical works resembled the analysis of Italian republican theorists. Dutch authors cherished liberty, which they saw threatened by both faction and an external enemy. They emphasized that, to overcome the internal forces of discord and the external threat of Spain, concord and a disciplined army were necessary. This required civic virtue at all levels of society. It required the willingness to make personal sacrifices for the protection of the liberty of the fatherland, and thereby of one's own personal liberty. Dutch citizens were urged to lead a life of *negotium*, of virtuous acts of public service.

Eventually the quest for the best state of government resulted in a fundamental debate which focused both on the merits of the respective forms of government and on the implications of the idea of

---

[157] See also Geurts, *De Nederlandse Opstand*, 274–9. See Skinner, 'Machiavelli's *Discorsi* and the pre-humanist origins of republican ideas', for an account of Cicero's and Sallust's influence on the development of Renaissance republicanism. Other studies concerning their influence on late medieval political thought include B. Smalley, 'Sallust in the Middle Ages', in R. R. Bolgar (ed.), *Classical influences on European culture AD 500–1500* (Cambridge, 1971), 165–75, and Cary J. Nederman, 'Nature, sin and the origins of society: the Ciceronian tradition in medieval political thought', *JHI* 49 (1988), 3–26.

popular sovereignty. As such this debate touched the heart and soul of the political thought of the Dutch Revolt.

The differences of opinion were subtle, yet of overriding importance. Wilkes' interpretation of popular sovereignty reduced the States to a group of provincial civil servants, with whom the Governor-General at least in theory had hardly to reckon. There was a direct link between the people and the Governor-General, the administrator of sovereignty.

Holland accepted that the States were delegates of nobles and towns. However, in making a distinction between the residence and administration of sovereignty, Vranck was able to pursue the celebration of the States as upholders of liberty and leading sovereign powers while retaining a notion of popular sovereignty.

There has been some debate about the proper interpretation of the notions of popular sovereignty such as those developed by both Wilkes and Vranck. At stake are the proper meanings of the terms 'popular' and 'representation' in late sixteenth-century political thought.

It has been argued that the great pleas for popular sovereignty, as formulated by the *Vindiciae contra tyrannos* and Althusius, were developed in connection with 'holistic' and corporatist notions of the community and as such were following late medieval political thought. Here the term 'popular' did not refer to 'a group of independent individuals, who somehow or other have united themselves together', but rather to 'the permanent social framework by which they are united'.[158] Sovereignty did not, as later notions would hold, belong to a 'quantifiable collection of real living beings' but to 'a network of ancient institutions, of councils, parliaments, colleges and estates, and secondarily, those who have a place in them'.[159] Accordingly, when Althusius or authors such as Wilkes and Vranck referred to certain colleges, such as the States, in terms of representative institutions, this did not 'mean that these assemblies are appointed by the people to give expression to popular will'.[160] Rather it meant that such institutions more or less personified the people, embodying 'the social bond which unites people in society'.

However, late medieval notions of popular sovereignty were, in spite of holism, certainly not by definition incompatible with more

---

[158] See E. H. Kossmann, 'Popular sovereignty at the beginning of the Dutch *ancien régime*', *LCHY* 14 (1981), 4.
[159] Ibid.   [160] Ibid. 23.

individualistic notions of society.[161] The Commentators and Decreta-
lists employing 'holistic' language themselves often recognized that
the *populus* was both an 'abstract unitary entity' and a 'plurality of
human beings'. In fact jurists such as Baldus and even holistic
thinkers such as Marsilius of Padua described a corporation as a
'fiction of the law', attributing actual reality only to the individual
members.[162] Moreover, the Roman-law maxim that 'what touches
all is to be approved by all' promoted the development of influential
theories of government by (popular) consent, in which the position of
the individual was, one way or the other, of great importance.

With regard to representation, a powerful tradition in late
medieval political thought exemplified by, amongst others, Marsilius
had interpreted it in terms of delegation.[163] As is well known, the
question, and the fundamental ambiguities involved, whether the
delegate could be said to personify the community or corporation he
represented was addressed with particular vehemence by William of
Ockham, whose nominalist philosophy not only resulted in the view
that, as Ockham put it, 'the people is not an individual, it is an
aggregate of individuals', but also led to the idea that, therefore,
representation had to involve 'individual delegation by members of
the community'.[164]

With regard to the issues of popular sovereignty and representation, the political thought of the Dutch Revolt reflected and
elaborated the riches of medieval political thought. Endorsing holistic
notions, the 1576 *Address*, for example, argued that the States
represented 'the entire corps', adding that they should do 'in its
name what otherwise the generality should have done itself'. Vranck
himself consistently described the town councils as colleges, representing 'the whole state and the entire body of the inhabitants'. More
and more, however, representation was explicitly interpreted in
terms of delegation, the States' members being delegates, who, as
Vranck pointed out so amply and in close correspondence with
political reality, could only act in virtue, and on the order and

---

[161] The point is made by Anthony Black, 'Society and the individual from the Middle Ages to Rousseau: philosophy, jurisprudence and constitutional theory', *HPT* 1 (1980), 157-9.

[162] See most recently J. P. Canning, *The political thought of Baldus de Ubaldis* (Cambridge, 1987), 185ff., and Brian Tierney, 'Marsilius on rights', *JHI* 52 (1991), 6.

[163] See Jeannine Quillet, 'Community, counsel and representation', in J. H. Burns (ed.), *The Cambridge history of medieval political thought* (Cambridge, 1988), 554-72, and Brian Tierney, *Religion, law, and the growth of constitutional thought, 1150-1650* (Cambridge, 1982), 26-7.

[164] Arthur P. Monahan, *Consent, coercion, and limit: the medieval origins of parliamentary democracy* (Leiden, 1987), 239-49. See also Quillet, 'Community, counsel and representation', 561-5.

instruction, of the 'corporation of the nobles' and the 'colleges' of the town councils. Although this language was undoubtedly reminiscent of holistic traditions, some passages, for example in the *Brief discourse*, indicated that the relation between the representatives of the people, the States and the people was not always interpreted purely in holistic terms. In defending the States' demand for freedom of religion, the treatise argued that, as the States represented 'the whole people and all the inhabitants of the country', it was 'reasonable' for them to 'conform themselves to the dispositions and desires of the inhabitants in just and proper matters for the common good of the country'.[165]

Such formulations not only contained a conception of representation not in terms of personification, but in terms of delegation, they also moved towards the articulation of the idea that the States were the delegates of the individual inhabitants of the country, to whose desires the States were to conform.

---

[165] *Brief discours sur la negotiation de la paix, que se tracte presentement à Coloigne entre le Roy d'Espaigne, & les Estats du Pays Bas* (Leiden, 1579), fol. B1.

CHAPTER 6

Politics and religion (1572–1590): the debates on religious toleration and the substance of liberty

6.1. INTRODUCTION: REFORMED PROTESTANTISM BETWEEN 1572 AND 1590[1]

In the history of Reformed Protestantism 1572 was a turning-point, opening up new perspectives especially in Holland.[2] In some towns small Calvinist minorities had remained which had been active in the decision of the towns to join William of Orange's armed resistance. These minorities were weak in numbers but strong in discipline and organization. None the less, for the most part the Reformed Protestant church had to be built up from scratch. Thus in the years following 1572, amidst the hazard of war, Reformed Protestants were preoccupied with constructing a proper church order along Calvinist lines as determined during the Emden synod. The Emden policy was confirmed by the 1574 provincial synod of Dordrecht. It reaffirmed allegiance to the 1561 *Confession of Faith* and to the Heidelberg Catechism and took steps to set up a proper church organization in Holland and Zeeland, dividing the provinces into fourteen classes. The classis, the assembly of representatives of the Reformed

---

[1] There is no English survey available of the history of the Reformed Protestant church in this period, although A. Duke, 'The ambivalent face of Calvinism in the Netherlands, 1561–1618', in M. Prestwich (ed.), *International Calvinism 1541–1565* (Oxford, 1985), also covers this period. Recent Dutch surveys include J. J. Woltjer, 'De religieuze situatie in de eerste jaren van de republiek', in *Ketters en papen onder Filips II* (The Hague, 1986), and W. Nijenhuis, 'De publieke kerk veelkleurig en verdeeld, bevoorrecht en onvrij', in *AGN* vi. 325–43. The most comprehensive study of Reformed Protestant church life in the times of Oldenbarnevelt and Maurice of Nassau is A. T. van Deursen, *Bavianen en slijkgeuzen: kerk en kerkvolk ten tijde van Maurits en Oldenbarnevelt* (Assen, 1974). An orthodox view is offered by R. H. Bremmer, *Reformatie en rebellie: Willem van Oranje, de Calvinisten en het recht van opstand: tien onstuimige jaren: 1572–1581* (Franeker, 1984).

[2] For the process of reconstructing the Reformed Protestant church in Holland, see A. Duke and R. L. Jones, 'Towards a reformed polity in Holland, 1572–1578', *TvG* 89 (1976), 373–93.

Protestant congregations within a certain area, was of crucial importance in building up the Reformed Protestant church. It controlled the observance of proper discipline, doctrine and charity in the congregations. It examined candidate ministers and was deeply involved in the appointment of new ministers.

In suspending the placards concerning the persecution of protestants, the 1576 Pacification of Ghent gave new impetus to the growth of the Reformed Protestant church in the Dutch Provinces. Many exiles returned to their homes, and from about 1578 Reformed Protestant churches sprang up like mushrooms in provinces such as Friesland, Guelders, Brabant and especially Flanders.

As the Ghent committee of XVIII embraced the Calvinist cause and embarked on a revolutionary course to make Ghent the Geneva of the north, Reformed Protestantism began to gain momentum in Flanders and in Brabant.[3] The process was far from peaceful. Pursuing a violent policy of expansion the Ghent republic and revolutionary committees in other towns not only contributed to the growing polarization and the collapse of the Pacification, they also more or less imposed Calvinism on Flanders. This policy of forceful ' protestantization' was not without success. By 1579 the organization of the Calvinist church was completed in Flanders. Ghent itself had become a centre of radical Calvinism. It has been estimated that between 1578 and 1584 about 15,000 people adopted the Calvinist faith, which amounts to 30 per cent of the population.[4]

The rise of Flemish and Brabant Calvinism practically coincided with the first national synod of the Reformed Protestant churches, held at Dordrecht in the summer of 1578.[5] The organization of the church was the main theme of the synod's deliberations. Its objective was to bring unity and conformity in church order and doctrine.[6] The synod devised 102 articles to regulate the appointment and

---

[3] See J. Decavele, 'Gent, het "Geneve van Vlaanderen"', in J. Decavele (ed.), *Het eind van een rebelse droom* (Ghent, 1984), 32–60; J. Decavele, 'Het herstel van het Calvinisme in Vlaanderen in de eerste jaren na de Pacificatie van Gent (1577–1578)', in Dirk van de Bauwhede and Marc Goetinck (eds.), *Brugge in de Geuzentijd: bijdragen tot de geschiedenis van de hervorming te Brugge en in het Brugse Vrije in de 16e eeuw* (Bruges, 1982), 9–33; Guido Marnef, *Het Calvinistisch bewind te Mechelen*, Ancien pays et Assemblées d'Etats, lxxxvii (Kortrijk-Heule, 1987), 227–306.

[4] See J. Briels, *Zuid-Nederlanders in de Republiek 1572–1630: een demografische en cultuurhistorische studie* (Sint-Niklaas, 1985), 27.

[5] See D. Nauta and J. P. van Dooren (eds.), *De nationale synode van Dordrecht 1578: Gereformeerden uit de noordelijke en de zuidelijke Nederlanden bijeen* (Amsterdam, 1978).

[6] See W. van't Spijker, 'De kerkorde van Dordrecht (1578)', in D. Nauta and J. P. van Dooren (eds.), *De nationale synode van Dordrecht*, 131.

duties of ministers, to reaffirm the presbyterian church order, to promote Reformed education, to reformulate the church doctrine on catechism, sacraments and ceremonies, to regulate marriage and to set up a proper procedure for admonishing and excommunicating the 'stubborn sinner'.

The work on the church order was taken up by the national synod of 1581 held at Middelburg in Zeeland.[7] The synod commissioned four of its members to develop a *corpus disciplinae*. Probably in co-operation with the important Genevan theologian Lambert Daneau, who had recently accepted a post as professor at Leiden University, the commission devised a Reformed church order which fully affirmed the presbyterian organization and doctrine.[8] The *corpus disciplinae* delineated the duties of the church servants, ministers, elders and deacons, and affirmed that church government consisted of consistories and the so-called 'greater assemblies', classes, par-ticular (provincial) synods and finally the national synod. At the same time, the *corpus* endorsed the non-hierarchical principle, accepted already by the 1571 synod of Emden, that no church or church official should rule over other churches or church officials.

The synods of Dordrecht and Middelburg bore witness to the energy and organizational capacities of Reformed Protestants. Starting from scratch, they succeeded to build up, within less than ten years, a more or less nation-wide church order and government. How successful the Reformed Protestant drive had been during these years from a missionary point of view is difficult to assess. Available figures indicate that the members of the Reformed Protestant church were at best a substantial minority. Growth was steady yet slow. A major impetus was the exodus of Reformed Protestants from the southern provinces in the 1580s to northern towns, which meant that within a relatively short period the Reformed churches in the north acquired thousands of new and mostly radical Calvinist members. Yet even in 1587 the States of Holland, at that moment subject to strong criticism from Reformed ministers supporting Leicester, asserted that less than 10 per cent of the population of Holland

---

[7] See J. P. van Dooren (ed.), *De nationale synode te Middelburg in 1581: Calvinisme in opbouw in de noordelijke en zuidelijke Nederlanden* (Middelburg, 1981).

[8] See W. van't Spijker, 'De Acta van de synode van Middelburg (1581)', in van Dooren (ed.), *De nationale synode te Middelburg*, 64–128, and R. H. Bremmer, 'De nationale synode van Middelburg (1581): politieke achtergronden van kerkelijke besluitvorming', in van Dooren (ed.), *De nationale synode te Middelburg*, 1–63.

belonged to the Reformed church. In fact it has been argued that until 1619 (the year of the synod of Dordrecht) there were more Roman Catholics than Reformed Protestants in the Dutch Republic.[9]

It is difficult to assess such assertions, if only because the allegiance to the Reformed church was not confined to its members. In addition there was a group of what were called 'lovers'. The 'lovers' were persons who more or less frequently attended Reformed Protestant services but had not been confirmed as communicant members, either because they did not want to become members of the church or because they were as yet unacceptable to the Reformed church itself.[10] The importance and influence of this group should not be underestimated. They played an important role in community life and were involved in the appointment of new ministers; in the formative years of the Reformed church many town magistrates were amongst them.

As the various attempts, led by William of Orange in particular, to establish religious peace in the Low Countries failed, the position of the Reformed church became more and more privileged. Already in 1573 most towns in Holland decided to forbid the Roman Catholic mass. Eight years later a similar decision was taken by the States General in issuing a placard which forbade all 'papal exercises'. The magistrates, regardless of their private religious preferences, accepted the Reformed church as the principal church of the Dutch Provinces. They were willing to protect the church, for example by means of Sunday laws, and called upon it to fulfil public tasks, such as the spiritual care of the army. Accepting these 'public duties', the Reformed church gradually became the 'public church', as it is usually called, of the Dutch Provinces. For example, in spite of its own stress on discipline, it adopted a very lenient approach to non-members who wanted to get married in church or who wanted their children baptized. In these respects the Reformed church stood open to everyone.

Yet the Reformed Protestant church had no intention of becoming the church of all people regardless of their moral standing and faith. The community of the saints admitted only members whose moral and spiritual standing was acceptable according to Reformed Protestant standards and who were willing to submit themselves to

[9] See Briels, *Zuid-Nederlanders in de Republiek*, 265.
[10] For the 'lovers' see in particular van Deursen, *Bavianen en slijkgeuzen*, 128ff., and A. van Deursen, *Het kopergeld van de Gouden Eeuw: hel en hemel* (Assen, 1980), 41ff.

the severe demands of church discipline. As the church demanded a total regeneration of spiritual and daily life of its members, many seem to have hesitated to enter church ranks and perhaps preferred the less demanding role of 'lover'.

Thus people were never forced to become members of the church. This was also the policy of the public authorities. In spite of their recognition and support of the Reformed Protestant church, both States and town magistrates were unwilling to follow a religious policy of coercion. The principle of freedom of conscience was accepted by the States of Holland from the outset; it was enshrined in the 1579 Union of Utrecht. In addition, although Roman Catholic worship was forbidden by law, actual policy was more tolerant and Roman Catholic services were often though certainly not always condoned. More freedom was given to other protestant churches, those of the Mennonites and the Lutherans, who were in general permitted to hold services.[11]

In the process of constructing their church between 1572 and 1590, Reformed Protestants had to address new questions concerning politics and religion. This chapter reconstructs the debates in the Dutch Provinces on the key issues of religious peace, the relationship between church and political government and the issue of toleration. These debates were of fundamental importance for the character of the Reformed Protestant church, for its place in the United Provinces, for the political and religious culture of the Dutch Republic and, last but not least, for the development of political thought during the Dutch Revolt.

6.2. THE DEBATE ON RELIGIOUS PEACE

On 22 June 1578 the synod of Dordrecht presented a *Supplication* to Archduke Matthias and the Council of State on behalf of 'the inhabitants of these Netherlands...who desire to live after the Reformation of the Gospel'.[12] It reiterated the view that the purpose of the Spaniards was to bring the Netherlands 'under the pretext of

---

[11] For a fine study about the complexities of Dutch churches in one of the major towns of Holland, see Joke Spaans, *Haarlem na de Reformatie: Stedelijke cultuur en kerkelijk leven* (The Hague, 1989).

[12] *Supplicatie aen sijne Hoocheyt, en Heeren des Raets van State, overgegeven door de inwoonders deser Nederlanden, welcke protesteren dat sy te begeren te leven nae de Reformatie des Evangeliums* (1578).

devotion and religion' under their unbearable tyranny. The *Supplication* asserted that 'the good patriots and lovers of the Republic' should have resisted this policy from the outset in concord, 'without distinction of religion', in order to maintain their privileges and liberties. It explained that resistance was weakened due to growing discord between Roman Catholics and Reformed Protestants and presented religious peace as the key solution to this problem, assuring that 'protestants' had no intention of exterminating the Roman Catholic religion by force, or of acting against their 'fellow citizens' but were willing to do what was in their power for the 'protection of the whole fatherland'.[13] The *Supplication* referred to the experience of Germany and France, which after considerable bloodshed had shown that permitting the exercise of both religions was the only way to stop further killing.

The argument of the *Supplication* was remarkably political. It presented religious peace not as a preference of principle but as the solution to the political problem of growing discord which threatened to undermine the resistance against Spanish tyranny. This political call for religious peace was undoubtedly meant to support William of Orange, who considered religious peace to be the answer to the growing polarization in the provinces.[14] As such, the *Supplication* fitted well into the prince's campaign to get his proposal for religious peace accepted.

Although the States General rejected Orange's proposal, his campaign was not entirely without success, for a number of towns decreed a form of religious peace. One of the towns to do so was Antwerp, where religious peace was declared on 12 June 1579.[15] The declaration of peace asserted that 'no religion may be maintained or impressed with violence or weaponry'. As religion was a 'special gift of God' all Christian people should live with each other in peace and

---

[13] Ibid., pp. ix–x.

[14] It has long been debated whether the *Supplication* was in fact a request of the Reformed Protestant synod. For a summary of the debate, see R. H. Bremmer, 'De nationale betekenis van de synode van Dordrecht (1578)', in Nauta and van Dooren (eds.), *De nationale synode van Dordrecht*, 92ff., and Bremmer, *Reformatie en rebellie*, 128ff., who shows that the *Supplication* was indeed commissioned by the synod. Its author was probably Villiers, who played an important role as intermediary between the synod and Orange.

[15] See *De Religions-vrede: Gheaccordeert ende gepubliceert binnen Antwerpen den xijen Junij MDLXXIX* (Antwerp, 1579). Utrecht, Brussels and eventually even Ghent also declared some form of religious peace. For Ghent, see *Ordonnantie ende edict opt faict van beede de religien ghestatueert by Bailliu, Schepenen van beede de bancken, beede de dekenen der stede van Ghendt, by advise van mijnen Heere den Prince van Oraengen ende adveu van de drye leden der selver steden, den 16e decembris, anno 1578* (1578).

concord, respecting those who had chosen another church. Thus the Antwerp citizens were ordered not to hinder, disturb or slander fellow citizens of a different denomination.

Orange's campaign was supported by a series of treatises. Some of them defended the idea of religious peace on essentially political grounds. A fine example of this line of reasoning was the attempt of a number of Antwerp officials to convince Ghent of the necessity for religious peace. Their argument was built on the idea 'that the sole means to prosperity, maintenance and conservation of countries, towns and republics has always been unity and concord'.[16] Concord was seen as 'the stay and foundation' of countries and towns, whereas 'discord or dissension' were the causes of 'all adversity, total ruin, spoliation and desolation'.[17] This principle, the Antwerp officials pointed out, applied to the Dutch Provinces, and Flanders in particular, as they, more than ever, were afflicted by discord and were confronted with a grave military threat. Appealing to civic duty the Antwerp deputies, obviously referring to the persecution of Roman Catholics by Ghent, asserted that 'for all wise and political governors and magistrates, and everyone involved, the general and common welfare should be of greater weight and consideration than any interest or particular affection of zeal, or vengeance'.[18] Pledging Ghent to abandon its particular affections, the town was urged to accept religious peace, as no war was more damaging than a civil war based on religious differences.[19] In short, endorsing the view that concord was the foundation of all countries and towns, the Antwerp officials defended religious peace as a necessary remedy for the discord afflicting the Dutch Provinces.

This argument was also propounded by a number of treatises published in 1579. The *Warning to those of the Low Countries* argued that without unity and concord the provinces would fall victim to 'malicious and shrewd Machiavellians'. Such considerations, the treatise asserted, 'should move all patriots who love the liberty and

---

[16] *Openinghe ende Propositie ghedaen van weghen myne Heeren den Bailliu, Schepenen van beede de bancken, beede de Dekenen, Edelen ende Notabelen der Stede van Ghendt ter vergaderinghe vanden drye Leden der selver Stede* (Ghent, 1578), fol. A3.

[17] Ibid.   [18] Ibid., fol. B.

[19] Ibid., fols. C2–C3. For a similar argumentation in favour of religious peace, see the 1579 *Clare vertoninge ende bericht der articulen ende conditien nu onlancz tot Cuelen inde vredehandel byden Churfursten, fursten ende andere Keyserlycke Maiesteyts Ghesanten, gheproponeert*, fol. D4, and *Een Goede waerschouwinghe voor den borgheren ende besonder dien vanden leden van Antwerpen, dat sy hen niet en souden laten verlocken met het soet aengheven vande bedriechlijcke artijckelen van peyse onlancx ghecomen van Cuelen*, fol. 8.

conservation of their fatherland and the expulsion of the enemy and
its adherents to do their utmost in order to maintain union, a gift of
God'.[20] According to the *Warning*, without concord and union the
Dutch could 'neither achieve the liberty' for which they had 'taken
up arms nor escape from the eternal servitude in which we and our
posterity will fall because of our disunion'.[21]

Another call to concord was the *Friendly warning to the States of Artois,
Hainaut and Douay*. This treatise, explicitly addressed to the provinces
which were on the verge of reconciling with Philip II, warned
forcefully against the dangers of internal discord, 'the true cause' of
the destruction of famous monarchies and republics. As religious
peace was the unique means of obtaining peace and concord, the
treatise demanded 'the free exercise and worship' of the Reformed
religion.[22]

A mixture of political and religious arguments in favour of religious
peace was presented by the *Admonition and advice for the Netherlands*,
which not only wanted to discuss whether 'one should force
consciences' but also intended to show both the cause and the remedy
of the internal discord of the provinces. The treatise asserted that the
principal cause of the civil war, 'the sickness of the Netherlands', was
'the constraining and forcing of consciences', of which both Roman
Catholics and 'evangelicals', who from persecuted had turned into
persecutors themselves, were guilty. According to the *Admonition* the
constraint of conscience was a grave crime, in fact 'worse than cruelly
taking somebody's life'.[23]

In denouncing the constraint of conscience, the *Admonition* first
referred to the rule of nature, imprinted by God 'in the heart of all
nations', of not doing 'unto others what you do not want to be done
to yourself'.[24] It went on to reject the argument, presented as the
principal cause of the French religious troubles, that it was the holy
office of princes and magistrates to persecute and execute heretics in
accordance with the law of the Old Testament, which proscribed the
execution of blasphemers and false prophets. The *Admonition* argued
at length that interpreting the Bible differently on issues such as the
sacraments was not by implication a form of blasphemy. Neither did
heretics fit the description of false prophets as given by Moses.

---

[20] *Advertissement à ceulx du pais Bas* (1579), 13.   [21] *Ibid.*

[22] *Vriendelijcke waerschouwinghe aen de Staten van Artois, van Henegouwen en van Douay* (1579), fol. B.

[23] *Vermaninghe ende raet voor de Nederlanden, waer in doorsake bewesen wort vanden tegenwoordigen
inlantschen twist, ende oock de Remedie daer teghen, maer principalijck wort hier bewesen oftmen de
conscientien behoort te bedwinghen* (1578), fol. A8.   [24] *Ibid.*, fol. C. See also fols. B3, B6.

Pleading for toleration, the treatise urged to follow Christ's example and command of meekness. It argued that God's word ordered only admonishment and, if necessary, excommunication of those who sinned, but this was a task of the church, not of the magistracy.

The third and final argument of the *Admonition* was again political in character. It argued that the origin of the 'sedition and domestic dispute' tormenting the Netherlands was 'that one has tyrannized and persecuted those who are held for heretics'.[25] In the opinion of the author of the *Admonition*, heretics would not have risen to sedition if they had not been persecuted. The treatise asserted that in this case the remedy was worse than the disease. There were so many sects that persecution could only lead to considerable bloodshed. Therefore, as 'a wise man always chooses the lesser of two evils if he cannot eschew them both',[26] the treatise arrived once again at the conclusion that the constraint of conscience was unwarranted.

It has been argued that the *Admonition* was essentially an adapted version of Castellio's *Conseil à la France désolée* and was written by Philippe Duplessis-Mornay, the putative author of the *Vindiciae contra tyrannos*.[27] The *Admonition* was not without followers. It was mentioned in another treatise, also probably written by Duplessis-Mornay, the *Discourse on the permission of liberty of religion, called 'religions vrede' in the Low Countries*,[28] which was published in 1579. In line with the *Admonition* this discourse defended freedom of religion on both political and religious grounds. The religious peace as proposed by Orange was presented as the necessary remedy to cure the sick Netherlands, to re-establish the provinces in 'repose, peace, accord and union'.[29] Duplessis-Mornay reasserted that concord was the foundation of the community, arguing that 'if the good or evil of the Republic is at stake, one can not doubt that welfare depends on union and total ruin on division'.[30] He admitted that it was preferable to have one single religion in a country but endorsed the view that it was

[25] Ibid., fols. F4–F5.   [26] Ibid., fol. F6.

[27] See P. A. M. Geurts, *De Nederlandse Opstand in de pamfletten 1566–1584* (Utrecht, 1983; first pub. 1956), 79–80, and G. Güldner, *Das Toleranzproblem in den Niederlanden im Ausgang des 16. Jahrhunderts* (Hamburg, 1968), 52–4.

[28] See Geurts, *De Nederlandse Opstand*, 81, Güldner, *Das Toleranzproblem in den Niederlanden*, 52, and Raoul Patry, *Philippe Du Plessis-Mornay: un Huguenot homme d'etat (1549–1623)* (Paris, 1933), 51–2, who argues that the *Discourse* was an adapted version of Duplessis-Mornay's 1576 *Remonstrance aux Etats de Blois*, combined with the treatise *Si l'on doit laisser à un chacun la liberté de servir Dieu selon sa maniere et phantaisie*, which made up the last pages of the *Discourse*.

[29] Philippe Duplessis-Mornay, *Discours sur la permission de liberte de religion, dicte Religions-vrede au Pais Bas* (1579), 3.   [30] Ibid. 47. See also p. 4.

better to suffer from diversity of religion than to ruin the country. In this context he reiterated the argument that the cure was worse than the disease.

In addition to these political arguments for religious peace, Duplessis-Mornay propounded the thesis that it was improper amongst Christians to persecute each other. As he put it, both Roman Catholics and Reformed Protestants sought their own 'welfare: both are afraid to offend Christ: both tend to the same Christ. Or should it be said that for following different roads we should cut each other's throat?'[31] Instead Christians of different denominations should try to persuade each other in an open dialogue, for, as Duplessis-Mornay put it, 'the voice of truth is (Scripture says) stronger than kings themselves'. In this respect Christ, who did not appeal to Caesar or other 'lieutenants' to chase the Pharisees from the temple but did so by 'the force of truth', should be the leading example. Thus Duplessis-Mornay asserted that, although it was 'a dignified objective of all Christians to advance the true religion', this should be achieved by proper means such as 'to preach carefully the word of God, to teach their neighbours properly and to instruct hearts by good examples instead of destroying the others'.[32] He retained the idea of a free general council which eventually would settle all issues.

Duplessis-Mornay's arguments were reiterated in *A friendly admonition to all lovers of liberty and religious peace*, also published in 1579. This treatise, which was mainly a summary of Duplessis-Mornay's *Discourse*, endorsed the view that two groups of Christians, which both sought to fear and serve the Lord, should not 'cut each other's throat, plunder or oppress, only because they take different ways'.[33] Likewise the *Friendly admonition* pleaded for dialogue, arguing that 'reasonable human beings' should convince each other 'by reason, by gentle and loving conduct, by a free council and assembly to demonstrate of both sides their truthful reasons'.[34]

In recognizing that 'the welfare of the community' depended on 'concord and union', the *Friendly admonition* was again on familiar ground. The treatise joined those who had warned against religious strife, which could only lead to 'internal civil war'. The *Friendly admonition* did not plead for freedom of religion for all 'sects'. In line with Duplessis-Mornay's discourse, it argued that those who dis-

---

[31] Ibid. 9.   [32] Ibid. 44.
[33] *Een vriendlijcke vermaninghe tot allen Liefhebbers der Vryheyt ende des Religions-vreden* (1579), fol. A2.
[34] Ibid.

turbed the 'common peace' should not be included. In addition, religious freedom should not be given to some groups of Anabaptists, libertarians and followers of Hendrik Niclaes, the founding father of the Family of Love. Only those who had been 'seduced by ignorance' could be tolerated 'in their weakness of conscience'.[35]

Another fundamental plea for religious peace, also emphasizing the necessity of remaining 'in good concord' and of preventing faction, was the *Good admonition to the good citizens of Brussels*. This treatise pointed out that attempts were made to subvert the Pacification of Ghent. While the purpose of the Pacification was to 'dispel and avert all faction and discord from the country', it was now abused to create disunion on the issue of religion. Thus the heart of the Pacification was at stake. According to the *Good admonition* the Pacification, the 'foundation of our common freedom', had been concluded to maintain the inhabitants in 'their old liberty, using their old rights, customs and privileges'.[36] At this point the *Good admonition* made the important move of arguing that the essence of liberty was freedom of conscience. As the treatise put it, 'everyone knows, that the liberty of the human lies especially in the soul, which is the principal part of us, and because of which we are called humans. Its liberty is the freedom of conscience, which lies in this, that a human may accept and keep such religion as his conscience guides, and that no one hath the right nor power to hinder or prohibit him this.'[37] Religion was a 'covenant' between a human being and God, therefore man should 'account for it to no one but God'.[38] This fundamental idea was the source of the 'natural right of freedom of conscience', which was inalienable, as conscience and soul could not be touched by humans.

According to the *Good admonition* the ancestors, who had always laboured to maintain not only 'the freedom of body and goods but also of soul, that is of conscience', had had the wisdom of 'conserving' this natural right of freedom of conscience in the laws of the country. References were made to the 1339 treaty between Brabant and Flanders and the Joyous Entry, which were said to guarantee freedom of body and goods and freedom of conscience. The *Good admonition* recognized that although conscience itself could not be

---

[35] Ibid., fol. A7. See also Duplessis-Mornay, *Discours*, 53–4. Duplessis-Mornay's treatise did not include the reference to the Family of Love.
[36] *Een goede vermaninghe aen de goede borghers van Bruessele* (Ghent, 1579), 13.
[37] Ibid.   [38] Ibid.

affected by human violence this did not apply to the external dimensions of freedom of conscience, which consisted of the 'profession of the mouth and the external exercise of ceremonies'.[39]

In the view of the *Good admonition* freedom of conscience of necessity entailed freedom of worship, and the treatise forcefully condemned Roman Catholics who still wanted to oppress the Reformed religion. The judgment of Roman Catholics as expounded in the treatise was harsh, presenting them as enemies of the liberty of the country. None the less, calling for toleration, the treatise pleaded unequivocally for religious peace.

The idea of liberty, as expounded in the *Good admonition*, was also developed by the *Discourse containing the true understanding of the Pacification of Ghent*, one of the most refined pleas in favour of religious toleration. The *Discourse* was an attempt to refute the arguments of 'sophists' who were sowing discord under the pretext of the authority of the king and the issue of religion in particular. Their main argument regarded the Pacification of Ghent, which in the view of the 'sophists' left no room for religious peace. In their opinion the States themselves had started the war not only for the maintenance of liberty but also for the maintenance of the authority of Philip II and for the protection of Roman Catholicism. The *Discourse* denounced this interpretation. Reaffirming the view, so essential in the resistance ideology of the Revolt, that preserving liberty was of overriding concern, the *Discourse* pointed out that the States would rather 'demand the assistance of the Turk' than subject the country to tyranny.[40] As the *Discourse* put it, in taking up arms the principal intention of the States was 'none other but to defend the liberty of the fatherland, to free oneself from servitude, to reform all the abuses and orders, which, under the shadow of the religion and the authority of His Majesty held the States and the whole country in bridles, in sum to redress everything that is against liberty, under whatever title it may have been introduced, be it religion, the authority of His Majesty or whatever else'.[41]

In addition, it had been the intention of the States to 're-establish the country in repose and tranquillity'. As this could only be effected by unifying the provinces, the States had worked 'to reunite all the members of the *res publica* in one body'.[42] The Pacification of Ghent

---

[39] Ibid. 15. [40] *Discours contenant le vray entendement de la Pacification de Gand* (1579), 12.
[41] Ibid. 23. As the *Discourse* added, the authority of Philip II and the religious issue were mere 'accessoires' in comparison. [42] Ibid. 23–4.

and subsequent treaties were the outcome of this policy. They were attempts to re-establish the Netherlands 'in its pristine and proper liberty' and to create 'perpetual amity' amongst the provinces.

In accordance with the intentions of the States, the *Discourse* argued, the Dutch had 'been restituted in full liberty, which is to say, of goods, of body and of conscience'.[43] Thus the discourse asserted that freedom of conscience was an essential part of liberty. It was claimed to consist of 'two members, namely of the internal and external cultivation of God'. The external dimension referred to 'the profession of the mouth and the exercise of ceremonies'.[44] While the 'liberty of internal cultivation' could never be ousted by men, however gruesome their tyranny might be, the *Discourse* recognized that the 'external cultivation' was 'subject to the violence of men' and it asserted that the 'principal benefit' of the restoration of liberty was the freedom of religion and worship. According to the *Discourse* to have such liberty was an individual natural right. As the *Discourse* itself concluded, 'the principal point of liberty is to have liberty of conscience, to which all are entitled by natural right'.[45]

The *Discourse* took great pains to distinguish religion from politics, asserting that, if a religious doctrine did not incline to subversion of the political order, religion 'does not affect politics in any sense'.[46] The 'office of governors of policy with regard to religion' was none other but to take care that the political order was 'not disrupted because of religion'. Repeating its claim that freedom of conscience was an individual natural right, the *Discourse* asserted that religion was a matter for each individual to decide. It was 'of no concern to the *res publica* where or whether the souls are going after the death, if each serves it as a good patriot during his life'.[47] Thus if it was impossible to 'avoid diversity of religions' the only task of the magistrates was to make good order so as to ensure 'peace and amity'. As the *Discourse* underlined, denouncing Plato, Aristotle and Plutarch, 'the principal goal of a political man cannot be the supreme good or eternal felicity but rather the public repose and tranquillity, which is the supreme good that men can pursue in this life'.[48] Thus religious peace should be effected, being 'the unique

---

[43] Ibid. 31.
[44] Ibid. 31–2. The point was also made in some French treatises, see Joseph Lecler, *Histoire de la tolérance au siècle de la Réforme*, 2 vols. (Paris, 1954), ii. 185.
[45] *Discours*, 95. See also p. 64, where the individual character of this right is emphasized.
[46] Ibid. 35.   [47] Ibid. 64. See also pp. 37ff.   [48] Ibid. 55–6.

means to conserve peace and accord amongst the inhabitants of the provinces'.[49]

Another elaborate and principled defence of religious peace was provided by Pieter de Zuttere, who dedicated his dialogue *A gentle conversation of Cephas and Arnolbius* to William of Orange. The support for a policy of toleration and freedom of conscience brought de Zuttere, at the time of publication working as a Reformed minister in his home town of Ghent, into conflict with his colleagues and the town's radical authorities, who eventually put him temporarily under arrest.

De Zuttere based his plea for toleration on a number of arguments, which were inspired by the works of Erasmus and Augustine, but also Luther and Melanchthon.[50] First, de Zuttere pointed out with reference to Matthew 7 that Christ did not permit men to judge others. Invoking Christ's famous words, the Ghent minister argued that he 'who examined himself will lightly understand that he cannot pull the mote out of his brother's eye, before he has thrown out the beam from his own eye'.[51] This fundamental human weakness should, in de Zuttere's view, exert man above all to punish and better himself, instead of judging others. In matters of religion and conscience God had kept all judgment to himself, as he alone could investigate the human heart. The world, as de Zuttere put it, 'can neither understand nor receive the spirit of truth'. This applied as well to worldly authorities. Though instituted by God, the government was 'a human, temporary order locked within certain limits', which ruled only over earthly affairs. Only 'the bodies and transitory goods of mortal man' were subject to the laws of government, whose 'right and power' was restricted to this earthly realm. The 'mind of man', over which only God ruled, was 'not tied to the human laws of the government'.[52] Governments should follow Gamaliel's famous advice and leave heresy untouched. This led to a bold assertion of freedom of conscience and worship, as de Zuttere emphasized that 'nothing is so free as faith and the service to God which follows therefrom, to which no one may be forced, as it is a work of God through the Holy Spirit and can by no means be exacted by human violence'.[53]

[49] Ibid. 85.
[50] See Pieter de Zuttere, *Een Saechtmoedighe tsamensprekinghe van Cephas ende Arnolbius* (Ghent, 1581), fol. A5. In fact the closing pages of de Zuttere's book offered a series of quotations from a number of church fathers, from Erasmus, but also from Luther, Calvin and Beza.
[51] Ibid., fol. B1.   [52] Ibid., fol. B6.   [53] Ibid., fol. B8.

De Zuttere's Spiritualist arguments resembled those of Aggaeus van Albada, whose *Acts of the peace negotiations which took place at Cologne* contained an authoritative plea for freedom of conscience and religion. Albada's arguments, scattered throughout the *Acts*, were manifold. First of all, Albada referred to the 'law of nature', which taught man that 'what you do not want to be done to yourself, do not do unto others'.[54] Applied to religious persecution this meant, as no one would want to be persecuted himself, that one should not persecute others.

Albada's second argument was based on the fundamental difference between matters concerning the body and matters concerning the soul. Heresy, Albada argued, 'is a spiritual matter, which should not be destroyed with iron, nor consumed by fire, nor washed away or drowned with worldly water'.[55] The worldly powers should not and could not touch the soul. As it was in no one's power to 'close or open heaven and hell', no one was able to force someone to belief or disbelief. Boldly Albada asserted that 'nothing should be as free as faith and religion, to which no one can be forced, as it is a divine work in the Holy Spirit'.[56] Political authorities had been instituted to govern 'body and goods', not conscience. Religion, Albada expounded during the negotiations, was an individual affair. Each should serve the Lord 'after his conscience'. The office of government had no concern with 'the spiritual empire of Christ'. The 'worldly magistrate', whose 'external worldly office' was to govern 'earthly affairs', differed 'from the heavenly empire of Christ and of his spiritual regiment as heaven from earth'.[57] Since faith was a gift of God it could be 'neither obtained, nor taken, nor protected, nor kept with the sword of flesh'.[58] Heresy should only be opposed with spiritual powers, with the truth and with God's word.

Referring to Hieronymus, Albada reiterated the view that man's judgment differed from God's judgment as earth differed from heaven.[59] Since religion was a 'spiritual mystery', as Albada called it, one should beware and not judge lightly. Since only someone who was 'in the truth' could fully grasp it, 'the world can neither comprehend nor understand the spirit of the truth'.[60] In Albada's view, 'the truth is set so that no one may judge of her' unless he himself was 'in the truth'. Since 'the world not only cannot

---

[54] Aggaeus van Albada, *Acten van den Vredehandel gheschiet te Colen* (Antwerp, 1581), 129.
[55] Ibid. 171.   [56] Ibid. 168.   [57] Ibid. 194.
[58] Ibid. 54.   [59] Ibid. 48.   [60] Ibid. 48.

understand these matters, but on the contrary seeks and loves the lie ', Albada asked, 'how might it judge and sentence the matter?'[61] Finally, Albada, who repeatedly stressed the importance of concord and the negative effects of discord and faction,[62] referred to the political necessity of religious toleration, without which there could in his view be no peace.

Thus in line with the other pleas for religious peace Albada's argumentation underlined the pivotal role of concord in the political thought of the Dutch Revolt. Once again concord and union were presented as the foundation of the community, while discord and faction were seen as the principal means of destruction. Religious differences were recognized as the most important seeds of discord. Religious peace was therefore a sheer political necessity in the situation of the Netherlands. In this respect Dutch arguments in favour of religious peace marked, just like French pleas such as the *Conseil à la France desolée* and also Junius' *Brief discourse* had done, the beginning of the political justification of religious toleration.[63]

Other arguments in favour of religious peace had a far more religious background, derived from Spiritualist and humanist sources, with Sebastian Castellio and Sebastian Franck as outstanding examples. The 'law of nature' not to do to others what you do not want to be done to yourself, the notion that man simply lacked the capacity to grasp God's truth and the idea that religion was a spiritual realm which could not be touched by the sword of the flesh, all led to the conclusion that, regardless of the political situation in the country, religious peace was desirable and just.

Finally, it should be noted that some authors made the radical move of advocating freedom of conscience because it should be regarded as an individual natural right which was said to be the very essence of liberty. From this perspective the Dutch Revolt as a defence of liberty was principally a fight for individual freedom of conscience and worship.

[61] Ibid. 46. [62] See e.g. pp. 6 and 299.
[63] See Hans R. Guggisberg, 'Wandel der Argumente für religiöse Toleranz und Glaubens-freiheit im 16. und 17. Jahrhundert', in Heinrich Lutz (ed.), *Zur Geschichte der Toleranz und Religionsfreiheit* (Darmstadt, 1977), 455–81, and, for a study of the French *Conseil* in this context, Hans R. Guggisberg, 'Castellio und der Ausbruch der Religionskriege in Frankreich: einige Betrachtungen zum *Conseil à la France désolée*', *ARG* 68 (1977), 253–67.

6.3. THE RELATIONSHIP BETWEEN CHURCH AND POLITICAL AUTHORITIES[64]

Although, as pointed out, the Reformed Protestant church was soon accepted and supported by States and town magistrates as the public church in the United Provinces, Orange's policy of religious peace and the pleas for religious freedom accompanying it, soon indicated that this support was by no means unqualified. From the beginning, the relationship between the Reformed Protestant churches and government officials in Holland was full of tension.

Reformed Protestants clung to their views on the nature and role of political authority as developed during the 1560s. For example, in 1571 Peter Dathenus and other Reformed Protestants strongly defended the necessity for and authority of government in a debate with a group of Anabaptists. Dathenus emphasized that government was a divine institution, ordained on the one hand 'to punish the evil and shelter and protect the good' and on the other hand 'to maintain the honourable, peaceable life in all godliness and virtue'.[65] Thus the religious duty of political authorities to support true godliness, incorporated in article 36 of the *Confession of faith*, was reaffirmed. This somewhat 'theocratic' idea of political authority remained an essential element of Reformed Protestant thought throughout the Revolt and afterwards. Although it meant that Reformed Protestants expected political authorities to support their church, time and again they defended the independence of the Reformed Protestant church from governmental interference. In the church order as outlined by the 1571 Emden synod political authorities had no role whatsoever. The 1578 national synod of Dordrecht reaffirmed this view. Article 4 of its acts, regulating the appointment of church ministers, said ministers should be appointed by the consistory in co-operation with the deacons and the classis. Having elected a minister, he was to be presented to the 'Reformed government' and the congregation, which both had two weeks to protest against the appointment. Thus

---

[64] There is of course a large body of literature on this topic. Most of it concentrates on the debates of the 17th century. For the importance of the debates in the 16th century, see (amongst others) H. A. Enno van Gelder, *Vrijheid en onvrijheid in de Republiek* (Haarlem, 1974), and H. A. Enno van Gelder, *Getemperde vrijheid* (Groningen, 1972). Available in English is: R. L. Jones, 'Reformed church and civil authorities in the United Provinces in the late sixteenth and early seventeenth centuries, as reflected in Dutch state and municipal archives', *Journal of the Society of Archivists*, 4 (1970–3), 109–23.

[65] *Protocol, dat is: alle handelinge der Tsamensprekinghe tot Franckenthal...metten genen diemen Wederdoopers noemt* (1571), fol. 173.

by way of minor concession the synod recognized that in the procedure of appointing ministers town magistrates had a limited right of protest. However, the eventual decision to appoint a minister belonged to the consistory. In answering one of the 'particular questions', the synod asserted explicitly that the government was not entitled to appoint or dismiss ministers at its own will. With regard to the appointment of elders the synod claimed an even more exclusive right, not acknowledging any right of confirmation on behalf of the town government.

This bold reassertion of the independence of the Reformed Protestant church was unacceptable to a majority of the towns and States of Holland. Already in 1576 a committee of the States argued that as the ministers were paid out of public finances they should be appointed by public authorities. Referring to the 'confusion of religion and the troubled state of our republic' the committee warned against the creation of two different forms of magistracy in one community.

One of the sternest opponents of the mainstream Reformed Protestant view on the relationship between church and political authorities was the town magistrate of Leiden. In the summer of 1579 Leiden openly declared itself in disagreement with the church order of the Dordrecht synod, asserting that the appointment of ministers, elders and deacons belonged to the magistrate. An elaborate defence of this position was articulated in the famous *Justification of the magistrate at Leiden in Holland,* which discussed the conflict between the magistrate and the consistory of Leiden on the appointment of ministers. The *Justification,* probably written by Dirck Volckertsz Coornhert, accused the consistory of trying to 'usurp' the 'magistrate's rule' and avowed that the magistrate, 'being relieved of the awkward yoke of the tyrannic Romanists', did not intend to bear 'a new form of yoke from anyone else'.[66]

As the treatise pointed out, the Reformed Protestant consistory demanded the 'prohibition, constraint and punishment' by the town magistrate of Mennonites, Roman Catholics and all other religious groupings. Thus the town magistrate, which was not allowed to interfere in church affairs in any way, was expected to execute the orders of the Reformed Protestants. With this policy, the *Justification* argued, Reformed Protestants trod in the footsteps of the Inquisition, as they demanded the forcing of conscience, which had been 'the root

---

[66] *Justificatie des magistraets tot Leyden in Hollant* (1579), fol. A4.

cause of this bloody war'. Moreover, as Reformed Protestants denied the magistrate independent judgment in religious affairs, the *Justification* concluded that the consistory wanted to subjugate it, to control its sword and to make it like Pilate, who followed the wishes of the Pharisees without making a proper judgment himself.

The *Justification* denounced these claims forcefully, arguing that the magistrate was instituted by God 'for the defence of the pious and the chastisement of the evil'.[67] If its divinely ordained power was not to be abused, as had happened under the Inquisition, it needed to have 'lawful knowledge' of the people to be appointed 'as shepherds in the church or fold of Christ'.[68] Thus on the basis of its divinely ordained duty the magistrate had a rightful claim to authority over the 'election and approbation' of 'church servants'.

Moreover, according to the *Justification* the 'office' of the magistrate was to take precautions and to settle disputes in both political and ecclesiastical affairs, especially if these tended to 'a common sedition'. This did not imply complete control over ecclesiastical affairs. The magistrate merely wanted to prevent the appointment of 'seditious spirits' in the consistory in order to safeguard the church from a new form of popery.

The claims of the Leiden magistrate were supported by one of the Reformed ministers in Leiden, Caspar Coolhaes.[69] Coolhaes, who became one of the most prolific authors on church affairs during the Revolt, was born in 1534 in Cologne, where he studied at the university before becoming a Carthusian monk. In 1566 Coolhaes served the Reformed congregation of Deventer. In 1574 he received his appointment in Leiden. His support of the Leiden magistrate in the conflict over the appointment of church officials, and his unorthodox views, made Coolhaes a rather controversial figure in Reformed Protestant circles. To defend himself he published in 1580 his *Apology: a Christian and fair account of Caspar Coolhaes, servant of God's word in Leiden.*

Coolhaes' apology, which took the form of a dialogue between himself and Theophilus, contained an elaborate defence of the magistrate's authority in church affairs. Coolhaes rejected accusations addressed to the Leiden magistrates of being 'godless Epicurists, libertarians, papists, Franckists, Schwenckfeldians and such-

---

[67] Ibid., fol. B6. [68] Ibid.
[69] On Coolhaes see Bremmer, 'De nationale betekenis', 35ff., and J. P. van Dooren, 'Caspar Coolhaes: het een en ander uit zijn leven voor en na de synode van Middelburg', in van Dooren (ed.), *De nationale synode te Middelburg*, 174–83.

like'.[70] He pointed out that the office of the magistrate was to protect
and uphold the word of God and 'to punish without distinction all
persons who wilfully violated it, be they ministers, elders, deacons,
rich, poor, noble or ignoble, men or women, young or old'.[71] As
custodian of both Tables of Moses' law and promoter of the church
of God, the magistrate had the duty of safeguarding the proper
preaching of God's word.

As far as the subjects were concerned Coolhaes pointed out that
they were obliged to obey the magistrate in all 'that is not expressly
incompatible with God's word'.[72] As this rule applied even to godless
magistrates, it certainly applied to Christian authorities, such as the
magistrate of Leiden.

Having reasserted, on the one hand, the duty of the magistrate to
foster the church and to safeguard the proper preaching of God's
word, and on the other hand, the duty of the subjects to obey the
magistrate in all that was not against God's word, Coolhaes defended
the lawfulness of the magistrate's claim of appointing the consistory,
as it meant that eventually the election of church servants resided
with the community. Coolhaes argued that the election of the
consistory was 'nothing without the election by the government' and
that 'the election of the government' was 'nothing without the
election by the community'.[73] Both minister and magistrate were,
according to Coolhaes, servants of the community and as such the
community, the one being served, was 'greater, higher and worthier'
than ministers and magistrates. Since 'common men' were 'like
unemancipated children' in these affairs, the magistrate had to act as
guardian of the community in the election of ministers, elders and
deacons.

Coolhaes recognized that such ideas were in conflict with the
church order as determined by the synod of Dordrecht. However, as
he put it, the divine command to obey 'the government in all things
which are not in conflict with God's word' did not mean that the
faithful should by definition obey 'five or six, ten or twenty, indeed a
hundred or a thousand ministers' who had gathered to 'make some
statutes'.[74] The Leiden minister acknowledged that God's word commanded the faithful to be part of the church or the community, but
reasserted the view that, as the magistracy was the 'most principal

---

[70] Caspar Coolhaes, *Apologia, Een Christelijcke ende billijcke verantwoordinge Caspari Coolhaessen,
Dienaer des Goddelijcken woorts tot Leyden* (1580), fol. 8.   [71] Ibid., fol. 22.
[72] Ibid., fol. 32.   [73] Ibid., fol. 28.   [74] Ibid., fol. 48.

part of the community', it should certainly not be excluded from the church. In fact Coolhaes went as far as to argue that his colleagues were on the way to a new 'popery', if they wanted to put the synod (which Coolhaes considered a superfluous body) above the magistrate and make regulations binding each individual Christian. Coolhaes favoured toleration and meekness, arguing that love was the 'unique, truthful and unmistakable characteristic' of Christianity and that only God was to judge the 'heart and kidneys' of men.[75]

The ideas of the Leiden *Justification* and Coolhaes' *Apology*[76] formed a direct threat to the independent presbyterian church order as adopted by the Reformed Protestant church. In 1581 Coolhaes was summoned to appear for the national synod held at Middelburg.[77] He was put under strong pressure to denounce his views and to accept ten theses of which half dealt with the church order. One of these addressed the role of the magistrate in church affairs. Reflecting the views of the synod, it asserted that it was a 'godly office to sanction the church order made by the church (unless there was something unlawful in it), and to execute it with its authority'.[78]

The Middelburg synod reaffirmed the independence and the presbyterian character of the Reformed Protestant church, although it acknowledged that the government 'professing the Reformed religion' had a right of 'approbation and approval' with regard to the appointment of church servants.[79]

Coolhaes eventually accepted the Middelburg theses. However, he refused to confess his guilt, to denounce his own books and to subscribe to the confession and discipline of the church. As he refused full capitulation he was excommunicated in 1582. Coolhaes responded with a series of publications. His *Missive* denounced the Middelburg synod and reaffirmed his broad and tolerant view on the Christian community as consisting of those who 'confess Christ, love his word, do not champion life without Christ [and] advocate the

---

[75] Ibid., fol. 19.

[76] In 1580 Coolhaes published also the *Breeder bericht van de scheuringe der kercken Christi tot Leyden*, restating his case.

[77] See Bremmer, 'De nationale betekenis', 35ff., and Olivier Fatio, *Nihil pulchris ordine: contribution à l'étude de l'établissement de la discipline ecclésiastique aux Pays-Bas ou Lambert Daneau aux Pays-Bas (1581–1583)* (Leiden, 1971), 36ff.

[78] See Fatio, *Nihil pulchris ordine*, 115, for the theses Coolhaes was urged to accept. The theses are also included in the *Cort eenvoudich ende waerachtich verhael waeromme Caspar Coolhaes ... byden Synode Provinciael van Hollandt vander kercke Christi is gheexcommuniceert* (Dordrecht, 1582).

[79] See 'Kerckenordeninghe inden generalen synode der Nederlandtschen kercken vergadert tot Middelburch', in van Dooren (ed.), *De nationale synode te Middelburg*, 82.

people of God in God's word'.[80] He re-emphasized the role of the magistrate in ecclesiastical affairs and the subordinate position of the synod with regard to the magistrate and to the Gospel.

This time Coolhaes was countered in print by a *Short, simple and truthful story of why Caspar Coolhaes...is excommunicated from Christ's church by the provincial synod of Holland.* This elaborate defence of the excommunication reasserted the view on the relationship between church and political authority as propounded by the synods of Dordrecht and Middelburg. Thus the treatise explicated the difference between the offices of magistrate and minister. As 'a servant of God' the government should govern life on earth and 'maintain both Tables of God', which meant that it should 'foster God's truth with its protection and nutrition'. The office of the ministers, who 'in other affairs' were 'subject with body and goods to the government' was 'to teach, instruct, steer, admonish and move the conscience and soul of men to blessedness'.[81]

Thus while the objectives of minister and magistrate overlapped, each office had its distinctive duty. The treatise emphasized that the synod and ministers of the Reformed Protestant church had no intention of ruling the 'political regiment' and pledged they were willing to obey political authorities 'with body and goods'. However, the government should permit the ministers 'to live in free conscience in accordance with God's word, administering their office (commanded to them by God) after the prophetic and apostolic scriptures'.[82]

Thus the relative independence of the church and its ministers was reasserted. In addition the *Short, simple and truthful story* endorsed the synod's view on the appointment of church servants and rejected the accusation that Reformed Protestants advocated the constraint of conscience. On the contrary, the Reformed Protestant church was claimed to foster true freedom of conscience. Its essence was, and here the wording was almost identical to Calvin's in the *Institutes*, that man, whose 'conscience' testified that 'he was guilty before God's judgment and to eternal death, because of his sins', had learnt in the Gospel 'that God Almighty forgives the sins and accepts the faithful as his children, not because of their dignity or merits, but because of his undeserved mercy'.[83]

---

[80] Caspar Coolhaes, *Sendtbrief Caspars Coolhaes, dienaers des godlicken woorts, residerende tot Leyden* (1582) fol. C3.   [81] *Cort eenvoudich ende waerachtich verhael*, 4.   [82] Ibid. 11.
[83] Ibid. 117. For Calvin's analysis of freedom of conscience and Christian liberty, see John Calvin, *Institutes of the Christian religion*, ii (Grand Rapids, Mich., 1983), 3, ch. 19.

Such true freedom of conscience brought peace with God. It liberated the faithful from 'external things, which are of themselves mediocre and free'. Thus true freedom of conscience did not mean that 'someone may feel and believe as pleases him, as if (as some now say) each can become blessed in his faith'.[84] The treatise rejected this 'libertarian' view on freedom of conscience in the strongest terms. True freedom of conscience could only be found in Christ and in the true Christian doctrine, and, instead of depriving people of their freedom of conscience, it was the deepest wish of the Reformed church to give everybody such true freedom.

Coolhaes responded with a new series of treatises, published in 1584 and 1585. Again he championed a tolerant, open church which respected freedom of conscience and which permitted all who attended the public services to participate in the sacraments.[85] The office of the minister was not to gather a 'new special church'[86] but 'to preach in its true understanding the doctrine of Christ, the prophets and apostles, left to us in writing in the Bible, without subtracting or adding anything'.[87] Coolhaes urged the ministers to remain within the limits of their office and not to usurp their power by trying to enforce upon the consciences of the audience their 'opinions and feelings' as if these were equal to the word of God. According to Coolhaes 'if they want to trap us with laws and regulations, in the way of the world, robbing us of the liberty we have in Jesus Christ, we are not bound to listen to them'.[88] He denounced claims to the monopoly of the truth by the various religious groupings and, referring to Sebastian Franck, argued that the faithful were to be found amongst all denominations.

Thus once again Coolhaes warned against the formation of a new popery, and urged neighbourly love and toleration. He claimed that the scriptures of the apostles and prophets in themselves were sufficient to teach people all that was necessary for their bliss. Every further attempt to tie man's conscience to some particular interpretation of the scriptures should be regarded as tyrannic, as 'antichristian'.[89] Coolhaes did not regard interpreting the scriptures

[84] Ibid. 119.
[85] See e.g. Caspar Coolhaes, *Conciliatio: Dat is verghelijckinghe van sekere poincten der Leere* (Gouda, 1585), fol. 35.
[86] Caspar Coolhaes, *Seekere poincten uut die Heylighe Godtlijcke Schriftuer* (1584), fol. 1.
[87] Caspar Coolhaes, *Toutzsteen tot een seekere proeve welcx in der waerheydt die Apostolische, Catholijcke, Evangelische, Gereformeeerde reyne kercke sy* (1584), fol. B3.
[88] Coolhaes, *Seekere poincten*, fol. 3.
[89] Ibid., fol. 18. See also Coolhaes, *Toutzsteen*, fol. E2, and Caspar Coolhaes, *Een christelijcke vermaninghe aen alle onpartydighe Predicanten* (1584), fol. C3.

as useless but warned against any attempt to present a specific interpretation as the ultimate truth. Interpretations, as he put it, should be 'proposed to the listeners and readers on trial, leaving it in the Christian liberty to understand, accept and feel them or not'.[90] Of course this idea of the church entailed a much looser view on discipline and a much broader idea of freedom of conscience than the conception as articulated in the *Short, simple and truthful story*.

In Coolhaes' view the Dutch Revolt was essentially a fight for freedom of conscience, which should mean that 'each to the best of his knowledge' could 'serve the Lord in good conscience without fear', while 'maintaining mutual peace amongst the inhabitants' which was, 'next to God, the right, true and invincible strength of a town, yes, of a country and kingdom'.[91]

It would be wrong to see Coolhaes as an isolated, eccentric exponent of Reformed Protestantism. Though his conception of the church surely deviated from what the main stream of Reformed Protestant ministers had agreed upon during the various provincial and national synods, Coolhaes was by no means alone in endorsing views which were seen by more orthodox Reformed as latitudinarian. In fact, according to Reinier Donteclock, a Reformed minister in Delft who denounced such libertarian views, such ideas appealed 'to the mentality of a great number of people, especially in Holland'.[92]

Leiden, and the Leiden town magistrate for sure, formed a stronghold of these libertarian ideas. In 1582 a *Remonstrance or representation by those of Leiden* was published which denounced the synod of Middelburg's ideas on church order and its own authority. The *Remonstrance*, written by Coornhert, accused the synod of attempting to raise itself above the magistrate to which it was subject. Its articles on the appointment of ministers were presented as a deliberate attempt of the synod to 'become head of the government'. This policy, the *Remonstrance* declared, was unacceptable to those of Leiden, who would use all their might to prevent the reintroduction of the 'old popery'. For the *Remonstrance*, the essence of popery was its attempt to induce political authorities to support a certain 'true religion with its power', and any form of such coercion in religious affairs should be rebutted.

The *Remonstrance* argued that from the perspective of the common good and the 'conservation of policy' it was much better to

---

[90] Coolhaes, *Seekere poincten*, fol. 25.   [91] Coolhaes, *Toutzsteen*, fol. C2.
[92] Quoted in Fatio, *Nihil pulchris ordine*, 7.

acknowledge the right of each and everyone to have some 'particular opinion'. This stimulated the inhabitants to contribute to the 'common matter' as they would realize that to preserve the common good was to protect their own freedom of conscience and liberty. The treatise pointed out that in the protests against the 'popish government' liberty had played an eminent role and argued that the Revolt's call for liberty had essentially been a call for freedom of conscience and opinion. For, as the *Remonstrance* put it, 'liberty has always consisted principally in this, that one could voice one's opinion freely. It has been the unique mark of tyranny that one could not voice one's thoughts freely.'[93]

This forceful attack on the Reformed Protestant church provoked a fierce rejoinder of the ministers and elders in Holland. In the *Response of the servants of the word and elders of the churches in Holland... to the Remonstrance of the government of Leiden*, which, like the Leiden *Remonstrance*, was addressed to the States of Holland, the Reformed Protestant position was defended. The *Response* rejected the suggestion that the synod wanted to impose its regulations concerning the church order on the government and denounced the accusations of alleged Reformed Protestant pretensions to political rule. The ministers and elders of Holland, the treatise argued, acknowledged fully the authority of the States and confessed their duty to be subject to the States with 'body and goods'. Meanwhile, the ministers and elders reasserted the independence of the church, arguing that 'with regard to the administration of God's word, we are not servants of the government or any other man but of Christ, to whom both the government and we are subject'.[94] In matters of church and faith, people were obliged to obey 'the ministers and mentors' for, as the *Response* put it, 'who hears them, hears Christ himself and who rejects them, rejects Christ himself'.[95] Each Christian was held to submit himself to the 'spiritual government' of these 'governors and housekeepers or dispensers of God'.

The *Response* claimed that nothing in the church order of the Reformed Protestant church 'conflicted with the Holy Scriptures'. The synod itself, whose authority stood under attack, was defended as being of apostolic origin. If 'difficulties and questions cropped up because of an article of doctrine', a synod had been taken 'as an

---

[93] *Remonstrance of vertooch by die van Leyden* (1582), fol. B4.
[94] *Antwoorde der Dienaren des woordts ende ouderlinghen der kercken van Hollandt... op de remonstrantie by de overicheyt van Leyden* (Delft, 1582), fol. A4.   [95] Ibid.

appropriate remedy' by the apostles, not of their own accord but 'inspired by the spirit of Christ'. This was still the proper function of the synod. In this context governmental interference in ecclesiastical affairs was again ruled out. The *Response* urged magistrates 'not to intermingle the political government with the ecclesiastical, as it has pleased God to distinguish them, like the human body and soul'.[96]

The appointment of ministers was, according to the *Response*, undoubtedly part of the ecclesiastical domain. As only capable persons should be allowed to serve the church of Christ, 'natural reason itself' indicated 'that the judgment of capability belongs to those who have received the gift of God hereto'.[97] The *Response* argued that nobody was more capable of making up such judgments than those who themselves served the church as minister or elder. Therefore, it was the proper office of ministers and elders, the 'shepherds of the community, [and] the housekeepers or dispensers of God', 'to govern and lead' the community in this 'principal' matter. In line with the synod of Middelburg, the *Response* merely recognized a right of approbation on behalf of the magistrate in appointing ministers. Church servants should not be appointed by politicians as this could lead to schism caused by appointments of ministers unfavourable to the 'pure religion', and to popery due to politically motivated appointments.

The *Response* also rejected the conception of liberty as propounded in the Leiden *Remonstrance*. In particular, the *Response* attacked the idea of liberty as consisting primarily in freedom of conscience and opinion. It argued that 'without restriction' this idea 'opens the door for a despicable licentiousness and dissoluteness'.[98] Such liberty would give room to atheistic and godless expressions. The fear of tyranny and oppression of conscience, so the *Response* emphasized, should not result in 'libertarian licentiousness' unchecked by proper ordinances and laws. It was still the task of government to punish evil and to foster piety and virtue. Licentiousness should not be equated with liberty. For, as the *Response* asserted, 'Christian liberty does not consist in our doing everything we can do freely as we like, but in our being free in our conscience, and in the meantime serving each other with love.'[99]

Another elaborate analysis of what Christian liberty should mean was presented by the Ghent minister Nicasius van der Schuere in his *Small or short institution, that is instruction of the Christian religion,*

---

[96] Ibid., fol. C3.   [97] Ibid., fol. C4.   [98] Ibid., fol. D3.   [99] Ibid., fol. E3.

published in 1581. Van der Schuere, who had already been active during the *Annus mirabilis*, became minister in Ghent in 1581. His *Institution*, presented as an alternative to Calvin's, which according to van der Schuere many people found too long, was condemned by the synod of Middelburg as 'unedifying'.[100]

Van der Schuere argued that Christian liberty should not be seen as the equivalent of the 'liberty of the flesh'. It was neither physical freedom from the violence of tyrants nor 'liberty from obedience to the magistrate and its political laws or ordinances'. Likewise it was not the slave's freedom from service and obedience to his lord, nor the freedom to live in accordance with lust of the flesh, with disregard to divine and civil laws. Finally, it was not the freedom to act as you liked. The essence of Christian liberty consisted of 'freedom from devilish sin and the law's doom', on the one hand, and service to 'God, Christ and justice', on the other.[101]

Van der Schuere raised a dissenting voice with regard to the relationship between ecclesiastical and political authority. Though he asserted that political officials should not administer the ecclesiastical office and vice versa, he favoured a role for the government in ecclesiastical affairs. In this context he called the appointment of ministers a task of the government.[102]

The *Institution* affirmed that there was no strict uniformity among Reformed Protestants with regard to the position of political authorities in church affairs. The Reformed Protestant view as articulated by the national synods, however, seemed to have the dominant position, at least among the ranks of church officials. This view was not without complexities. On the one hand, it sought to reassure the independence of the church from governmental interference. On the other hand, recognizing freedom of conscience, it emphasized the duty of political authority to foster piety and virtue, which meant that conceptions of liberty as the freedom of opinion were unacceptable.

In addition, Reformed Protestants were rejecting Anabaptist views on the role of government. The treatises published to denounce Anabaptism generally included a chapter on political authority. Thus in the twelfth chapter of the *Protocol, that is, all acts of the conversation with the Anabaptists at Emden*, Menso Alting, minister of the

---

[100] See the synod's acts in van Dooren (ed.), *De nationale synode te Middelburg*, 74. The acts do not indicate the reasons for this judgment.
[101] Nicasius van der Schuere. *Een cleyne of corte Institutie, dat is onderwysinghe der Christelijcker Religie* (Ghent, 1581), fol. 58. [102] Ibid., fol. 94.

Reformed Protestant community at Emden and principal Reformed Protestant participant to the Emden debate, emphasized the active role of the government in fostering the true religion. The purpose of Alting's analysis was to refute the Anabaptist idea of government as an institution whose authority was confined to human affairs. As the Anabaptist spokesman Peter van Ceulen put it, 'in all countries God has ordained governmental rule, but over Israel he himself is lord'.[103]

According to Alting the government had been instituted by God to govern the inhabitants 'in accordance with all piety and justice', to punish evil 'with the external sword' and to protect and maintain the good. Thus, Alting asserted, the government was instituted 'in order that we together can serve the Lord in all piety and good peace, and may live with our neighbours in justice and virtue'.[104] This meant, as Alting pointed out, that the government had a duty to protect and promote the spread of the true religion amongst the inhabitants. In fulfilling this task the government should not touch the conscience of men. Alting acknowledged that 'no man has to judge conscience and faith, for only God knows the heart'.[105] As Alting emphasized, 'if the word faith and the word conscience are understood as a feeling which man hides in his heart and keeps to himself, no one can judge this but God'.[106] However, while respecting such freedom of conscience, Alting pointed out that the words 'faith' and 'conscience' did not encompass 'the external fruits of belief or disbelief'. As far as religious expressions and worship were concerned the government retained in Alting's view its duty to maintain 'both Tables of God's Ten Commandments'.[107]

In 1590 one of the most eminent Reformed Protestant ministers, Jean Taffin, published his *Instruction against the errors of the Anabaptists*. Taffin had served William of Orange as court chaplain. He has been characterized as the first Dutch representative of 'Reformed pietism'. In dogmatic questions Taffin supported the Calvinist line, yet his sermons and actions bore witness to piety, moderation and eirenism.[108]

In his analysis of the 'office, power and authority of the government' Taffin reiterated the familiar Reformed Protestant view

---

[103] *Protocol, dat is, alle handelinghe des gesprecks tot Embden in Oostvrieslandt, met den wederdooperen* (Emden, 1579), fol. 327.   [104] Ibid., fol. 316.   [105] Ibid., fol. 318.
[106] Ibid., fol. 322.   [107] Ibid., fol. 318.
[108] For Taffin, see C. Boer, *Hofpredikers van Prins Willem van Oranje* (The Hague, 1952), and W. Nijenhuis, 'Variants within Dutch Calvinism in the sixteenth century', *LCHY* 12 (1979), 48–64.

that the government had a double task. On the one hand, as 'a pillar and stay of the truth' the government should support and foster the true church. On the other hand, the government should bring peace and order in civil society, for 'without the authority and power of the government the common people would behave as rats in the straw'.[109] As the strongest would oppress the weakest and the greatest would eat the smallest, it was better even 'to be governed by a tyrant than to have no government at all'. In this context Taffin recognized the usual division of forms of government into monarchy, aristocracy and democracy, but did not express any preference. He endorsed the view that the faithful, too, were in need of a political government, not only to let them live in peace with the infidels, with whom they had certain political and civic affairs in common, but also because the faithful themselves had their weaknesses, which could not be corrected by ecclesiastical means.

Taffin acknowledged the crucial difference between ecclesiastical and political powers. Ministers and elders could only admonish or, as a last resort, excommunicate to purify the church and to bring the unrepentant to repentance. Political authority, not carrying the sword of the flesh in vain, could punish the criminal, repentant or not, 'to satisfy God's wrath and to make the others think and fear'.[110] Such distinctions were also made in another 1590 discussion of governmental authority. In his *Fifty-four sermons on the Christian, based on God's word, catechism which is preached and taught in the churches and schools of these Netherlands and the Palatinate*, Baltasar Copius pointed out that, whereas all were affected by political authority, ecclesiastical authority belonged only to the members of the church. Moreover, while the political government was entitled to carry and use the sword of the flesh, the punishment by the church was spiritual, not physical. Finally, unlike the political government, which punished criminals regardless of repentance, this often sufficed for the church.[111]

Taffin's and Copius' studies confirmed the delicacy of the Reformed Protestant analysis of political authority during the 1580s. Essentially it was based on two principles. On the one hand, the

[109] Jean Taffin, *Onderwijsinghe teghens de dwalinghe der wederdooperen* (Haarlem, 1590), 171–2.
[110] Ibid., fol. 219.
[111] See Baltasar Copius, *Vier en vijftich Predicatien over den Christelijcken en in Godswoort ghegronden Cathechismum, die inder kercken ende scholen deser Nederlanden ende der keur-Vorstelijcke Paltz gepredickt en geleert wort* (Amsterdam, 1590).

importance of political government as protector and fosterer of the true religion was emphasized. This idea had to be defended against the Anabaptists, who, though recognizing the civil use of political authority, dismissed the idea of any role for the government in the affairs of 'Israel' and argued that Christians should not hold political offices.

On the other hand, Reformed Protestants insisted on the independence of the church. Although government and church had overlapping objectives, Reformed Protestant authors took great pains to distinguish ecclesiastical from political authority, accentuating the spiritual character of church government. Above all, they dismissed any claim of political authorities to have a voice in church government.

It is clear that these views were not supported unanimously in the Reformed Protestant church but were criticized within its own ranks. The critique centred on the outright refusal of the church to accept governmental influence in its affairs and on freedom of conscience, which was defined differently by the main protagonists of the debate. By 1590 this debate had only just begun to gain momentum. In the decades up to the famous synod of Dordrecht the relationship between ecclesiastical and political authority became more and more important, turning out to be one of the key issues in the debates between Remonstrants and Contraremonstrants.

In the struggle over the relationship between political and ecclesiastical authorities Reformed Protestants in Holland failed to get their policy accepted. Bit by bit the government encroached upon the independence of the church. The synodal acts give some indications of this development. While the 1578 synod of Dordrecht only wanted to present appointed ministers to the magistrate, the 1581 synod of Middelburg already recognized a governmental right of approbation. The 1586 synod of The Hague accepted the presence of 'political commissioners' in the consistory. Thus, although the Reformed Protestant church never relinquished its presbyterian claims, it had to accept the realities of power politics.

6.4. THE DEBATES OF DIRCK VOLCKERTSZ COORNHERT

One of the sternest critics of the Reformed Protestant church was undoubtedly Dirck Volckertsz Coornhert.[112] Coornhert was one of the most prolific, provocative and original political theorists of the Dutch Revolt. He was deeply involved in the politics of the Dutch Revolt, and in various functions, such as agent of William of Orange and secretary of the 1572 free States assembly, he had worked actively for the cause.

Above all, however, Coornhert was a versatile author. The sheer number of his publications is amazing. He wrote several plays and published Dutch translations of many classical works, including Cicero's *De officiis* in 1561, Seneca's *De beneficiis* in 1562, parts of Homer's *Odyssey* and Boethius' *De consolatione philosophiae*. Coornhert wrote primarily in Dutch. It was one of his aims to promote a purified, clear and concise Dutch language, and indeed his contribution to the development of Dutch was considerable.

Coornhert was a highly independent thinker. He developed an ethical system, outlining why and how spiritual perfection could be achieved, wrote influential treatises on theological and social issues and published important political treatises. From 1578 he was almost constantly engaged in polemics and public disputes, for example with the eminent theologian Adrianus Saravia and with Lipsius. In these debates, as in his political treatises, Coornhert's leading theme was the fight for freedom of conscience, freedom of expression, freedom of printing and freedom of public worship, which he considered inseparably intertwined.

One of his first treatises to provoke public, that is printed, response was his 1582 publication *Means to abate the sects and factional strife in this civil war until such will be provided by common concord*. This treatise contained a conversation between Romanista, representing a Roman Catholic, Sectae, representing the sects, and Catholijc, who was impartial and represented Coornhert's view. Catholijc argued that the ultimate cause of the disastrous war was Charles V and Philip II's policy of religious persecution, which had been a wrong and counterproductive attempt to remedy dissension. According to Coornhert, religious dissension could only be overcome through persuasion. As

---

[112] For a recent biography of Coornhert see H. Bonger, *Leven en werk van D. V. Coornhert* (Amsterdam, 1978), and the collection of essays in H. Bonger *et al.* (eds.). *Dirck Volckertszoon Coornhert: dwars maar recht* (Zutphen, 1989). See also Lecler, *Histoire de la tolérance*, ii. 233–46.

this proved extremely difficult, and in fact impossible to achieve, Catholijc proposed an interim solution which was built on the argument that no one but God had perfect knowledge. As Coornhert put it, 'God alone knows everything, but no man on earth does. Who knows everything may err in nothing. However, each may, yes must, err where he does not know and none the less acts.'[113]

After some discussion, Catholijc succeeded in persuading the others to accept the basic principle 'that all naturally born men may, yes must, err somewhere.'[114] Coornhert pointed out that this principle also applied to churches and treatises, both human artefacts. Of all writings only the holy scripture was without erring. The divine scripture was 'a pure spring or fountain, springing and flowing from the pure and undiluted truth of the Holy Spirit'. 'Human glosses', however, were 'as cisterns not free from polluted phlegm and dirt coming from the depraved genius of man'.[115]

In order to avoid 'soul-killing errors', Coornhert proposed that human interpretations of the scriptures should be set aside until in good concord it was decided which doctrine should be adopted. In practice this meant that all 'ministers on the pulpit' should confine themselves in their preaching to reading the holy scripture, without adding anything to it. In Coornhert's view this should be regulated by the government.

Of course the implementation of Coornhert's proposal would have silenced Reformed Protestant ministers. As such, it was unacceptable to them. In 1582 the Reformed Protestant ministers of Delft, the influential Arent Cornelisz and Reinier Donteclock, published the *Examination of the unheard means recently made up and published by Dirck Volckertsz Coornhert to abate the sects and factional strife*. In the form of a dialogue between the examiner and the teacher, the treatise denounced Coornhert's ideas, accusing him of creating merely another sect. Referring probably to the argument of the 1582 Leiden *Remonstrance*, which Coornhert had written, that liberty consisted principally in freedom of opinion, the Delft ministers accused Coornhert of terrible inconsistency as he now proposed governmental interference in religious affairs to avert further error. As the ministers pointed out, this meant that Coornhert had in fact endorsed the Reformed Protestant view of the magistrate as a champion of the true

---

[113] D. V. Coornhert, *Middel tot mindringe der Secten ende Partijschappen staende dese inlantsche Oorloghen tot dat by gemeene eendracht daer in voorsien sal zijn* (Haarlem, 1582), fol. A6.
[114] Ibid., fol. B2.   [115] Ibid., fol. B4.

religion. However, he had proposed a false policy. The Delft ministers, reasserting a standard Reformed Protestant argument, argued that it was the task of the government to support the preaching of the true religion and to prohibit 'false teachers'.[116]

The Delft ministers acknowledged that men, and human assemblies such as general councils and synods too, erred. Yet this did not imply that it was always impossible for man to make good ordinances or to write good treatises. There were, they argued, great differences between one type of error and another for, as they put it, 'one error is such that it conflicts with an article of faith or with God's commandment; the other error is that (for example) the natural meaning of some difficult sentence or word of the scripture is not pertinently caught by the interpreter'.[117] Fundamentally, however, it was possible for human scriptures to 'correspond with the holy scripture'. In short, the Delft ministers rejected what was in their interpretation an outright plea for relativism and stressed the importance of the proper teaching of the true meaning of the Gospel.

In addition, the Delft ministers presented Coornhert's argument as a shrewd trick to 'plant his own particular religion' with the help of the government, and accused him of propounding a new form of Inquisition. They expounded a somewhat distorted interpretation of Coornhert's views. His rather vague appeal to governmental interference, however, could be exploited to accuse him, as the Delft ministers did with apparent eagerness, of attempting to introduce a new form of Inquisition, an accusation which had been raised against Reformed Protestants by the 1578 *Justification* and the 1582 *Remonstrance*, both written by Coornhert.

However, taking Coornhert's other writings into consideration his emphasis on the fallibility of human judgment in religion was more likely to be meant as an argument in favour of toleration than of governmental prohibition of religious expressions. This becomes especially clear in Coornhert's first main defence of freedom of conscience, the *Synod of the freedom of conscience*, published in 1582. The *Synod* had the form of a debate with 'Gamaliel' representing Coornhert himself. This form enabled Coornhert to invoke Calvin, Beza, Bullinger, Musculus and Duplessis-Mornay as participants in the debate.

---

[116] Arent Cornelisz and Reinier Donteclock, *Ondersoeck des ongehoorden middels, onlangs verciert and uutghegheven van Dirck Volckertsz. Cornhert, tot minderinge der Secten ende partijschappen* (Delft, 1582), fol. B. [117] Ibid., fol. C2.

The first book of the *Synod* dealt with the question whether the 'true visible church of Christ may err or not'.[118] It was essentially an elaboration of the argument that erring was inherent to humanity, and thus to Christians as well. However, erring did not by implication distort Christianity. Gamaliel argued that 'the true members of Christ may err, without falling off their faith'.[119] Having ascertained that the church as a whole could also err, Coornhert concluded that it was best to renounce all 'faction, dispute, condemnation, banishment and persecution'. Such 'would avert all tyranny from the church, and augment sweet concord'.[120]

As Coornhert emphasized, in religious disputes 'the interpretation and not the truth of the holy scripture' was at stake. He pointed out that so far no one had been able to prove his right in a 'free general council for impartial judges'. Accepting the truthfulness of all denominations, Gamaliel concluded that the chances of agreeing on which was the true church were indeed very slim. Therefore, his advice was to 'hold up in such a dark time our judgment of others, not to damn and denounce each other so odiously, but to tolerate and bear each other amicably in love'.[121]

Gamaliel reminded the participants to the debate of the principal difference between the judgment of man and the judgment of God, arguing that 'God's way and judgment differ from ours as heaven differs from earth.'[122] In the end, the 'Magister Consistorium Reformatorium' asserted, as the adherence to a true or false religious doctrine affected the blessedness or doom of the soul, the choice of religion should be left to the individual subject. As Gamaliel put it, 'each shall judge for himself, and not for somebody else, which is the true doctrine, or at least which has the least defects, of the interpretation of the holy scripture'.[123]

The second book of the *Synod* discussed whether the judgment of heresy belonged to 'the civil or the church government'.[124] Coornhert used this part of the *Synod* to refine his attack on Reformed Protestants. He tried to show that Reformed Protestants such as Beza were of the opinion that although civil authorities should condemn heresy, defined 'as perturbation under the common people', they should judge it not of their own accord but on the basis of knowledge provided by the true, that is Reformed Protestant, church. Thus, in

---

[118] D. V. Coornhert, 'Synodus van der Conscientien Vryheydt' (1582), in D. V. Coornhert, *Wercken*, 3 vols. (Amsterdam, 1630), vol. ii, fol. 1. [119] Ibid., fol. 3. [120] Ibid.
[121] Ibid., fol. 9. [122] Ibid., fol. 13. [123] Ibid., fol. 15. [124] Ibid., fol. 18.

debate with Beza, Gamaliel concluded that the former was 'making the civil government, by its ignorance of the matter, the servant of other people's cruelties, rather than the protector of God's truth'. In the margin Coornhert wrote that Beza wanted 'to abuse the power of the magistrate' against other Christians, 'just as the Pharisees abused Pilate's power against Christ'.[125]

At the same time Coornhert recognized that Reformed Protestants respected freedom of conscience. While in the debate on freedom of conscience the 'Doctor Consistorium Catholicorum' left no room whatsoever for freedom of conscience, both Beza and the 'Magister Consistorium Reformatorium' argued that God's law prohibited the force of conscience. The Catholic doctor, however, retorted that in the past years Reformed Protestants had changed their opinion as they now prohibited the exercise of the Catholic religion. This was confirmed by Gamaliel, who pointed out that in obtaining power Reformed Protestants seemed to have changed their conscience. Gamaliel's own argument was an elaborate defence of the freedom of conscience. He reiterated the view that man did not have 'the power to dispel religion from the hearts of man'.[126] Only God could rule the human conscience. Therefore, referring to Calvin, Gamaliel concluded that constraint of conscience was 'a tyranny in the church' as 'faith should be excepted and free from all human subjection'.[127]

In this context Gamaliel attacked forcefully the persecution of heretics as a glaring violation of freedom of conscience. Deviating opinions, he asserted, should be conquered by the weapons of debate and persuasion: 'this spiritual fight of spiritual captains in the spiritual empire of Christ should be waged with spiritual weapons'.[128] Likewise Coornhert, at this point invoking 'Mr Remonstrance of Leiden', condemned the prohibition of the publication of books. He reasserted that liberty consisted principally in freedom of opinion and expression, and defended the freedom to print religious books. Gamaliel could understand that, for the sake of the common good, the government acted against politically seditious books. As far as religious publications were concerned, however, any form of prohibition was useless and in conflict with the freedom of conscience. In the religious realm the government should refrain from interfering. Quoting Albada's *Acts* the 'Magister Consistorium Reformatorium' argued that princes overstepped the limits of their jurisdiction as

---

[125] Ibid., fol. 19.   [126] Ibid., fol. 22.   [127] Ibid., fol. 23.   [128] Ibid., fol. 30.

ordained by God if they tried to rule conscience. The worldly powers should not and could not touch the soul. As the Reformed master put forward, 'if it is so that the government's power is capable of oppressing neither the true doctrine nor heresy, as only the truth can do easily, then this is as it should be: therefore would it not be pure folly to ruin these countries and their people, just for trying to do something which, one should confess, is impossible?'[129]

It is remarkable that Coornhert put these words into the mouth of the Reformed master. In fact, in his conclusion, the president of the fictional debate, Jezonias, recognized explicitly that there was pluriformity amongst Reformed Protestants on the question of the role of government in religious affairs.[130] Gamaliel also, as Coornhert's representative the most outspoken adversary of governmental interference in religious affairs, recognized this pluriformity.

While the *Synod* attacked the views of some Reformed Protestants on freedom of conscience, Coornhert's *Examination of the Catechism of Heidelberg*, attacked the essentials of Reformed Protestant theological doctrine. In the preface Coornhert accused Reformed Protestants of trying to impose the teachings of the Heidelberg Catechism on the Netherlands. The *Examination* was a warning against what Coornhert considered the poison of the youth, described in a later attack on the Heidelberg Catechism as 'Genevan popery'.[131] With his *Examination* Coornhert wanted to promote 'one of the desirable fruits' of the war, namely freedom of religion, which implied 'that in matters of religion one may speak the truth modestly and freely without fear of punishment and for the benefit of one's neighbour'.[132]

Coornhert's *Examination* was principally an attack on the Reformed Protestant image of man. In particular, Coornhert dismissed the idea that by nature man tended to do evil and that he was incapable of fulfilling God's commandments perfectly. From Coornhert's perspective these ideas implied a denial of Christ's salvation. Defending his own theology of human perfection, Coornhert argued that 'the commandments of Christ', being principally 'to love God and your

[129] Ibid., fol. 37.   [130] Ibid., fol. 38.
[131] D. V. Coornhert, 'Dolingen des Catechismus, anderwerven blijckende in des selfs proeve', in Coornhert, *Wercken*, vol. ii, fol. 293 (first pub. 1586).
[132] D. V. Coornhert, *Proeve van de Heydelbergsche Catechismo* (1582), 5. For an analysis of this treatise, see, in addition to Bonger's study, W. Nijenhuis, 'Coornhert en de Heidelbergse catechismus: moment in de strijd tussen humanisme en Reformatie', *Nederlands Theologisch Tijdschrift*, 18 (1963), 271–88, and W. Nijenhuis, *Adrianus Saravia* (c. *1532–1613*), *Dutch Calvinist: first reformed defender of the English episcopal church on the basis of the ius divinum*, Studies in the history of Christian thought, xxi (Leiden, 1980), 85–91.

neighbour', were 'not heavy but light to fulfil'.[133] A man filled with Christ's power and spirit was, Coornhert claimed, able to attain 'human perfection in love'. In the face of Christ sin dwindled. Articulating the essence of his religious thought, Coornhert argued that 'where Christ governs, he dispels sin, as much as the sun through its clarity dispels darkness, namely completely'.[134]

Coornhert's fierce attack on the Heidelberg Catechism resulted in a public debate, held in The Hague in 1583, with Adrianus Saravia defending Reformed Protestant views. The debate was an intellectual clash between two different conceptions of basic elements of the Christian faith and of different images of human nature.[135] Coornhert reasserted his perfectionist claims, arguing again that it was 'not heavy but light' to fulfil the commandment of love. Saravia retorted to Coornhert's claims that 'reborn men can keep God's commandments but not completely'.[136] Saravia drew an analogy between the situation of a child and that of a reborn man. As a child grows to become an adult, so a reborn man grew in keeping God's commandments until finally, in the hereafter, he would receive 'perfect salvation from all sin' and reach a state of perfection.

The debate between Saravia and Coornhert was subtle and polite, at times even friendly, but both adhered to their opinions. Coornhert retained his view, so he wrote to William of Orange, that Reformed Protestantism, as articulated in the Heidelberg Catechism, was a threat to freedom of conscience whose preservation had been the principal motive of the war and of the abjuration of Philip II, as Coornhert pointed out with reference to Orange's own *Apology*.[137] Coornhert reasserted his view, quoting the 1582 Leiden *Remonstrance*, that the essence of liberty was to be free 'to speak one's opinion freely'.[138]

Although the question of liberty was not discussed during the debate with Saravia, it played a pivotal role in the dispute that

---

[133] Ibid. 6.   [134] Ibid. 27.

[135] Nijenhuis has interpreted the dispute as 'a point in the eternal struggle between Humanism and Reformation' (*Adrianus Saravia*, 88; also Nijenhuis, 'Coornhert en de Heidelbergse catechismus', 286–7). Perhaps this is partly true, but such a characterization is in danger of playing down the interconnections between humanism and the Reformation. In this particular case it plays down the humanist influences in Saravia's thought and the Reformational aspects of Coornhert's.

[136] *Disputatie over den Catechismus van Heydelbergh, openbaarlijck voor den Volcke ghehouden op't Hof van s'Gravenhage in Hollandt, anno 1583* (Gouda, 1617), 33.

[137] See 'Request aen sijne Princelijcke Extie', in *Disputatie*, 107.   [138] Ibid. 110.

followed between Coornhert and Reformed Protestant ministers. Coornhert's accusation concerning the new 'Genevan popery', as formulated in the preface of his *Examination*, was dismissed by the *Remonstrance to my lords the States of the country of Holland*, written again by the Reformed Protestant ministers of Delft, Arent Cornelisz and Reinier Donteclock. The Delft ministers rejected strongly the suggestion that Reformed Protestants wanted to 'make themselves lord over each man's faith' and rule people's conscience. By no means did Reformed Protestants pretend to have 'the right and authority to do everything in religious affairs, tying and untying the human conscience at will, as is done by the Pope'.[139] On the contrary, the sole weapons of the ministers as 'servants' and 'teachers' were 'praying', 'admonishing' and 'teaching'.

The Delft ministers acknowledged freedom of conscience fully, agreeing that with regard to the 'faith and feeling of mind no man can give, hinder or avert another'.[140] However, they contested Coornhert's argument that freedom of conscience entailed freedom of opinion. If each and everyone was entitled to express freely his opinion on religion, this could only lead to the 'public desecration' of God's name. 'To do so freely', the Delft ministers asserted, 'we do not regard as liberty but as pernicious licence.'[141] True freedom of conscience did not consist of allowing vicious sects and persons to speak freely, thus seducing innocent hearts and creating discord. On the contrary, in the view of the Delft ministers the public authorities, as champions of the true religion, had a duty to silence those who undermined the true religion if they, being heard and corrected, refused to accept the true religion.

In 1585 the Delft ministers published another treatise against Coornhert, the *Refutation of a book called Examination of the Dutch Catechism by D. Coornhert*, which was primarily an attack on Coornhert's doctrine of perfectionism. They reiterated the view that it was impossible for man to keep God's commandments perfectly during his stay on earth. The reborn man was in a state of gradual growth in the love of God and neighbour. In a way typical of Reformed Protestantism, the Delft ministers emphasized that 'as the reborn can keep, though not perfectly, God's commandments', their nature was starting to 'be improved by God's spirit, so that they are inclined to

---

[139] Arent Cornelisz and Reinier Donteclock, *Remonstrantie aen mijn Heeren de Staten slandts van Hollandt* (Delft, 1583), 12. See also p. 9.

[140] Ibid. 13.   [141] Ibid.

love God and their neighbour although much is still wanting in this inclination'.[142]

In the meantime Coornhert became involved in a dispute with Lambert Daneau, who had immersed himself in Dutch church affairs.[143] He played, for example, an important advisory role during the synod of Middelburg and intervened frequently in the Coolhaes case. Daneau attacked Coornhert in his *Living chalk*, which Coornhert translated and published, together with his response, in 1583 under the title *Living lime with which Dirck Coornhert's soap is lightly annulled*, to which Coornhert added a translation of an attack on Calvin by Castellio.[144]

The dispute between Daneau and Coornhert lacked the subtlety and the intellectual standing which had marked Coornhert's debate with Saravia. Basically Daneau and Coornhert were engaged in a barely concealed slanging match. Daneau in particular did not shy away from slander, putting Coornhert on a par with 'murderers and wretches',[145] and accusing him of 'idle conceit and beastly folly'.[146]

Coornhert's final dispute was with Justus Lipsius.[147] Coornhert admired Lipsius' *De constantia*, although not without criticism. Lipsius' discussion of the role of *fatum* in human life was criticized by Coornhert, as he felt it was incompatible with a notion of free will. The main cause of the dispute, however, was Lipsius' plea for the persecution of public heresy in the *Politics*. Coornhert reacted with the *Trial of the killing of heresy and the constraint of conscience*.

The first, 'political' part of the *Trial* was directed against Lipsius. The form of a trial enabled Coornhert, as previously in the *Synod*, to invoke participants in the debate such as the States of Holland, the town of Leiden and above all the 'annotator'. The annotator was Coornhert's friend Albada, whose *Acts* were a main source of

[142] Arent Cornelisz and Reinier Donteclock, *Wederlegginghe eens boecxkens ghenoemt Proeve canden Nederlantsche Catechismo by D. Cornhert* (Delft, 1585), 60.

[143] For Daneau's stay in the Netherlands, see Fatio, *Nihil pulchris ordine*.

[144] See *Levende-Kalck waarmede Dirijck Koornharts Zeepe lichtelijck te niet wert gemaackt* (1607; first pub. 1583). Coornhert had translated the *Defensio adversus libellum cujus titulus est Adversus nebulonem Joannis Calvini*. Castellio had denied being its author (see Güldner, *Das Toleranzproblem in den Niederlanden*, 159).

[145] See *Levende-Kalck*, 11. [146] Ibid. 15.

[147] See Bonger, *Leven en werk van D. V. Coornhert*, 140ff., Güldner, *Das Toleranzproblem in den Niederlanden*, 65–158, and, for the role of this conflict in Lipsius' decision to leave Leiden, Francine de Nave, 'De polemiek tussen Justus Lipsius en Dirck Volckertsz Coornhert (1590): hoofdoorzaak van Lipsius' vertrek uit Leiden (1591)', *De Gulden Passer*, 48 (1970), 1–39, and especially M. E. H. N. Mout, 'In het schip: Justus Lipsius en de Nederlandse Opstand tot 1591', in Groenveld *et al.* (eds.), *Bestuurders en geleerden*.

inspiration for him. For example, Coornhert accepted Albada's conception of the Dutch political order. The *Trial* contained a paragraph full of quotes from Albada's *Acts* in which the 'States' explained the character of the political order, underlining that both people and States were above every prince and limiting the role of worldly government strictly to political affairs. The government should protect the 'good, the widows and orphans' and administer proper justice. However, the government was not ordained to 'punish the errant in matters of faith and even less to exterminate the weeds on God's field'.[148] Thus, once again, Coornhert denounced governmental interference in religious affairs. He reasserted that religion was ultimately a special relationship between God and the individual human being. The subjects, Coornhert argued, 'are not bound to obey the government in all its commandments'. In times of conflict they should 'obey God rather than man'.

In the *Trial* Coornhert reiterated his attack on the persecution of heresy and summarized the main arguments he had developed throughout his life in favour of religious toleration. Most of them sprang from his view on the nature of religion and the basic rules of Christianity. Thus Coornhert first referred to the 'natural law, mentioned in God's word [that] what you wish people to do unto you, do that also unto them'.[149] Since no one wanted to be persecuted himself, this imperative ruled out the persecution of heretics.

Coornhert's second argument was based on the notion that 'the Christian religion is a great mystery in whose furtherance God does not use godless warriors, nor bow, nor sword, but his spirit and the pastors or shepherds, which are sent by him'.[150] In other words, because of the very essence of religion only spiritual weapons were allowed in religious disputes.

Thirdly, Coornhert argued, appealing to an essential element of the Reformed doctrine, that faith was a gift of God. It was not up to man to give or take away this gift. From this perspective the unfaithful were people who had not (yet) been awarded the gift of God. It was unjust to demand from a heretic 'the gift of the true faith, which God has not yet given to him and which no human being can give him'. Consequently, it was grossly unjust to kill someone because

---

[148] D. V. Coornhert, 'Proces van't ketterdooden ende dwangh der Conscientien. Tusschen Justum Lipsium...ende Dirck Coornhert. Het eerste deel politijck' (1589), in Coornhert, *Wercken*, vol. ii, fol. 60.

[149] Ibid., fol. 54. See also fols. 58, 69.   [150] Ibid., fol. 64.

he had not received the gift of faith and to 'deprive him of the time of mercy during which God might give it to him'.[151]

Fourthly, Coornhert reiterated the argument that it was up to God alone to know and judge the soul. Therefore, if the prince entered the religious realm, he stepped outside the limits of his office into the office of God.

Of course these considerations entailed a powerful defence of freedom of conscience. Coornhert quoted the Leiden *Remonstrance* to make clear that in his view freedom of conscience and opinion was the essence of liberty. He rejected the conception of liberty as articulated by the Delft ministers, pointing out that they had confounded the notions of Christian liberty and freedom of conscience. Coornhert recognized that the liberation from the devil and the entrance to the empire of Christ formed the essence of Christian liberty but emphasized that this had little to do with the notion of freedom of conscience.

The second, 'ecclesiastical' part of the *Trial* was directed against Theodore Beza. It consisted of a trial between Coornhert and 'Wolfaert Bisschop', Beza's lawyer. The similarity in argument between the first and the second part of the *Trial* was apparent from the outset. In this fictional debate with Beza, Coornhert reiterated, and at some points refined, the arguments he had raised against Lipsius. The main thrust of Coornhert's argument was again that the worldly authorities should abstain from interfering in religious affairs. As before, this argument was based on the principal difference between the empire of Christ and that of the earth. Coornhert reasserted the view that 'the worldly princes have no commanding power over the souls of the subjects, but only over their bodies and goods'. Princes were 'overstepping their limits and are venturing to command in God's empire if they order their subjects (even if without the threat of punishment) to believe this or that and to use this or that ceremony'.[152] The choice of religion should be left to the individual common man. In Coornhert's words, 'each common man may, yes should, judge whether a doctrine is true or false'.[153]

---

[151] Ibid., fol. 87.

[152] D. V. Coornhert, 'Proces van 't ketterdooden ende dwangh der Conscientien. Tusschen Wolfaert Bisschop, Advocaet van Theodore de Beza...ende Dirck V. Coornhert. Het tweede deel, Kerckelijck' (1589), in Coornhert, *Wercken*, vol. ii, fol. 127.

[153] Ibid., fol. 166. See also fols. 168, 169, where Coornhert refers at length to the work of Luther.

Coornhert also contended that it was impossible to judge heretics in a trial which met the demands of a fair and just legal procedure. If heresy was, and here Coornhert invoked a definition taken from Peter Martyr, 'the election and stubborn protection of doctrines which conflict with the divine scripture' with the purpose of satisfying private 'lusts and benefit', then the proper judgment of heresy required a judge who should not only be able to decide which of the various religious doctrines was the true one, but should also know the hearts of the accused heretics, and, finally, should himself be impartial. Such requirements, Coornhert argued, could not be met by any judge. It was simply impossible to find an 'impartial judge, who knows and loves the truth, who is neither in one nor in the other religion, and to whose judgment both the accused and the accuser voluntarily have put the matter'.[154]

On the one hand, this argument was based on the notion that man could err and had no certainty yet about which religious doctrine was the true one. On the other hand, Coornhert pointed out that as 'God alone knows the heart',[155] it was 'temerity' to accredit man with this faculty. The third and final part of the argument was built on the alleged impossibility of finding a sincere and impartial judge acceptable to all parties.

This meant that the persecution of heresy was in practice impossible, and, as it was better not to punish than to punish unjustly, it also meant that from the legal point of view toleration was the only viable alternative. In response to Beza's proposal that the judgment of what heresy was should be left to the church, Coornhert repeated the accusation that it turned the prince into the 'ministers' headsman', while the ministers themselves were usurping the sword of government.

Coornhert's views on religion as articulated in both parts of the *Trial* were fundamentally at odds with the ideas Lipsius had expressed in the *Politics*. Lipsius argued that 'one religion is the author of unity', whereas 'confused religion' always resulted in 'dissension'. Therefore, although Lipsius fully respected the freedom of conscience, allowing people to think and believe as they thought best in private, he judged it a matter of civil prudence to 'burn' and 'saw asunder' public heresy, as it was 'better' – and here Lipsius quoted Cicero – 'that one member be cast away, than that the whole body runs to

---

[154] Ibid., fol. 120.   [155] Ibid., fol. 117.

ruin'.[156] Only if the prince was too weak to 'check and control' should he 'let the matter slip for a time' and tolerate the exercise of more than one religion.

At this point the conflict between Lipsius and Coornhert was twofold. First, whereas Coornhert urged worldly authorities to refrain from intruding in the realm of religion, Lipsius had emphasized the political usefulness of religion. In Coornhert's view, Lipsius, as a disciple of Machiavelli, saw religion basically as an instrument of the 'body's comfort and peace', fully neglecting the truthfulness of religious views and the blessedness of man. Thus Coornhert repudiated Lipsius' alleged scepticism.[157]

Secondly, whereas Lipsius felt that religious unity would foster political unity, Coornhert emphasized the disastrous social and political consequences of the persecution of heresy, which above all led to 'weeds of discord'. In Coornhert's view discord was one of the main causes of the Dutch troubles. The danger of discord and the necessity of concord were the dominant themes of one of Coornhert's final works, *The root of the Dutch wars with instruction to indigenous concord*. *The root* consisted of a conversation between a Roman Catholic, a Reformed Protestant and the pacifier, Pacifijc. Pacifijc, doubtless representing Coornhert, described 'faction and injustice' as the country's principal problems. According to Pacifijc, faction 'dissipated concord and unity', while injustice generated 'hateful dispute'.[158]

The pacifier, Coornhert, impressed upon the Roman Catholic and the Reformed Protestant the need for toleration and understanding of each other. As the pacifier urged, toleration was absolutely necessary in the troubled Netherlands. For without toleration, Coornhert explained, there could be no hope of 'amiable concord, which is a mother of peace, richness and power, which makes small things big, ties divided hearts together, and unites man with God'.[159] In other words, whereas Lipsius argued that unity in religion was best for political unity while religious faction was said to cause discord

---

[156] Justus Lipsius, *Six bookes of politickes or civile doctrine* (London, 1594; repr. in The English experience, no. 287, Amsterdam, 1970), 64. The reference was to Cicero, *Philippics*, 8.

[157] 'Proces', fol. 67. For Lipsius and scepticism and Coornhert's reaction, see Richard Tuck, 'Scepticism and toleration in the seventeenth century', in Susan Mendus (ed.), *Justifying toleration: conceptual and historical perspectives* (Cambridge, 1988), 21–30.

[158] D. V. Coornhert, 'Wortel der Nederlantsche oorloghen met aenwijsinghe tot inlantsche eendracht' (1590), in Coornhert, *Wercken*, vol. ii, fol. 180.   [159] Ibid.

Coornhert maintained that religious diversity was not only inevitable but also that toleration truly fostered concord. When the liberty of the community was at stake its individual members would realize that freedom of conscience, the essence of their individual liberty, was threatened directly and would therefore be much more willing to act as dutiful patriots.[160] Lipsius, so Coornhert argued, had misunderstood the basic argumentation of both Cicero and Sallust.[161]

In short, Coornhert was an apostle of toleration for religious and political reasons. Throughout his life he sought, in writing and in action, to promote freedom of conscience, of religion and of opinion, which in his view were inseparably intertwined. Many of the arguments Coornhert used and developed to support his plea for toleration had been articulated before. The appeal to the law of nature, the emphasis on the principal difference between matters concerning the body and matters concerning the soul, and the argument that disastrous consequences come from discord were not original. Coornhert himself recognized his indebtedness to others. Both the *Synod* and the *Trial* contained a bibliography of books attacked or exploited by Coornhert. These lists show that, in developing his argument for toleration, Coornhert offered a fine overview of the whole gamut of arguments, as developed during the sixteenth century in favour of freedom of conscience and opinion.

It is, of course, tempting to see Coornhert as the successor of Erasmus. With his plea for toleration, which stemmed from Coornhert's religious persuasion, his attention to social issues and his translations of the classics, Coornhert fitted the pattern of Christian humanism very well. However, although he sometimes quoted him, Coornhert did not hold Erasmus in great esteem. Coornhert criticized the great humanist from Rotterdam for the latter's 'scrupulous subjection' to the Roman Catholic church.[162] Unlike Erasmus, Coornhert was a Christian humanist of the Reformation.

6.5. CONCLUSIONS

As Reformed Protestants started to build up their church after 1572 they were faced with the challenge to do so in provinces which sympathized with, but often were also hesitant if not hostile to, their doctrines. Reformed Protestants were constantly in debate with

---

[160] Coornhert, 'Proces', fol. 83.   [161] Ibid., fols. 85–6.
[162] See Bonger, *Leven en werk van D. V. Coornhert*, 261.

people of different persuasions. These debates were often dogmatic in character, such as the confrontations with Mennonites or the growing debate within the church itself on the issue of predestination. To the development of the political thought of the Dutch Revolt the debates on freedom of conscience and religion and on the relationship between church and political authorities turned out to be of particular importance.

The debate on the relationship between ecclesiastical and political powers showed that certainly not everyone in the United Provinces, and in Holland in particular, was willing to accept the Reformed Protestant church as an independent institution organized along presbyterian lines. The Reformed Protestant view, as accepted by various synods, emphasized this independence, which was based on the principal difference between church and political government. The church was a spiritual regiment with no place for the sword of the flesh. The difference between church and political government was essentially a difference of means, for in the Reformed Protestant doctrine both had the same objective of protecting and fostering the true religion. The Reformed Protestant church expected the worldly authorities to fulfil their religious task in accordance with Reformed Protestant doctrine, sanctioning and executing decisions of the church. It did not try to minimize the role of the government. On the contrary, in the debates with the Mennonites the authority of the government was emphasized and defended.

For its adversaries in Holland such Reformed Protestantism merely propounded a new form of popery, as the church practically ordered the political government what to do in religious affairs. Coolhaes, and also the treatises which Coornhert wrote on behalf of the Leiden magistrate, contested the special status of the Reformed Protestants as the bearers of truth. They propounded a different and, from the mainstream Calvinist point of view, latitudinarian conception of the character and role of the church. The church should be an ecumenical institution which had room for different interpretations and which stood under the control of the whole community, whose representatives, the magistrate, elected and appointed church servants.

The debate on the proper relationship between church and political authorities was closely related to the debates on religious peace and freedom of conscience. It should be underlined that freedom of conscience was unanimously favoured by the authors who supported the Dutch Revolt. This is of fundamental importance as it shows that in the conceptions of liberty developed during the Dutch Revolt personal liberty was not merely seen as the freedom of body and goods but above all as the freedom of conscience. If the Dutch Revolt was a defence of liberty it was seen as a fight for freedom of conscience in particular. Staunch defenders of Reformed Protestantism acknowledged freedom of conscience just as much as a fundamental right as Coornhert, Albada and de Zuttere. All agreed that freedom of conscience was an essential part if not the essence of liberty; all agreed that no one should try to control conscience by means of violence.

At this point consensus broke down. During the debates on religious peace and the disputes between Reformed Protestant authors and Coolhaes, the Leiden magistrate and Coornhert, conceptions of liberty centring around the idea of freedom of conscience were developed which were fundamentally in conflict with each other. On the one hand, there was the mainstream Reformed Protestant view, as articulated by Calvin and propounded by the Delft ministers, that true freedom of conscience was liberation from devilish sin and the recognition of such liberation through faith. True freedom of conscience was to live in Christ, which in practice implied adherence to the Reformed Protestant faith.

Reformed Protestants who articulated this conception of freedom of conscience unequivocally recognized that conscience could not and should not be touched by human violence, but dismissed the idea that freedom of conscience entailed freedom of worship and of opinion, which in their view could only lead to pernicious licentiousness.

An alternative conception was developed in treatises which defended religious peace and in the work of Coornhert in particular. In this alternative conception, freedom of worship and opinion were simply the external dimensions of freedom of conscience. A whole battery of arguments was developed and used to defend this view and the radical plea for toleration it entailed. An important part of these arguments concerned the nature of religion and as such was obviously inspired by and derived from the works of previous advocates of religious toleration such as Franck and Castellio. Thus the claim was put forward that not only was it impossible for man to touch conscience and soul, as all Reformed Protestants recognized, but that the matters of the soul were also beyond human grasp and understanding. Religion was a great mystery, of which ultimately only God knew the truth. The idea of human fallibility, also popular in Reformed Protestant circles, was used to argue that, since each man and church could err, it was unwarranted to prohibit other interpretations of the holy scripture. In addition the law of nature was invoked, which prescribed that 'you should do unto others as you want done unto yourself'.

In addition, many – and some exclusively – advocated religious toleration on political grounds. Like some French studies and Junius' *Brief discourse*, a number of Dutch authors dismissed the traditional idea that religious unity was a pre-condition of political unity. In France L'Hôpital, Castellio in his *Conseil à la France désolée* and later Montaigne and Bodin emphasized that the preservation of the French nation and state required the sacrifice of religious unity and the toleration of religious diversity. For those celebrating the case of the so-called Politiques, religious toleration was the recipe for the preservation of the French nation as demanded by reasons of state.[163] As such, it was endorsed by Lipsius.

Coornhert and others disagreed. They favoured religious toleration not so much for reasons of state but because they felt, in the spirit of Renaissance political philosophy, that concord and union as the foundation of all communities was threatened principally by faction arising out of religious diversity. Their solution was not to suppress this form of faction but to canalize it with a policy of religious toleration. Seeing freedom of conscience as a natural right of each individual, some authors, Coornhert being the leading example, went as far as to argue that religion was the realm of the individual. Coornhert more or less propounded the view that religion should be regarded as in the private sphere. This did not mean that one should not discuss religion; on the contrary. However, ultimately the choices made by individual citizens should be respected. This was a highly controversial claim, and in 1590 the debate on this issue was far from closed.

[163] See Lecler, *Histoire de la tolérance*, ii. 43ff.

CHAPTER 7

Conclusions: the Dutch Revolt and the history of European political thought

7.1. THE POLITICAL THOUGHT OF THE DUTCH REVOLT

The principal aim of this study has been to reconstruct the ideas on the issues of obedience and resistance and on the character of the best state of the commonwealth as developed during the Dutch Revolt. By way of conclusion this final chapter will relate the political thought of the Dutch Revolt to some of the main streams of sixteenth-century European political thought. By comparing the political thought of the Dutch Revolt with the political ideas of the Lutheran and Calvinist Reformation, with the monarchomach ideology of French Huguenots, and with the republican theories of the Italian Renaissance, an attempt will be made to arrive at some conclusions about its character and origins, and, last but certainly not least, to indicate its significance for the history of European political thought.

Formulating the essentials of this study, two conclusions should be emphasized. First, that during the Dutch Revolt a substantial body of Reformed Protestant treatises was published which, employing a highly biblical vocabulary, presented a more or less unified conception of the origins and duties of political authority, elaborated a multivalent plea for freedom of conscience, entailed a right of disobedience for individual subjects and, finally, sought to indicate the lines of demarcation between ecclesiastical and political authority.

Unanimously, Reformed Protestant authors, mostly ministers, assumed that political authority was ordained by God to temper the wickedness of man, punishing the wrongdoer and protecting the good. Most argued that political authority was instituted to protect both Tables of Moses' law, and that therefore its principal duty was to fight idolatry and foster the true religion. In this respect, church and government had identical objectives, but, as Dutch Reformed

Protestants continually emphasized, to realize these objectives, church and government should employ essentially different means. The church was a spiritual realm, which should remain unaffected by the powers of the flesh. Although not all Reformed Protestants agreed, and this issue gave rise to a provocative debate on the relationship between church and political authorities, Reformed Protestant synods continued to defend the independence of the church.

A further limit to the scope of the governmental power was the argument that, in fostering the true religion, political authorities should refrain from using the sword of the flesh. Unequivocally, Reformed Protestant authors rejected the use of physical violence and persecution in affairs of religion and stressed freedom of conscience. Dutch political thinkers emphasized that freedom of conscience was of paramount importance, forming the essence of liberty.

From the outset, however, there was, also amongst Reformed Protestants, a difference of opinion between the proponents of the Revolt over what freedom of conscience meant in practice. This led to a profound and unprecedented debate on the character of liberty, and of freedom of conscience in particular. During this debate different conceptions of liberty were developed. On the one hand, there was the Reformed Protestant idea that true freedom of conscience could only be found in Christ, which in practice meant in the true Reformed faith. On the other hand, there was the view held by such leading libertarians as Coornhert, Albada and de Zuttere that freedom of conscience of necessity implied freedom of expression and public worship, which were simply the external dimensions of freedom of conscience.

Equally problematic were the issues of obedience and resistance. Dutch Reformed Protestants did not develop a specific Reformed Protestant idea of resistance. On the contrary, they generally felt that the issue was a problem to which political and legal answers should be given. With regard to the issue of obedience, the situation was different. Although emphasizing the duty of the subjects to obey political authorities, Reformed Protestants pointed out that obedience was not without limits. As God should be obeyed rather than man, the subjects had a duty to disobey a ruler who commanded against God's word.

Significantly, the discussion on both freedom of conscience and the issue of obedience led to the articulation of views which proposed a considerable curtailment of traditional governmental powers. Perhaps the political thought of Dutch Reformed Protestants was revolutionary primarily because it extended the spectrum of individual rights as developed until the Reformation.[1] In the minimal formulation the private person was awarded the right of freedom of conscience and, if the government ordered against God, of disobedience. In the maximum libertarian formulation the individual had, as far as religion was concerned, the rights of freedom of worship, freedom of opinion and freedom of printing. In this view religion was a private sphere, where political interference was unwarranted. It should be recognized that the articulation of these rights was often Spiritualist in argument if not in inclination. Albada, Coornhert, de Zuttere and also the authors who supported William of Orange's policy of religious peace during the 1570s developed ideas which were not only inspired by Christian humanists, such as Erasmus and Cassander, but were also highly similar to, and sometimes explicitly derived from, authors such as Castellio and Franck. The Spiritualist contribution to this aspect of the political thought of the Revolt should not be underestimated.

In addition, these libertarians urged for religious toleration on political grounds. In the spirit of Renaissance political philosophy, they argued that concord was the foundation of the *res publica*. Its main internal threat, faction, was, in the Low Countries above all, caused by religious diversity. The solution was not to suppress this form of faction, and thus to persecute heretics, but to control it with a policy of religious toleration.

The debates of the 1570s on the relationship between ecclesiastical and political authority and on the nature and political consequences of freedom of conscience did not, of course, come to an end in 1590. In retrospect, they can probably be interpreted as preludes to the great debates on these issues which dominated the United Provinces at the beginning of the seventeenth century.

The second major conclusion from this study is that during the Revolt an ideology of the Dutch political order and of political resistance was developed which celebrated liberty, arguing that in the Low Countries freedom was protected by a political framework which was based on the notion of popular sovereignty and functioned

[1] For an authoritative overview see Brian Tierney, 'Origins of natural rights language: texts and contexts, 1150–1250', *HPT* 10 (1989), 615–46.

through fundamental constitutional guarantees, and representative institutions and virtuous citizens who were the guardians of liberty.

From the very beginning of the protests against Philip II's policy, liberty was presented as the political value *par excellence*, the 'daughter of the Netherlands', the source of prosperity and justice. It was put on a par, if not identified, with the common good of the community, whose maintenance and furtherance was held to be the supreme law of politics. An essential element of this idea of liberty was the emphasis on the inseparability of the liberty of the country and the personal liberty and welfare of its inhabitants. Time and again, it was reasserted that the loss of liberty of a country, mainly seen in terms of self-government, not only implied the ruin of that country but would also turn its inhabitants into the most oppressed slaves in the world.

The resistance against Philip II was essentially presented as the defence of liberty threatened by the lust for power and tyrannical ambitions of Philip II's government. The political order itself was argued to have been deliberately created by the forebears of the Dutch with the purpose of safeguarding liberty. It tried to achieve this goal by means of what can be called a constitutional framework consisting of a set of fundamental laws, the privileges, charters and customs of the provinces, and a number of institutions, in particular the States. The charters won during the late Middle Ages by provinces and towns were the constitutional guarantees of liberty. To become lord of the country, a prince had to take a solemn oath to uphold the privileges. They bridled the prince and contained the terms on which he had been accepted, some said elected, by the States on behalf of the people. The States were representative institutions and they owed their authority to their constituent principals, in the case of Holland, especially the towns. They had been created to check and bridle the prince and to take the important political decisions. As it turned out in this Dutch ideology the States did not hold the position of 'inferior magistrates'. On the contrary, they were presented as leading sovereign powers whose principal task was to protect the privileges and thus the common good. The States, in short, were the guardians of liberty.

However, as many authors urged, the States were not the only guardians of liberty. Political treatises and the States of Holland themselves continually emphasized that protection of the freedom and welfare of the community ought 'to be observed with diligence by each one in accordance with his profession and abilities'. The ideology of liberty, privileges, States and popular sovereignty as developed during the Revolt contained a strong sense of civic duty, inspired by a Ciceronian view on citizenship. It was a principal duty of a good patriot to fight for liberty and to serve the fatherland, which was increasingly identified with the Netherlands or the United Provinces as a whole instead of the home town or province.[2] Civic virtue was considered necessary for the preservation of the country. The citizens of the Low Countries were urged to lead a life of *negotium*, of virtuous public service. Perhaps the finest expression of Dutch political thought on this point is a stained-glass window in the Church of St Jan in Gouda. The theme of the window is freedom of conscience.[3] It shows a carriage on which two female figures, representing freedom of conscience and freedom of religion, are seated. The carriage is pulled by five other female figures, representing the virtues of love, justice, fidelity, concord and constancy. With the help of these virtues freedom of conscience is able to crush tyranny, who is lying on the ground, his sword and spear broken.

In the formation of the ideology of liberty, privileges and States, the issue of resistance played a pivotal role. Appealing to the privileges, and the Joyous Entry of Brabant in particular, an evolution took place which, starting from a reaffirmation of the right of disobedience as contained in the Joyous Entry, led to the articulation of a political right of resistance that allowed the States, as representatives of the people, to disobey and oppose by force a prince who violated the privileges and to replace him by a regent. It was also suggested that following from the privileges the States had a right of abjuration.

In the ultimate defence of the abjuration, however, the treatises of the Revolt moved beyond the privileges. The right of abjuration was built on the idea that the prince had been created by and because of the people to serve them in accordance with right and reason and, in addition, with certain conditions which followed from the rights of the country. If the prince exceeded the limits of his authority, as demarcated by nature and by his covenant with the people, and turned into a tyrant, the people, that is their representatives, the States, were fully entitled to resume the power and authority they had given to the prince. In addition, it was pointed out that, if there

---

[2] For a more sceptical view on this issue see S. Groenveld, 'Natie en nationaal gevoel in de zestiende-eeuwse Nederlanden', *Nederlands Archievenblad*, 84 (1980), 372–87.

[3] In fact the window was probably a tribute to Coornhert's *Synodus van der Conscientien Vryheydt* (1582). For the window see the jacket illustration of this book.

was a choice to be made between loyalty to a prince who had become a tyrant and the preservation of the common good, loyalty to the prince should be sacrificed for the sake of the supreme value of the common good.

The notion of popular sovereignty entailed by these formulations was elaborated during the quest for the best state of the commonwealth of the 1580s. In a fundamental debate amongst the proponents of the Revolt, dealing with the political implications of the idea of popular sovereignty, an interpretation was developed which strengthened the position of the States. The States were presented as the foundation of the country, essential to the common good. As upholders of liberty and privileges, they were entrusted with the administration of sovereignty. Thus a crucial distinction was made, according to which sovereignty resided with the people, but was administered by the representatives of the people, the States.

This notion of sovereignty can be seen as a forceful rebuttal of late medieval theories defending *plenitudo potestates* and theocratic notions of sovereignty. As such this ideology of liberty, privileges, States and popular sovereignty was, in retrospect, more than a conservative attempt to stabilize the dynamic of the formation of the rising state. It was, perhaps above all, an attempt to direct the formation of the state in an alternative direction. The ideological works justifying and motivating the Revolt were creative forces for the development of a form of state built on liberty, popular sovereignty, constitutional charters, a number of individual rights and a republican form of government.[4]

This version of the best state of the commonwealth was not uncontested. First, in answering the question how the peace and welfare of the community and its members was served best, some proponents of the Revolt argued, for practical and principled considerations, in favour of princely rule. The most impressive work in this respect was Lipsius' *Politics*, published in 1589, which defended strong, virtuous princely rule as the superior way to attain the *vita civilis*. Although the *Politics* should not be reduced to a singular attempt to repudiate the political order of the emerging Dutch Republic, it is still striking that this influential plea for a Neostoical, absolutist prince was written and published in the United Provinces of the 1580s.

Secondly, it has been shown that the notion of popular sovereignty

---

[4] Whether this ideology offered an empirically adequate interpretation of the political reality of the United Provinces in 1590 is, of course, an altogether different question.

was subject to manifold interpretations. In fact the view on sovereignty as propounded by Vranck and the States of Holland was a reaction to opposing views defended by Prouninck and Wilkes. By 1590 the debate on this issue was far from closed.

Throughout this study it has been noted that the development of the ideology of the Dutch political order as based on liberty, constitutional charters, representative institutions and popular sovereignty coincided with the political developments of the Revolt. The political thought of the Dutch Revolt was the result of a permanent confrontation with political reality. Political developments challenged political thinkers to reassert and extend their arguments, while each ideological innovation conditioned political action and subsequent political argumentation.

7.2. THE REFORMATION AND THE POLITICAL THOUGHT OF THE DUTCH REVOLT

Although more and more the pluriformity of Dutch Reformed Protestantism has come to be appreciated, John Calvin is still held to be one of the spiritual fathers of the Dutch Republic. As far as the political thought of the Dutch Revolt is concerned, however, it remains difficult to assess Calvin's influence.

It is clear that, predominantly, Reformed Protestant authors shared Calvin's ideas on the origins, nature and purpose of political authority. Throughout the Dutch Revolt they underlined the necessity of a civil and sword-bearing magistracy, which had the principal task of maintaining public order, protecting the good and punishing wrongdoers. Similarly, starting with Veluanus in 1554, Dutch Reformed Protestants propounded the view that political authorities should be champions of the true religion, fighting idolatry and blasphemy. Thus, they invoked the idea of what Calvin had called the 'double regime', which held that God had instituted two forms of authority for 'the management of human affairs', the one ecclesiastical, employing the power of the word, and the other political, employing the power of the flesh.

With regard to the character and organization of the church, Dutch Reformed Protestants also followed Calvin's ideas. The presbyterian organization of the church was definitely inspired by the situation in Geneva and France, although it was adapted to the particular (and varying) conditions in the Netherlands. Likewise, the emphasis on discipline and the role and authority of ministers and consistory, to mention but a few examples, betray Calvin's influence.

Like Calvin, Dutch Reformed Protestants expected the political authorities to collaborate with the true Reformed Protestant church. As physical coercion was alien to the spiritual nature of the church, Calvin expected the secular authorities to sustain the church in furthering the true religion. In the Netherlands such views were repeatedly expressed by Reformed Protestants, who called upon the political authorities to sanction and execute their decisions. This was completely in the spirit of Calvin, who, according to Höpfl, wanted the Geneva magistrates to act as 'tame instruments of the clergy'.[5] As Calvin had not delimited the respective spheres of competence in detail, this led repeatedly to conflicts between church and magistrates in Geneva.[6] A similar situation occurred in the Netherlands. There was, however, an important difference, which concerned the focal point of the conflict in the United Provinces, the appointment of ministers. In Geneva, Calvin and his supporters accepted that, ultimately, ministers, elders and deacons were appointed by the elected councils that governed the town.[7] Although in the Netherlands Reformed Protestants gradually had to make concessions to secular authorities, they emphasized that the appointment of ministers was the touchstone of the independence of the church. Thus in this respect, perhaps due to different political circumstances, Dutch Reformed Protestants adopted a stricter approach than Calvin. Their adversaries in the debate on the relationship between church and political authority were aware of this difference. Both Coolhaes and Coornhert referred to the situation in Geneva in order to repudiate Reformed Protestant claims that the appointment of ministers was the unique competence of the church.

The most important point of divergence between the political thought of Dutch Reformed Protestants and Calvin concerned freedom of conscience. As Bouwsma has noted in his 'sixteenth-century portrait' of the Genevan reformer, Calvin was not at ease with notions of liberty. In contrast with Luther, Calvin even distrusted the idea of Christian liberty, as many had abused it to 'shake off all obedience to God and [to] break out into unbridled

---

[5] See Harro Höpfl, *The Christian polity of John Calvin* (Cambridge, 1982), 123 and 196.

[6] See Gillian Lewis, 'Calvinism in Geneva in the time of Calvin and of Beza (1541–1605)', in Prestwich (ed.), *International Calvinism 1541–1565*, 39–70, esp. pp. 50, 53.

[7] See Robert Kingdon, 'John Calvin's contribution to representative government', in Phyllis Mack and Margaret C. Jacobs (eds.), *Politics and culture in early modern Europe: essays in honour of H. G. Koenigsberger* (Cambridge, 1987), 186.

licentiousness'.[8] If only because of the execution in Geneva of Servetus, for which Calvin is often held responsible, the record of the latter with regard to freedom of conscience is somewhat blemished. In Calvin's defence of Servetus' execution, the principle that magistrates had a duty to suppress and punish heresy, if necessary even by means of executing heretics, was simply taken as a matter of course.[9] According to Calvin, true freedom of conscience could only be acquired through the true religion, when man was in his conscience spiritually liberated from all human power by the blood of Christ. A similar view on freedom of conscience was expounded in the debates between Dutch Reformed Protestants and Coolhaes and Coornhert during the late 1570s and the 1580s. Reformed Protestants also followed Calvin in his argument that it was the duty of political authorities to foster religion by prohibiting public worship to other denominations, as no room should be given to licentiousness. None the less, much stronger than Calvin, even the sternest Dutch Reformed Protestant authors recognized that, as the Union of Utrecht ordained, the conscience of man should not be manipulated by violence. From the outset Dutch Reformed Protestants had acknowledged this interpretation of freedom of conscience. Perhaps some did so grudgingly, accepting the political *fait accompli*, but, as has been shown throughout this study, between 1555 and 1590 Reformed Protestant authors frequently put forward pleas for freedom of conscience. Such pleas were reminiscent of Christian humanism, which in this respect seems to have left its mark on Dutch Reformed Protestantism.

As far as the issue of obedience was concerned, the ideas of Reformed Protestants in the Low Countries were, as noted, fully in line with the main stream of the Lutheran and Calvinist Reformation. The dogma that the faithful were obliged to obey the established political authorities under almost all circumstances was cherished by Reformed Protestants. Especially in their writings of the 1550s and 1560s, but also later in repudiating Mennonite doctrines, they endorsed the Pauline doctrine of non-resistance and obedience. Suffering, patience, humility and martyrdom were unceasingly presented as existential characteristics of the earthly life of the

---

[8] John Calvin, *Institutes of the Christian religion*, ii (Grand Rapids, Mich., 1983; trans. of the definitive 1559 edn.), 131. See also W. J. Bouwsma, *John Calvin: a sixteenth century portrait* (New York, 1988), 50, 86, and Höpfl, *The Christian polity of John Calvin*, 35–8.

[9] See J. W. Allen, *A history of political thought in the sixteenth century*, rev. edn. (London, 1957), 83ff.

faithful. At the same time Dutch Reformed Protestants endorsed the common view that obedience was not without limits. If political authorities ordered against God, the faithful had the right and duty of passive disobedience.

Moreover, adopting the 'private law' theory as developed since 1530 by Lutherans and Calvinists, some authors referred to the natural right of self-defence and to the maxim that it was permitted to repel unjust force by force. However, as far as the legitimization of resistance was concerned, most Reformed Protestants seemed to be inclined to the constitutionalist line of thought, also developed since 1530. Thus Dutch authors discussed whether, as with superior magistrates, the inferior magistrates had been instituted by God to protect the good and to punish the evil,[10] and arrived at the conclusion that the specific office of inferior magistrates was to bridle evil princes. The precise formulation of this principle and its implications for the situation in the Netherlands aroused vigorous debate amongst Reformed Protestants. Following the Lutheran move of the 1530s, during the 1560s Dutch Reformed Protestants concluded that the legitimacy of resistance depended on the laws and privileges of the country. Thus, as had happened throughout the Lutheran and Calvinist Reformation, the debate on the crucial issue of resistance was transferred from the religious to the constitutional and therefore political realm.

7.3. MONARCHOMACH IDEOLOGY AND THE POLITICAL THOUGHT OF THE DUTCH REVOLT

As noted, as far as the issue of resistance was concerned the political thought of the Dutch Revolt has been presented as a rather straightforward application of French Huguenot political thought. In justifying and motivating their own resistance Dutch authors, so the argument goes, applied the fundamental ideas of monarchomach ideology, as exemplified by the 'monarchomach triumvirs',[11] which

---

[10] In addition to various treatises, there was the famous letter of Du Hames (also mentioned by Skinner, *The foundations of modern political thought*, ii. 210), in which he urged Louis of Nassau, the younger brother of William of Orange, to clarify the role and rights of inferior magistrates.

[11] See Ralph E. Giesey, 'The monarchomach triumvirs: Hotman, Beza and Mornay', *Bibliothèque d'Humanisme et Renaissance*, 32 (1970), 41–56. For the claim that the triumvirate should be extended to a quartet by including the *Discours politique des diverses puissances* in the list of monarchomach classics, see Sarah Hanley, 'The *Discours politique* in monarchomaque

included François Hotman's *Francogallia*, published in 1573, Theodore Beza's 1574 *Du Droit des magistrats*, and the *Vindiciae contra tyrannos*.

The *Vindiciae*, published in 1579 by a certain Junius Brutus, which was probably a pseudonym for Philippe Duplessis-Mornay,[12] has probably become the most famous and surely the most comprehensive treatise of 'monarchomach' ideology. In discussing four questions, the *Vindiciae* expounded the ideology of resistance as developed by Huguenot political thinkers in France throughout the 1570s.

The argument of the *Vindiciae* centred around two covenants.[13] The first consisted of a contract between God, the king and the inferior magistrates. On the basis of this covenant the *Vindiciae* pointed out that, since both king and inferior magistrates were 'ordained by God to govern justly and rule on his behalf', the inferior magistrates had the religious duty to resist a king 'who overturns the law and the Church of God'.

The second covenant concerned a contract between the king and the people. The *Vindiciae* argued that, in a position of natural liberty, the people had decided to create a king, to pursue their welfare and to uphold their rights. Kings should always remember, according to the *Vindiciae*, 'that it is from God, but by the people and for the people's sake that they do reign'.[14] However, since it was, of course, physically impossible for all inhabitants of (for example) France to get together and conclude a contract with the king, the people had, according to the *Vindiciae*, vested its authority in a body of lesser magistrates which concluded the contract with the king. As the *Vindiciae* emphasized, the conclusion of such a contract did not imply that the people had given up their original sovereignty. Putting forward an idea of popular sovereignty the *Vindiciae* argued that kings should not 'be esteemed other than servant to the public'.[15] Thus, if the king broke the contract, the people would have the moral right to resist him. As the *Vindiciae* argued, 'if the prince fails in his promise,

---

ideology: resistance right in sixteenth century France', in *Assemblee di Stati e istituzioni rappresentative nella storia del pensiero politico moderno* (Rimini, 1983), 121–34.

[12] The debate on the authorship of the *Vindiciae* is endless. As alternative candidates Hubert Languet and Johan Junius de Jonghe, the author of the 1574 *Discourse*, have been mentioned. See M. N. Raitière, 'Hubert Languet's authorship of the *Vindiciae contra tyrannos*', *Il Pensiero Politico*, 13 (1981), 395–420, and D. Visser, 'Junius: the author of the *Vindiciae contra tyrannos*', *TvG* 84 (1971), 510–25.

[13] See Junius Brutus, *A defence of liberty against tyrants: a translation of the 'Vindiciae contra tyrannos' by Junius Brutus with an historical introduction by Harold J. Laski* (London, 1924). Refs. are to this edn.   [14] *Vindiciae*, 120.   [15] Ibid. 125.

the people are exempt from obedience, the contract is made void, the right of obligation of no force'.[16] However, this right did not belong to each individual citizen, for the people had created the king as a collectivity. Only the lesser magistrates, to whom the people, as a collectivity, had transferred their 'authority and power', were morally entitled and obliged to resist a tyrant. In the words of the *Vindiciae*, 'every magistrate is bound to relieve, and as much as it in him lies, to redress the miseries of the commonwealth, if he shall see the prince, or the principal officers of state, his associates, by their weakness or wickedness, risk the ruin thereof'.[17]

It is easy to see why the ideological defence of the Dutch Revolt has been subsumed under the heading of monarchomach theory. First, there were manifold connections between French and Dutch revolutionaries. William of Orange himself spent some time in France, to assist Coligny, and leading Huguenot political thinkers such as Languet and Duplessis-Mornay spent considerable time in the Netherlands, actively contributing to the cause of the Revolt.[18] Thus Duplessis-Mornay is held to be the author of a political treatise which supported William of Orange's policy of religious peace.[19]

Secondly, there are obvious and striking parallels between the arguments used to justify the Dutch Revolt and monarchomach ideas. Without going into an elaborate comparison it can be pointed out that the justifications of both the Dutch and the French resistance were ultimately based on notions of popular sovereignty, noting that the rulers had been made by and because of the people; in Dutch and French conceptions, the prince was first and foremost the servant of the community, to be elected and accepted, by way of contract, by the representatives of the people. As far as the right of resistance is concerned, the similarity between Dutch and French political thought is again striking. Dutch and French thinkers alike argued that the representatives of the people had the right to resist a prince who violated the law of nature and the terms of the contract on which he had been appointed. Another parallel was that, generally, Dutch and French political thinkers confined this right of resistance to the representatives of the people, that is to the people as a collectivity.

Thirdly, there are certain parallels to be discerned in the evolution

---

[16] Ibid. 199. One of the historical examples to support this argument was in fact the Joyous Entry of Brabant (see *Vindiciae*, 180), which played such a pivotal role in the political thought of the Dutch Revolt.   [17] *Vindiciae*, 209.

[18] For Duplessis-Mornay, see Raoul Patry, *Philippe Du Plessis-Mornay: un Huguenot homme d'état (1549–1623)* (Paris, 1933), 45–94.   [19] See ch. 6, pp. 221–2.

of Dutch and Huguenot political thought. In both countries the first
manifestations of protest and resistance were presented as acts of
loyalty to protect the prince. In both countries 'protestants' insisted
on the legality of their position.[20] Subsequently, in both France and
the Netherlands, a process of radicalization occurred. In France
hopes of reconciliation and tolerance lasted until 1572, when they
were demolished by the massacre of St Bartholomew, which meant a
decisive turning-point in Huguenot political thought. In the Netherlands the ideological development was more gradual. Armed
resistance was already defended in the treatises of 1568 but the fiction
of loyalty, which presented Philip II as cruelly misled, was retained
until well in the 1570s. The difference in the political situation made
it possible for Dutch authors to avoid an open disavowal of Philip II
(who, after all, resided far away, somewhere in Castile) while taking,
from 1568, major steps in the articulation of an ideology of resistance,
which as the events of the 1570s showed could easily be extended to
the case of Philip II himself.

Fourthly, both the monarchomach and the Dutch justification of
resistance were essentially legalistic in character. French political
thought was, to an important extent, the outcome of publications by
and debates between lawyers who, as Kelley has pointed out, formed
'a unique lay class analogous to the clergy, a sort of secular
intellectual corporation whose vocation was the analysis and regulation of human relations – the cure, in a sense, not of souls but of
citizens'.[21]

The political justification of the Dutch was equally (perhaps even
more) legalistic in argument. As in France, the history of the
Burgundian–Habsburg Netherlands had been marked by the rise of
professional jurists at both the central and the local level. Before the
foundation of the University of Louvain in 1425, Dutch students of
law were compelled to matriculate at foreign universities if they
aspired to a training at university level. The universities of their
preference were Orléans, Padua and Bologna.[22] After 1425, students

---

[20] For France, see Skinner, *The foundations of modern political thought*, ii. 241, and Donald R.
Kelley, *The beginning of ideology: consciousness and society in the French Reformation* (Cambridge,
1981), 255ff. For the Netherlands, see ch. 4.

[21] Kelley, *The beginning of ideology*, 185.

[22] See Hilde de Ridder-Symoens, 'Internationalismus versus Nationalismus an Universitäten
um 1500 nach zumeist südniederländischen Quellen', in *Europa 1500: Integrationsprozesse im
Widerstreit* (Stuttgart, 1986), 400. This article offers a synthesis of a number of more detailed
studies. Of particular importance for the Dutch, especially Brabantine, *peregrinatio* to the
(law) University of Orléans, is Hilde de Ridder-Symoens, 'Brabanders aan de rechtenuni-

of law from the Low Countries continued, in fact in increasing numbers, to visit Orléans, a centre of constitutionalist studies, during their *peregrinatio academica*. In the first half of the sixteenth century 480 students from the southern provinces of the Netherlands studied there. Thus, a substantial number of Dutch lawyers must have shared the intellectual background of their French colleagues.

Together with ministers, lawyers seem to have had a dominant influence in constructing the political thought of the Dutch Revolt. Authors such as Albada, Aldegonde, Junius de Jonghe and Jacob van Wesembeeke had either studied law or had a legal professional background. Many anonymous treatises also appealed to positive or natural law, sometimes displaying detailed legal knowledge.[23] In short, it is very possible that, to an important extent, the ideologists of the Dutch Revolt and Huguenot resistance had a legal (professional and university) background in common. Therefore, it is no great surprise that, both in Dutch and French political thought, use was made of the works of the great medieval commentators on Roman law and indeed of Roman law itself.

Ironically, this common intellectual background may explain some of the differences between the political justification of the Revolt and monarchomach ideology. For, to justify their resistance, both Huguenot and Dutch thinkers turned to the ancient customs, laws and privileges of their countries, which, of course, were not identical. In France, this reflected the methodological twist in the study from the *mos Italicus* to the *mos Gallicus*, the study of the history of ancient indigenous French law. In the Netherlands, the ancient customs and privileges had traditionally been used in conflicts with central institutions. In France the turn to ancient indigenous law led to the impressive, but controversial, analysis of French legal history in Hotman's *Francogallia*. In the Netherlands it led to the, in itself traditional, rearticulation and far more controversial extension of the right of disobedience as formulated in the various editions of the Joyous Entry of Brabant and other privileges. As has been shown, the political justification of the Revolt was largely built on an appeal to, and interpretation of, indigenous Dutch constitutional charters, themselves the outcome of struggles for power between towns, provinces and lords. Dutch constitutional traditions, exemplified by

---

versiteit van Orléans (1444–1546) : een socio-professionele studie', *Bijdragen tot de Geschiedenis*, 61 (1978), 198–347.
[23] For principal examples, see the 1576 *Address* and the 1582 *Political education*.

the great charters of the late medieval period, were the principal point of reference for the justification of the Revolt and the articulation of the ideology of the Dutch political order as based on liberty, constitutional charters, representative institutions and popular sovereignty.[24] The essentials of this ideology were formulated in the treatises which were published between 1566 and 1573, well before publication of the monarchomach triumvirs.

In this respect two other important differences between the Dutch and the monarchomach ideology should be mentioned. The first concerns the role of the States. Whereas in Dutch political thought the role of the States was emphasized from the outset, the position of the States General in French political thought was much more ambiguous.[25] Being aware of the institutional inability of the States assemblies to respond to emergencies, the monarchomach theorists indicated different institutions as the principal representatives of the community.[26] Thus, in pointing out who, as representatives of the people, had the right of resistance, the *Vindiciae* referred to the 'officers of the kingdom' and the *Discours politique* to what Hanley has called the 'Assembly of public assessors'.[27] In the ideology of the Revolt, however, the role of the States was celebrated from the outset. Unequivocally, the States were designated as the guardians of liberty and as the executors of the right of resistance and abjuration. Moreover, the States were not seen as 'inferior magistrates'. As noted, already in 1568 Wesembeeke elevated to an imperative of politics the principle that the prince, in matters of great importance, should seek the advice and consent of the States, and in 1571 the *Defence* argued that princes were 'subject to the power of general parliaments'. In 1579, the year when the *Vindiciae* was published, the *Brief discourse* presented the States as leading sovereign powers.

Thus by 1579 Dutch political thinkers were well on the way to articulating a right of abjuration. In France, of course, an abjuration did not take place. On the contrary, the accession of Henry of Navarre to the French throne led to a distinct decline of monarcho-

---

[24] For a similar conclusion, see W. P. Blockmans, 'Du contrat féodal à la souveraineté du peuple: les précédents de la déchéanche du Philippe II dans les Pays Bas (1581)', in *Assemblee di stati e istituzioni rappresentative*, 150.   [25] See also ibid., 143–4.

[26] See Hanley, 'The *Discours politique* in monarchomaque ideology', 128, and Giesey, 'The monarchomach triumvirs', 44, who concluded that the ideological position of the States 'is impotent in Hotman's scheme, as likely as not ineffectual in Beza's, and superseded in Mornay's'.

[27] See Hanley, 'The *Discours politique* in monarchomaque ideology', 129ff.

mach ideology.[28] With the reversal of the political situation, celebrated monarchomachs such as Hotman and Duplessis-Mornay started to defend the importance of the king and diverged a long way from their former ideas. In the Netherlands no such reversal occurred. On the contrary, in the United Provinces the ideology of resistance was further extended, especially with regard to the right of abjuration and, during the 1580s, the issue of sovereignty. While in France Huguenot thinkers welcomed and defended the kingship of a well-disposed, gracious king, political thinkers in the Netherlands started to reflect on a political future without princely rule.

In short, although the Dutch and Huguenot ideologies of resistance were obviously related, the Dutch ideology should not be interpreted as a mere application of monarchomach ideas to the situation in the Netherlands. To subsume the political justification of the Revolt under the heading of French monarchomach ideology is to misunderstand the origins and character of the political thought of the Dutch Revolt.

This is not to deny the importance of Huguenot political thought. On the contrary, as Quentin Skinner has argued, in sixteenth-century Europe the monarchomach ideology of resistance was a sort of intellectual breakthrough. The Huguenots, as Skinner put it,

> were able to make the epoch-making move from a purely religious theory of resistance, depending on the idea of a covenant to uphold the laws of God, to a genuinely political theory of revolution, based on the idea of a contract which gives rise to a moral right (and not merely a religious duty) to resist any ruler who fails in his corresponding obligation to pursue the welfare of the people in all his public acts.[29]

This intellectual breakthrough was not confined to France. It should be concluded that a similar 'epoch-making move', to the articulation of a 'genuinely' political ideology of resistance, was made by the political thinkers of the Dutch Revolt.[30] As such, Dutch and

---

[28] See Kelley, *The beginning of ideology*, 328ff., and Myriam Yardeni, 'French Calvinist political thought, 1534–1715', in Prestwich (ed.), *International Calvinism*, 324ff.

[29] Skinner, *The foundations of modern political thought*, ii. 335.

[30] Recently Carlos M. N. Eire, *War against the idols: the reformation of worship from Erasmus to Calvin* (Cambridge, 1986), 276–310, has attacked Skinner's interpretation of Huguenot political thought on this point, arguing that it distorts the Calvinist character of monarchomach ideology. According to Eire, although the Huguenot ideology of resistance was political in argument, it was religious in motivation. In Eire's view, Huguenot political thought should be regarded as the outcome of a Calvinist crusade against idolatry, and he readily includes the Dutch Revolt in this argument. Although I do not want to dismiss the contribution of Reformed Protestants to the Revolt, it should be pointed out that to

French political thought of the late sixteenth century formed the culmination of an intellectual development which had started in the German empire during the 1530s. Absorbing and transcending late medieval political thought commenting on Roman law, on the value of contracts and on issues such as sovereignty and representation, the Dutch and the French established some of the 'foundations of modern political thought'.

7.4. RENAISSANCE REPUBLICANISM AND THE DUTCH REVOLT[31]

In the first half of the sixteenth century, when their republic was starting to collapse, Florentine political theorists confronted the problem of the instability of the republic. As trained humanists, standing in the tradition of fifteenth-century Florentine political thought, they conceptualized the fight for the stability of the republic in terms of a battle between *virtù* and *fortuna*, thus elaborating a distinct republican political language which in itself was another major foundation of modern political thought. According to Pocock's analysis, the political language of Renaissance republicanism, with Machiavelli as one of the greatest authors, has been of tremendous importance for the history of political thought in shaping an Atlantic republican tradition up to seventeenth- and eighteenth-century Britain and the American Revolution.[32]

The position of early modern Dutch political thought in the history of republican thought has remained a matter of controversy. It has been frequently argued that Dutch political thought does not fit in the paradigms of the Atlantic republican tradition.[33] Academic

interpret the Dutch Revolt as a fight against idolatry is a gross simplification of its complexities and a denial of political motives. Oldenbarnevelt would turn in his grave.

[31] The following paragraph seeks to refine the argument as developed in Martin van Gelderen, 'The Machiavellian moment and the Dutch Revolt: the rise of Neostoicism and Dutch republicanism', in G. Bock *et al.* (eds.), *Machiavelli and republicanism* (Cambridge, 1990), 205–23.

[32] See J. G. A. Pocock, *The Machiavellian moment: Florentine political thought and the Atlantic republican tradition* (Princeton, NJ, 1975).

[33] Pocock himself has studied the relation between the republican tradition and Dutch 17th-and 18th-century political thought in J. G. A. Pocock, 'The problem of political thought in the eighteenth century: patriotism and politeness (with comments of E. O. G. Haitsma Mulier and E. H. Kossmann)', *Theoretische Geschiedenis*, 9 (1982), 3–37, and J. G. A. Pocock, 'Spinoza and Harrington: an exercise in comparison', *BMGN* 102 (1987), 435–49. For recent comments on his interpretations, see E. H. Kossmann, 'Dutch republicanism', in *L'età dei lumi: studi, storici sul settecento Europeo in onore di Franco Venturi*, i (Naples, 1985), 455–86 (also in E. H. Kossmann, *Politieke theorie en geschiedenis: verspreide opstellen en*

political theory in particular seemed to concentrate 'on the advantages and disadvantages of monarchy' until well into the seventeenth century.[34] Republican ideas were not completely absent but were 'more opinion than doctrine'.[35] A republican breakthrough took place in the second half of the seventeenth century with the studies of the brothers de la Court and, above all, Spinoza.[36] However, even though Machiavelli was an important source of inspiration for these authors, Dutch republicanism remained eclectic. Thus it has been argued that, although the republican works of authors such as Spinoza in the seventeenth century and Luzac in the eighteenth century were 'most interesting and rewarding', Dutch republicanism 'was ever developed...into a peculiarly Dutch intellectual tradition which it would be correct to define as the Dutch paradigm'.[37]

At first sight the relation between the political thought of the Dutch Revolt and republican theory as developed in particular by Italian Renaissance theorists seems intriguing and in a way ironic. The first political thinker in the Netherlands to acknowledge openly Machiavelli's value as a political analyst was Lipsius;[38] indeed it is

voordrachten (Amsterdam, 1987), 211-34), and E. O. G. Haitsma Mulier, 'The language of seventeenth-century republicanism in the United Provinces: Dutch or European?', in Anthony Pagden (ed.), *The languages of political theory in early modern Europe* (Cambridge, 1987), 179-95. For a proficient and somewhat sceptical view on the importance of republican ideas in Dutch political thought in the late 16th and early 17th centuries, see Nicolette Mout, 'Ideales Muster oder erfundene Eigenart', in H. G. Koenigsberger (ed.), *Republiken under Republikanismus im Europa der frühen Neuzeit* (Munich, 1988).

[34] Haitsma Mulier, 'The language of seventeenth-century republicanism', 179. The classic study on this issue is E. H. Kossmann, *Politieke theorie in het zeventiende-eeuwse Nederland* (Amsterdam, 1960). See also E. H. Kossmann, 'The development of Dutch political theory in the seventeenth century', in J. S. Bromley and E. H. Kossmann (eds.), *Britain and the Netherlands*, i (London, 1960), 91-110.

[35] Kossmann, *Politieke theorie*, 10. For somewhat different interpretations see Mout, 'Ideales Muster', H. Schilling, 'Der libertär-radikale Republikanismus der holländischen Regenten', *Geschichte und Gesellschaft*, 10 (1984), 498-533, and H. Schilling, 'Calvinismus und Freiheitsrechte: die politisch-theologische Pamphletistik der Ostfriesisch-Groningischen "Patrioten-partei" und die politische Kultur in Deutschland und in den Niederlanden', *BMGN* 102 (1987), 403-34.

[36] The decisive study on this point is E. O. G. Haitsma Mulier, *The myth of Venice and Dutch republican thought in the seventeenth century* (Assen, 1980). For Spinoza, see also Hans Blom, 'Virtue and republicanism: Spinoza's political philosophy in the context of the Dutch Republic', in Koenigsberger (ed.), *Republiken und Republikanismus*, 195-213.

[37] E. H. Kossmann, 'Dutch republicanism', 486. For Luzac, see also W. R. E. Velema, 'God, de deugd en de oude constitutie: politieke talen in de eerste helft van de achttiende eeuw', *BMGN* 102 (1987), 476-97.

[38] Others did so in private. For example Albada, who, in a letter written in 1571 to Hector of Aytta, recommended Machiavelli's historical work. See K. van Berkel, 'Aggaeus de Albada en de crisis in de Opstand (1579-1687)', *BMGN* 96 (1981), 5.

tempting to put his *Politics* next to Machiavelli's. For both, the essence of the art of politics was to establish how virtue could conquer fortune or fate, in order to realize a *vivere civile*. Both Machiavelli's and Lipsius' accounts stood squarely within the humanist tradition of the study of politics. As trained humanists, both employed the language and the 'organizing categories' of this tradition. Their analyses of princely rule elaborated on the humanist mirror-for-princes tradition, while dismissing it at crucial points.[39]

Thus Neostoicism was developed out of the same classical tradition as Machiavellian republicanism. To an important extent Neostoicism had the same epistemological foundation, employed the same 'language' and used the same conceptual scheme and similar organizing categories. None the less, there were essential differences between Neostoicism and the republicanism of the Machiavellian moment. For Lipsius was by no means the 'philosopher of liberty' Machiavelli had been.[40] On the contrary, Lipsius' *Politics* contained no conception of liberty whatsoever. Moreover, the philosopher of Neostoicism certainly did not endorse a republican view of politics. In fact, in arguing that the *vita civilis* could only be attained in a political order which was marked by unified, virtuous princely rule and obedient citizens, Neostoicism plainly rejected republicanism.

In Renaissance republicanism liberty was the key political value. Thus, following great predecessors such as Leonardo Bruni's *Laudatio florentinae urbis*, Machiavelli pointed out that liberty was the key to greatness and prosperity.[41] The argument was derived from Sallust's *Bellum Catilinae*,[42] which emphasized that Rome had risen to greatness only after it had attained a state of liberty, which essentially meant that the community had obtained the freedom to govern itself. In the republican conception liberty entailed self-government.

Machiavelli emphasized that self-government was a pre-condition for the personal liberty of the members of a community. The essence of the republican argument was that, unless a community is maintained 'in a state of liberty', being able to govern itself, its individual members 'will find themselves stripped of their personal

---

[39] See ch. 5, pp. 104–5.

[40] The term is Quentin Skinner's. See Quentin Skinner, *Machiavelli* (Oxford, 1981), 48ff.

[41] See Niccolò Machiavelli, 'Discorsi sopra la prima deca di Tito Livio', in Niccolò Machiavelli, *Tutte le opere* (Florence, 1971), 148 (*Discorsi*, book 2, ch. 2).

[42] See Quentin Skinner, 'Political philosophy', in Charles B. Schmitt and Quentin Skinner (eds.), *The Cambridge history of Renaissance philosophy* (Cambridge, 1988), 419.

liberty'.[43] Citizens could only hope to escape from political servitude and to have the freedom to pursue their own goals if the community, of which they were members, governed itself in accordance with its own will. As Quentin Skinner has pointed out, 'this conclusion – that personal liberty can only be fully assured within a self-governing form of republican community – represents the heart and nerve of all classical republican theories of citizenship'.[44]

As republican theorists recognized, the liberty of the community to govern itself in accordance with its own will could be threatened both from inside, by the *grandi*, the rich and powerful factions whose ambition it was to dominate over others, and from outside, by other ambitious communities, which had the same ambition for dominance. Faction and foreign conquest were the existential threats to liberty.

According to republican theory, in order to protect the community against internal divisions, a proper set of laws and ordinances was needed which bridled the ambitions of factions and prevented any faction from dominating the will of the community. Discord should be warded off, concord promoted. In general, republican theorists felt that the best form of government to preserve concord and thereby liberty was a mixed form of elective government. As Machiavelli, like so many inspired by Sallust, explained, monarchs scarcely ever promoted the common good.[45]

In order to protect the community against the threats of ambitious foreign powers, the importance of a vigilant military defence was underlined, which Machiavelli insisted should be based on a virtuous civic militia.

In order to make both the military and the constitutional machinery work, virtuous acts of public service were required. Time and again republican theorists urged citizens to lead a life of *negotium*, which was marked by the virtuous exercise of the cardinal virtues of justice, prudence, fortitude and temperance.

Thus, in order to preserve the free and self-governing republic through time, *virtù* was vital. The *res publica* should be what Pocock

---

[43] Quentin Skinner, 'The idea of negative liberty: philosophical and historical perspectives', in Richard Rorty *et al.* (eds.), *Philosophy in history* (Cambridge, 1984), 213.

[44] Ibid. 207–8.

[45] See Machiavelli, 'Discorsi', 148. For Machiavelli's indebtedness to Sallust, see Quentin Skinner, 'Machiavelli's *Discorsi* and the pre-humanist origins of republican ideas', in Bock *et al.* (eds.), *Machiavelli and republicanism*, 139.

has called a 'structure of virtue', which meant that it should be 'a structure in which every citizen's ability to place the common good before his own was the pre-condition of every other's, so that every man's virtue saved every other's from that corruption part of whose time-dimension was *fortuna*'.[46]

If it is the essence and defining characteristic of Renaissance republicanism that, as supreme political values, liberty, the common good of the community and the personal freedom of its members were preserved and furthered best by a political system characterized by a set of sound laws, a refined form of mixed government based on elections (and thus on representation) and virtuous acts of public service by the citizens, then it is worth while to compare the ideology developed during the Dutch Revolt, which contained a vision of the political order as based on liberty, constitutional charters, representative institutions and popular sovereignty, with Renaissance republicanism.

At certain points the pattern of ideas concerning the preservation of liberty as developed during the Dutch Revolt parallels republican philosophy rather strikingly. Both regarded liberty as one of the key political values, to be practically equated with the supreme law of the common good; both conceived of liberty in terms of self-governance; both recognized that preservation of the liberty of the community was a pre-condition of personal liberty; both saw faction and foreign conquest as the existential threats to liberty; both emphasized the necessity of concord, endorsing Sallust's proverb that concord made small commonwealths great but discord disrupted even the greatest ones; both argued that, in order to preserve the liberty of the community, proper laws and institutions were essential; both favoured a mixed republican form of government; both underlined the importance of civic virtue for the preservation of liberty.

Thus, if it is the essence and defining characteristic of the republican ideology of liberty that unless a community is maintained in a state of freedom its inhabitants will lose their personal liberty, and that to uphold the liberty of the community good laws, proper institutions and civic virtue are required, then the conclusion should be that the ideology of the Dutch political order as based on liberty, constitutional charters (privileges), representative institutions (States and town governments) and popular sovereignty, as developed during the Revolt, was principally republican. As this ideology lay at

---

[46] Pocock, *The Machiavellian moment*, 184. See also Skinner, *Machiavelli*, esp. pp. 53–7.

the heart of the political thought of the Dutch Revolt, to an important extent, the political thought of the Dutch Revolt should be qualified as republican. In other words, like the republicanism of the Italian Renaissance, the political thought of the Dutch Revolt has its place in the history of early modern republican thought.

Of course, if only because they were developed in different historical settings, and were addressing the political problems of their own time and country, there are important differences to be noted between the republicanism of the Italian Renaissance, as exemplified, for example, by Machiavelli, and Dutch late sixteenth-century republicanism.

First, almost unanimously Dutch authors disagreed with Machiavelli on the importance of the virtue of justice. Throughout the political literature of the Revolt, it was argued that justice was indispensable. In this respect Dutch ideas were more in line with Machiavelli's republican predecessors. Machiavelli's ideas were condemned as sheer viciousness. He was presented only as the author of *The Prince*, as 'the compass of the Italian princes' (such as Philip II's Governor Farnese), teaching them to lie and cheat, and to discard justice.[47] It was not unusual to present the alleged Machiavellianism of Philip II as the root cause of the Dutch troubles.

Secondly, although the recognition of the freedom of the community as a pre-condition of the personal liberty of its members was essential to both Machiavellian republicanism and the ideology of the Dutch political order as based on liberty, privileges, States and popular sovereignty, the conceptions of what personal liberty was strongly diverged. For Machiavelli the essence of personal liberty was that men were free 'to marry as they chose; to bring up their families without having to fear for their honour or their own welfare; and to be in a position "freely to possess their own property"'.[48] The Dutch also conceived of personal liberty as the free enjoyment of 'body and goods'. However, at the heart of the conceptions of personal liberty

---

[47] Willem Verheyden, *Nootelijcke consideratien die alle goede liefhebbers des Vaderlandts behooren rijpelijck te overweghen opten voorgeslaghen Tractate van Peys met den Spaengiaerden* (1587), fol. B. In the French version Verheyden put it this way: 'Nicholas Machiavelli, l'oreillier, le guide & miroir des Italiens, n'apprend il point un Prince à se tourner selon les ventz, disant, qu'il faut qu'il apparoisse humain, loyal & pitoiable, & qu'il n'est tenu d'estre tousiours garny de vertu, moyennant qu'il ai apparance de l'estre?' See Willem Verheyden, *Considerations necessaires sur un traicté avec l'espagnol* (1587), fol. B. For the reception of Machiavelli's works in the Dutch Republic, see E. O. G. Haitsma Mulier, 'A controversial republican: Dutch views of Machiavelli in the seventeenth and eighteenth centuries', in Bock *et al.* (eds.), *Machiavelli and republicanism*, 247–63.

[48] Quentin Skinner, 'Machiavelli on the maintenance of liberty', *Politics*, 18 (1983), 4.

developed during the Dutch Revolt was the idea that freedom of conscience formed the essence of personal liberty. As noted, the precise meaning and contents of freedom of conscience was a matter of dispute amongst the proponents of the Revolt. None the less, the fundamental view that no one should be questioned or persecuted because of his religion was unanimously endorsed by the political thinkers of the Revolt and was incorporated into the 1579 Union of Utrecht, which became one of the fundamental laws of the Dutch Republic.

The emphasis on freedom of conscience reflected a fundamental shift in conceptions of personal liberty. What was at stake in the debates on freedom of conscience was the freedom of individuals to believe, as far as religion was concerned, what they wanted and to speak freely about their beliefs. Such a conception of liberty was alien to the republican conceptions of the Italian Renaissance. It indicates the profound influence of the Reformation on the political thought of the Dutch Revolt.

Thirdly, whereas Machiavelli had acknowledged the inevitability of civic discord and, referring to the history of Rome, had emphasized that civic conflict was a necessary pre-condition for the survival and glory of a community,[49] Dutch thinkers emphatically underlined the necessity for concord. Faced with growing discord due especially to the religious polarization of the late 1570s, the Dutch clung to the classical Ciceronian maxim that concord and union formed the foundation of the *res publica*. Of course religious diversity as the origin of faction was relatively new and was unknown to Machiavellian republicanism. It posed a new challenge, which the Dutch, in political theory and even more in political praxis, sought to answer by means of religious toleration. Thus the cause of faction, religious diversity, was not removed. By means of good laws and a pragmatic policy Dutch authorities sought to control the discordant effects of religious diversity. Therefore, as a political principle religious toleration can be seen as the outcome of an ideology which celebrated liberty and concord: because freedom of conscience was seen as the essence of liberty and because concord was regarded as the foundation of a community, religious toleration became an important value in Dutch political thought.

---

[49] See Machiavelli, 'Discorsi', 81–8 (ch. 1.3–1.7). For a refined analysis, see Gisela Bock, 'Civil discord in Machiavelli's *Istorie Fiorentine*', in Bock *et al.* (eds.), *Machiavelli and republicanism*, 181–201.

The final difference between Machiavellian republicanism and the ideology of the Dutch political order as built on liberty, constitutional charters, representative institutions and popular sovereignty concerns the epistemological foundations of the political languages used by Dutch and Italian authors to articulate republican ideas. It seems that, unlike the republican theorists of the Italian Renaissance, the political thinkers of the Dutch Revolt did not conceive of the fight for the preservation of the old freedom and the political order – for that is how they represented the resistance and abjuration – so much in terms of a fight between *virtù* and *fortuna*. Research has not yet shown whether the language of civic humanism was of importance to the development of humanism in the Low Countries and to the rise of Christian humanism. Florentine political thought does not seem to have exerted a positive appeal to the theorists of the Dutch Revolt. Unlike Venice, praised by some authors, Florence had suffered the very fate the Dutch were trying to avoid.

In this respect the Reformation may again have left its mark, for it seems, at first sight, difficult to reconcile notions of politics as a battle between *virtù* and *fortuna* with Reformed Protestant ideas of Providence. Calvin himself explicitly warned against the temptation to think 'that human affairs are whirled about by the blind impulse of Fortune'.[50] Instead of 'foolishly' imagining that fate and fortune controlled incomprehensible events, some authors, influenced by Reformed Protestantism, might have preferred the idea of the Providence of God, whose ways were beyond human comprehension.

With many inhabitants of the Low Countries being imbued with neither humanism nor Calvinism, it is tempting to speculate, as Simon Schama has done, that many Dutch conceived of the fight against Spanish tyranny as a parallel to their centuries-old existential fight against the principal enemy of the Netherlands, water.[51] Like the defence against Spanish tyranny, the defence against the tyrant water required concord, good laws, representative institutions and civic virtue. Without concord, good laws and polder boards (which in fact were amongst the most participatory in the Low Countries) an effective system of dikes and other forms of protection could never have been set up. Without virtuous acts of public service by all participants the challenge of sea and rivers could never have been met. As one single hole in the dike was enough to cause catastrophe,

---

[50] Calvin, *Institutes of the Christian religion*, i. 183 (book 1, ch. 17, para. 1). See Bouwsma, *John Calvin*, 167.   [51] See Schama, *The embarrassment of riches*, 37–50.

courage, constancy, and also prudence and temperance, were permanently required. Thus the articulation of republican ideas during the Revolt may well have been the result of transposing the age-old existential experience of the fight against water to the art of politics.

Probing into the origins of the political thought of the Dutch Revolt, it should of course be pointed out that both the republicanism of the Machiavellian moment and the articulation of republican ideas during the Dutch Revolt had in common the Renaissance and the rediscovery of the classics as important sources of inspiration. Dutch printers, Plantin's office in Antwerp being the most spectacular example, published editions of classical works in impressive numbers. The classics were also translated into the vernacular. As has already been noted, Coornhert translated, amongst others, Cicero's *De officiis* into Dutch. In pursuing their analyses on the best state of the commonwealth and in discussing civic virtue, Dutch authors dwelt upon the classics, on Cicero and Sallust in particular, just as Italian republican theorists had done before. In this respect the articulation of republican ideas during the revolt was the offspring of the Dutch Renaissance.

On the other hand there is a remarkable similarity to be noted between Dutch republican conceptions of liberty and what Skinner has called 'the scholastic defence of liberty', as developed in the course of the fourteenth century by seminal authors such as Bartolus of Sassoferrato.[52] Conceiving of liberty in republican terms as political independence and self-government, Bartolus too saw civil discord as the main danger to liberty. To ensure that sectional interests were set aside and that citizens equated their own good with the good of the community as a whole, scholastic theorists felt that an efficient and complex constitutional framework was needed. Its leading principle was that the people (conceived of as a *universitas*, not as a mere sum of individuals) were and remained the sovereign authority in a body politic. If the people conceded authority to a 'ruling part', it was essential to ensure that that ruling part was kept firmly under control and represented 'the mind of the people', as Bartolus put it.[53] To achieve this goal the scholastic theorists of liberty favoured a number of constitutional arrangements: rulers were to be elected, they were

---

[52] See Skinner, *The foundations of modern political thought*, i. 53–66. See also Walter Ullmann, *Medieval political thought* (Harmondsworth, 1975), 200–28, and, more generally, Brian Tierney, *Religion, law, and the growth of constitutional thought, 1150–1650* (Cambridge, 1982).

[53] See J. P. Canning, *The political thought of Baldus de Ubaldis* (Cambridge, 1987), 198.

only allowed minimal discretion in administering the law (which was the basic task) and a complex network of checks of magistrates and ruling councils was to be devised.

Bartolus and his pupil Baldus in particular were the first to develop a juristic theory of the *de facto* sovereignty of Italian city republics which entailed a powerful notion of popular sovereignty. Faced with the *de facto* situation that imperial rule was no longer effective in the Italian city republics Bartolus and Baldus made the important move of arguing 'that the consent of the people could be a complete alternative to the will of a superior'.[54] And since the city republic no longer recognized a superior, its population was a *populus liber* fully entitled to self-government.

This 'radical version of early modern constitutionalism'[55] had lasting influence. It entered the sixteenth century through the writings of authors such as Salomonio. Undoubtedly the 'scholastic defence of liberty' influenced the political thought of the Dutch Revolt. Famous Commentators on Roman law such as Bartolus and Baldus, and the work of Salomonio, were well known in the Netherlands, as exemplified by Albada's 1581 *Acts* and the 1582 *Political education*. As has been noted, Albada built his argument concerning popular sovereignty to an important extent on Salomonio's work, and Bartolus featured prominently in the theory of resistance as developed in *Political education*.[56] Thus, as in the case of monarchomach theory, the Dutch ideology of resistance was to an important extent an elaboration of late medieval 'scholastic and Roman law traditions of radical constitutionalism'.[57]

The connections between the scholastic and Roman-law traditions of constitutional thought and Renaissance republicanism have been a matter of some controversy. In Pocock's analysis, Bartolus' work is presented as typical of the 'language of jurisprudence', the other dominant political language of early modern Europe, which, at least according to Pocock, was essentially different from the republican language. While the 'republican vocabulary...articulated the positive conception of liberty', contending 'that *homo*, the *animale politicum*, was so constituted that his nature was completed only in a *vita activa* practised in a *vivere civile*', the 'juristic presentation of liberty' is said to be basically negative as 'it distinguished between

---

[54] Ibid. 96.   [55] Skinner, *The foundations of modern political thought*, i. 65.
[56] See p. 158 for a full analysis.
[57] For monarchomach theory on this point, see Skinner, *The foundations of modern political thought*, ii. 320.

libertas and *imperium*, freedom and authority, individuality and sovereignty, private and public'.[58] Whereas in republican language liberty was seen as the freedom to participate, in the language of jurisprudence it was essentially regarded as freedom from authority.[59] In juristic vocabulary the essence of citizenship was the possession of rights, whereas in republican vocabulary the essence of citizenship was participation. The difference should be regarded as essential. As Pocock has put it, the basic concept of the republican language is *virtus*, the basic concept of 'all language of jurisprudence is necessarily *ius*', and there is no known way of representing virtue as a right.[60]

On the basis of this analysis it should be concluded that the Dutch conception of political order as built upon liberty, constitutional charters, representative institutions and popular sovereignty ought also to be located in the history of the political language of jurisprudence, of which Grotius is said to be one of the leading representatives. Surely, for the thinkers of the Dutch Revolt, as in scholastic theory, the defence of liberty was essentially based on a constitutional framework of fundamental laws and a balanced system of institutions. Moreover, the political thought of the Dutch Revolt of course emphasized the importance of rights and contained powerful notions of popular sovereignty.

However, the use of the language of jurisprudence during the Dutch Revolt was by no means incompatible with the articulation of republican ideas. As the interpretation of the political order as built upon liberty, constitutional charters, representative institutions and popular sovereignty contained a conception of republican self-government as marked by civic virtue, the political thinkers of the Dutch Revolt seemed to merge the language of jurisprudence with elements of the republican language. For example, while the argument of the 1582 *Political education* to justify the abjuration of Philip II was obviously inspired by the scholastic and Roman-law traditions of constitutional thought, its analysis of concord, civic virtues and citizenship, being inspired by Cicero in particular, paralleled crucial elements of Renaissance rep ᴌlicanism.

---

[58] J. G. A. Pocock, 'Virtues, rights and manners: a model for historians of political thought', in Pocock, *Virtue, commerce and history*, 40–1.

[59] See John Robertson, 'The Scottish Enlightenment at the limits of the civic tradition', in Istvan Hont and Michael Ignatieff (eds.), *Wealth and virtue: the shaping of political economy in the Scottish Enlightenment* (Cambridge, 1983), 140.

[60] J. G. A. Pocock, 'Cambridge paradigms and Scotch philosophers: a study of the relations between the civic humanist and the civil jurisprudential interpretation of eighteenth-century social thought', in Hont and Ignatieff (eds.), *Wealth and virtue*, 248.

In this respect the political thinkers of the Dutch Revolt followed and elaborated on the constitutional traditions of the Low Countries. As has been noted,[61] the Joyous Entry of Brabant and the 1477 privileges were principal vehicles for formulating both civil rights and claims to political participation. When the political thinkers of the Dutch Revolt appealed to the privileges, they were not merely asking for the protection of rights, they were also demanding participation in the decision-making process for the States and therefore for the towns and communities and their citizens. Of course constitutional charters and the Revolt's appeal to them were bathed in the language of the law. For the political thinkers of the Dutch Revolt the language of jurisprudence was often perfectly suitable to express republican claims.[62] In fact Dutch political thinkers in the late sixteenth century seemed to emphasize that civil rights and civic virtue were entwined. Whilst the constitutional guarantee of self-government and civil rights was a pre-condition for the possibility and protection of the civic freedom to participate, permanent virtuous acts of public service were necessary to uphold the rule of law.[63] Just as a dike, to speculate once more, needed a well-balanced plan and authorities to supervise it, so its maintenance needed permanent virtuous observation.

In short, in employing elements of both the language of jurisprudence and republican language the political theorists of the Revolt articulated attitudes which had a long and powerful tradition in the Low Countries. As this study has emphasized, the constitutional traditions of the Dutch Provinces were undoubtedly major sources of inspiration for the political thought of the Dutch Revolt. To justify the resistance against Philip II and to reflect on the political future of the United Provinces after the abjuration, the political thinkers of the Revolt principally elaborated on an indigenous tradition of constitutionalism which had found its expression in the great constitutional charters of the Low Countries. The political thought of the Revolt was as much the Dutch appropriation of the intellectual innovations of Renaissance and Reformation as it was the articulation of long-standing traditions of Dutch constitutionalism.

---

[61] See ch. 2, pp. 27–30.

[62] As it was, of course, as Skinner has shown, for figures such as Marsilius of Padua and Bartolus. See Skinner, *The foundations of modern political thought*, i. 53–66.

[63] See Robertson, 'The Scottish Enlightenment', 160ff., where it is shown how a similar line of argumentation was developed in 18th-century Scotland, by Hume in particular.

Appendix: a note on primary sources

The interpretation of the political thought of the Dutch Revolt offered in this study is primarily based on the exploration and analysis of treatises published between 1555 and 1590. As the year of Charles V's abdication and Philip II's accession to the throne of Spain and the lordship of the Netherlands, 1555 is an obvious starting-point. As terminus the year 1590 has been chosen. The defeat of the Spanish Armada in 1588, new military initiatives by Maurice of Nassau and the political course under the leadership of Johan van Oldenbarnevelt meant the territorial and political consolidation of what from that time can be called the Dutch Republic.

Focusing on political treatises, the primary sources of this study overwhelmingly consist of printed material. It has become habit to conceive of the political literature of the Revolt in terms of pamphlets. This has been stimulated by the inventory of the collections of main libraries in what was usually called catalogues of pamphlets.[1] Unfortunately, these pamphlet catalogues rarely give any indication of the criteria for listing titles. A simple comparison between them shows that there must have been strong variation on this point. For example, whereas some catalogues of pamphlets list such official government publications as ordinances, resolutions and placards, others do not. The problem is that the term 'pamphlet' refers neither to a distinct form of printed material nor to a distinct genre of publication.[2] Craig Harline has defined 'pamphlets' as printed 'writings of immediate and direct or indirect political significance'.[3] Of course Lipsius' *Sixe bookes of politickes or civile doctrine*, Albada's *Acts* and Coornhert's *Trial of the killing of Heresy and the constraint of concience* fall under this head, yet in common language they are generally not described as pamphlets.

This has important consequences for the study of the political thought of the Dutch Revolt, which has often centred on pamphlets. Although the catalogues of pamphlets made up by Knuttel, Petit and van der Wulp undoubtedly include works of great importance for such a study, it should

---

[1] For a list of the main catalogues, see Bibliography.

[2] In this study the 'printed writings' which discuss political issues have been generally described by the term 'political treatises'. If the term 'pamphlet' is used, it denotes a 'political treatise', which has no more than 50 pages.

[3] See Harline, *Pamphlets, printing, and political culture in the early Dutch Republic*, 3.

be realized that a study of sixteenth-century political thought has to move beyond these catalogues.

The selection of material for this book was therefore based on an alternative approach. The foundation of this study is formed by the major collections of sixteenth-century literature in the Netherlands and Belgium.[4] Of each collection an inventory was drawn up of all treatises published between 1555 and 1590. The selection of works for exploration was then made on the basis of titles. Fortunately, a great number of sixteenth-century authors and publishers had a preference for elaborate titles which often give a reasonable indication of the publication's contents. Where titles left room for doubt, the treatises concerned were invariably consulted. In short, of the collections consulted, all works which were of potential interest to the subject of this book were explored. In total about 800 treatises were read, almost half of them (370 titles to be exact) coming from the Knuttel collection in the Royal Library at The Hague.

It is difficult to describe the function, importance and reception of political treatises in the society of the sixteenth-century Netherlands. There was a booming printing culture in the Dutch Provinces, with the Antwerp publishing house of Christopher Plantin as the outstanding example. These printing offices published respectable quantities of political treatises.[5] It has been estimated that as, per run, about 1,000 copies were printed of a single treatise, in any given year in the 1570s about 50,000 copies of pamphlets would have been available.[6]

Due to the fragmentation of political authority in the Netherlands and the lack of effective governmental control over authors, it was probably relatively easy to publish political treatises during the Dutch Revolt.

As titles indicate, authors of political treatises often anticipated the 'common people' of the provinces as their audience. Apparently authors of political treatises such as the 1583 *Warning to all good inhabitants of the Netherlands, who, for the protection of the liberty of their religion, persons, privileges, and old customs, are allied and united against the tyranny of the Spaniards and their adherents* considered it useful, if not necessary, to address their works to rather general audiences. They probably felt that the 'common people' were a political factor to reckon with, and that it was important to influence them.

It is, however, difficult to ascertain whether, and to what extent, political treatises were read by the 'common people' during the Revolt. A number

---

[4] The collection of the Royal Library in The Hague has been taken as the starting-point. The other collections consulted are those of the Royal Library of Brussels, the university libraries of Amsterdam, Ghent and Leiden, the library of the Plantin-Moretus Museum in Antwerp, and the City Archives in Antwerp. Additional research has been done in the university libraries of Utrecht and Liège, the municipal library of Antwerp, the British Library in London and the library of Trinity Hall in Cambridge.

[5] Following his definition Harline has counted the publication of 2,104 pamphlets between 1555 and 1590 (*Pamphlets, printing, and political culture in the early Dutch Republic*, 4). It should be pointed out that a substantial part of these pamphlets have not survived the whirls of history. [6] Ibid. 21.

of important pre-conditions for widespread reading of political treatises probably were fulfilled in the Netherlands.[7]

First, due to a highly developed school system the Netherlands had a relatively high level of literacy. In Flanders, for example, a network of schools had been developed which gave an exceptional boost to humanist education. Secondly, the overwhelming majority of the Revolt's political treatises were published in the vernacular, either in French or in Dutch, or, as was frequently the case, in both languages. Thirdly, as political treatises were printed in respectable quantities they may have been generally available to the reading public. The range of availability depended, of course, on the effectiveness of networks of transport and distribution of printed material. Although in the Dutch Republic such networks seem to have functioned rather well, it is likely that the uncertainties of war hampered distribution and communication during the Revolt. Fourthly, as far as prices are concerned, it can be argued that, although some of the smaller political treatises were probably relatively cheap, in general political treatises must be regarded as luxury items for a majority of the population. Finally, it has been argued that, during the early modern period, there was a steady rise of interest in political affairs amongst the people of Western Europe, especially the Dutch Provinces.[8]

The influence of books and pamphlets on the population was, in general, perceived as considerable by contemporaries. Both magistrates and ministers repeatedly complained about it. In 1578, for example, the national synod of the Reformed Protestant church decreed that books on religion should not be published without being examined and approved by a number of ministers or professors of theology; three years later several books were indeed condemned by the national synod of Middelburg. However, the attitude of Reformed Protestants was ambiguous. On the one hand, they often despised the relative freedom of publication in the Dutch Provinces and pleaded for effective censorship. On the other hand, they thought that the best way to rebut 'seditious' libels was to repudiate them through the printing-press. Thus Reformed Protestantism contributed considerably to the use of printed material as a medium for political and religious discussion and its use during the Dutch Revolt was without precedence in the albeit still short history of the Dutch printing-press.[9] The Dutch Revolt most definitely established books and treatises as the principal media for public dispute.

[7] See ibid. 57–71, and, more generally, Peter Burke, *Popular culture in early modern Europe* (New York, 1978), 253ff.

[8] See ibid., 264–5, and also Harline, *Pamphlets, printing, and political culture in the early Dutch Republic*, 67.

[9] It was not entirely new. During the revolt of the 1480s against Maximilian of Habsburg contestants had already resorted to printing as a medium of expressing political ideas. In scope, however, the literature of the 1480s is not comparable to the political literature of the Revolt.

Bibliography

PRIMARY SOURCES

After every title a code is given, which refers to the library where the treatise has been consulted (which does not of course mean that it can only be found in this library), and to the reference number of the title.

ANONYMOUS (IN CHRONOLOGICAL ORDER)

Die blijde incomste, den hertochdom van Brabant in voortijden by heuren Landsheeren verleent ende van Keyser Carolus den V. gheconfirmeert ende by Philips sijnen sone, Coninck van Spaignien, solemnelijck ghesworen, anno 1549, various edns. (1564, RLB-LP-1398-A; 1565, RLB-LP-3860-A1; 1566, RLB-LP-1441A; 1574, RLB-LP-2772A).

Requeste aen de Eerweerdighe, Wijse en seer voorsienighe heeren, Borghemeestern en Raet der vermaerder Coopstadt Antwerpen, ghepresenteert byde gemeyne Borgerscha der selver Stadt (1565, UBL-121-A; CAA-SA-641).

Requeste aen myn vrouwe d'Hertoghinne van Parme, Plaisance, &c Regent, ende andere gouverneurs ende regeerders deser Nederlanden, ghepresenteert van wegen der armen, verstroeyden ende verdructen gheloovighen, die tonrecht ghediffameert vervolcht ende gheaffligeert werden ter cause haerder religie nae den heylighen evangelium ghereformeert, in *Historie ende geschiedenisse van de verradelicke ghevangenisse der vromer ande godsaligher mannen, Christophorij Fabritij dienaer des goddelicken woords binnen Antwerpen ende Oliverij Bockij professeur der Latijnsche sprake in de hooghe en vermaerde schole van Heydelberch* (1565, RLB-VH-26-244, 199–210; repr. in S. Cramer and F. Pijper (eds.), *BRN,* viii (The Hague, 1911), 282–460).

Advertissement bijde goede ende ghetrauwe ondersaten ende inwoonderen der CM. Erfnederlanden gedaen aende gouverneurs en Staten derselver landen van t'ghene dat sijlieden verstaen ende versuecken geordonneert te worden opt stuck van der religie, 12 juni 1566 (1566, MPM-A-2213; also pub. in French as *Advertissement que sont les bons et loiaux suiets et habitants du Pais Bas*).

Copie des lettres patentes en forme d'asseurance que la Ducesse de Parme, Regente etc. a donne aux Gentilzhommes confederez, ayans presente la Requeste au mois d'Avril Soixantecinq avant Pasques. Ensemble des Reversalles desdictz Gentilhommes. Et aussi des Lettres closes escriptes par son Alteze pour le mesme effect aux Consaulx et principalles Villes de pardeca (Brussels, 1566, KN-139).

Copye vande Requeste ghepresenteert aen de Hertoghinne van Parma etc. Regente, opten vijfsten dach van April, anno XVC. vijffentsestich voer Paesschen, bij diversche Edelmannen van Herwaertsovere, opt feyt van de Inquisitie ende executie vande Placcaten vande Catholijcke Religie. Met de Apostille van heure Hoocheyt op de voerschreven Requeste ghestelt (Brussels, 1566, KN-137A).

Cort bewijs uit de schriften Lutheri en Brentij dat het lichaem Christi niet en sy een lichamelijcke maer een gheestelijcke spijse (1566, RLTH-1704-F10).

Derde waerschouwinge ende vermaninghe aende goede, getrouwe regeerders en gemeinte vanden lande van Brabant teghen de calumnien vanden Cardinael van Granvel, nieu Bisscoppen, Viglius, Morillon, theologiennen van Loeven, dekens, prochianen, monniken, Alonso Delcanto ende andere Inquisiteurs haren aenhangers (1566, RLB-II-59-249A).

Geschiedenisse aengaende t'feyt der religien, gebeurt t'Antwerpen int'iaer MDLXVI (1566, ULG-MEUL-151; also pub. in French, as *Recueil des choses advenues en Anvers, touchant le fait de la Religion, en l'an MDLXVI,* 1566, KN-142).

Gheboden ende uutrhoepen (Antwerp, 1566, RLB-VB-334-C1-3).

Les subtils moyens par le Cardinal Granvelle avec ces complices inventez pour instituer l'abnominable inquisition avec la cruelle observation des placcartz contre ceulx dela religion (1566, MPM-A-2213).

Libellus supplex (1566), in van Toorenenbergen (ed.), *Eene bladzijde uit de geschiedenis der Nederlandsche geloofsbelijdenis,* pp. lvii–lxiv.

Neuwe Zeittung ausz Niderland, von dem Ummgang oder Procession, so in Antorff gehalten mitten im Augsten, diese 66. Jars... (1566, ULL-THYS-129).

Newe Zeittung. In welcher kurtzlich, ordentlich und warhafftiglich nach aller umstendigkeit erzelet wird, was sich in der beruhmten Kauffstadt Antorff zwischen den 18. und 28. Augusti diese 1566. Jars in Religion Sachen, unnd anderen grossen hendelen zu getragen und verlauffen hat (1566, KN-141).

Propositie ende Requeste opt stuk van de Inquisitie, ghedaen ende overgegeven aen...dHertoginne van Parme ende Plaisance etc. Bij...Hendrick Heer tot Brederoede...Vergeselschapt met andere Heeren ende Edelen van dese Nederlanden opten v. sten April MDLXVI, naer gemeyn stijl. Mitsgaders dApostille bi haer Hoocheit daer op doen stellen, met tgeen daer van dependeert (Vianen, 1566, KN-138).

Remonstrance a la Majeste du Roy Catholique faite par ses suiets des pays bas, sur les inconveniens qui se resentent, par l'establissement de l'inquisition d'Espagne esdits pays (1566, KN-143).

Responce de la noblesse a la Duchesse de Parme regente &c. sur les articles proposez par les seigneurs Prince d'Orenge & Conte d'Egmont a l'assemblee faicte par les confederez a Saint-Trou... (1566, MPM-A-2213).

Supplication: So im Namen aller Evangelischen Kirchen in Niderlanden, an den Konig ausz Spanien, umb gnedige ab und Einstellung, der vorhabenden Kriegszrustung, geschickt worden (1566, KN-144).

Verclaringhe van die menichvuldighe losse practijcken en listen so van d'Inquisitie, observantie en onderhoudinghe van die Placcaten en andersins, dye de Cardinael

Grandvelle, met zyn adherenten, gheinventeert en ghebruyckt hebben om de vervloecte en Tyrannighe Spaensche Inquisitie in dese vermaerde Eedele Nederlanden in te voeren (1566, ULG-MEUL-124).

Andtorffischer Empörung so sich zwischen den Papisten und den Geusen, als man sie nennet, nechts den 13. 14 und 15 tag Martij zugetragen (1567, KN-153).

Artikelen des Contratz van den generalen peyse ghesloten binnen Antwerpen den veertiensten dach van Meerte MDLXXVII, tusschen den edelen Heere, mijn Heere den Prince van Aurangien den Magistraet ende alle de ghemeyne borgers ende ingesetene der selver stadt (1567, RLB-III-42-952).

De redenen waeromme dat die coomenschappe zeer floreren, de cooplieden zeer multipliceren, ende die Landen des to meer frequenteren en d'Accysen seer augmenteren zullen, ende dat oick al tot zeer groot proffyt van de ghemeyne welvaert (1567, ULL-121-B).

Der predicanten des heylighen Evangelij Jesu Christi binnen Antwerpen, der confessien van Ausburg toeghedaen, vermaninghe tot waerachtighe penitentie, ende vierighen ghebede in dese teghenwoodighe nooden ende periculen aen haere toehoorders (1567, CAA-64/11).

Eenen troostelijcken sentbrief, voor alle die om der waerheyt en om Christus naem vervolcht worden (1567(?), CAA-64/9).

Newe Zeittung, Der Niderlendische Stette, an die Königliche Kron ausz Hispanien ubergeben... (1567, KN-154).

Supplicatien ende requesten uut den name der Christelicker Ghemeynte binnen Antwerpen: Ende van sommigher ghevangenen Broeders ende lidtmaten der selver Ghemeenten wegen: over weynighe Iaren aen de Overicheyt der selve Stadt, en aen andere edele overighe Heeren ghepresenteert ende overghegheven (Antwerp, 1567, KN-152AA).

Vallenzin. Die feste Statt, inn den Grentzen Franckreich und Niderland, von wem und warumb dieselbige belegert... (1567, ULL-THYS-136).

Complainte de la desolée terre du Pais Bas (1568, KN-172).

De Artijckelen ende besluyten der Inquisitie van Spaegnien, om die vande Nederlanden to overvallen ende verhinderen (1568, KN-157B).

Derthien artijckelen: Gheintituleert: Het advijs der Spaengiaerden op den teghenwoordighen staet vanden Nederlanden (Tübingen, 1568, ULG-MRUL-193).

Fidelle exhortation aux inhabitants du pais bas, contre les vains et faux espoirs dont leurs oppresseurs les font amuser (1568, KN-171).

New Erschrockliche und Tyrannische Zeittung ausz den Niderlanden... (1568, KN-158A).

Procedures tenues à l'endroit de ceux de la religion du Pais Bas. Ausquelles est amplement deduit comme Guy du Bres et Peregrin de la Grange fideles ministres à Valenciennes, ont signe par leur sang non seulement la doctrine de l'evangile par eux purement annoncee: mais aussi les derniers assaults, et disputes soustenues contre certains apostats et ennemis de la croix et verité du fils de Dieu (1568, ULL-1368-F30).

Supplication. An die Rom. Keys. Mayestat. Item Chur und Fursten und alle andere des Heyl. Rom. Reichs Stande, auff dem Reichstage zu Speijer, im October ubergeben (1570, KN-184A; trans. of part of *Libellus supplex*, 1570).

Bewijsinghe dat die commissie die Ducq Dalve als Capiteyn Generael over de Nederlanden heeft laten uutgaen, By den Paus met zijn tyrannighe adherenten op den naem vanden Coninck onwetelijcken versiert, gedicht ende hem verleden is (1571, ULG-ACC-MEUL-1571(9)).

Het Advijs, der ijnquizicie van Spaengien bewijzinghe dat in alle de Nederlanden geen Papist oft Catholijcke persoonen en sijn na het geluyt der selver ijnquisicie van Spaengien (1571, KN-191).

Protocol, dat is: alle handelinge der Tsamensprekinghe tot Franckenthal...metten genen diemen Wederdoopers noemt (1571, RLTH-1704-F31).

Waerhafftige Supplicatie ofte Requeste...1571 Maximiliano...Keyser...alletijdt vermeerder des Rijcx, by die Churvorsten, Vorsten, Stenden, unde Verwanten der Augsburger Confession...tot Speyr opten Rijcxdach overgegeven den negenden dach Decembris in jaer 1570 (1571, KN-188).

Eine bewegliche Demonstration zu lob und ehren des...Printzen zu Uranien (1572, KN-198).

Antwoorde ende waerachtighe onderrichtinghe op eenen brief nu onlancx onder den name des Hertoghen van Alba, by forme van pardoen aen die van Aemstelredamme gheschreven... (Delft, 1573, KN-200B).

Copie eens sendtbriefs der Ridderschap, Edelen, ende Steden van Hollandt...aen...die Staten vanden Landen van Herwaerts overe, Hen vermanende, om eendrachtelick ten dienste vande Coninklicke Maiesteyt, die Landen te helpen brenghen in haren ghewoonlicken voorspoet ende vryheyt (Dordrecht, 1573, KN-210).

Sendbrief in forme van supplicatie aen de Conincklijcke Maiesteyt van Spaengien: van wegen des Princen van Oraengien, der Staten van Holland ende Zeeland, mitsgaders alle andere zijne getrouwe ondersaten van desen Nederlanden... Aenwijsende den rechten oorspronck van alle teghenwoordige beroerten indese landen, om daer inne by zijne Coninclijcke Majesteyt voorsien te moghen werden (Delft, 1573, KN-216).

Vriendelicke Vermaninghe aen de...Staten van Brabandt (Delft, 1574, KN-220).

Warachtighe waerschouwinghe teghens de absolute gratie ende generael pardoen by Don Loys de Requesens (Dordrecht, 1574, RLB-LP-793A).

Cort ende warachtich verhael, van het gene dat op de handelinge vanden Vrede nu coreelinghe tusschen den Prince van Oranegien, met die Staten van Hollandt ande Zeelandt...aen de eene zyde: Ende die Spaensche Gouverneure der Nederlanden met den synen aen de andere zijde, tot Breda geschiet is (1575, KN-239).

Certaine letters wherein is set forth a Discourse of the peace that was attempted and sought to have bin put in effecte by the Lords and States of Holland and Zelande in...1574 (London, 1576, KN-242; first pub. in Dutch, as *Sekere brieven waer inne den aenghevanghen vredehandel deses Jaers LXXIIII vervaetet is*, Delft, 1574).

Copie autentyck, Vanden Payse, Verbontenisse ende Unie...besloten ende gheaccordeert tot Ghendt, opten viij, Novembris, 1576 (Delft, 1576).

Vertoog ende openinghe om een goede, salighe ende generale vrede te maken in dese Nederlanden, ende deselven onder de ghehoorsaemheyt des Conincx, in haere oude voorspoedicheyt, fleur ende welvaert te brenghen. By maniere van supplicatie aen de...genereale staten (1576, RLB-II-59-252A).

Copie. Van de redenen ende cort verclaers waeromme het saisissement ende arrest van diversche Heeren binnen Ghent geschiet is den XXVIIJ en Octobris MDLXXVIJ, 15-11-1577 (Ghent, 1577, KN-322).

Response aux lettres de Don Juan d'Austrice sur le faict des troubles derniers advenuz au Pays-Bas (Antwerp, 1577, ULL-VH-26-527).

Sendtbrieven bijde Ridderschappen, Edelen ende Steden van Hollandt, representerende den Staten vanden selven Lande, laestgheschreven ende ghesonden aenden burghermeesteren en regeerders van Amsterdam... (Delft, 1577, KN-277).

Accord ende verbondt ghemaeckt tusschen mijn Heere de Hertoghe van Anjou... ende de Prelaten, Edelen ende ghedeputeerde vande Landen ende Steden, representerende de generale Staten van de Nederlanden (Antwerp, 1578, KN-378).

Articulen ende puncten, geconcipieert bij die generale Staten, waer op... Matthias... van Oostenrijck aengenomen is voor Gouverneur over dese Nederlanden (Leeuwarden, 1578, KN-323).

Lettre contenant l'eclaircissement des actions et deportemens de Monsieur filz & frere de Roy Duc d'Anjou, d'Alençon &c. (Rouen, 1578, KN-360).

Lettre contenant un avis de l'estat auquel sont les affaires des Pais-bas, tant pour le regard des principales provinces & villes en particulier, comme de toutes ensemble en general, avecq la recherche du party, le plus promt & plus asseuré, que les Estats puissent prendre contre l'Espagnol, pour leur conservation & salut (Reims, 1578, KN-358).

Lettre d'un gentilhomme de Haynault, a monsieur de la Mothe, Gouverneur de Gravelines (1578, KN-390).

Openinghe ende Propositie ghedaen van weghen myne Heeren den Bailliu, Schepenen van beede de bancken, beede de Dekenen, Edelen ende Notabelen der Stede van Ghendt ter vergaderinghe vanden drye Leden der selver Stede (Ghent, 1578, ULL-THYS-271).

Openinghe ende vertooch by mijne Heere Schepenen van beede de bancken ende beede de Dekenen aende de drye Leden deser Stede van Ghendt, december 1578 (ULL-VH-27-654).

Ordonnantie ende edict opt faict van beede de religien ghestatueert by Bailliu, Schepenen van beede de bancken, beede de dekenen der stede van Ghendt, by advise van mijnen Heere den Prince van Oraengen ende adveu van de drye leden der selver steden, den 16e decembris, anno 1578 (1578, RLB-LP-1896).

Supplicatie aen sijne Hoocheyt, en Heeren des Raets van State, overgegeven door de inwoonders deser Nederlanden, welcke protesteren dat sy te begeren te leven nae de Reformatie des Evangeliums (1578, KN-363).

Vermaninghe ende raet voor de Nederlanden, waer in doorsake bewesen wort vanden tegenwoordigen inlantschen twist, ende oock de Remedie daer teghen, maer principalijck wort hier bewesen oftmen de conscientien behoort te bedwinghen (1578, KN-369).

Wachtgeschrey. Allen liefhebbers der eeren Gods, des Vaderlandts en der privilegien ende Vryheden des selven tot waerschouwinghe ghestelt (1578, KN-379).

Advertissement à ceulx du pais Bas (1579, KN-423).

Advertissement et conseil au peuple des Pays-Bas (Roucelle, 1579, ULL-THYS-403).

Advijs van eenen liefhebber des Nederlandts (1579, KN-507).

Artikelen des pays vanden Nederlanden, by den Eerwerdichsten, doorluchtichsten, Doorluchtighen, ende Welgeboren heeren Commisarizzen der Keyserlicke Mayesteyt geconcipeert, ende beyde partyen den 18. Julij gecommuniceert (Cologne, 1579, KN-473).

Brief discours sur la negotiation de la paix, qui se tracte presentement à Coloigne entre le Roy d'Espaigne, & les Estats du Pays Bas (Leiden, 1579, KN-492; also pub. as *Petit traicté servant d'instruction à messieurs les estatz et touts bons patriots, à fin qu'ils s'efforcent pour remectre le pais en repos par moyen d'une paix asseuree sans se laisser abuser des offres amiellees qui ne tendent que pour nous reduire soubz le iouq de pristine servitude* (1579, KN-512).

Brieven der Keurvorsten, die te Cuelen versamelt zijn om den Peys vande Nederlanden te maken (Antwerp, 1579, KN-484).

Clare vertoninge ende bericht der articulen ende conditien nu onlancx tot Cuelen inde vredehandel byden Churfursten, Fursten ende andere Keyserlycke Maiesteyts Ghesanten, gheproponeert (1579, KN-500).

Copije des ghenes, soo by den Legaten der Nederlandischen Staten der Cheurvorsten den 4. Julij verthoont is (1579, RLB-LP-883A).

Cort Verhael, op eenighe feyten, der generale Staten van den Nederlanden (1579, KN-405).

De Religions-vrede : Gheaccordeert ende gepubliceert binnen Antwerpen den xijen Junij MDLXXIX (Antwerp, 1579, KN-455/456/457).

Declaratie der redenen ende causen om welcke wille de Schepenen ende wethouders der stede van Ghendt voor den ghewoenelicken tijt en sonder die ghecostumeerde forme te observeren op den 28ste Juli vernieut zijn (Ghent, 1579, MPM-R-16-27).

Discours contenant le vray entendement de la Pacification de Gand, de l'union des Estats & aultres traictez y ensuyviz touchant le faict de la Religion. Par lequel est clairement monstre que le Religionsfridt ne repugne pas ny ne contrarie aucunement a ladicte Pacification, Union, &c. (1579, RLB-VH-26-572A).

Een corte openinghe der causen, waerome het niet raedsam zy, dat de Prince van Oraignen nu ter tijt commen soude binnen der Stede van Ghendt (Ghent, 1579, ULG-GENT-503(1)).

Een goede vermaninghe aen de goede borghers van Bruessele (Ghent, 1579, KN-479).

Een Goede waerschouwinghe voor den borgheren ende besonder dien vanden leden van Antwerpen, dat sy hen niet en souden laten verlocken met het soet aengheven vande bedriechlijcke artijckelen van peyse onlancx ghecomen van Cuelen (1579, KN-493).

Een Vriendlijcke vermaninghe tot allen Liefhebbers der Vryheyt ende des Religions-vreden (1579, KN-426).

Eersame goede mannen, het is nu hooch tijt dat ghy lieden eenmael besluyt oft ghy het Spaensch iock wilt teenemael afleggen ofte niet (1579, KN-427).

Exhortation faicte par monseigneur l'Archiduc d'Austrice, gouverneur & capitaine general des pais bas, aux Estats generaux desdits pais…avec la harangue de messire Elbert Leoninus, Docteur és droits, et Conseiller d'estat (Antwerp, 1579, KN-442).

Openinghe ghedaen den drie leden der Stede van Ghendt, augustus 1579 (Ghent, 1579, MPM-R-16-27).

Poincts et articles par maniere d'instruction, pour estre proposez par monsieur le Duc d'Arschot, & autres Seigneurs deputez par les Estats generaux a l'assemblee qu'on tiendra a Couloigne pour appoincter, deliverer & conclure une bonne et ferme paix, entre le Mate. Catholique nostre Seigneur & Prince naturel & lesdicts Estats generaux, 9-4-1579 (1579, RLB-LP-916A).

Protest van de christelijcke ghemeynte binnen Antwerpen, toeghedaen der Confessien van Ausborch op de articulen vande pacificatie van Nederlant, ghemaeckt tot Cuelen der xviij. Julij (Antwerp, 1579, KN-486).

Protocol, dat is, alle handelinghe des gesprecks tot Embden in Oostvrieslandt, met den wederdooperen (Emden, 1579, RLTH-1701-E14).

Rapport faict par le Seigneur Guillaume vanden Hecke…à messieurs du Magistrat d'icelle ville…reiteré…en l'assemblee des Estats generaux en Anvers (Antwerp, 1579, KN-440).

Remonstrantie oft vertooch in maniere van beclach aen mijne Heeren, de gedeputeerde vande generale Staten, ende vanden gheunieerden Provincien, by den inwoonderen ende ghemeynte der Stadt van Antwerpen, met advijs om te voorsiene tot de quade orden van desen lande (1579, KN-475).

Sommiere verclaringhe vande sware perikelen en de miserien die den inghesetenen van dese Nederlanden te verwachten soude hebben soo verre het concept vande artikelen ende conditien van de pacificatie tot Coelen uytgegeven, ende voorts al omme in dese landen gestroyt, gevolcht ende aengenomen worde (Leiden, 1579, KN-490).

Verhandelinghe van de Unie, eeuwigh Verbont ende Eendracht (Utrecht, 1579, KN-407).

Vriendelijcke waerschouwinghe aen de Staten van Artois, van Henegouwen en van Douay (1579, KN-422).

Advertissement et conseil au peuple des pays-bas (1580, MPM-R-16-26; MPM-R-16-13).

Articulen gheraemt en ghestelt by myn Heere den Prince van Oraengnen en de ghedeputeerde Heeren van de Generale Staten, op den welcken men zoude moghen handelen met mijn Heere den Hertoghe van Anjou (1580, RLB-LP-947A).

Treuwe Vorwarnung und guthertziger hochzeitiger raht an das betrangte Volck inn Nederland auss billichem und schuldigem Mitleiden inn gegenwartigen misslichen laufften gestellet (1580, RLB-LP-936A).

Broederlijcke waerschouwinghe: aen allen Christen broeders, die van God verordent sijn tot de verkiesinghe der Overicheyt ende Magistraten inde Steden der gheunieerde Provincien (Antwerp, 1581, KN-577).

Discours faict par un gentilhomme Tournesien, a un Seigneur de Henault, sur le droit que Monseigneur d'Anjou fils de France, à de faire guerre au Roy d'Espaigne (1581, KN-553).

Een trouwe waerschouwinghe aen de goede mannen van Antwerpen (Antwerp, 1581, KN-575).

Sommaire discours sur le moyen de conserver, et maintenir la vraye religion christiene, & garder & assuerer les provinces unies (1581, KN-574).

Antwoorde der Dienaren des Woordts ende ouderlinghen der kercken van Hollandt…op de Remonstrantie by de overicheyt van Leyden (Delft, 1582, KN-622).

Cort eenvoudich ende waerachtich verhael waeromme Caspar Coolhaes…byden Synode

Provinciael van Hollandt vander kercke Christi is gheexcommuniceert (Dordrecht, 1582, KN-624).

De blijde ende heerlijcke Incomste van mijnheer Franssois van Vranckrijck ... in sijne zeer vermaerde stadt van Antwerpen (Antwerp, 1582, KN-586).

Politicq onderwijs (Mechelen, 1582, KN-581).

Premiere apologie pour Monseigneur, et les Estats des Pays-Bas (1582, KN-613).

Discours verclaerende wat forme ende manier van regieringhe dat die Nederlanden voor die alderbeste ende zekerste tot desen tyden aenstellen mochten (1583, KN-651).

Een Christelijcke waerachtige Waerschouwinge ende wederlegghinge ... (1583, KN-657).

Een claer vertooch der heymelijcke raetslaghen ende practijcken die de ghemeyne vyanden ghebruycken om dese Nederlanden wederomme der Spaensche tyrannie ende Inquisitie te onderworpen (1583, KN-661).

Een ootmoedich vertooch ende eenvoudighe verclaringhe vanden eenighe middel, waer deur men voordaen dese arme Nederlanden sal behoeden van voorder verwoestinghe (1583, KN-658).

Spraecke ghehouden tusschen twee vrienden, den eenen wesende vande ghereformeerde, ende den anderen vande Martinisten religie (1583, ULG-GENT-MEUL-548(1)).

Van den staet der tegenwoordiger Nederlandtsche regierung (1583, KN-652A).

Vriendelick Vertooch. Daerby ghediscoureert werdt wat middelen dese bedruckte Landen te wercke moghen legghen tot haerlieder conservatie en onderhout van de Religie, Liberteyt ende Privilegien (1583, ULG-MEUL-561).

Waerschouwinghe aen alle goede inghesetenen vanden Nederlanden, die tot beschermenisse vande vrijheydt van hunne Religie, persoonen, Previlegien, ende oude hercomen, teghens die tyrannie vande Spaingnaerden ende heuren aenhanck, t'samen verbonden en vereenicht sijn (1583, KN-656).

Discours van eenen oprechten, onpartijdighen ende ongheveynsden Patriot opden teghenwoordighen staet van dese Nederlantsche Provincien (1584, KN-704).

Een advertissement aen de goede Patriotten ende inwoonders des Vaderlandts, nopende den rechten middelen om te bewaren ons Vaderlantsche Vryheyt ... (1584, MPM-R-12-11, 35).

Het beclach vande Stadt van Ghent, waer in sy verhaelt ende beclaecht de ruwine ende verderfenisse, waer inne si ghecomen is, deur den raet ende het toedoen van heur Spaensche gesinde tot waerschouwinghe van alle vreedsamighe steden (1584, ULL-THYS-592).

Middelen ende conditien door de welcke d'Inghesetenen der gheunieerde Provincien, met der Majesteyt vanden Coninck van Spaignen, haren natuerlicken Heere, met goeder conscientie, mits behoorlicke versekertheyt zouden moghen accorderen (1584, KN-676).

Remonstrantie by forme van discours aen allen en eenen yeghelijcken Landen, Provintien, Steden en Ghemeenten, inhoudende t'Epitaphium op de doot des ... Prince van Oraingien (Delft, 1584, KN-697).

Verhael vande rechte middelen om so wel den standt van de ghemeynse saecke als de Religie in den Nederlanden te moghen behouden (1584, KN-702).

Vertooch aen mijn Heeren de Staten Generael op de wederoprichtinghe ende behoudenisse vanden Staet der Nederlanden (1584, KN-700).

Vertoogh ghedaen der inghesetenen der Stede van Ghendt, verclaerende, waerom die reconciliatie, so wel met den Spaignaerden als mit den Franchoysen niet radtsaem en sy (Ghent, 1584, ULG-GENT-7432).

Antwoorde vande Ridderschap, Edelen ende meeste Steden van Hollandt ende Westvrieslandt op de verclaringhe ende Remonstrantie van syne Excell (Delft, 1587, KN-786).

Naerder verclaringhe van de Staten van Hollandt waerby int corte verthoont wort dat de poincten aen zijne Excie, binnen Dordrecht versocht, zijn nootelick voor de welstant der Landen, en dat sonder het onderhout der selver, de Landen daerinnen niet gheconserveert en moghen worden (Delft, 1587, KN-789).

Remonstrantie by de Ridderschap, Eedelen ende Steden van Hollandt ende West-Vrieslandt, ghepresenteert aen syne Excellentie binnen der Stadt Dordrecht in Augusto, XVe zevenentachtich (Delft, 1587, KN-782).

Seyndtbrief ... aen de Staten slandts van Holland (Utrecht, 1587, KN-798).

Vertooch ende Remonstrantie by ... Robert Grave van Leycester ... ghedaen aen den Staten Generael ... den vij. September anno 1587 stilo novo (Dordrecht, 1587, KN-784).

Levende-Kalck waarmede Dirijck Koornharts Zeepe lichtelijck te niet wert gemaackt (1607, KN-671; first pub. 1583).

Disputatie over den Catechismus van Heydelbergh, openbaarlijck voor den Volcke ghehouden op't Hof van s'Gravenhage in Hollandt, anno 1583 (Gouda, 1617, KN-673).

Alardts, Francoys, *Een heerlicke troostbrief van des mensen leven ende wesen* (1567, BLL-35-05-de3; CAA-64/13).

Albada, Aggaeus van, *Acten van den Vredehandel gheschiet te Colen* (Antwerp, 1581, RLTH-1703-E39).

Barbier, Gervais, *Conseil sacré d'un Gentilhomme Francois aux Eglises de Flandre, qui peut servir d'humble exhortation a l'excellence des tresillustres Princes Protestans du Sainct Empire: et d'advertissement certain aux seigneurs des Pais Bas* (Antwerp, 1567, KN-152).

Bartolus of Sassoferrato, *De tyranno*, in Quaglioni (ed.), *Politica e diritto nel trecento Italiano*, 171–213.

In prima Codicis partem (Turin, 1589).

Beutterich, Petrus, *Le vray patriot aux bons patriots* (1578, KN-392).

Bloccius, Petrus, *Een claghe Jesu Christi, tot dat ongehoorsaeme menschelijcke gheslachte, seer profijtelijck ende nuttelijck in dese perijckeloose ende vaerlycke tijden voor alle den ghenen die den Heere van herten begheert na te volghen* (Delft, 1595, RLTH-1703-D29; first pub. 1562).

Meer dan tweehondert ketterijen, blesphemien, en nieuwe leeringen welcx uut de misse zyn ghecomen (1566, RLTH-1708-E15).

Bor, Pieter Christiaansz, *Oorsprongk, begin en vervolgh der Nederlantsche oorlogen, beroerten en borgerlijke oneenigheden*, i and ii (Amsterdam, 1679; first pub. 1595).

Bray, Guy de(?), *Confession de foy. Faicte d'un commun accord par les fideles qui conversent és Pais Bas, lesquels desirent vivre selon la purete de l'Evangile de nostre*

Seigneur Jesus Christ. Geneve. Presentee au Roy d'Espagne (Rouen, 1561, RLTH-1714-E15).

De wortel, den oorsponck ende het fundament der wederdooperen oft herdooperen van onsen tijde (Amsterdam, 1589, RLTH-1702-F36; Dutch trans. of *La Racine, source et fondement des anabaptistes ou rebaptisez de nostre temps* (1565)).

Declaration sommaire du faict de ceux de la ville de Valencienne (1566, KN-145).

Oraison au seigneur, contenant les gemissements, et complaintes des poures fideles espers per le pais bas, Flandre, Artois, Hainaut et autres contrées : affamez du desir de la predications de l'evangile, et pure administration des sacraments du seigneur (1564, RLTH-1714-E6).

(?), *Remonstrance et supplication de ceus de l'eglise reformée de la ville de Valenciennes sur le mandement de son Altesse, fait contre eus le 14. jour de Decembre 1566, a messeigneurs les chevaliers de l'ordre* (1567, MPM-A-2213).

Brederode, Hendrik van, *Copie de la lettre escripte par le Seigneur Brederode, tant en son nom, que au nom des Gentilzhommes confederez, du VIIIe de Fevrier XVe Soixante Sept...* (Brussels, 1567, KN-151).

C.D.W., *Een troostelicke sendtbrief aen de Christen ghemeynte der reynder bekentenisse, van den edelen wygaert onses Heeren Jesu Christi, doer syn goddelijck woordt gheplantet binnen Antwerpen* (1567, CAA-64/12).

Calvin, John, *Institutes of the Christian religion*, ii (Grand Rapids, Mich., 1983; trans. of the definitive 1559 edn.).

Castaldus, Restaurus, 'De imperatore', in *Duodecimum Volumen Tractatuum e variis iuris interpretibus collectorum* (Lyons, 1549).

Cicero, *De officiis*, Loeb edn. (Cambridge, Mass., 1975).

Clerq, Gilles le, *Remonstrantie ofte vertoogh aen den grootmachtigen Coninck van Spaengen etc. op de Requeste byden Edeldom der Co. M. erfnederlanden den 5. april 1565 aen mijn Vrouwe de Hertoginne van Parme gepresenteert* (Antwerp, 1566, KN-139B).

Coolhaes, Caspar, *Apologia. Een Christelijcke ende billijcke verantwoordinge Caspari Coolhaessen, Dienaer des Goddelijcken woorts tot Leyden* (1580, KN-548A).

Breeder bericht van de scheuringe der kercken Christi tot Leyden (1580, KN-548B).

Conciliatio : Dat is verghelijckinghe van sekere poincten der Leere (Gouda, 1585, KN-758).

Een christelijcke vermaninghe aen alle onpartydighe Predicanten (1584, KN-716).

Seekere poincten uut die Heylighe Godtlijcke Schriftuer (1584, KN-717).

Sendtbrief Caspars Coolhaes, dienaers des godlicken woorts, residerende tot Leyden (1582, KN-623(.

Toutzsteen tot een seekere proeve welcx in der waerheydt die Apostolische, Catholijcke, Evangelische, Gereformeerde reyne kercke sy (1584, KN-718).

Cooltuyn, Cornelis, *Dat Evangeli der Armen* (1559, RLTH-1705-G30; repr. in S. Cramer and F. Pijper (eds.), *BRN*, ix (The Hague, 1912), 217–480).

Coornhert, Dirck Volckertsz, 'Dolingen des Catechismus, anderwerven blijckende in des selfs proeve', in Coornhert, *Wercken*, vol. ii, fols. 268–340.

Justificatie des Magistraets tot Leyden in Hollant (1579, KN-516).

Middel tot mindringe der Secten ende Partijschappen staende dese inlantsche

Oorloghen tot dat by gemeene eendracht daer in voorsien sal zijn (Haarlem, 1582, ULL-1498-F15-7).

'Overweginghe van de teghenwoordighe gelegentheyt der Nederlantsche saken', in Coornhert, *Wercken*, vol. i, fols. 551–4.

'Proces van't ketterdooden ende dwangh der Conscientien. Tusschen Justum Lipsium…ende Dirck Coornhert. Het eerste deel politijck' (1589), in Coornhert, *Wercken*, vol. ii, fols. 42–109.

'Proces van't ketterdooden ende dwangh der Conscientien. Tusschen Wolfaert Bisschop, Advocaet van Theodore de Beza…ende Dirck V. Coornhert. Het tweede deel, Kerckelijck' (1589), in Coornhert, *Wercken*, vol. ii, fols. 109–73.

Proeve van de Heydelbergsche Catechismo (1582, KN-625).

Remonstrance of vertooch by die van Leyden (1582, KN-621).

'Synodus van der Conscientien Vryheydt' (1582), in Coornhert, *Wercken*, vol. ii, fols. 1–42.

Wercken, 3 vols. (Amsterdam, 1630, RLTH-3200-C3/4/5).

'Wortel der Nederlantsche oorloghen met aenwijsinghe tot inlantsche eendracht' (1590), in Coornhert, *Wercken*, vol. ii, fols. 173–83.

Coornhert, Frans, *Cort Onderwijs eens Liefhebbers des welstandts deser Nederlanden, waerinne allen Christenen, goede ghemeenten en Patriotten claerlijck bewesen wort: Dat het wel gheoorloft is tegen te staen een Coning ofte Here vande landen, die Godt ende zijn heylich woort onderstaet te verdrijven ende…de selve Landen onderstaet te beroven van hare gherechticheyden, Privilegien, ende Vrijheyden* (Amsterdam, 1586, KN-767).

Copius, Baltasar, *Vier en vijftich Predicatien over den Christelijcken en in Gods woort ghegronden Cathechismum, die inder kercken ende scholen deser Nederlanden ende der keur-Vorstelijcke Paltz gepredickt en geleert wort* (Amsterdam, 1590, RLTH-1708-D22).

Cornelisz, Arent, and Donteclock, Reinier, *Ondersoeck des ongehoorden middels, onlangs verciert and uutghegheven van Dirck Volckertsz. Cornhert, tot minderinge der Secten ende partijschappen* (Delft, 1582, ULA-402-G27).

Remonstrantie aen mijn Heeren de Staten slandts van Hollandt (Delft, 1582, KN-672).

Wederlegginghe eens boecxkens ghenoemt proeve vanden Nederlandsche catechismo by D. Cornhert (Delft, 1585, RLTH-1702-C37).

Corro, Antonio, *Epistre et amiable Remonstrance d'un ministre de l'evangile de nostre Redempteur…envoyee aux pasteurs de eglise Flamengue d'Anvers lesquelz se nomment de la Confession d'Augsbourg, les exhortant a concorde et amitie avec les autres ministres de l'evangile* (1567, KN-152A).

Dathenus, Peter, *Catechismus ofte onderwijsinghe in de christelijcke leere gelijck in die kercken en scholen der cheurvorstelicken Paltz ghedreven oft gheleert wordt* (1566, RLTH-1714-E29).

Een christelijcke verantwoordinghe op die disputatie, ghehouden binnen Oudenaerde, tusschen M. Adriaen Hamstadt, ende Jan Daelman beschreven met onwaerheyt, ende uutghegheven door Jan Daelman voorseyt, 2nd edn. (Antwerp, 1582, MPM-R-23-4; first pub. 1559).

Erasmus, Desiderius, 'Moriae Encomium id est stultitiae laus' (Praise of

Folly), in Desiderius Erasmus, *Opera Omnia. Desiderii Erasmi Roterodami*, series 4, vol. iii, ed. Clarence Miller (Amsterdam, 1979), 67–196.

Gnapheum, Wilhelmum, *Tobias ende Lazarus mit grooter neersticheyt ghecorrigeert, verbetert, ende in die Dialogus oft t'samen sprekinghe, underscheydelicken ghedeelt, alle krancken, bedroefden, ende eenvoudighe menschen seer profytelick om te lesen* (Emden, 1557, ULG-GENT-343(1)).

Grotius, Hugo, *Tractaet vande Oudtheyt vande Batavische nu Hollandsghe Republique* (The Hague, 1610, KN-1735).

Guicciardini, Lodovico, *Descrittione di tutti i Paesi Bassi* (Antwerp, 1581).

Haemstede, Adriaen Cornelis van, *De geschiedenisse ende den doodt der vromer martelaren, die om het ghetuyghenisse des Evangeliums haer bloedt ghestort hebben, van den tijden Christi af totten jare 1559 toe, bijeen vegadert op het kortste* (1559, RLB-VB-8631E).

Vermanighe tot de Overheyt (1559), in Haemstede, *De geschiedenisse ende den doodt der vromer martelaren.*

or Wybo, Joris(?), *Historie ende geschiedenisse van de verradelicke ghevangenisse der vromer ende godsaligher mannen, Christophorij Fabritij dienaer des goddelicken woords binnen Antwerpen ende Oliverij Bockij professeur der Latijnsche sprake in de hooghe en vermaerde schole van Heydelberch* (1565, RLB-VH-26-244A; repr. in S. Cramer and F. Pijper (eds.), *BRN* viii (The Hague, 1911), 282–460).

Historien oft geschiedenissen der vromer martelaren, die om het ghetuyghenisse des Evangely haer bloet vergoten hebben, van den tijde Christi af, tot den jar MDLXXIX toe... Wederom van nieus oversien, verbetert ende veel vermeerdert (Dordrecht, 1579, RLB-VB-8631F).

Heere, Lucas d', *Beschrijvinghe van het ghene dat vertoocht werd ter incomste van dExcellentie des Princen van Orangien binnen der stede van Ghendt, den xxix. Decembris, anno 1577* (1577, RLB-VH-26-530A).

Hoefnaghel, Joris, *Traité de la Patience* (1569), in *Patientia. 24 politieke emblemata door Joris Hoefnaghel*, ed. R. van Roosbroeck (Antwerp, 1935).

Houwaert, Jean Baptist, *De Vier Uuterste, van de doot, van het oordeel, van d'eeuwich leven, van de pyne der hellen* (Antwerp, 1583, RLB-1497-C29).

Oratie der Ambassadeuren vanden doorluchtighen Prince Matthias Aertshertoge van Oostenrijck, etc. Gouverneur van die Nederlanden (Antwerp, 1578, ULG-ACC-MEUL-1578(16)).

Sommaire bechrijvinghe van de triumphelijcke incomst vanden... Aerts-hertoge Matthias binnen... Brussel (Antwerp, 1578, KN-329).

Illyricus, Matthias Flacius, and Houwaert, Balthazar, *Corte verantwoordinghe oft bescherminghe der confessien oft bekentenisse des gheloofs der Christelijcken ghemeinten van Antwerpen der Ausborcher Confessien toegedaen* (1567, CAA-64/2).

Ionghe, Johan Junius de, 'Discourse', in *Certaine letters wherein is set forth a Discourse of the peace that was attempted and sought to have bin put in effecte by the Lords and States of Holland and Zelande in... 1574* (London, 1576, KN-242).

Junius, Franciscus, *Een corte verhalinge gesonden aen Coninc Philips... tot welvaert ende profijt sijnder Maiesteit, ende sonderlinghe van syne Nederlanden* (1566; KN-144A first pub. in French, as *Brief discours envoyé au roy Philippe nostre sire et souverain Seigneur, pour le bien et profit de la Maiesté, et singulierement de ses pays bas, auquel est monstré le moyen qu'il faudroit tenir pour obvier aux troubles et emotions pour le faict de la religion, et extirper les sectes et heresies pullulantes en sesdicts pays* (1566, UNG-Meulm 1565(3)).

Junius, Brutus, *A defence of liberty against tyrants: a translation of the 'Vindiciae contra tyrannos' by Junius Brutus with an historical introduction by Harold J. Laski* (London, 1924).

Kiele, Jan van den, *Redene exhortatyf* (Antwerp, 1582, ULL-1497-G4).

L.P., *Een schoone christelijcke waerschouwinghe, om alle grouwelicke ende verdoemelicke dwalinghen ofte secten (waerdoor in dese ghevaerlicker tijdt veel eenvoudighe christen jammerlicken vervoert worden) te schouwen* (1568, RLTH-1702-G8).

Leoninus, Elbertus, *Waerachtighe antwoorde op de opene brieven ende bedrieghelicke persuasien van don Jan van Oostenryck...* (Antwerp, 1578, KN-339).

Lipsius, Justus, *Sixe bookes of politickes or civile doctrine, written in Latine by Iustus Lipsius: which doe especially concerne Principalitie* (London, 1594; repr. in The English experience, no. 287, Amsterdam, 1970).

Twee boecken van de Stantvasticheyt (Leiden, 1584, MPM-R-573).

Machiavelli, Niccolò, 'Discorsi sopra la prima deca di Tito Livio', in Niccolò Machiavelli, *Tutte le opere* (Florence, 1971), 73–254.

Marnix, Philips van St Aldegonde(?), *A Defence and true Declaration of the things lately done in the lowe Countrey whereby may easily be seen to whom all the beginning and cause of the late troubles and calamities is to be imputed* (London, 1571, RLTH-1709-F17; trans. of *Libellus supplex Imperatoriae Maiestati*, 1570, KN-179).

Advis d'un affectione au bien publique a la bourgeoisie d'Anvers (1580, KN-534).

Advys aengaende den twist in de Nederduytsche kercke tot London in Engellandt 1568, in *Philips van Marnix van St. Aldegonde*, ed. van Toorenenbergen, i, 135–82.

Cort Verhael vande rechte oorsaecken ende redenen die de Generale Staten ghedwongen hebben, hen te versiene tot hunder beschermenisse, teghen den Heer Don Jehan van Oostenrijck (Antwerp, 1577, KN-310).

Ernstighe vermaninghe vanden standt ende ghelegentheyt der Christenheyt, ende vande middelen haerder behoudenisse ende welvaren (1583, KN-627).

Oraison des ambassadeurs du serenissime prince Matthias archiduc d'austriche &c. Gouverneur des pais bas: & des Estats generaux desdits pais (Antwerp, 1578, KN-355).

(?), *Oratio ecclesiarum Christi* (1566), in van Toorenenbergen, *Eene bladzijde uit de geschiedenis der Nederlandsche geloofsbelijdenis*, pp. lxv–xcvii.

Philips van Marnix van St. Aldegonde: Godsdienstige en kerkelijke geschriften, i, ed. J. J. van Toorenenbergen (The Hague, 1871).

Responce d'un bon patriot et bourgeois de la ville de Gand au libelle fameux... (1583, KN-633).

Van de Beelden afgheworpen in de Nederlanden in Augosto 1566, in *Philips van Marnix van St. Aldegonde*, ed. J. J. van Toorenenbergen, 3–34.

Vraye Narration et apologie des choses passees au Pays-Bas, touchant le fait de la religion en l'an MDLXVI (1567), in *Philips van Marnix van St. Aldegonde*, ed. J. J. van Toorenenbergen, 35–133.

Michaellam, Johannes, *De collecteur des nieuwen boeckskens. Geïntituleert uutsprake van der kerkcken etc. gedruckt anno 1567. Bevesticht ende bewijst breeder met wichtighen redenen ende ook by publiken acten der protestanten ende predikanten, so wel in Vranckricke als in den Nederlanden t'gene dat hy van het ampt en officie der Overheit over den onderdanen ende wederomme der onderdanen tot heure, geschreven heeft in den voornoemden boeckskens: mit verklaringe syns naems* (1567, RLTH-1704-F12(2)).

(?), *Uutsprake van der Kercke of Ghemeynte Godes: welcke, wat ende hoedanich sy sy* (1567, RLTH-1704-F12(1)).

Micron, Marten, *De christlicke ordinancien der Nederlantscher Ghemeinten Christi... te London* (London, 1554; re-ed. W. F. Dankbaar, *Marten Micron: de Christlicke ordinancien der Nederlantscher Ghemeinten te London (1554)* (The Hague, 1956)).

De kleyne catechismus, oft kinderleere der Duytscher ghemeynte van London (London, 1561, RLTH-7-C16-2).

Een waerachteghe historie van Hoste (gheseyt Jooris) van der Katelyne, te Ghendt om het vry opentlick straffen der afgodischer leere, ghebrant, ten grooten nutte ende vertroostinghe aller christenen (Emden, 1555, RLB-VH-25-260; repr. in F. Pijper (ed.), *BRN*, vol. viii, (The Hague, 1911), 187–253).

Moded, Herman, *Apologie ofte verantwoordinghe Hermanni Modedt teghens de calumnien ende valsche beschuldinghen ghestroeyet, tot lasteringhe des H. Evangelij, ende zijnen persoon door de vianden der christelijcker religie* (1567), repr. in G. J. Brutel de la Rivière (ed.), *Het leeven van Hermannus Moded, een der eerste Calvinistische predikers in ons vaderland* (Haarlem, 1879).

Montanus, Eusebius, *Een clare beantwoordinge wt Gods Woort op dese vraghe oft een Christelicke Onder-overheyt, haerder hoogher-overheyt, dewelcke om der oeffeninghe der warer religie, over haer Ondersaten, met confiscatie aller Privilegien, lijfs ende goets, tyranniseert, met vrijer conscientie wederstaen mach* (Middelburg, 1588, KN-852; BLL-T-1716(41)).

Mornay, Philippe de (Philippe Duplessis-Mornay), *Discours sur la permission de liberte de religion, dicte Religions-vrede au Pais Bas* (1579, KN-425).

Orange, William of, *Alle ende elckerlicken Capiteynen, Volck van wapenen ende anderen goeden ende ghetrovven Crijchsluyden van Nederlant, wenschet de Prince van Oraengien... gheluck ende salicheyt* (1568, KN-170A).

Apologie, ofte verantwoordinghe des doerluchtighen ende hooghgeborenen Vorsts ende Heeren, Heeren Wilhelms van Godes ghenade prince van Orangien (Leiden, 1581, KN-554); English edn.: *The Apologie of Prince William of Orange against the proclamation of the king of Spaine*, ed. H. Wansink (Leiden, 1969).

Corte vermaninghe aende naerdere gheunierde Provincien ende Steden der Nederlanden (1580, KN-526).

D. Guilielmi Nassavii Principis Avrantii etc. Germaniam inferiororem libertati vindicantis ad ordines et poulum denuntiatio. 16 junij 1572 (KN-194; also in Bor (ed.), *Oorsprongk der Nederlantsche oorlogen*, 131–40).

Remonstrantie ghedaen bij zijne Excellentie binnen Antwerpen. Desen eersten dach van December, 1581 (1582, MPM-R1-12).

Verantwoordinghe des Princen van Oraengien (1568, KN-161), repr. in Schenk (ed.), *Prins Willem van Oranje*, 23–98.

Verklaringhe ende uutschrift des Duerluchtighsten, Hoochgeborenen Vorsten ende Heeren... Willem, Prince van Oranien, etc. ende zijner Excellentien nootsakelicken Defensie teghen den Duca de Alba, ende zijne grouwelicke tyrannie (1568, KN-164), repr. in Schenk (ed.), *Prins Willem van Oranje*, 99–116.

Waerschouwinge des Princen van Oraegnien, aende inghesetenen ende ondersaten van den Nederlanden (1568, KN-168), in Schenk (ed.), *Prins Willem van Oranje*, 117–28.

Willem... Prince toe Orangien, Grave toe Nassaw... Allen ondersaten des Con. Mai. in den Nederlanden, Salyt (1568, KN-167A).

Pneumenander, *Vermaninghe aen die gemeyne Capiteynen ende Krijchsknechten in Nederlandt* (1568, ULG-MEUL-187).

Prouninck van Deventer, Gerard, *Antwoorde teghens verscheyde quade opspraken die hem by sommige persoonen van de teghenwoordighe regeringhe onwaerachtelijck zijn nagehouden* (Utrecht, 1587, ULL-THYS-696; also in Bor, *Oorsprongk der Nederlantsche oorlogen*, ii, 914–18).

Een corte errinneringhe ende waerschouwinghe opt schandelyck verraedt daer mit de Colonnel Stanle ende Hopman Jorck de Stadt Deventer ende de schanse teghens Zutphen, den Spaengiaerden om gelt verraden ende ghelevert hebben (Utrecht, 1587, ULL-THYS-313).

Emanuel–Erneste. Dialogue de deux personnages sur l'Estat du Pais Bas (Antwerp, 1580, KN-545).

Saliger, Johannis, *Een troostelijcken Seyndtbrief, ghesonden aen die Christelicke gemeente Christi, tot Antwerpen* (Wesel, 1567, ULG-ACC-1389).

Sallust, *Bellum Jugurthinum*, in *Sallust*, Loeb edn. (Cambridge, Mass., 1985).

Saravia, Adrianus, *Een hertgrondighe begheerte van den edelen, lanckmoedighen hoochgeboren Prince van Oraengien* (1568), repr. in Schenk (ed.), *Prins Willem van Oranje*, 129–55.

Schetz, Caspar, Heer van Grobbendock(?), *Grondelycke onderrichtinghe aen de gemeene inghesetenen van Nederlandt* (Cologne, 1579, KN-498).

Schuere, Nicasius van der, *Een cleyne of corte Institute, dat is onderwysinghe der Christelijcker Religie* (Ghent, 1581, ULG-GENT-302).

Soto, Domingo de, *Libri decem de Iustitia et Iura* (Lyons, 1569).

Spangenberg, M. Cyr, *Notwendige Warnunge an alle Ehrliebende Deutsche Kriegsleute* (1568, KN-154B).

Steven, Simon, *Het Burgherlick Leven* (Leiden, 1590; repr. Amsterdam, 1939).

Taffin, Jean, *Onderwijsinghe teghens de dwalinghe der wederdooperen* (Haarlem, 1590, RLTH-1703-A13).

Veluanus, Anastasio, *Kort bericht in alle principalen punten des christen geloves, mit klair ghetuichnis der hilligher schriffturen un guede kunstschafft der alden doctoren, mit anwysung wanneer unde durch welcke personen die erroren opgestanden unde vermeert zijnen, bereit vur den simpelen ongelerden christen, un is des halven genant der leken wechwyser* (Strasburg, 1554), repr. in S. Cramer and F. Pijper (eds.), *BRN* iv (The Hague, 1906), 123–376.

Verheyden, W., *Considerations necessaires sur un traicté avec l'espagnol* (1587, ULL-THYS-743).

Nootelijcke consideratien die alle goede liefhebbers des Vaderlandts bohooren rijpelijck te overweghen opten voorgeslaghen Tractate van Peys met den Spaengiaerden (1587, KN-816).

Vranck, François, *Corte vertoninghe van het recht byden Ridderschap, Eedelen ende Steden van Hollandt ende Westvrieslant van allen ouden tijden in den voorschreven Lande gebruyckt tot behoudenisse vande vryheden, gherechticheden, Privilegien ende Loffelicke ghebruycken vanden selven Lande* (Rotterdam, 1587, KN-790). See also Bor, *Oorsprongk der Nederlantsche oorlogen*, ii, 921–9.

Wesembeeke, Jacob van, *Corte Vermaninghe aen alle christenen oft vonnisse oft advis, met grooter wreetheit te wercke ghestelt teghen Heer Anthonis van Stralen, Borghemeester van Antwerpen ende commissaris generael vanden Staten der Nederlanden* (1569, ULU-PAMFLET-43).

De beschriivinge van den geschiedenissen in der Religien saken toegedraghen in den Nederlanden (1569, KN-147).

De bewijsinghe vande onschult van mijn heere Philip Baenreheere van Montmorency, Grave van Hoorne etc. (1568, RLTH-1704-F27).

La defence de Jacques de Wesenbeke jadis conseiller et pensionnaire de la ville d'Anvers, contre les indevës et iniques citations contre luy décrétées (1569, RLB-VH-26-464), in Rahlenbeck (ed.), *Mémoires de Jacques de Wesenbeke*, 1–45.

La défense de messire Antoine de Lalaing, comte de Hoochstrate (Mons, 1838; first pub. 1568).

Wilkes, Thomas, *Remonstrance* (1587), in Bor, *Oorsprongk der Nederlantsche oorlogen*, ii. 918–21.

Zuttere, Pieter de, *Een saechtmoedighe tsamensprekinghe van Cephas ende Arnolbius* (Ghent, 1581, ULG-GENT-301).

Eyne korte bewysung mit die getuygenis der heyliger Schrift, hoe dat alle rechte gelovige der sunden gestorven syndt, und in Christo warachtich leven (1563, ULG-GENT-7989(2)).

Eyne korte Leerung wie dat alle Geloovigen in Christo, alss eyn koren in der aerden, hitze und kalde lyden, unde sterven moeten, eer dat men tot den eewigen leven, in Christo vermenichfuldicht, unde hondertfalt fruchten fortbrengt (1563, ULG-GENT-7989(1)).

Eyne korte unde eynvaldige underwisung uut die Goddelicke Schrift, of man oock lasteren, ordeylen und schelten sal tegen die ongeloovige Secten und Gotzlasteren. Item eyne korte Leerung, wie dat Marter geyn Christen maeckt : unde geyn Christen ungemartert is (1563, ULG-GENT-7989(0)).

CATALOGUES OF PAMPHLETS

Knuttel, W. P. C., *Catalogus van de Pamfletten-verzameling berustende in de koninklijke bibliotheek*, i (The Hague, 1889) (KN).

Petit, L. D., *Bibliotheek van Nederlandse pamfletten. Verzameling van Joannes Thysius en de bibliotheek der rijksuniversiteit te Leiden*, i (The Hague, 1882).

Tiele, J. P., *Bibliotheek van Nederlandsche pamfletten. Eerste afdeling. Verzameling van Frederik Muller te Amsterdam*, i (Amsterdam, 1858).

Wulp, J. K. van der, *Catalogus van de tractaten, pamfletten, enz. over de geschiedenis van Nederland, aanwezig in de bibliotheek van Is. Meulman*, i (Amsterdam, 1866).

SECONDARY SOURCES

Abel, Günter, *Stoizismus und frühe Neuzeit: zur Entstehungsgeschichte des modernen Denkens im Felde von Ethik und Politic* (Berlin, 1978).

Allen, J. W., *A history of political thought in the sixteenth century*, rev. edn. (London, 1957).

Arnould, Maurice-A., 'Le lendemain de Nancy dans les "pays de par deça"', Janvier–Avril 1477', in Blockmans (ed.), *1477*, 1–78.

Ashcraft, Richard, *Revolutionary politics and Locke's 'Two Treatises of Government'* (Princeton, NJ, 1986).

Augustijn, C., 'Godsdienst in de zestiende eeuw', in *Ketters en papen*, 26–40.

Avonds, P., 'Beschouwingen over het onstaan en de evolutie van het saamhorigheidsbesef in de Nederlanden (14de–19de eeuw)', in *Cultuurgeschiedenis in de Nederlanden van de Renaissance naar de Romantiek* (Leuven, 1986), 45–58.

Brabant tijdens de regering van Hertog Jan III (1312–1356): de grote politieke krisissen (Brussels, 1984).

Backhouse, M. F., 'The official start of armed resistance in the Low Countries: Boeschepe 12 July 1562', *Archiv für Reformationsgeschichte* 71 (1980), 198–212.

Baelde, M., *De collaterale raden onder Karel V en Filips II, 1531–1578: bijdrage tot de geschiedenis van de centrale instellingen in de zestiende eew* (Brussels, 1965).

and Peteghem, P. van, 'De pacificatie van Gent (1576)', in *Opstand en pacificatie*, 1–62.

Bakhuizen van den Brink, J. N., *De Nederlandse belijdenisgeschriften* (Amsterdam, 1976).

Bergsma, Wiebe, *Aggaeus van Albada (c. 1525–1587), schwenckfeldiaan, staatsman en strijder voor verdraagzaamheid* (Meppel, 1985).

Berkel, K. van, 'Aggaeus de Albada en de crisis in de Opstand (1579–1587)', *BMGN* 96 (1981), 1–25.

Bie, J. P. de, Lindeboom, J., Itterzoon, G. P. van, and Nauta, D., *Biografisch woordenboek van protestantsche godgeleerden in Nederland*, 5 vols. (The Hague, 1907–43).

Black, Anthony, 'Society and the individual from the Middle Ages to Rousseau: philosophy, jurisprudence and constitutional theory', *HPT* 1 (1980), 145–66.

Blockmans, W. P., 'Alternatives to monarchical centralization: the great tradition of revolt in Flanders and Brabant', in Koenigsberger (ed.), *Republiken und Republikanismus*, 145–54.

308   Bibliography

'Breuk of continuiteit? De Vlaamse privilegien van 1477 in het licht van
   het staatsvormingsproces', in Blockmans (ed.), *1477*, 97–125.
'Corruptie, patronage, makelaardij en venaliteit als symptomen van een
   ontluikende staatsvorming in de Bourgondische Nederlanden', *Tijdschrift voor sociale geschiedenis*, 11 (1985), 231–47.
Culturele geschiedenis van Vlaanderen, ii (Deurne, 1983).
'De representatieve instellingen in het zuiden 1384–1482', in *AGN* iv,
   156–63.
*De volksvertegenwoordiging in Vlaanderen in de overgang van middeleeuwen naar
   nieuwe tijden (1384–1506)* (Brussels, 1978).
'Du contrat féodal à la souveraineté du peuple: les précédents de la
   déchéanche du Philippe II dans les Pays Bas (1581)', in *Assemblee di
   Stati e istituzioni rappresentative nella storia del pensiero politico moderno*
   (Rimini, 1983), 135–50.
'Le régime représentatif en Flandre dans le cadre européen au bas Moyen
   Age avec un projet d'application des ordinateurs', in *Album Elemér
   Mályusz: studies presented to the International Commission for the History of
   Representative and Parliamentary Institutions*, lvi (Brussels, 1976), 211–45.
'La signification constitutionnelle des privilèges de Marie de Bourgogne
   (1477)', in Blockmans (ed.), *1477*, 495–516.
(ed.), *1477: le privilège général et les privilèges régionaux de Marie de Bourgogne
   pour les Pays-Bas*, Ancien pays et assemblées d'états, lxxx (Kortrijk-
   Heule, 1985).
and Herwaarden, J. van, 'De Nederlanden van 1493 tot 1555: binnen-
   landse en buitenlandse politiek', in *AGN* v, 443–91.
and Peteghem, P. van, 'La pacification de Gand à la lumière d'un siècle
   de continuité constitutionnelle dans les Pays-Bas: 1477–1576', in
   Rudolf Vierhaus (ed.), *Herrschaftsverträge, Wahlkapitulationen, Fundamentalgesetze* (Göttingen, 1977), 220–34.
Blom, Hans, 'Virtue and republicanism: Spinoza's political philosophy in
   the context of the Dutch Republic', in Koenigsberger (ed.), *Republiken
   und Republikanismus*, 195–213.
Bock, Gisela, 'Civil discord in Machiavelli's *Istorie Fiorentine*', in Bock *et al.*
   (eds.), *Machiavelli and republicanism*, 181–201.
Skinner, Quentin, and Viroli, Maurizio (eds.), *Machiavelli and republicanism* (Cambridge, 1990).
Boer, C., *Hofpredikers van Prins Willem van Oranje: Jean Taffin en Pierre Loyseleur
   de Villiers* (The Hague, 1952).
Bonger, H., *Leven en werk van D. V. Coornhert* (Amsterdam, 1978).
Hoogervorst, J. R., Mout, M. E. H. N., Schöffer, I., and Woltjer, J. J.
   (eds.), *Dirck Volckertszoon Coornhert: dwars maar recht* (Zutphen, 1989).
Boogman, J. C., 'De overgang van Gouda, Dordrecht, Leiden en Delft in de
   zomer van het jaar 1572', *TvG* 51 (1942), 81–109.
'The Union of Utrecht: its genesis and consequences', in J. C. Boogman,
   Van spel tot spelers: verspreide opstellen (The Hague, 1982), 53–82.
Boon, Louis Paul, *Het Geuzenboek* (Amsterdam, 1979).

Bouwsma, W. J., *John Calvin : a sixteenth century portrait* (New York, 1988).
'The two faces of humanism : Stoicism and Augustinianism in the Renaissance', in W. J. Bouwsma, *A usable past : essays in European cultural history* (Berkeley, Calif., 1990), 19–73.
Braekman, E. M., 'Anvers – 1562 : le premier synode des églises réformées', in *Bulletin de la Société de l'Histoire du Protestantisme Belge*, 102 (1981), 25–37.
'La pensée politique de Guy de Brès', *Bulletin de la Société de l'Histoire du Protestantisme Français*, 115 (1969), 1–28.
'Les courants religieux de la reforme aux Pays-Bas', in Michel Baelde and Herman van Nuffel (eds.), *The century of Marnix van St. Aldegonde* (Antwerp, 1982).
Bremmer, R. H., 'De nationale betekenis van de synode van Dordrecht (1578)', in Nauta and van Dooren (eds.), *De nationale synode van Dordrecht*, 53–68.
'De nationale synode van Middelburg (1581) : politieke achtergronden van kerkelijke besluitvorming', in van Dooren (ed.), *De nationale synode te Middelburg*, 1–63.
Reformatie en rebellie : Willem van Oranje, de Calvinisten en het recht van opstand : tien onstuimige jaren : 1572–1581 (Franeker, 1984).
Briels, J., *Zuid-Nederlanders in de Republiek 1572–1630 : een demografische en cultuurhistorische studie* (Sint-Niklaas, 1985).
Bruin, C. C. de, 'De spiritualiteit van de moderne devotie', in C. C. de Bruin, E. Persoons and A. G. Weiler, *Geert Grote en de moderne devotie* (Zutphen, 1984), 102–44.
Burke, Peter, *Popular culture in early modern Europe* (New York, 1978).
Burns, J. H. (ed.), *The Cambridge history of medieval political thought, c. 350–c. 1450* (Cambridge, 1988).
Caenegem, R. C. van, 'Coutumes et legislation en Flandre aux XIe et XIIe siècles', *Collection Histoire*, 19 (1968), 245–79.
Canning, J. P., *The political thought of Baldus de Ubaldis* (Cambridge, 1987).
Cargill Thompson, W. D. J., *The political thought of Martin Luther* (Brighton, 1984).
Cellarius, Helmut, 'Die Propagandatätigkeit Wilhelms von Oranien in Dillenburg 1568 im Dienste des niederländischen Aufstandes', *Nassauische Annale*, 76 (1968), 120–48.
Coopmans, J. P. A., 'De herkomst van het plakkaat van Verlatinge', in G. van Dievoet and G. Marcours (eds.), *Justicie ende gerechticheyt* (Antwerp, 1983), 36–52.
'Het privilege als vorm van wetgeving in de late middeleeuwen', in Willem Frijhoff and Minke Hiemstra (eds.), *Bewogen en bewegen : de historicus in het spanningsveld tussen economie en cultuur* (Tilburg, 1986), 95–116.
Decavele, J., *De dageraad van de Reformatie in Vlaanderen* (Brussels, 1975).
'De mislukking van Oranje's "democratische politiek" in Vlaanderen', *BMGN* 99 (1984), 626–50.

'Het herstel van het Calvinisme in Vlaanderen in de eerste jaren na de Pacificatie van Gent (1577–1578)', in Dirk van Bauwhede and Marc Goetinck (eds.), *Brugge in de Geuzentijd: bijdragen tot de geschiedenis van de hervorming te Brugge en in het Brugse Vrije in de 16e eeuw* (Bruges, 1982), 9–33.

'Het ontstaan van de evangelische beweging en ontwikkeling van de protestantse kerkverbanden in de Nederlanden tot 1580', in *Ketters en papen*, 41–57.

'Reformatie en begin katholieke restauratie 1555–1568', in *AGN* vi. 166–85.

'Tolerantie, de moeilijke weg van ideaal naar praktische erkenning', in *Apologie van Willem van Oranje: hertaling en evaluatie na vierhonderd jaar* (Tielt, 1980), 49–70.

'Willem van Oranje, de "vader" van een verscheurd "vaderland" (1577–1584)', *Handelingen der Maatschappij voor Geschiedenis en Oudheidkunde te Gent*, ns 38 (1984), 69–86.

(ed.), *Het eind van een rebelse droom: Opstellen over het calvinistisch bewind te Gent (1577–1584) en de terugkeer van de stad onder de gehoorzaamheid van de koning van Spanje (17 september 1584)* (Ghent, 1984).

Despretz, A., 'De instauratie der Gentse Calvinistische Republiek (1577–1579)', *Handelingen der Maatschappij voor Geschiedenis en Oudheidkunde te Gent*, ns 17 (1963), 119–229.

Deursen, A. T. van, *Bavianen en slijkgeuzen: kerk en kerkvolk ten tijde van Maurits en Oldenbarnevelt* (Assen, 1974).

'Between Unity and independence: the application of the Union as a fundamental law', *LCHY* 14 (1981), 50–65.

Het kopergeld van de Gouden Eeuw: hel en hemel (Assen, 1980).

'Staatsinstellingen in de noordelijke Nederlanden 1579–1780', in *AGN* v. 250–387.

and Schepper, H. de, *Willem van Oranje: een strijd voor vrijheid en verdraagzaamheid* (Weesp, 1984).

Dooren, J. P. van, 'Caspar Coolhaes: het een en ander uit zijn leven voor en na de synode van Middelburg', in van Dooren (ed.), *De nationale synode te Middelburg*, 174–83.

'Der Weseler Konvent 1568: neue Forschungsergebnisse', *Monatshefte für die Evangelische Kirchengeschichte des Rheinlandes*, 31 (1982), 41–55.

(ed.), *De nationale synode te Middelburg in 1581: Calvinisme in opbouw in de noordelijke en zuidelijke Nederlanden* (Middelburg, 1981).

Duke, A., 'The ambivalent face of Calvinism in the Netherlands, 1561–1618', in Prestwich (ed.), *International Calvinism*, 109–34.

'Building heaven in hell's despite: the early history of the Reformation in the towns of the Low Countries', in Duke and Tamse (eds.), *Britain and the Netherlands*, vii. 45–75.

'From king and country to king or country? Loyalty and treason in the Revolt of the Netherlands', *Transactions of the Royal Historical Society*, 32 (1982), 113–35.

'Salvation by coercion: the controversy surrounding the "Inquisition" in the Low Countries on the eve of the Revolt', in P. N. Brooks (ed.), *Reformation principle and practice: essays in honour of A. G. Dickens* (London, 1986), 137–56.

and Jones, R. L., 'Towards a reformed polity in Holland, 1572–1578', *TvG* 89 (1976), 373–93.

and Kolff, D. H. A., 'The times of troubles in the county of Holland, 1566–1567', *TvG* 82 (1969), 316–37.

and Tamse, C. A. (eds.), *Britain and the Netherlands*, vii: *Church and state since the Reformation* (The Hague, 1981).

Easton, David, *A framework for political analysis* (Chicago, Ill., 1979).

Eire, Carlos M. N., *War against the idols: the reformation of worship from Erasmus to Calvin* (Cambridge, 1986).

Elias, Norbert, *Über den Prozess der Zivilisation*, 2 vols., 8th edn. (Frankfurt am Main, 1982).

Faber, J. A., 'De Noordelijke Nederlanden van 1480 tot 1780', *AGN* v. 196–251.

Fatio, Olivier, *Nihil pulchris ordine: contribution à l'étude de l'établissement de la discipline ecclésiastique aux Pays-Bas ou Lambert Daneau aux Pays-Bas (1581–1583)* (Leiden, 1971).

Fernandez-Santamaria, J. A., *The state, war and peace: Spanish political thought in the Renaissance, 1516–1559* (Cambridge, 1977).

Fontaine Verwey, H. de La, 'De Blijde Inkomste en de Opstand tegen Filips II', in H. de La Fontaine Verwey, *Uit de wereld van het boek i: humanisten, dwepers en rebellen in de zestiende eeuw* (Amsterdam, 1970), 113–32.

Galston, William A., 'Moral personality and liberal theory', *Political Theory*, 10 (1982), 492–519.

Gelder, H. A. Enno van, *Getemperde vrijheid* (Groningen, 1972).

Vrijheid en onvrijheid in de Republiek (Haarlem, 1974).

Gelderen, Martin van, 'A political theory of the Dutch Revolt and the *Vindiciae contra tyrannos*', *Il Pensiero Politico*, 19 (1986), 163–82.

'Conceptions of liberty during the Dutch Revolt (1555–1590)', *Parliaments, Estates and Representation*, 9 (1989), 137–53.

'The Machiavellian moment and the Dutch Revolt: the rise of Neo-stoicism and Dutch republicanism', in Bock *et al.*, *Machiavelli and republicanism*, 205–23.

'The position of the States in the political thought of the Dutch Revolt', *Parliaments, Estates and Representation*, 7 (1987), 163–76.

(ed.), *The Dutch Revolt*, Cambridge texts in the history of political thought (Cambridge, 1992).

Geurts, P. A. M., *De Nederlandse Opstand in de pamfletten 1566–1584* (Utrecht, 1983; first pub. 1956).

Geurts, Paul, *Overzicht van Nederlandsche politieke geschriften tot in de eerste helft der 17e eeuw*, i (Maastricht, 1942).

Geyl, Pieter, 'An interpretation of Vrancken's deduction of 1587 on the nature of the States of Holland's power', in Charles H. Carter (ed.), *From the Renaissance to the Counter-Reformation* (London, 1966), 230–46.

The Revolt of the Netherlands, 1555–1609 (London, 1932; repr. 1988).

Giesey, Ralph E., 'The monarchomach triumvirs: Hotman, Beza and Mornay', *Bibliothèque d'Humanisme et Renaissance*, 32 (1970), 41–56.

Gilbert, Felix, *Machiavelli and Guicciardini: politics and history in sixteenth century Florence* (New York, 1984; first pub. 1965).

Graafland, C., Kamphuis, J., van't Spijker, W., and Exalto, K. (eds.), *Luther en het gereformeerd protestantisme* (The Hague, 1982).

Grapperhaus, Ferdinand, *Alva en de tiende penning* (Deventer, 1982).

Grayson, J. C., 'The civic militia in the county of Holland, 1560–1581: politics and public order in the Dutch Revolt', *BMGN* 95 (1981), 35–63.

Griffiths, Gordon, 'Democratic ideas in the revolt of the Netherlands', *Archiv für Reformationsgeschichte*, 50 (1959), 50–63.

'Humanists and representative government in the sixteenth century: Bodin, Marnix, and the invitation to the Duke of Anjou to become ruler of the Low Countries', in *Representative institutions in theory and practice: historical papers read at Bryn Mawr College, 1968: studies presented to the International Commission for the History of Representative and Parliamentary Institutions* (Brussels, 1970), 61–83.

Groenveld, S., 'Natie en nationaal gevoel in de zestiende-eeuwse Nederlanden', *Nederlands Archievenblad*, 84 (1980), 372–87.

Leeuwenberg, H. L. P., Mout, N., and Zappey, W. M., *De kogel door de kerk? De Opstand in de Nederlanden en de rol van de Unie van Utrecht* (Zutphen, 1979; 2nd rev. edn. 1983).

Groenveld, S. and Leeuwenberg, H. L. P. (eds.), *De Unie van Utrecht. Wording en werking van een verbond en een verbondsacte* (The Hague, 1979).

Mout, M. E. H. N., and Schöffer, I. (eds.), *Bestuurders en geleerden* (Amsterdam, 1985).

Guggisberg, Hans R., 'Castellio und der Ausbruch der Religionskriege in Frankreich: einige Betrachtungen zum *Conseil à la France désolée*', *Archiv für Reformationsgeschichte*, 68 (1977), 253–67.

'Wandel der Argumente für religiöse Toleranz und Glaubensfreiheit im 16. und 17. Jahrhundert', in Heinrich Lutz (ed.), *Zur Geschichte der Toleranz und Religionsfreiheit* (Darmstadt, 1977), 455–81.

Güldner, G., *Das Toleranzproblem in den Niederlanden im Ausgang des 16. Jahrhunderts* (Hamburg, 1968).

Gunnell, John G., *Political theory: tradition and interpretation* (Cambridge, 1979).

Haitsma Mulier, E. O. G., 'A controversial republican: Dutch views of Machiavelli in the seventeenth and eighteenth centuries', in Bock *et al.* (eds.), *Machiavelli and republicanism*, 247–63.

'The language of seventeenth-century republicanism in the United Provinces: Dutch or European?' in Pagden (ed.), *The languages of political theory*, 179–95.

The myth of Venice and Dutch republican thought in the seventeenth century (Assen, 1980).

Hamilton, Alistair, *The Family of Love* (Cambridge, 1981).

Hanley, Sarah, 'The *Discours politique* in monarchomaque ideology: resistance right in sixteenth century France', in *Assemblee di Stati e istituzioni rappresentative nella storia del pensiero politico moderno* (Rimini, 1983), 121–34.

Harline, Craig E., *Pamphlets, printing, and political culture in the early Dutch Republic* (Dordrecht, 1987).

Hessels, J. H. (ed.), *Ecclesiae Londino Batavae Archivum*, ii: *Epistulae et tractatus* (Cambridge, 1889).

Hibben, C. C., *Gouda in revolt: particularism and pacifism in the revolt of the Netherlands 1572–1588* (Utrecht, 1983).

Holt, M. P., *The Duke of Anjou and the politique struggle during the wars of religion* (Cambridge, 1986).

Hont, Istvan, and Ignatieff, Michael (eds.), *Wealth and virtue: the shaping of political economy in the Scottish Enlightenment* (Cambridge, 1983).

Höpfl, Harro, *The Christian polity of John Calvin* (Cambridge, 1982).

Houtte, J. A. van, 'Die Städte der Niederlande im Übergang vom Mittelalter zur Neuzeit', in J. A. van Houtte, *Essays on medieval and early modern economy and society* (Louvain, 1977), 203–26.

IJsewijn, Jozef, 'The coming of humanism to the Low Countries', in Heiko A. Oberman and Thomas A. Brady (eds.), *Itinerarium italicum: the profile of the Italian Renaissance in the mirror of its European transformations* (Leiden, 1975), 193–301.

Janssen, A. E. M., 'Het verdeelde huis: Prins Willem van Oranje en Graaf Jan van Nassau bij de totstandkoming van de Unie van Utrecht', in Groenveld and Leeuwenberg (eds.), *De Unie van Utrecht*, 101–36.

Janssen, Peter L., 'Political thought as traditionary action: the critical response to Skinner and Pocock', *History and Theory*, 24 (1985), 115–46.

Janssens, G., 'Barmhartig en rechtvaardig: visies van L. de Villavencio en J. Hopperus op de taak van de Koning', in W. P. Blockmans and H. van Huffel (eds.), *Etat et religion aux XVe et XVIe siècles* (Brussels, 1986), 25–42.

'Brabant in verzet tegen Alva's tiende en twintigste penning', *BMGN* 89 (1974), 16–31.

'Brabant strijdt voor vrede', in *Opstand en pacificatie*, 63–74.

Jelsma, Auke Jan, *Adriaan van Haemstede en zijn martelaarsboek* (The Hague, 1970).

Johnston, Andrew George, 'The eclectic reformation: vernacular evangelical pamphlet literature in the Dutch-speaking Low Countries, 1520–1565', Ph.D. thesis, University of Southampton, 1986.

Jones, R. L., 'Reformed church and civil authorities in the United Provinces in the late sixteenth and early seventeenth centuries, as reflected in Dutch state and municipal archives', *Journal of the Society of Archivists*, 4 (1970–3), 109–23.

Jong, O. J. de, *Nederlandse kerkgeschiedenis*, 3rd rev. edn. (Nijkerk, 1986).

'Union and religion', *LCHY* 14 (1981), 29–49.

Jonge, C. de, *De irenische ecclesiologie van Franciscus Junius (1545–1602):*

onderzoek naar de plaats van het geschrift ' Le paisible Chrestien' (1593) in zijn denken (Leiden, 1980).

Jongkees, A. G., 'Vorming van de Bourgondische staat', in *AGN* iv. 184–200.

Jongste, J. A. F. de, 'Hollandse stadspensionarisssen tijdens de Republiek: notities bij een onderzoek', in Groenveld *et al.* (eds.), *Bestuurders en geleerden*, 85–96.

Kelley, Donald R., *The beginning of ideology: consciousness and society in the French Reformation* (Cambridge, 1981).

'Horizons of intellectual history: retrospect, circumspect, prospect', *JHI* 48 (1987), 143–69.

Ketters en papen onder Filips II (The Hague, 1986).

Kingdon, Robert, 'John Calvin's contribution to representative government', in Phyllis Mack and Margaret C. Jacobs (eds.), *Politics and culture in early modern Europe: essays in honour of H. G. Koenigsberger* (Cambridge, 1987), 183–98.

Koenigsberger, H. G., *Dominium regale or Dominium politicum et regale: monarchies and parliaments in early modern Europe* (London, 1975).

'Orange, Granvelle and Philip II', *BMGN* 99 (1984), 554–72.

'The organization of revolutionary parties in France and the Netherlands during the sixteenth century', in H. G. Koenigsberger, *Estates and revolutions: essays in early modern European history* (Ithaca, NY, 1971), 224–53.

'Why did the States General of the Netherlands become revolutionary in the sixteenth century?' *Parliaments, Estates and Representation*, 2 (1982), 103–11.

(ed.), *Republiken und Republikanismus im Europa der frühen Neuzeit* (Munich, 1988).

Koopmans, J. W., *De Staten van Holland en de Opstand: de ontwikkeling van hun functies en organisatie in de periode 1544–1588* (The Hague, 1990).

Kossmann, E. H., 'Bodin, Althusius en Parker, of: over de moderniteit van de Nederlandse Opstand', in Kossmann, *Politieke theorie en geschiedenis*, 93–111 (first pub. 1958).

'Dutch republicanism', in *L'età dei lumi: studi, storici sul settecento Europeo in onore di Franco Venturi*, i (Naples, 1985), 455–86 (also in Kossmann, *Politieke theorie en geschiedenis*, 211–34).

Politieke theorie en geschiedenis: verspreide opstellen en voordrachten (Amsterdam, 1987).

Politieke theorie in het zeventiende-eeuwse Nederland (Amsterdam, 1960).

'Popular sovereignty at the beginning of the Dutch *ancien régime*', *LCHY* 14 (1981), 1–28.

'The development of Dutch political theory in the seventeenth century', in J. S. Bromley and E. H. Kossmann (eds.), *Britain and the Netherlands*, i (London, 1960), 91–110.

and Mellink, A. F. (eds.), *Texts concerning the revolt of the Netherlands* (Cambridge, 1974).

Kuyper, A., *Kerkeraadsprotocollen der Hollandsche gemeente te London, 1569–1571*, Werken der Marnix-vereeniging, series 1, vol. i (Utrecht, 1870).

Lagomarsino, Paul David, 'Court faction and the formulation of Spanish policy towards the Netherlands (1559–1567)', Ph.D. thesis, Cambridge University, 1973.

Lancée, J. A. L., *Erasmus en het Hollands humanisme* (Utrecht, 1979).

Langeraad, L. A. van, *Guido de Bray: zijn leven en werken* (Zierikzee, 1884).

Lecler, Joseph, *Histoire de la tolérance au siècle de la Réforme*, 2 vols. (Paris, 1954).

Leupen, P. H. D., 'De representatieve instellingen in het noorden, 1384–1482', in *AGN* iv. 164–72.

Lewis, Gillian, 'Calvinism in Geneva in the time of Calvin and of Beza (1541–1605)', in Prestwich (ed.), *International Calvinism*, 39–70.

Lindeboom, J., *Austin Friars: geschiedenis van de Nederlandse hervormde gemeente te Londen, 1550–1950* (The Hague, 1950).

Lockyer, Andrew, 'Traditions as context in the history of political theory', *Political Studies*, 27 (1979), 201–17.

Lovett, A. W., 'A new governor for the Netherlands: the appointment of Don Luis de Requesens, Comendador Mayor de Castilla', *European Studies Review*, 1 (1971), 89–103.

Early Habsburg Spain 1517–1598 (Oxford, 1986).

'The governorship of Don Luis de Requensens, 1573–1576: A Spanish view', *European Studies Review*, 2 (1972), 187–99.

Lynch, John, *Spain under the Habsburgs*, i: *Empire and absolutism 1516–1598*, 2nd edn. (Oxford, 1981).

Mack Crew, Phyllis, *Calvinist preaching and iconoclasm in the Netherlands 1544–1569* (Cambridge, 1978).

Mann Philips, Margaret, *Erasmus and the northern Renaissance* (Woodbridge, 1981).

Marnef, Guido, *Het Calvinistisch bewind te Mechelen*, Ancien pays et assemblées d'états, lxxxvii (Kortrijk-Heule, 1987).

Marshall, Sherrin, 'Protestant, Catholic and Jewish women in the early modern Netherlands', in Sherrin Marshall (ed.), *Women in Reformation and Counter-Reformation Europe* (Bloomington, Ind., 1989), 120–39.

Mellink, A. F., 'Prereformatie en vroege reformatie 1517–1568', in *AGN* vi. 146–65.

Mesnard, Pierre, *L'essor de la philosophie politique au XVIe siècle*, 3rd edn. (Paris, 1969).

Monahan, Arthur P., *Consent, coercion, and limit: the medieval origins of parliamentary democracy* (Leiden, 1987).

Monte Verloren, J. P. de, and Spruit, J. E., *Hoofdlijnen uit de ontwikkeling der rechterlijke organisatie in de noordelijke Nederlanden tot de Bataafse omwenteling*, 5th edn. (Deventer, 1972).

Moreau, Gérard, *Histoire du protestantisme à Tournai jusqu'à la veille de la Révolution des Pays-Bas* (Paris, 1962).

Morsink, G., *Joannes Anastasius Veluanes* (Kampen, 1986).

Motley, J. L., *The rise of the Dutch Republic*, 3 vols. (Leipzig, 1858).

Mout, M. E. H. N., 'Heilige Lipsius, bid voor ons', *TvG* 97 (1984), 195–206.

'Het intellectuele milieu van Willem van Oranje', *BMGN* 99 (1984), 596–625.

'In het schip: Justus Lipsius en de Nederlandse Opstand tot 1591', in Groenveld *et al.* (eds.), *Bestuurders en geleerden*, 55–64.

Plakkaat van verlatinge 1581: inleiding, transcriptie en vertaling in hedendaags Nederlands (The Hague, 1979).

'The Family of Love (Huis der Liefde) and the Dutch Revolt', in Duke and Tamse (eds.), *Britain and the Netherlands*, vii. 76–93.

'Van arm vaderland tot eendrachtige republiek: de rol van politieke theorieën in de Nederlandse Opstand', *BMGN* 101 (1986), 345–65.

Mout, Nicolette, 'Ideales Muster oder erfundene Eigenart: republikanische Theorien während des niederländischen Aufstands', in Koenigsberger (ed.), *Republiken und Republikanismus*, 169–94.

Nauta, D., 'De synode van Emden (1571) en de Hugenoten', *Gereformeerd Theologisch Tijdschrift*, 73 (1973), 76–98.

'Emden toevluchtsoord van ballingen', in Nauta *et al.* (eds.), *De synode van Emden*, 7–22.

'Les Réformés aux Pays-Bas et les huguenots spécialement à propos du synode d'Emden (1571)', in *Actes du Colloque: l'amiral de Coligny et son temps* (Paris, 1974), 577–600.

'Marnix auteur van de *Libellus supplex* aan de rijksdag van Spiers (1570)', *Nederlands Archief voor Kerkgeschiedenis*, 55 (1975), 151–70.

and Dooren, J. P. van (eds.), *De nationale synode van Dordrecht 1578: Gereformeerden uit de noordelijke en de zuidelijke Nederlanden bijeen* (Amsterdam, 1578).

and Jong, O. J. de (eds.), *De synode van Emden Oktober 1571* (Kampen, 1971).

Groot, A. de, Berg, J. van den, Jong, O. J. de, Kentsch, F. R. J., and Posthumus Meyes, G. H. M., *Biografisch lexicon voor de geschiedenis van het Nederlands protestantisme*, ii (Kampen, 1983).

Nave, Francine de, 'De polemiek tussen Justus Lipsius en Dirck Volckertsz Coornhert (1590): hoofdoorzaak van Lipsius' vertrek uit Leiden (1591)', *De Gulden Passer*, 48 (1970), 1–39.

'Peilingen naar de oorspronkelijkheid van Justus Lipsius' politiek denken' *Tijdschrift voor Rechtsgeschiedenis*, 38 (1970), 449–83.

Nederman, Cary J., 'Nature, sin and the origins of society: the Ciceronian tradition in medieval political thought', *JHI* 49 (1988), 3–26.

Nierop, H. F. K. van, 'Willem van Oranje als hoog edelman: patronage in de Habsburgse Nederlanden?', *BMGN* 99 (1984), 651–76.

Nijenhuis, W., *Adrianus Saravia (c. 1532–1613), Dutch Calvinist: first reformed defender of the English episcopal church on the basis of the ius divinum*, Studies in the history of Christian thought, xxi (Leiden, 1980).

'Coornhert en de Heidelbergse catechismus: moment in de strijd tussen humanisme en Reformatie', *Nederlands Theologisch Tijdschrift*, 18 (1963), 271–88.

'De grenzen der burgerlijke ongehoorzaamheid in Calvijns laatstbekende preken: ontwikkeling van zijn opvattingen aangaande het verzetsrecht', in *Historisch bewogen: Opstellen over de radicale reformatie in de 16e en 17e eeuw* (Groningen, 1984), 67–99.

'De publieke kerk veelkleurig en verdeeld, bevoorrecht en onvrij', in *AGN* vi. 325–43.

'De synode te Emden 1571', *Kerk en Theologie*, 23 (1972), 34–54.

'Variants within Dutch Calvinism in the sixteenth century', *LCHY* 12 (1979), 48–64.

Noordegraaf, L., 'Dearth, famine and social policy in the Dutch republic at the end of the sixteenth century', in Peter Clark (ed.), *The European crisis of the 1590s* (London, 1985), 67–83.

Hollands welvaren? Levensstandaard in Holland 1450–1650 (Bergen, NH, 1985).

'Nijverheid in de noordelijke Nederlanden', in *AGN* vi, 12–26.

Oestreich, Gerhard, *Antiker Geist und moderner Staat bei Justus Lipsius (1547–1606)* (Göttingen, 1989).

Neostoicism and the early modern state (Cambridge, 1982).

Opstand en pacificatie in de lage landen: bijdrage tot de studie van de pacificatie van Gent (Ghent, 1976).

Pagden, Anthony (ed.), *The languages of political theory in early modern Europe* (Cambridge, 1987).

Parker, Geoffrey, *Philip II* (London, 1978).

The Dutch Revolt, rev. edn. (Harmondsworth, 1985).

Patry, Raoul, *Philippe Du Plessis-Mornay: un Huguenot homme d'état (1549–1623)* (Paris, 1933).

Petri, Franz (ed.), *Kirche und gesellschaftlicher Wandel in deutschen und niederländischen Städten der werdenden Neuzeit* (Cologne, 1980).

Pettegree, Andrew, 'The exile churches and the churches "under the cross": Antwerp and Emden during the Dutch Revolt', *Journal of Ecclesiastical History*, 38 (1987), 187–209.

Plomp, J., 'De kerkorde van Emden', in Nauta *et al.* (eds.), *De synode van Emden*, 88–121.

Pocock, J. G. A., 'Cambridge paradigms and Scotch philosophers: a study of the relations between the civic humanist and the civil jurisprudential interpretation of eighteenth-century social thought', in Hont and Ignatieff (eds.), *Wealth and virtue*, 235–52.

'Introduction: the state of the art', in Pocock, *Virtue, commerce and history*, 1–34.

'Spinoza and Harrington: an exercise in comparison', *BMGN* 102 (1987), 435–49.

'The concept of language and the *métier d'historien*: some considerations on practice', in Pagden (ed.), *The languages of political theory*, 19–38.

The Machiavellian moment: Florentine political thought and the Atlantic republican tradition (Princeton, NJ, 1975).

'The problem of political thought in the eighteenth century: patriotism and politeness (with comments of E. O. G. Haitsma Mulier and E. H. Kossmann)', *Theoretische Geschiedenis*, 9 (1982), 3–37.

Virtue, commerce and history (Cambridge, 1985).

'Virtues, rights and manners: a model for historians of political thought', in Pocock, *Virtue, commerce and history*, 37–50.

Press, V., 'Wilhelm von Oranien: die deutschen Reichsstande und der niederlandische Aufstand', *BMGN* 99 (1984), 677–707.

Prestwich, M. (ed.), *International Calvinism 1541–1565* (Oxford, 1985).

Prevenier, Walter, and Blockmans, Wim, *The Burgundian Netherlands* (Cambridge, 1985).

Quaglioni, Diego (ed.), *Politica e diritto nel trecento Italiano: il 'De tyranno' di Bartolo da Sassoferrato (1314–1357)* (Florence, 1983).

Quillet, Jeannine, 'Community, counsel and representation', in Burns (ed.), *The Cambridge history of medieval political thought*, 554–72.

Rahlenbeck, C. (ed.), *Mémoires de Jacques de Wesenbeke* (Brussels, 1859).

Raitière, M. N., 'Hubert Languet's authorship of the *Vindiciae contra tyrannos*', *Il Pensiero Politico*, 13 (1981), 395–420.

Raus, Louisa, 'De dialoog Emanuel–Erneste en zijn auteur', *De Gulden Passer*, 10 (1932), 25–39.

Rawls, John, *A theory of justice* (Oxford, 1973).

Reitsma, Rients, *Centrifugal and centripetal forces in the early Dutch Republic: the States of Overijssel, 1566–1600* (Amsterdam, 1982).

Ridder-Symoens, Hilde de, 'Brabanders aan de rechtenuniversiteit van Orléans (1444–1546): een socio-professionele studie', *Bijdragen tot de Geschiedenis*, 61 (1978), 198–347.

'Internationalismus versus Nationalismus an Universitäten um 1500 nach zumeist südniederländischen Quellen', in *Europa 1500: Integrationsprozesse im Widerstreit* (Stuttgart, 1986), 397–414.

Robertson, John, 'The Scottish Enlightenment at the limits of the civic tradition', in Istvan Hont and Michael Ignatieff (eds.), *Wealth and virtue*, 137–78.

Roosbroeck, R. van, *Het wonderjaar te Antwerpen (1566–1567): inleiding tot de studie der godsdienstonlusten van den beeldenstorm af (1566) tot aan de inneming der stad door Alexander Farnese (1585)* (Antwerp, 1930).

'Wunderjahr oder Hungerjahr? Antwerpen 1566', in Petri (ed.), *Kirche und gesellschaftlicher Wandel in deutschen und niederländischen Städten*, 169–96.

Rowen, Herbert H., 'Neither fish nor fowl: the stadtholderate in the Dutch republic', in Herbert H. Rowen and Andrew Lossky (eds.), *Political ideas and institutions in the Dutch republic* (Los Angeles, 1985), 3–31.

The Princes of Orange: the Stadtholders in the Dutch Republic (Cambridge, 1988).

Rutgers, F. L. (ed.), *Acta van de Nederlandsche synoden der zestiende eeuw*, 2nd edn. (Dordrecht, 1980).

Ruys, T., *Petrus Dathenus* (Utrecht, 1919).

Ruystinck, Symeon, Calandrinus, Caesar, Culenborgh, Aemilius van,

Gheschiedenissen ende handelingen die voornemelick aengaen de Nederduytsche Natie ende Gemeynten wonende in Engelant ende int bysonder tot Londen, ed. J. J. van Toorenenbergen, Werken der Marnix-vereeniging, series 3, vol. i (Utrecht, 1873).

Saunders, J. L., *Justus Lipsius: the philosophy of Renaissance Stoicism* (New York, 1955).

Schama, Simon, *The embarrassment of riches: an interpretation of Dutch culture in the Golden Age* (London, 1987).

Scheerder, J., *De beeldenstorm* (Bussum, 1974).

'De werking van de Inquisitie', in *Opstand en pacificatie*, 153–66.

Schelven, A. A. van, *De Nederduitsche vluchtelingenkerken der 16e eeuw in Engeland en Duitschland in hunne beteekenis voor de reformatie in de Nederlanden* (The Hague, 1908).

'De opkomst van de idee der politieke tolerantie in de 16e eeuwsche Nederlanden', *TvG* 46 (1931), 235–47, 337–88.

'De staatsvorm van het Zwitsersch Eedgenootschap den Nederlanden ter navolging aanbevolen', in *Miscellanea historica in honorem Leonis van der Essen*, ii (Brussels, 1947), 747–56.

'Het begin van het gewapend verzet tegen Spanje in de 16e-eeuwsche Nederlanden', *Handelingen en mededelingen van de maatschappij der Nederlandsche Letterkunde te Leiden over het jaar 1914–1915* (Leiden, 1915), 126–56.

(ed.), *Kerkeraads-protocollen der Nederduitsche vluchtelingen-kerk te London 1560–1563* (Amsterdam, 1921).

Schenk, M. G. (ed.), *Prins Willem van Oranje: geschriften van 1568* (Amsterdam, 1933).

Schepper, Hugo de, *Belgium nostrum 1500–1650: over integratie en desintegratie van het Nederland* (Antwerp, 1987).

'De burgerlijke overheden en hun permanente kaders, 1480–1579', in *AGN* v. 312–49.

'De Grote Raad van Mechelen, hoogste rechtscollege in de Nederlanden?', *BMGN* (1978), 389–411.

'Vorstelijke ambtenarij en bureaukratisering in regering en gewesten van 's konings Nederlanden, 16e–17e eeuw', *TvG* 90 (1977), 358–77.

Schilling, H. 'Calvinismus und Freiheitsrechte: die politisch–theologische Pamphletistik der Ostfriesisch–Groningischen "Patrioten-partei" und die politische Kultur in Deutschland und in den Niederlanden', *BMGN* 102 (1987), 403–34.

'Der libertär–radikale Republikanismus der holländischen Regenten', *Geschichte und Gesellschaft*, 10 (1984), 498–533.

Niederländische Exulanten im 16. Jahrhundert: ihre Stellung im religiösen Leben deutscher und englischer Städte, Schriften des Vereins für Reformationsgeschichte, vol. 78–9, no. 187 (Gütersloh, 1972).

Schöffer, I., 'The Batavian myth during the sixteenth and seventeenth centuries', in J. S. Bromley and E. H. Kossmann (eds.), *Britain and the Netherlands*, v: *Some political mythologies* (The Hague, 1975), 78–101.

Wee, H. van der, and Bornewasser, J. A., *Geschiedenis der Nederlanden*, ii: *Noord en Zuid in de nieuwe tijd (van c. 1500 to 1780)* (Amsterdam, 1977).

Scholliers, E., and Vandenbroeke, C., 'Structuren en conjuncturen in de Zuidelijke Nederlanden, 1480–1800', in *AGN* v. 252–310.

Schutte, G. J., *Het Calvinistisch Nederland* (Utrecht, 1988).

Skinner, Quentin, 'Ambrogio Lorenzetti: the artist as political philosopher', *Proceedings of the British Academy*, 72 (1986), 1–56.

'Hermeneutics and the role of history', *New Literary History*, 7 (1975–6), 209–32.

Machiavelli (Oxford, 1981).

'Machiavelli on the maintenance of liberty', *Politics*, 18 (1983), 3–15.

'Machiavelli's *Discorsi* and the pre-humanist origins of republican ideas', in Bock *et al.* (eds.), *Machiavelli and republicanism*, 121–41.

'Meaning and the understanding of speech acts', in Tully (ed.), *Meaning and context*, 29–67.

'Motives, intentions and the interpretation of texts', in Tully (ed.), *Meaning and context*, 68–78.

'Political philosophy', in Charles B. Schmitt and Quentin Skinner (eds.), *The Cambridge history of Renaissance philosophy* (Cambridge, 1988), 389–452.

'Social meaning and the explanation of social action', in Tully (ed.), *Meaning and context*, 79–96.

'Some problems in the analysis of political thought and action', in Tully (ed.), *Meaning and context*, 97–118.

The foundations of modern political thought, i: *The Renaissance*, ii: *The age of Reformation* (Cambridge, 1978).

'The idea of negative liberty: philosophical and historical perspectives', in Richard Rorty, J. B. Schneewind and Quentin Skinner, *Philosophy in history* (Cambridge, 1984), 193–211.

Smalley, B., 'Sallust in the Middle Ages', in R. R. Bolgar (ed.), *Classical influences on European culture AD 500–1500* (Cambridge, 1971).

Smit, J. W., 'The Netherlands revolution', in R. Forster and J. P. Greene (eds.), *Preconditions of revolution in early modern Europe* (Baltimore, Md., 1970), 1–55.

Soly H., 'Le grand essor du capitalisme commercial: villes et campagne', in E. Witte (ed.), *Histoire de Flandre* (Brussels, 1983), 105–20.

and Thys, A. K. L., 'Nijverheid in de zuidelijke Nederlanden', in *AGN* vi. 27–57.

Spaans, Joke, *Haarlem na de Reformatie: stedelijke cultuur en kerkelijk leven* (The Hague, 1989).

Spijker, W. van 't, 'De Acta van de synode van Middelburg (1581)', in van Dooren (ed.), *De nationale synode te Middelburg*, 64–128.

'De kerkorde van Dordrecht (1578)', in Nauta and van Dooren (eds.), *De nationale synode van Dordrecht*, 126–42.

Steggink, O., 'De religieuze en mystieke literatuur 1380–1520', in *AGN* iv. 421–6.

Swart, K. W., 'Wat bewoog Willem van Oranje de strijd tegen de Spaanse overheersing aan te binden?' *BMGN* 99 (1984), 557–8.

William the Silent and the Revolt of the Netherlands (London, 1978), 5–40.

Tex, J. den, *Oldenbarnevelt*, i: *Opgang, 1547–1588* (Haarlem, 1960).

Tierney, Brian, 'Marsilius on rights', *JHI* 52 (1991), 3–17.

'Origins of natural rights language: texts and contexts, 1150–1250', *HPT* 10 (1989), 615–46.

Religion, law, and the growth of constitutional thought, 1150–1650 (Cambridge, 1982).

Tjaden, A. J., 'De reconquista mislukt: de opstandige gewesten 1579–1588', in *AGN* vi. 244–58.

Todd, Margo, *Christian humanism and the Puritan social order* (Cambridge, 1987).

Toorenenbergen, J. J. van, *Eene bladzijde uit de geschiedenis der Nederlandsche geloofsbelijdenis* (The Hague, 1861).

Tracy, James D., *Holland under Habsburg rule, 1506–1566: the formation of a body politic* (Berkeley, Calif., 1990).

The politics of Erasmus: a pacifist intellectual and his political milieu (Toronto, 1978).

Tuck, Richard, 'Scepticism and toleration in the seventeenth century', in Susan Mendus (ed.), *Justifying toleration: conceptual and historical perspectives* (Cambridge, 1988), 21–35.

Tully, James H. (ed.), *Meaning and context: Quentin Skinner and his critics* (Oxford, 1988).

Review article: 'The pen is a mighty sword: Quentin Skinner's analysis of politics', in Tully (ed.), *Meaning and context*, 7–25.

Ullmann, W., *Medieval political thought* (Harmondsworth, 1975).

Uytven, R. van, '1477 in Brabant', in Blockmans (ed.), *1477*, 253–85.

'De rechtsgeldigheid van de Brabantse Blijde Inkomst van 3 januari 1356', *TvG* 82 (1969), 39–48.

'Stadsgeschiedenis in het noorden en zuiden', in *AGN* ii. 187–253.

'Vorst, adel en steden: een driehoeksverhouding in Brabant van de twaalfde tot de zestiende eeuw', *Bijdragen tot de Geschiedenis*, 59 (1976), 93–122.

and Blockmans, W. P., 'Constitutions and their application in the Netherlands during the Middle Ages', *Revue Belge de Philologie et d'Histoire*, 47 (1969), 399–424.

Vandamme, L., 'Het calvinisme te Brugge in beweging (1560–1566)', in Dirk van de Bauwhede and Marc Goetinck (eds.), *Brugge in de Geuzentijd* (Bruges, 1982), 102–22.

Velema, W. R. E., 'God, de deugd en de oude constitutie: politieke talen in de eerste helft van de achttiende eeuw', *BMGN* 102 (1987), 476–97.

Verheyden, A. L. E., *Le conseil des troubles: liste des condamnés (1567–1573)* (Brussels, 1961).

Visser, D., 'Junius: the author of the *Vindiciae contra tyrannos*', *TvG* 84 (1971), 510–25.

Vrankrijker, A. C. J. de, *De motiveering van onzen opstand* (Nijmegen, 1933; repr. 1979).

Vries, Jan de, *The Dutch rural economy in the Golden Age, 1500–1700* (New Haven, Conn., 1974).

Waterbolk, E. H., 'Humanisme en de tolerantiegedachte', in *Opstand en pacificatie*, 302–15.

Wells, Guy, *Antwerp and the government of Philip II, 1555–1567* (Ann Arbor, Mich., 1982).

Woltjer, J. J., 'De politieke betekenis van de Emdense synode', in Nauta et al. (eds.), *De synode van Emden*, 22–49.

'De religieuze situatie in de eerste jaren van de republiek', in *Ketters en papen*, 94–106.

'De vrede-makers', in Groenveld and Leeuwenberg (eds.), *De Unie van Utrecht*, 56–87.

'De wisselende gestalten van de Unie', in Groenveld and Leeuwenberg (eds.), *De Unie van Utrecht*, 88–101.

Friesland in hervormingstijd (Leiden, 1962).

'Inleiding', in *Opstand en onafhankelijkheid: eerste vrije statenvergadering Dordrecht 1572* (Dordrecht, 1972), 5–29.

'Stadt und Reformation in den Niederlanden', in Petri (ed.), *Kirche und gesellschaftlicher Wandel in deutschen und niederländischen Städten*, 155–67.

Yardeni, Myriam, 'French Calvinist political thought, 1534–1715', in Prestwich (ed.), *International Calvinism*, 315–37.

Zijp, R. P., 'Spiritualisme in de 16de eeuw, een schets', in *Ketters en papen*, 75–93.

Index

Ideas in Context

Edited by Quentin Skinner (General Editor), Lorraine Daston,
Wolf Lepenies, Richard Rorty and J. B. Schneewind

Forthcoming titles include works by Martin Dzelzainis, Mark Goldie, Noel Malcolm, Roger Mason, James Moore, Nicolai Rubinstein, Quentin Skinner, Martin Warnke and Robert Wokler.

Titles marked with an asterisk are also available in paperback.

Printed in the United Kingdom
by Lightning Source UK Ltd.
116418UKS00001B/174